7/2020

P9-DYB-794

CONTEMPORARY
AFRICAN
AMERICAN
LITERATURE

BLACKS IN THE DIASPORA

FOUNDING EDITORS
Darlene Clark Hine
John McCluskey, Jr.
David Barry Gaspar

EDITORS
Herman L. Bennett
Kim D. Butler
Judith A. Byfield
Tracy Sharpley-Whiting

EDITED BY
LOVALERIE KING AND
SHIRLEY MOODY-TURNER

CONTEMPORARY AFRICAN AMERICAN LITERATURE

THE LIVING CANON

INDIANA UNIVERSITY PRESS

Bloomington & Indianapolis

This book is a publication of

Indiana University Press
Office of Scholarly Publishing
Herman B Wells Library 350
1320 E. 10th St.
Bloomington, IN 47405

iupress.indiana.edu

Telephone orders   800-842-6796
Fax orders   812-855-7931

© 2013 by Indiana University Press
All rights reserved

No part of this book may be reproduced
or utilized in any form or by any means,
electronic or mechanical, including
photocopying and recording, or by any
information storage and retrieval system,
without permission in writing from the
publisher. The Association of American
University Presses' Resolution on Permis-
sions constitutes the only exception to
this prohibition.

⊖ The paper used in this publication
meets the minimum requirements of
the American National Standard for
Information Sciences—Permanence
of Paper for Printed Library Materials,
ANSI Z39.48-1992.

Manufactured in the
United States of America
Library of Congress Cataloging-in-
Publication Data

Contemporary African American
literature : the living canon / edited
by Lovalerie King and Shirley Moody-
Turner.
       pages cm
   Includes bibliographical references and
index.
   ISBN 978-0-253-00625-7 (cloth : alk.
paper) — ISBN 978-0-253-00626-4
(pbk. : alk. paper) — ISBN 978-0-253-
00697-4 (ebook) 1. American literature—
African American authors—History
and criticism. 2. African Americans—
Intellectual life. 3. African Americans in
literature. I. King, Lovalerie, editor of
compilation. II. Moody-Turner, Shirley,
editor of compilation.
   PS153.N5C644 2013
   810.9'896073—dc23

                           2013016443

   1 2 3 4 5   18 17 16 15 14 13

THIS VOLUME IS DEDICATED TO THE ANCESTORS
AND TO THOSE SCHOLARS, AUTHORS, AND
AUTHOR/SCHOLARS WHO CONTINUE TO
CARRY THE TRADITION FORWARD.

CONTENTS

Foreword \ *Mat Johnson* ix

Acknowledgments xiii

Introduction \ *Lovalerie King and Shirley Moody-Turner* 1

Part 1. Politics of Publishing, Pedagogy, and Readership

1 The Point of Entanglement: Modernism, Diaspora,
and Toni Morrison's *Love* \ *Houston A. Baker, Jr.* 17

2 "The Historical Burden That Only Oprah Can Bear":
African American Satirists and the State of
the Literature \ *Darryl Dickson-Carr* 41

3 Black Is Gold: African American Literature, Critical Literacy,
and Twenty-First-Century Pedagogies \ *Maryemma Graham* 55

4 Hip Hop (feat. Women Writers): Reimagining Black Women
and Agency through Hip Hop Fiction \ *Eve Dunbar* 91

5 Street Literature and the Mode of Spectacular Writing:
Popular Fiction between Sensationalism, Education,
Politics, and Entertainment \ *Kristina Graaff* 113

Part 2. Alternative Genealogies

6 Portrait of the Artist as a Young Slave: Visual Artistry as Agency
in the Contemporary Narrative of Slavery \ *Evie Shockley* 137

7 Variations on the Theme: Black Family, Nationhood,
Lesbianism, and Sadomasochistic Desire in Marci Blackman's
Po Man's Child \ *Carmen Phelps* 155

8 Bad Brother Man: Black Folk Figure Narratives in Comics \
James Braxton Peterson 168

Part 3. Beyond Authenticity

9   Sampling the Sonics of Sex (Funk) in Paul Beatty's *Slumberland* \
    L. H. Stallings   189

10 Post-Integration Blues: Black Geeks and Afro-Diasporic
    Humanism \ *Alexander G. Weheliye*   213

11 The Crisis of Authenticity in Contemporary African American
    Literature \ *Richard Schur*   235

12 Someday We'll All Be Free: Considering Post-Oppression Fiction \
    Martha Southgate   255

Part 4. Pedagogical Approaches and Implications

13 Untangling History, Dismantling Fear: Teaching Tayari Jones's
    Leaving Atlanta \ *Trudier Harris*   269

14 Reading Kyle Baker's *Nat Turner* with a Group of Collegiate Black
    Men \ *Howard Rambsy II*   285

15 Toward the Theoretical Practice of Conceptual Liberation:
    Using an Africana Studies Approach to Reading African American
    Literary Texts \ *Greg Carr and Dana A. Williams*   302

Afterword \ *Alice Randall*   329

Annotated Bibliography \ *Pia Deas and David F. Green, Jr.*   333

Contributors   351

Index   359

FOREWORD
MAT JOHNSON

There is a fanpage on the popular networking site Facebook entitled "I Hate Reading." It's a very succinct title, and there's not much else to the page. If you hate reading, you simply click the button that says "Like," and you can become a "Fan" and proudly show your unabashed support for illiteracy. As of this writing, the site has over 450,000 members, all of whom presumably overcame the irony of having to read the page in the first place.

As a writer, I am of course disheartened by this lambasting of the written word. But as a human, I understand. Books are hard. My own art, the novel, is among the hardest. Novels are incomplete in their process, forcing the reader to use her or his imagination to bring the text to life. TV shows don't demand that; they do the work for you. Films as well, with millions of dollars spent to bring the creativity to life. People work hard, come home exhausted, they want the release, they want escape, they want someone else to carry the load. It's no wonder every time I write a book someone says to me, "Maybe they'll turn it into a movie." That knowledge keeps me from attacking them.

So why do novels matter? In this era of visual media, when one film's advertising budget alone can dwarf the incomes of entire publishing houses, what does the novel hope to offer? I ask myself this quite often. I ask it every time I happen upon a beautiful book that's been ignored, or as I struggle myself with the realities of trying to maintain my life as a writer. I'm asked this too, by writing students struggling to understand if the art they're dedicating their lives to still has a place in the world. And I usually answer them with one word. *Lolita.*

Lolita: Vladimir Nabokov's masterpiece, the story of a wretched pe-
dophile's obsession with stealing the innocence of a little girl. Stunning
in its poetry, its hypnotizing view of the world. It pulls the reader in from
its first rhythmic lines and yanks them into a narrative twisted and honest and breathtaking. It was a huge hit after it was first published in 1955,
and the inevitable need to see it enacted in film resulted in two film versions, one in 1962 and another in 1997. The great tale was visually translated by great and accomplished directors, Stanley Kubrick and Adrian
Lyne, respectively, with ample budgets to aid them. And both the cine-
matic versions failed to live up to the artistic accomplishment of their
source material. The visual reality of this forbidden relationship became
distasteful when presented in visual form: both movies cast the female
role with an older actress out of decency. And it was an impossible task,
to take the detailed reality of protagonist Humbert Humbert and fit it
into a few hours fare. But there are other reasons besides time that speak
to the strength of the novel form. Watching a film is a communal event,
the darkened theater is a group occasion. TV, while watched primarily
at home, is even more communal, with millions of others joining in the
shared experience. But the novel demands a solitary audience. You read,
and the words become images within the privacy of your own mind. And
within the darkened space of your imagination, anything can be said, any
truth can be uttered, with intimacy.

That is what the novel offers, like no other storytelling form: truth.
One person's truth. Not one person and a legion of collaborators. Not a
truth dictated in part by harsh market concerns and obligations to financial reward. Not just truth the majority of people want to hear. That same
money that floods into TV and film also brings with it the need for a mass
audience, and for a vision that can sacrifice its intimacy for leaps towards
the universal.

This becomes an increasingly difficult dilemma for telling the stories
of minorities, who by their nature garner smaller audiences directly familiar with their experiences. In order to combat that shrinkage, commercially viable minority storytelling is often aimed at the lowest level of
sophistication, so as not to exclude any of the already small pool. The result, as evidenced in African American TV and film, has been a paucity
of sophisticated depictions of Black life. It's not that there are not sophisticated visual storytellers of African descent, it's just that it is extremely
difficult for them to get the massive funding they need for their art, and

when they do it is usually weighted with the need to receive crossover approval from the majority, White, audience. And that is why African American literature, at this moment, is so important: it offers truth the best chance.

African American literature has always been about telling uncomfortable truths. It began its prose with the slave narrative, transitioned in the nineteenth century into the protest novel, and was often judged by both white and black critics more by how effectively it held a mirror to white oppression than by its artistic merits.

But our world has changed. In the time since Toni Morrison won the Pulitzer Prize in 1988 for her masterpiece set in the slave era, *Beloved*, a new generation of writers has come of age, a group of people from a dramatically different moment: the first generation of African American writers to produce work in a post–Civil Rights era, the last great battle in the centuries old war for equality that has defined African American experience. Contemporary writers of African descent have seized the freedom won for them, following their art where it's led. Issues of race and human rights are still common themes, but the rest of human experience is no longer Jim Crowed beyond access. This is an historic moment in the African American literary dialogue, a time when writers are hiking en mass to the artistic mountains once only viewed from the top of the racial one.

While great writing doesn't depend on massive budgets, or majority approval, it does depend on great criticism. Literature is a conversation. Without engaged criticism, literature is reduced to a monologue for an empty room. Sadly, sophisticated criticism rarely comes from newspaper reviews, which typically consist of only synopsis followed by two or three sentences of judgment. It serves to answer one question—"Should I buy this?"—and that answer is usually provided by rushed, underpaid reviewers forced to plow through stacks of the advanced reader copies piling up on their desks. Despite the abundance of reviewing opportunities in the various comment sections of book-focused websites, constructive public criticism is still a rarity—never before have so many people been so able to share such casual, cursory impressions: e.g., "Meh." That is why the role of the academic critic is such an essential one.

Through academic criticism, detailed, informed, and considered, literary fiction comes alive in all its facets and complexities, allowing its seeds to find ground. Through these critics, the work is digested, divined, revealed and reimagined. This is an historic moment in African American literature, when new social realities demand new questions be asked. And those questions demand new responses, new ways of discovering their nature. African American Literature is a living dialogue of ideas. *Contemporary African American Literature* is the lively discussion.

·

ACKNOWLEDGMENTS

We are deeply indebted to Mat, Houston, Darryl, Maryemma, Eve, Kristina, Evie, Carmen, Alice, James, L.H., Alex, Richard, Martha, Trudier, Howard, Dana, Greg, Pia, and David for trusting us with their work and for staying with us through multiple revisions. We could not have asked for a more agreeable and talented group of contributors.

We wish to recognize the following Penn State University persons and entities for their financial support of the fall 2009 conference upon which this volume is based: the College of the Liberal Arts, the Africana Research Center, the Institute for the Arts and Humanities, the Department of English, the Center for American Literary Studies, the George and Barbara Kelly Professor of American Literature Aldon Nielsen, and the Edwin Erle Sparks Professor of Literature Michael Bérubé, as well as the African American Literature and Culture Society.

We would like to acknowledge Penn State University Department of English faculty and graduate students, including Robin Schulze, Mark Morrison, Linda F. Selzer, Aldon Nielsen, Bernard W. Bell, Kevin Bell, Keith Gilyard, Iyun Osagie, Pia Deas, Nadia Wilson, Phylissa Smith-DeRoze, Gregory Pierrot, Michael New, David F. Green, Alexandria Lockett, Sarah Rude, William Woolfitt, Emily Sharpe, and Damon Cagnolatti for their support during the conference. Thanks go as well to Aqsa Ahmed, Natasha Lloyd-Owens, Julia Kramer, Trevon Pegram, and Dawn Noren for their clerical and other support. We would like to thank the staff at Indiana University Press, especially Angela Burton and our editor, Robert Sloan. We are grateful for the insightful feedback and comments provided during the review process, and we would like to extend appreciation to colleague Keith Mitchell who shared his expertise with us during the revision process.

Finally, we would like to recognize the Africana Research Center at Penn State University and the Rutgers University African Diaspora Literature Post-doctoral Fellowship for their financial support of this project. We are especially grateful to Erin King and TJ Turner, who share our living spaces and make us feel like we can do anything we want to do. We thrive on their unconditional love as well as that of the always present Ancestors.

CONTEMPORARY AFRICAN AMERICAN LITERATURE

INTRODUCTION

LOVALERIE KING AND
SHIRLEY MOODY-TURNER

But whether an author protested Jim Crow directly or strived to produce a work in which race didn't matter, what made African American literature a literature was the historical circumstance in which black literary achievement could count, almost automatically, as an effort on behalf of the "race" as a whole. That circumstance was Jim Crow or legalized segregation. We are no longer in that moment. Nothing makes the work of any individual black writer a matter for the "race" as a whole.

—KENNETH W. WARREN

But a funny thing happened on the way to the Civil Rights movement. Black writers started reading and revising each other's works, situating their representations of their own experiences and those of other black people, in the tropes and metaphors of other black writers. That is what a literary tradition is: it is a body of texts defined by signifying relations of revision. Like it or not, black literature, because of this, is here to stay.

—HENRY LOUIS GATES, JR.[1]

While *Contemporary African American Literature* was already conceived and well underway when Kenneth Warren's provocatively titled *What Was African American Literature?* appeared in early 2011, many of the questions Warren raises are covered in this volume. In his slender but spirited treatise, Warren ties literary achievement on behalf of the "race" (a separate and distinct African American Literary tradition) to Jim Crow–era politics, arguing that African American literature ceased to exist when the conditions that called it into being ended with Jim Crow's legal demise. Warren further reads contemporary articulations of a distinct and identifiable African American literary tradition as essentialist and nostalgic assertions of a monolithic racial identity; such imaginings, he asserts, are not viable in our post–Jim Crow world. If one accepts Warren's terms, it is difficult to challenge his argument. We do not, however, accept those terms.

By its very existence, *Contemporary African American Literature* enters into the debates spurred by Warren's central assertions. Its various chapters implicitly respond to a question that has been posed elsewhere by Aldon Nielsen: "Why would anyone be satisfied with such a procrustean definition of the field of African American literature?"[2] In other words, why would anyone identify the tradition as a mere response to racial oppression and a socio-political impulse to showcase the achievements of the race. Indeed, Warren's definition overstates the degree to which all African American writing counted in the political project he describes. There have always been "anomalous" African American literary texts that neither protested racial oppression directly nor showcased the achievements of prominent African Americans.[3] If these texts traditionally have not been counted as African American literature, it is a shortcoming of our definitions rather than a testament to the ability of Jim Crow to corral all African American literary production into one single rubric. While agendas have always been articulated regarding the proper function of African American literary production, African American literary creativity has rarely been contained by these various manifestos and pronouncements.

In the early twentieth century, W. E. B. Du Bois and others in the African American literary establishment grappled with questions about the "criteria of Negro art" and how African Americans should be portrayed— offering up a set of conventions for what constituted appropriate representations that in some ways echoed calls for portraits of respectability from an earlier era. The younger generation of artists protested, responding with their own sets of literary goals, realized in the short-lived literary journal, *FIRE!!* Artists such as Langston Hughes, Zora Neale Hurston, Wallace Thurman, and Richard Bruce Nugent refused to have their art confined to what they saw as the limiting criteria requiring that African American literature function only on behalf of "the race." They resisted attempts by others to delimit the meaning and parameters of their art, electing instead to engage in thematic and formal innovations in order to challenge these definitional strictures. By the middle of the twentieth century, the task for the Black Arts Movement (BAM) involved articulating a rubric for assessing the value of Black Art outside of Eurocentric aesthetic standards. And while the most vocal proponents of BAM promoted goals and agendas for African American literature that included the celebration of a revolutionary Afrocentric engagement with and reconstruction of black history, art and music, they were not able to restrain African American literary creativity to prescriptive criteria.[4] Prescription automatically curtails creativity.

Like each of these past literary moments, the contemporary moment is marked by tension and debate. Perhaps as Evie Shockley suggests, we should think of contemporary African American literature not in terms of how texts do or do not conform to one aesthetic; rather, we should consider how the African American literary tradition is characterized by multiple aesthetics accompanied by varied and diverse, rather than monolithic, strategies for grappling with questions of race, gender, identity and tradition.[5]

Reflecting this alternative approach to the study of contemporary African American literature, *Contemporary African American Literature* engages with conversations about *race* and *authenticity*, the *literary* versus the *popular*, and ideations of "post-racial," "post-black," "post-soul," "post–Civil Rights," or "post-oppression" literature. Contributors grapple with difficult questions: When did Blackness begin? What is authentic Blackness? Is Blackness over? How and when will we know? What are the implications of a post-racial America? Which scholars are most prone to the kinds of questions that anticipate an end to Blackness? What are the pros and cons of the commercialization of African American Literature? What are the signs of a crisis in African American narrative production, and how can the crisis be alleviated? How do we teach contemporary texts as part of an over 250-year tradition? Is a graphic novel "literary" or "popular"? Does it matter? Of what value is student preference in considering the readings for course syllabi? How can conventional scholars of literature assess the value of urban fiction, including Street and Hip-Hop Literature? How has the loss of racial homogeneity around the issue of racism influenced the debates, tensions, and anxieties in African American literary study? Questions such as these, we believe, speak to the tradition's vitality and dynamism, and serve the potential of reinvigorating established scholars' inquiries while bringing new interest to the field and new readers to the texts.

As we move into the second decade of the twenty-first century, we stand at a historical juncture where African American literature is as diverse as it has ever been, where genres such as a Street and Hip Hop literature are reaching unimagined levels of popularity among unexpected audiences, where Oprah's book club, Nikki Turner's urban fiction series, and Zane's publishing prowess have launched careers and created new and influential reading communities. Within the realm of so-called literary fiction, we are witnessing a new generation of writers who locate themselves firmly within an African American literary tradition, while refusing to be bound by monolithic and imaginary notions of authentic blackness or respectability. In the mid-1970s black feminist literary critics began a call for an expansion of the African American literary canon in order to include the works of black women writers. They insisted on the concomitant creation of new theories, paradigms, models and approaches to reading, writing about, and teaching these works to adequately account for black women's contributions to the African American literary tradition.[6] Similarly, the current moment in African American literary studies, rather than herald the end of African American literature, must call for new strategies, paradigms, and critical approaches to understanding and appreciating how contemporary African American literature facilitates a dynamic relationship of continuity and change in a centuries-old literary tradition.

As folklorist Henry Glassie explains, "If tradition is a people's creation out of their own past, its character is not stasis but continuity; its opposite is not change but oppression, the intrusion of a power that thwarts the course of development. Oppressed people are made to do what others will them to do. . . . Acting traditionally, by contrast, they use their own resources—their own tradition, one might say—to create their own future, to do what they will themselves to do."[7] In our understanding, tradition signifies a living, growing, changing, and expanding relationship between individual creativity and group practices, all of which takes place in specific socio-political and historical contexts. Tradition is influenced by the currents of past actions, customs, and practices, but it is shaped and molded through individual volition and contemporary circumstance. Tradition brings the past into a dynamic relationship with the future. This volume affirms that contemporary African American literature, as Gates suggests, continues a signifying relationship with earlier works in the tradition through its re-engagement with themes, tropes, and questions taken up in those earlier works. It does not argue for a fixed canon; nor does it deny that the African American literary tradition intersects in important and dynamic ways with other identifiable literary traditions within and beyond the United States. It does argue, however, that there is a tradition of writing by and about African Americans that began during the Colonial Era and continues today in a dynamic relationship of continuity and change, rewriting, and/or signifying. Such a tradition is distinguishable by a history of shared formal, thematic and other concerns that have been adapted to late twentieth-century and early twenty-first-century contexts.

CONTEMPORARY AFRICAN AMERICAN LITERATURE

In fall 2009 Penn State University hosted the Celebrating African American Literature conference, focusing specifically on the contemporary African American novel. The conference attracted some of the most respected and established scholars in the field, along with scores of enthusiastic beginning and intermediate scholars. Authors Mat Johnson, Alice Randall, and Martha Southgate played pivotal roles at the conference, and all three contributed to this volume. Author participation in the conference and the volume reflects part of a current generational shift as well as our self-conscious effort to encourage more sustained and vigorous dialogue between authors and the scholars and critics who write about and teach their works.

Indeed, we believe that the strength of this volume lies in its inclusion of multiple theoretical and critical approaches to the tradition. When scholars sit down to examine a text, they are always beginning from different places with different sets of ideological constructs. *Contemporary African American Literature* provides a space for critics, authors, and both young and seasoned scholars to benefit from shared knowledge; it highlights contemporary texts and makes them accessible to a variety of new readers; it reinforces the dynamic nature of a tradition that continues to develop in new directions. The volume's richness also derives from the contributors' varied intellectual backgrounds and theoretical orientations. Collectively, contributors earned their degrees over the past four decades—some in the 1970s, and others since the new millennium began. They were educated and have taught, or are teaching, at historically black colleges and universities (HBCUs), Ivy League universities, private liberal arts colleges, and large predominantly white public or private research institutions. Such variety facilitates a more complex and nuanced engagement with the subject matter and also demonstrates how such factors as historical and political context or a scholar's age, race, class, gender, social location, and academic background can influence and shape scholarly the perspective that s/he brings to criticism, pedagogy, and mentoring.

FORMAT

In order to focus reader attention, chapters have been grouped under the following sections: "Politics of Publishing, Pedagogy, and Readership"; "Alternative Genealogies"; "Beyond Authenticity"; and "Pedagogical Approaches and Implications." An annotated bibliography of selected novels by contemporary authors follows. The bibliography is meant only to hint at the great range and depth of contemporary African American literary production. Taken alongside the chapters herein, the bibliography can serve as a useful tool for syllabus planning, research projects, and focused reading, while pointing the interested reader and scholar in the direction of many more texts that could not make our necessarily limited list.

The volume opens with author Mat Johnson's foreword. Next, Houston A. Baker Jr.'s provocative "The Point of Entanglement: Modernism, Diaspora, and Toni Morrison's *Love*" reminds us how the past continues to impact the expressive creativity and literary imagination of contemporary African American writers. Baker poses a dual challenge, at once critiquing the dominant mainstream arbiters of literary merit who pass judgment on African American literary works by relying on standard codes of Western literary conduct and, simultaneously, challenging the current genealogies of modernism that do not locate the Black Diaspora at their center. Exposing the shortcomings of contemporary journalistic reviews, Baker argues that works such as those produced by Toni Morrison cannot be fully understood or appreciated outside of what he refers to as an *oceanic critical consciousness* or a consciousness attuned to the resonances of the transatlantic slave trade and its continuing effects as "a prerequisite for analyzing Black creativity." Reading Morrison as exemplar of this tradition, Baker insists that an informed approach to African American literary and cultural production must remember and recognize the transatlantic past rather than ignore or bury it. Considering an alternative manifestation of the contemporary publishing juggernaut, Darryl Dickson-Carr's "'The Historical Burden That Only Oprah Can Bear': African American Satirists and the State of the Literature" surveys the state of contemporary black cultural production, considering first the commercialization of black lives and cultural traditions that has taken place under the influential supervision of a few powerful figures, particularly Oprah Winfrey. He then reads Paul Beatty's *Slumberland* and Percival Everett's *Erasure* as utilizing satire to critique both the process of commodification and the resultant move toward conformity in representing black lives and experiences. Dickson-Carr thus calls for a heightened awareness about the potentially stultifying effects of the politics of the mainstream marketplace on African American literary and cultural production.

Chapters focused on popular literature complete the first section. In "Black Is Gold: African American Literature, Critical Literacy, and Twenty-First-Century Pedagogies," Maryemma Graham urges scholars and teachers to challenge what she identifies as a dangerous tendency to gain academic legitimacy by devaluing pedagogy and depoliticizing the study of African American literature. Graham's painstaking analysis includes a rich and detailed trek through the development of African American literary studies and literary production as only a senior scholar can make and which contemporary students will find invaluable. She begins by referencing Morrison's language from *Playing in the Dark:* "I want to draw a map, so to speak, of a critical geography and use that map to open as much space for discovery . . . as did the original charting of the New World—without the mandate for conquest." Graham then charts a path toward a "set of discoveries in a global context" that shifts the "attention from writer to reader" while considering developments in print culture and a "broader spectrum of cultural and intellectual practices" that helps us to consider the "implications and consequence of the radical shifts occurring in the creation, production, and distribution of literature in particular and the consumption of knowledge in general." Graham not only provides a critique of some of the underlying issues in Kenneth Warren's provocative theoretical formulation about the nature and foundations of African American literature, but she also considers the meaning of *literacy* in contemporary technology-driven culture.

Taking up Graham's call, Eve Dunbar and Kristina Graaff respond with critical and pedagogical approaches to Street, Urban, and Hip Hop fiction. Dunbar's "Hip Hop (feat. Women Writers): Reimagining Black Women and Agency through Hip Hop Fiction" provides a framework for reading stories collected in Nikki Turner's *Girls from Da Hood* series. She argues that female rappers find an outlet/voice in these stories that has often been closed off to them in the music industry. She also explains why the stories are meant to be cautionary tales rather than advance a specific lifestyle. Like Graham, Kristina Graaff calls attention to the widespread commercial success of Street and Urban fiction; her "Street Literature and the Mode of Spectacular Writing: Popular Fiction between Sensationalism, Education, Politics, and Entertainment" employs four "modes and functions of spectacular writing as sensationalist, didactic, political, and entertaining" in order to link Street Literature with drama. She posits that "spectacular writing can serve as an instrument not only to interpret Street Literature beyond a binary judgment of 'good' versus 'bad' but also to reveal how most of the popular novels possess multiple, often coexisting, interpretational layers." She proposes the "notion of spectacular writing" as "an interpretative framework that can be linked to the few ongoing research projects on Street Literature."

In the next section, Evie Shockley, Carmen Phelps, and James Braxton Peterson consider alternative genealogies and configurations of the African American literary tradition. In "Portrait of the Artist as a Young Slave: Visual Artistry as Agency in the Contemporary Narrative of Slavery," Shockley recovers the genealogy of the artist in historic and contemporary narratives of slavery. Shockley's chapter examines the role of visual artistry as a means of evoking subjectivity and resistance. Tracing this tradition back to Harriet Jacobs's *Incidents in the Life of a Slave Girl* before analyzing contemporary manifestations in Edward P. Jones and Thylias Moss, Shockley demonstrates how artistry and the visual artist have long been central, though understudied and under-appreciated, aspects of African American literary traditions. In "Variations on the Theme: Black Family, Nationhood, Lesbianism, and Sadomasochistic Desire in Marci Blackman's *Po Man's Child*," Phelps calls into question both the idea of a monolithic black identity and the marginalization of

GBLTQ texts within the African American literary tradition. She argues that GLBTQ texts occupy a contentious space within the black literary tradition, troubling heterosexist ideas about black community and creating visibility within the tradition for black gay and lesbian writers and themes. Phelps concludes that the experiences of invisibility, oppression, trauma, and violence expressed in Marci Blackman's *Po Man's Child*, and presaged in Ann Allen Shockley's *Loving Her* and Octavia Butler's *Kindred*, reveal the perspectives of GLBTQ writers and their characters to be integral to, rather than distinct from, the development of an African American literary tradition. Turning to the graphic novel, James Braxton Peterson offers instructive ways of exploring the "dense visual imagery" in Kyle Baker's *Nat Turner*, Mat Johnson and Warren Pleece's *Incognegro: A Graphic Mystery*, and Derek McCulloch and Shepherd Hendrix's *Stagger Lee*. Peterson undertakes an examination of the novels via the Bad-Brother-Man figure, which he suggests provides a more nuanced way to trace the lineage of the badman figure from African American folk tradition to its present guise in the graphic novel. Peterson concludes that the aforementioned graphic novels "recover various folkloric expressions" and "underwrite multiple points of view necessary for the development and transmission of black folk narrative." They also "serve as a corrective for certain (Hip Hop) scholars who may have been a bit too hasty and reductive in comparative analyses of the bad man and the rapper."

The next four chapters focus on "authenticity." L. H. Stallings's "Sampling the Sonics of Sex (Funk) in Paul Beatty's *Slumberland*" offers an alternative reading of Beatty's *Slumberland*, approaching the text not in relation to its marketplace critique, but rather through the novel's engagement with indeterminate blackness. Stallings argues that Beatty's novel offers an alternative to the linear and spatial approach to blackness and post-blackness, suggesting that terms like "post-soul," "post-black," and "post-racial" are wedded to United States movements and periods (i.e., configured as post–Civil Rights phenomena) and are inadequate in accounting for the indeterminacy of blackness. Stallings traces Beatty's alternative conceptualizations of time and space through formulations such as CPT (colored people's time), sampling, break beat, and the sonics of funk. Through these alternative configurations, Stallings asserts, we can "change the trajectory of future discourses about race and racial identity." In "Post-Integration Blues: Black Geeks and Afro-Diasporic

Humanism," Alexander Weheliye focuses not on the cool badman or outlaw but on the figure of the geek in exploring questions of authenticity via constructions of the black geek in African American literature. Weheliye shares actual experiences of teaching a blues structured course on recent African American literary history. The title of the course, "post-integration blues," "insists on coarticulating the positive and negative dimensions of integration without resolving the tensions between them." Taking the blues as "a structure of feeling rather than a particular musical genre, provides a pathway to understanding the central contradictions of the post-integration era," notes Weheliye. Next, Richard Schur and novelist Martha Southgate recognize and offer critical approaches to reading the narrative possibilities offered by some of today's most prominent authors of African American literary fiction. Reading Danzy Senna's *Causasia* and Colson Whitehead's *Sag Harbor* within the context of the post–Civil Rights era, Schur suggests in "The Crisis of Authenticity in Contemporary African American Literature" that these novels force us to re-imagine ideas about authenticity, blackness, and identity and to expand our definition of African American literature to encompass these "new" narratives. Contemporary novelist Martha Southgate offers, in "Someday We'll All be Free: Considering Post-Oppression Fiction," her insightful commentary on what she terms "post-oppression" African American fiction. While cognizant of the gains, advantages and freedoms achieved through the sacrifices of the Civil Rights generation, Southgate argues that this new kind of narrative includes works in which racial oppression is not a central theme and in which issues of race are not necessarily the defining features of the text. Southgate's chapter forces us to consider what will be the defining features of an African American literary tradition that includes increasingly diverse experiences of race, history, oppression, and liberation that continue to intersect in increasingly complex ways with gender, sexuality, and class.

Chapters focusing on pedagogical interventions are geared toward introducing the literature to new generations of scholars who will bring their own personal and educational backgrounds to bear on future critical and theoretical interventions. Contributors remind teachers and their students of the historical foundations of the tradition. Their chapters can help students who must meet challenges to rhetorics of authenticity that may be part of the critical tradition, or who want to challenge many aspects of the very grounds upon which the tradition has proceeded and been borne by their academic predecessors. Celebrated teacher Trudier Harris's reading of Tayari Jones's *Leaving Atlanta* points to the author's careful attention to, and incorporation of, American history. Noting that "one could just as easily chart a history of peoples of African descent on American soil by reading their imaginative writings as he or she could chart that history through nonliterary sources," Harris provides material for a number of pedagogical interventions into contemporary black literature with history as a rubric that assists in textual as well as intertextual analysis. Howard Rambsy II considers the genre of the graphic novel while examining the reading practices and learning styles of African American men through a case study of his reading group's engagement with Kyle Baker's graphic novel *Nat Turner*. Rambsy's chapter suggests that through such novels we gain both fresh insights on the development of the African American novel as well as new alternative perspectives on the visual literacy and competency of African American male readers—a population, as Rambsy reminds us, typically seen solely in terms of lack and deficiency. Rambsy's chapter also illustrates how contemporary technology can be factored into the teacherly process in a way that encourages greater student participation. In "Toward the Theoretical Practice of Conceptual Liberation: Using an Africana Studies Approach to Reading African American Literary Texts," Greg Carr and Dana Williams revisit Baker's opening injunction that we employ theoretical and pedagogical frameworks that recognize the influence of the diasporic past on contemporary African American literary and cultural production. A strong understanding of Africana approaches enables teachers and students to "leverage the social, political, and cultural capital that attend the production of Africana narratives, texts, and practices [in order] to discern intellectual connections and engagements necessary to widen the tributaries flowing from African contributions to human knowledge and advancement."

Authors who identify as African American have written and continue to write from a variety of political, ideological, and socio-economic vantage points. That fact has never prevented critics from setting out specific criteria and articulating grand frameworks regarding what constitutes African American literature, or suggesting provocatively that it no longer exists. It now seems inevitable that in the Age of Obama, the question of whether African American literature exists, or needs to exist, as a distinct tradition would *return* as a hot topic for debate. We hope you will find this to be an essential reference tool for your teaching and scholarly engagement with contemporary African American literature.

NOTES

1. March 19, 2011, *Chronicle of Higher Education,* online chat with Henry Louis Gates, Jr., and Kenneth W. Warren.

2. Aldon Nielsen, "Wasness" in "What Is African American Literature: A Symposium," *Los Angeles Review of Books* (June 13, 2001). Accessed July 26, 2011. http://lareviewofbooks.org/post/6482760433/what-is-african-american-literature-a-symposium

3. In *Psychoanalysis and Black Novels: Desire and the Protocols of Race,* Claudia Tate identifies anomalous texts in African American literary history as those that "resist, to varying degrees, the race and gender paradigms that we spontaneously impose on black textuality." See Claudia Tate, *Psychoanalysis and Black Novels: Desire and the Protocols of Race* (New York: Oxford University Press, 1998), 8. Drawing on Tate's definition, Gene Jarrett, in *African American Literature Beyond Race,* introduces a number of African American texts that resist traditional notions of what constitutes "the" African American literary tradition, from Paul Laurence Dunbar's *The Uncalled* to Frank Yerby's *The Foxes of Harrow* and Zora Neale Hurston's *Seraph on the Suwanee* to Octavia Butler's *Bloodchild.* See Gene Jarrett, editor, *African American Literature Beyond Race: An Alternative Reader* (New York: New York University Press, 2006), 7–8.

4. As Evie Shockley notes, even the notion of BAM as a monolithic entity with a unified goal and purpose has been challenged, citing recent work, by Carter Mathes for example, recognizing the diversity within BAM. See Evie Shockley, *Renegade Poetics: Black Aesthetics and Formal Innovation in African American Poetry* (Iowa City: University of Iowa Press, 2012), 2.

5. Ibid., 7.

6. See, for example, Mary Helen Washington, "Black Women Image Makers: Their Fiction Becomes Our Reality," *Black World* 23, no.10 (August 1974): 10–18; Barbara Smith, "Toward a Black Feminist Criticism," *Conditions: Two* 1, no. 2 (October 1977): 24–44; Deborah McDowell, "New Directions for Black Feminist Criticism," *Black American Literature Forum* 14, no.4 (Winter 1980): 153–59.

7. Henry Glassie, "Tradition," *Journal of American Folklore,* 108, no. 430 (Autumn 1995): 396.

WORKS CITED

Chronicle of Higher Education, March 19, 2011, online. Accessed July 26, 2011. http://chronicle.com/article/Live-Chat-The-End-of/126492/.

Glassie, Henry. "Tradition." *Journal of American Folklore.* 108.430 (Autumn 1995): 395–412.

Jarrett, Gene, editor. *African American Literature Beyond Race: An Alternative Reader.* New York: New York University Press, 2006.

Nielsen, Aldon Lynn. "Wasness" in "What is African American Literature: A Symposium." *Los Angeles Review of Books* (June 13, 2001). Accessed July 26, 2011. http://lareviewofbooks.org/post/6482760433/what-is-african-american-literature-a-symposium.

Shockley, Evie. *Renegade Poetics: Black Aesthetics and Formal Innovation in African American Poetry*. Iowa City: University of Iowa Press, 2012.

PART ONE

POLITICS OF PUBLISHING, PEDAGOGY, AND READERSHIP

ONE

THE POINT OF ENTANGLEMENT: MODERNISM, DIASPORA, AND TONI MORRISON'S *LOVE*

HOUSTON A. BAKER, JR.

We must return to the point from which we started. Diversion is not a useful ploy unless it is nourished by reversion: not a return to the longing for origins, to some immutable state of being, but a return to the point of entanglement, from which we forcefully turned away; that is where we must ultimately put to work the forces of creolization, or perish.

—EDOUARD GLISSANT, "REVERSION AND DIVERSION"

"The hooked C's on the silverware worried me because I thought he took casual women casually. But if doubled C's were meant to mean Celestial Cosey, he was losing his mind."

—L'S UTTERANCE IN *LOVE*

Erzulie always holds the idea of love in suspension, for those who serve are after recollections of those experiences that must defeat or question that love.

—COLIN (JOAN) DAYAN, "ERZULIE: A WOMEN'S HISTORY OF HAITI"

CONTINGENT MODERNISM, JOURNALISTIC CRITICISM, AND DIASPORA STUDIES

A glance at selected journalistic assessments of Toni Morrison's novel *Love* reveals the intellectual shallowness and implicit critical contempt that are hallmarks of journalistic reviews of Black expressivity.[1] Here is the judgment on Morrison provided for the *New York Times* by Michiko Kakutani:

> . . . while there are some beautifully observed passages in this book [*Love*], where the author's distinctive style (forged into something new from such disparate influences as Faulkner, Ellison, Woolf, and Garcia Marquez) takes over, the story as a whole reads like a gothic soap opera, peopled by scheming, bitter women and selfish predatory men: women engaged in cartoon-violent catfights; men catting around and going to cathouses.[2]

Kakutani even allows herself the insult that *Love* is "an awkward retread of *Sula* and *Tar Baby* combined."[3]

Writing for *The Guardian*, Elaine Showalter retreads journalistic ineptitude when she suggests that *Love* is "gothic," and written by an author who "braids the [African American] cultural background with stories of love and hate in a narrative style influenced by Garcia Marquez and Faulkner."[4] Showalter damns with faint praise. She salutes Morrison's skillful rendering of Christine, one of *Love*'s most damaged actors. According to Showalter, Christine's story "condenses material that would easily provide a dozen novels for another writer. . . . In the hands of, say, Philip Roth, [Christine's] life history would afford opportunities for rich, sardonic and profound reflections on human experience in the 20th century, beyond, nationality, race, sex, age, class, and ethnicity."[5] In Showalter's judgment, Faulkner and Marquez gave Morrison language, but the author of *Love* should have contracted Philip Roth to teach her how to use it. Showalter concludes:

> Morrison's imaginative range of identification is narrower by choice; although she would no doubt argue—and rightly—that African American characters can speak for all humanity. But in *Love,* they do not; they are stubbornly bound by their own culture; and thus, while *Love* is certainly an accomplished novel, its perfection comes from its limitations.[6]

Showalter's review differs in chronology only from the racialized presumptuousness of critic Louis Simpson, who in 1963 wrote of the Pulitzer Prize–winning African American poet Gwendolyn Brooks as follows:

> Gwendolyn Brooks' *Selected Poems* contains some lively pictures of Negro life. I am not sure it is possible for a Negro to write well without making us aware he [*sic*] is a Negro; on the other hand, if being a Negro is the only subject, the writing is not important.[7]

Finally, Laura Miller writing for the *New York Times* provides an example of a review that sketchily merges journalistic pseudo-profundity with African American class fantasy:

> What middle-class blacks in Morrison's fiction gain in order, stability and mutual support—no small blessing in a hostile white-run world—they lose in vitality, in wildness and perhaps in truth. All of her novels constellate around this perplexing transaction, none more so perhaps than *Sula,* and *Love* is the sister to the fiery 1974 book. *Sula*—wayward, ruthless, precious—personifies the kind of love that ransacks the lives of Morrison's characters, leaving them dazed and bereft, with blood on their hands.[8]

The following assumptions are implicit in the reviews cited. *Love* can be adequately understood in a traditional Western optic of the modern novel. The Black history required for reviewing *Love* is the twice-told tale of Southern slavery, Negro emancipation, and Civil Rights demonstrations. *Love's* rising and falling action, as well as its address to affections and spiritual relations of everyday Black life, can successfully be evaluated by standard codes of Western literary critical conduct. Such assumptions must be resisted if Morrison's novel is to be fitly critiqued. Upon further thought these assumptions are not merely to be resisted, they are to be *contested.*

Formal, disciplinary *contestation* alone produces regenerative accounts of expressive culture. Out of such contestation, "The Renaissance" has in recent scholarly shifts been rechristened "The Early-Modern Era." *Modernism* is the sign at stake for the criticism of Morrison's oeuvre. Morrison defines modernism's circuits of enunciation not as products of 1920s London intellectuals, but as resonances of the Transatlantic Slave Trade's violent concatenations.

The Transatlantic Slave Trade appropriated millions of African men, women, and children and violently transformed them into commodities to further enrich white men of property and wealth. The Atlantic is the domain of the trade and foregrounds an *oceanic critical consciousness* as a prerequisite for analyzing Black creativity. Oceanic consciousness is the analytical offspring of ships, trade, and nightmarish terror. It is littoral and tiller for a Black Diaspora Studies that unsettles familiar Western notions of modernism and provides regenerative knowledge and scholarly methods for reviewing and judging *Love* and its creative kindred.[9]

In recent years, scholars such as Marcus Rediker, Donna Weir-Soley, Paul Gilroy, Achille Mebembe, Edouard Glissant, Heather Russell, Brent Edwards, and others have acknowledged the Transatlantic as a space of dread, a Middle Passage and mass grave for millions. Gilroy and others brilliantly contest a present-day criticism akin to journalistic reviews that hypothetically entreats: Why not let the dead past bury its dead? To-day's artists and critics should invent new canvases to conceal historical horror. Isn't amnesia more nourishing and less painful for race relations? I emphasize that the foregoing is a *hypothetical* utterance. Despite its hypothetical cast, the utterance captures key tendencies of journalistic reviews. Such reviews are amnesiac with respect to oceans. Diaspora Studies *memorializes* the Transatlantic and effectively addresses its attendant creativity.[10]

In *The Slave Ship: A Human History,* Marcus Rediker writes:

> In producing workers for the plantation, the [slave] ship-factory also produced "race." ... The ... [Middle Passage] thus transformed those who made it. War making, imprisonment, and the factory production of labor power and race all depended on violence. ... [A slave ship's] captain facing a "rage for suicide" [among the ship's African captives] seized upon a woman "as a proper example to the rest." He ordered the woman tied with a rope under her armpits and lowered into the water. "When the poor creature was thus plunged in, and about halfway down, she was heard to give a terrible shriek, which at first was ascribed to her fears of drowning; but soon after the water appearing all red around her, she was drawn up. And it was found that a shark, which had followed the ship, had bit her off from the middle."[11]

Rediker adds: "[The slave ship] was the historic vessel for the emergence of capitalism, a new and unprecedented social and economic system that remade large parts of the world beginning in the sixteenth century."[12]

Terror, torture, and murder were instrumental in the operation and discipline of the slave ship. However, as Rediker makes clear, any notion that Transatlantic violence gave birth to "instant" Black abjection like that defined by historian Stanley Elkins as a "Sambo Personality" is no more than dominant-culture fantasy.[13] Brutalized by slave-ship incarceration and surveillance, captive Africans were *never* en masse reduced to quivering "cargoes" devoid of language, affiliation, and collective strategies of revolt. African resilience and its propensity for insurrection were common knowledge among ship captains and ship builders. Armed sailors were in long supply to man the ships. In the center of many vessels was a high *barricado* fitted with cannons to be used in the event of "cargo insurrection." Eviscerating disciplinary terror was a staple. Still, as Rediker writes: "[captive Africans] managed a creative, life-affirming response:

they fashioned new languages, new cultural practices, new bonds, and a nascent community among themselves aboard the ship. They called each other 'shipmate,' the equivalent of brother and sister, and thereby inaugurated a 'fictive' but very real kinship to replace what had been destroyed by their abduction and enslavement in Africa."[14] Survival, resistance, and Black creative revolt were constants of the Transatlantic.

What remained (and remains) beyond repair, however, is the "unspeakable" trauma the Transatlantic Slave Trade and colonialism perpetrated in the destruction of African civilizations. In *Discourse on Colonialism*, Aimé Césaire writes: "*I am talking about societies drained of their essence, cultures trampled underfoot, institutions undermined, lands confiscated, religions smashed, magnificent artistic creations destroyed, extraordinary possibilities wiped out . . . I am talking about . . . food crops destroyed, malnutrition permanently introduced, agricultural development oriented solely toward the benefit of the metropolitan countries.*"[15] Armageddon presumes a clash of opposing forces. Colonialism and the slave trade were one-way genocidal assaults. They were bloodbaths for profit. Césaire cites General Gérard's description of the massacre at Ambike: "The native [Senegalese] rifleman had orders to kill only the men, but no one restrained them; intoxicated by the smell of blood, they spared not one woman, not one child. . . . At the end of the afternoon, the heat caused a light mist to arise: it was the blood of the five thousand victims, the ghost of the city, evaporating in the setting sun."[16]

In "Middle Passage," Robert Hayden celebrates the miracle of African survival as a "voyage *through* death/to life upon these shores" [my emphasis].[17] Yet given scenes of violence like Ambike and the evisceration described by Rediker, how can one imagine a cessation of Black Diaspora *trauma*? How can one in good faith ignore the enduring psychological and physio-behavioral pathologies of colonialism and enslavement? The smell of blood lingers. There is permanent somatic disorder felt along the pulses: Post Traumatic Stress Disorder (PTSD) is defined as "an anxiety that can develop after exposure to a terrifying event or ordeal in which grave physical harm occurred or was threatened."[18] The oceanic specificity of such trauma is a precondition for a critique of Toni Morrison's *Love*.

For nearly four decades, Toni Morrison has asserted her creative allegiance with Black Diaspora voices, rhythms, and signification. The

psyches and actions of her characters are always functions of Post Traumatic Slave Syndrome (PTSS). Joy Degruy Leary's *Post Traumatic Slave Syndrome* (PTSS) is mandatory for those who would get Morrison "right."[19]
Morrison's fiction presupposes trauma as never ending. It has no "cure"
and is *always* determinative in the under-consciousness of Black Diaspora everyday life. Psychology explains that trauma is "worked through."
But Black life knows PTSS as wake-up call and evening embrace. Flashbacks and dreams of irredeemable insult are its stock-in-trade. PTSS is
transgenerational, passing from great ancestors to descendants of the
ninth and tenth generations.

Genocide, Holocaust, and imperialist assault (read: Armenian, European Jewry, North Vietnamese Citizenry) are infinite in traumatic du-
ration. Leary reflects on the following: "In America, generations were
born into slavery and died there."[20] If dysfunctional, maladaptive, and
violent behaviors of other nations and ethnic groups are, at least in part,
results of trauma, how can one believe the same is *not* true for generations of sufferers and descendants of the Transatlantic Slave Trade?

The United States declared emancipation of Black millions in 1863.
Indissoluble debt, Jim Crow suppression, convict leasing, lynch law, and
white supremacist terror "enslaved" the Black majority (more than 90 percent of the Black population) at the end of the nineteenth century. In our
twenty-first millennium, the U.S. prison-industrial complex incarcerates
more than 2.2 million people, the majority of whom are Black and Latino.
According to a study by the American Civil Liberties Union (ACLU)
titled "Race and Ethnicity in America," in 2006, the U.S. penal population was 41 percent Black and 19 percent Latino.[21] In 2004, 21 percent of
Black men in their 20s who did not attend college were in jail or prison.[22]
In *Golden Gulag: Prisons, Surplus, Crisis, and Opposition in Globalizing
California*, Ruth Wilson Gilmore persuasively argues against claims that
the prison-industrial complex is a new millennial analogue of Southern
plantations.[23] She writes: "The problem with the 'new slavery' argument
is that very few prisoners work for anybody while they're locked up. Recall, the generally accepted goal for prisons has been *incapacitation:* a do-
nothing theory if ever there was one."[24] Gilmore's research and conclusions seem impeccable.

Yet if we consider the continuous genealogy of Black abjection from
the festering holds of transatlantic slave ships to our millennium's rot-

ting Black inner-city neighborhoods, we have little choice but to define the plight of the present-day Black majority as "worse than slavery," to borrow a title phrase from historian David Oshinsky.[25] Rampant unemployment, discriminatory criminal justice, remorseless assaults on (and among) Black males, denial of basic literacy, and infinite evictions—all of these and more appear to make twenty-first-century Black majority life inexorably purulent. A journey *through* Black inner-city death seems by far the exception rather than the rule. How, then, can one speak in good conscience of the *eradication* of the offices and effects of slavery? How can one believe—after surveying streets of Detroit, or observing certain nocturnal provinces of Kingston, Jamaica—that PTSS has vanished, has been "cured," or already "worked through"?

To a signatory, the Founding Fathers of our republic *embraced* a heinous crime against humanity. Their aboriginal affirmation has morphed into a U.S. criminal justice system that finds thousands of young Black men almost certain to spend time in jail, prison, or under the jurisdiction of the criminal justice system at some point in their lives. "The Law" is the new *Master.* Who does it serve? We might answer in the manner of former Jamaican prime minister Michael Manley when he speaks about the formation of the International Monetary Fund and the World Bank: "You ask whom do they serve? I ask you: Who set them up?"[26] Clearly, the laws of criminal incarceration in the United States have immemorially served the interests of capital and its imperious orders of dominion. In our century, those orders are global, governing manufacture, supply, consumption, and well-being of the planet. To paraphrase Faulkner: The Transatlantic Slave Trade is not dead; it is not even past. The *epistemological arrogance* that abetted the trade, albeit as a farcical return, has not been lost to journalistic criticism. Andrew O'Hehir's review of *Love* for Salon.com offers a case in point.

O'Hehir writes: "But while *Love* is indeed, in some large sense, a novel about the damaging legacy of slavery and racism, there is nothing simplistic anywhere in it. In no way does Morrison provide ideological excuses for Bill Cosey or the warring women around him, or apologize for the rape and murder, the petty torture and the money-grubbing and the malicious arson fires and the corruption that have poisoned the Cosey resort and the Cosey world."[27] O'Hehir's judgment has about it an air of clerical congratulations. His effusion suggests that he harbored (no matter how transiently) at least a suspicion that a Nobel Laureate might work in "simplistic" terms. Had he not entertained such a prospect, why does he robustly assure us: *It did not happen*? There is Euro-conquistador swagger in O'Hehir's review. It can be extrapolated as follows: Slavery and PTSS do not grant victim-survivors of the Transatlantic the prerogative of claiming trauma from historical and continuing crimes against them as in any way *causal* for their everyday behaviors. O'Hehir summarily "forgets" the ocean, considers its effects inadmissible for a critique of *Love*. In fact his dilettantish review implies that bad Black behavior is, perhaps, culturally autochthonous. It cannot legitimately be charged to traumatic revisitations of Transatlantic horror and harm. O'Hehir's is the arrogant logic of forgetting.

Those acquainted with Diaspora Studies and Morrison's contributions acknowledge Post-Traumatic Slavery Syndrome as a story one cannot ignore. "Forced disappearance" of PTSS from critical responses to Black expressivity is almost as great an insult as the three-fifths clause in the Constitution of the United States. Still there are afloat in seas of American punditry declarations that hard-won and compelling narratives of the Transatlantic Slave Trade and its entailments should be disappeared. These declarations are discursive avatars of slave masters, rapists, and murderers. Referencing the art of Francisco Goya, one might say that forced disappearances of the Transatlantic are opiates for the journalistic masses. So-called post-racial impulses to forgetfulness are willed ignorance. They induce a sleep of reason that produces "monsters."[28] To *speak* infamous acts and institutions of the Transatlantic in lyrical, unapologetic, and memorial forms is Toni Morrison's genius. She writes:

> ... modern life begins with slavery ... From a women's point of view,
> in terms of confronting the problems of where the world is now, Black
> women had to deal with the post-modern problems in the nineteenth
> century and earlier. These things had to be addressed by Black people
> a long time ago; certain kinds of dissolution, the loss of and the need to
> reconstruct certain kinds of stability. Certain kinds of madness, deliberately going mad in order, as one of the characters says ... [in *Beloved*] "in
> order not to lose your mind." These strategies for survival made the truly
> modern person. They're a response to predatory western phenomena.
> You can call it ideology and an economy, what it is is a pathology. Slavery
> broke the world in half, it broke it in every way.[29]

Creative engagement with *modernism* demands journeying to the world's "breaking point," to Black Diaspora unconscious and its myriad and entangled visitations.

In an afterword to the 1993 reissue of *The Bluest Eye,* Morrison provides a manifesto: "My choice of language (speakerly, aural, colloquial) my reliance for full comprehension of codes embedded in Black culture, my effort to effect immediate co-conspiracy and intimacy (without distancing, explanatory fabric), as well as my attempt to shape a silence while breaking it are attempts to transfigure the complexity and wealth of Black-American culture into a language worthy of culture."[30] "Worthy" and "explicable" are premiere judgments of Morrison's corpus by Diaspora Studies. Diaspora Studies share an extended West Indian, British, and post-colonial heritage. Their contemporary insights are as clear as a ship's bell and as materially and historically grounded as the enduring racial terror of the Americas. Diaspora Studies focus critical attention on Glissant's distinction between the complexities of a *Diaspora* created by terror and the exigencies of *Exilic Relocation.* Glissant writes:

> There is a difference between the transplanting (by exile or dispersion) of a people who continue to survive elsewhere and the transfer (by the slave trade) of a population to another place where they change into something different, into a new set of possibilities. It is in this metamorphosis that we must try to detect one of the best kept secrets of creolization.[31]

Paul Gilroy invokes Glissant to stake a claim for the existence of "countercultures of modernity," modes of survival and creativity that produce transnational community for sufferers of "transfer."[32] Achille Mbembe philosophically investigates the "post-colony" as an entanglement of temporalities, affiliations, and incompletions.[33] Morrison shares artistic and intellectual ground with Glissant, Gilroy, and Mbembe. She has repeatedly admonished that critical and scholarly neglect of Diaspora Studies and its oceanic consciousness produces grotesque assessments of Black expressivity. *El sueno de la razone produce monstrous.* The sleep of reason produces monsters.

Aware of her ideal audience's history and traumatic anxieties, Morrison is not shy to announce her singularity:

> Nobody was going to judge me [in my determination to write my first novel *The Bluest Eye*] because they didn't know what I knew. No African

American writer has ever done what I did—none of the writers I knew, even the ones I admired [had ever done what I did]—which was to write without the White Gaze. My writing wasn't about them [whites].[34]

The foregoing declaration makes clear that "modern whiteness" was not Morrison's chosen field of play. She has worked with singular purpose to reclaim and *regenerate* both the novel as form and *Diaspora Experience* as its subject.[35] Her dazzling inscription of formal "difference" has merited her place in the first rank of modern artistic achievement. She has altered forever the familiar Western definitions of the "modern novel." Journeying to Glissant's "point of entanglement from which we forcefully turned away,"[36] her accomplishments are fittingly designated "Morrisonian Modernism."

Love's modernism *changes the subject*. It invokes PTSS and summons goddesses who work a sea change on traditional lexicons, assumptions, and semantic fields of mainstream journalistic criticism. The propensity of such criticism to identify Faulkner's "gothic" and other haunting white-Southern or South American writing as *sole* stylistic roots for Morrison's oeuvre are, in a word, "irresponsible." Black Diaspora critique tells a very different story.

In her review of Marlon James's novel *John Crow's Devil,* Lisa Allen-Agostini writes: "In the West Indian canon, the gothic or horror novel is not common. Monsters in [West Indian expressivity] generally come in human form, as slavemasters, rapists, racists—the entirely earthy terrors that still plague a people too close to the dehumanizing collective anguish of slavery and indentureship."[37] In harmony with Allen-Agostini's projections, Morrison claims as her subject an unparalleled Black subjectivity shaped by terrors of slave masters, rapists, and racists. Her monsters are not imitation gothic dramatis personae. They are (and this is much more frightening) normal white people who "break the world in half."

In a quatrain from "Middle Passage," Robert Hayden writes: "Deep in the festering hold thy father lies, / of his bones New England pews are made, / those are altar lights that were his eyes."[38] Hayden's poem resonates with the economic compactness of trauma. "Passage," in its resilient expressivity, shakes the authority of *The Tempest*'s "Full fathom five they father lies." It also powerfully indicts the ethical debacle of Christian Enlightenment with its materialist "New England pews" and pious "altar lights." Against seemingly insurmountable odds African and Black Diaspora forged a legacy of readable love. This exceptional and readily discoverable survival and regeneration is not negligible. Nor should it abide, or honor, any designation other than *Diaspora*.

Modern history grants no privilege of *single* ownership on terrors of dispossession and denigrating racialization. And it would be naïve in the extreme to deny that capital investment dictates *whose* trauma takes precedence in the annals of displacement and suffering. Certainly an abundance of financial and cultural capital can prioritize and promote an interest group's claims to exceptionality in the archives of horror. However, any account of modernism that fails clearly to state that the Transatlantic Slave Trade *was* a Holocaust and did produce an African and Black *Diaspora* is uselessly uncritical. To deny the Transatlantic as Holocaust and Black Diaspora trauma as its consequence is a failure of history and imagination. Toni Morrison *invests* in Black Diaspora and adopts a legacy of the Transatlantic as subject and title of her eighth novel, *Love*.

LOVE AND GODDESSES OF THE DIASPORA

In *Love*, Romen, who is the grandson of Sandler and Vida Gibbons, sits in a classroom gazing dreamily out the window. He is musing on "what has already taken place and imagining new ways to do it."[39] The object of his distraction is Junior Viviane, ex-convict, seductress—a young and sensual Black woman blessed with addictive thighs. She is a recent arrival in the seacoast town of Silk. She and Romen are joined in an omnivorous, county-spanning, marathon of sexual "grapple and heat." Their lovemaking is fueled by abundant opportunity and physically rough desire. The fourteen-year-old Romen is transfixed. He is certain his relationship with Junior has converted him from a shamefaced pariah among his peers. His outsider status results from his refusal to participate in the gang rape of Pretty-Fay. With Junior at his call and service, Romen believes he has achieved a chiseled self and a fearless manhood. While his dutiful history teacher strains to convey fundamentals of the Eighteenth Amendment, the dreamy fourteen-year-old is flooded by images of Junior:

> How was he supposed to concentrate on a history lesson when Junior's face was a study? Her breasts, her armpits required focused explanation; her skin demanded closer analysis. Was . . . [her skin's] perfume flowery or more like rain? Besides, he had to memorize the thirty-eight ways she

could smile and what each one meant. He needed a whole semester to figure out her sci-fi eyes: the lids, the lashes, irises so shiny Black she could
be an alien. One he would kill to join on the spaceship.[40]

The subject of the history lesson is the Eighteenth Amendment, the constitutional revision prohibiting the "manufacture, sale, or transportation
of intoxicating liquor." Could there be a modification of the law more dis-
cordant with the grandson's intoxicating reverie of Junior? There could
not. The Eighteenth Amendment is the *only* constitutional amendment
to be repealed. The repeal suggests that God, man, and history miscal-
culated with prohibition. The cunning passages of historical cravings far
outweighed the seemingly reasonable dictums of the law. Prohibition
almost immediately produced what a famous reggae lyric declares: "So
much *trouble* in this world."

Official prohibitions, moralistic sanctions—whether from religion,
history, or law—are essentially moot in the everyday Black life of Morrison's modernism. Blackness and its people—geographies, affections,
mores, and especially its wild women graced with wondrous hair—do
not lightly suffer prohibition. Their refusal is a signal reality of Black Diaspora subversion. L, the narrator of Morrison's *Love* speaks as follows
about Celestial, the most majestically captivating figure in *Love:*

> Her hair, flat when she went . . . [into the nighttime waters of the bay] . . .
> rose up slowly and took on the shape of the clouds dragging the moon.
> Then she—well, made a sound. I don't know to this day whether it was a
> word, tune, or a scream. *All I know is that it was a sound I wanted to answer.*
> Even though, normally, I'm stone quiet. Celestial.[41]

The name "Celestial" is, in effect, the "amen" of L's reverie and remem-
brance. What L observes is a narrative scene when Black women's luxu-
riant and survival-burnished hair is foregrounded. Such sumptuous agency
defies the universe, shrugging aside with a mere rising from oceans'
depth all prohibitive codes of nature, history, and the law.

We know well in advance of *Love* that a grievous charge borne by
Black Diaspora Manhood has to do with hair. In Morrison's *Song of Solomon* the overindulged and potentially murderous Hagar indicts the novel's protagonist Milkman Dead as follows: ". . . [Milkman] don't like hair
like mine. . . . He don't love it at all. He hates it."[42] If such hair as Hagar,
Celestial, and Junior possess is not loved, countenanced, blessed, and

empowered, then redemptive love can never be the gift of Black community.

To undervalue such hair's wizardry is to court disaster. For when the "best self" of Black community is not empowered, then, truly, things fall apart. In *Love*, the *harmatia* or tragic flaw signaled by misevaluations (fictive and critical) of Junior and Celestial brings the thunder. Some commentators have named this flaw the "Misogynistic/Harmatia."[43] It extends from *early-modern* Hamlet to Morrison's Milkman Dead.

The seemingly impermeable Black and Up Beach community in *Love*—site of low-wage labor and a cannery—drowns in Hurricane Agnes's surge and flood. A venerable Black middle class—doctors, lawyers, musicians, teachers, and swaggering military officers—is charred and re-educated by flames of Black revolution. Sacrosanct codes of friendship, sex, matrimony, and mental health are unmoored by unembarrassed Black libertinism and dark indiscretion. *Celestial* forces, one might say, incite every resistive turn in *Love*. Sublime unconventionalities thwart prohibition and geld normative male codes of conduct.

For example, the administrator of the reform school where Junior Viviane has been incarcerated caresses her magical hair and praises her beauty as she is about to be released. Abruptly, the administrator pushes Junior's head down hard, causing her to fall to her knees. Panting, the administrator unbuckles his pants in anticipation. In less than a nanosecond, Junior grasps the back of his knees and topples him off a balcony. He survives a one-story fall. But it is Junior who is sentenced to three years in prison. The perjured testimony of the reform school's male guidance counselor (a witness to the fall) convicts her. The additional years of incarceration only amplify Junior's magic. She achieves an inviolate sense of who decisively she is and what precisely she wants.

How can mainstream criticism read Junior only as a dodgy, Black adolescent con artist? Such judgment represents a serious intellectual failure. It signals, in fact, the willed amnesia of a version of modernism endorsed by a few well-spoken white men and women "after the war." To merely skim the surface of *Love* is to miss completely its social and historical ancestry of oceans. An unloved child from the wilds of the Settlement, the adolescent Junior, is in the first instance a beautiful and bountiful survivor. Not a single phrase or paragraph by a reliable narrator in *Love* suggests she has either a serious criminal past or a proven (to borrow Heed's phrase for her adoptive sister Christine) "slut history." But mainstream modernist criticism, like mainstream American justice, needs only a hint of evidence to convict a "racial" offender. If Junior has "done time" she must be a criminal character. Such calumny and behaviorist judgment obscure historical and spiritual structures of feeling in *Love*.

Junior is an unorthodox and fearless counter force to the worst manifestations of the central crime in *Love*. If the fall that brings Black community to ruin is male dominance (the "Misogynist/Harmatia"), then its most brutal manifestation is rape. The character Fruit and his band of self-styled "revolutionary" brothers foment riots and speak passionately of Black community and power to the people. Yet their so-called nationalism is no more than a baggy and demonic masquerade. Their insecure posturing masks rapist bluster, a violence not at all distinct from the gang-rape sensibility of the young Theo and his brood of Black boys who sexually assault Pretty-Fay. It is Junior who neuters such terror. She does so through exquisite equipoise and stinging resistance to contempt. Junior (as I shall discuss more fully) is an amalgam of the many manifestations of the Vodoun goddess or loa Erzulie.[44]

Theo, son of Maceo who owns the café where L cooks, believes he has delivered the coup de grace of male contempt when he slops Junior's carryout order carelessly into Styrofoam containers. Junior says nothing as he "let the stewed tomatoes slide over the compartments to discolor the potato salad, and forked barbecue on top of the gravied chicken" (67). But, as she settles her check and turns to leave, she says to Theo: "I see why you need a posse. Your dick don't work one on one?" (67). L, who witnesses the scene, thinks:

> *This Junior girl—something about her puts me in mind of a local woman I know. Name of Celestial. When she was young, that is, though I doubt if Junior or any of these modern tramps could match her style.* (italics in original, 67)

Matchless in articulateness and self-reliance, Black women's will is the ethical arsenal of *Love*. There is a reason Junior reminds L of the divine Celestial.

Mainstream definitions and cartographies of "history" and "modernism" are narratively unhinged by *Love*. Modernism ineptly highlights in its journalistic criticism what I call the *ultra-excessive naturalness* of "the Settlement." But in *Love*, even the inbred Settlement dogs (in their hunting skills and aesthetic appeal) are more "civilized" than the traumatized human inhabitants. Likewise, the Settlement repudiates all normative definitions of "modern" and "conviviality" in its traumatic replay of, as it were, "the masters' pillage." The population is "unevolved and reviled" (54). "They used stream and rain water, drank cow's milk or home brew; ate game, eggs, domestic plants, and if they hired out in a field or a kitchen, they spent the earnings on sugar, salt, cooking oil, soda pop, cornflakes, flour, dried beans, and rice. If there were no earnings, they stole" (54). From subsistence to theft, what could be more descriptive of "slavemasters, rapists, racists" of the Transatlantic? Even empowered officials of District Ten—unwary modernists—come to dangerous crossroads when they enter Settlement boundaries. "Settlers" signals unsettling mayhem and theft. The marginal Settlement is, in reality, within shouting distance of Cosey's Hotel and Resort, and the voluptuous Junior (goddess) hails from it precincts.

Junior breaches primal codes of Settlement—"the only crime was departure" (55). "Civilization" has only one site for escapees such as Junior: Reform School and prison. However, nothing is calmly normal or ethically binary in Morrison's geographies. Her fictive landscapes, like Junior, are culturally voluptuous. For example, one cannot ignore the Settlement's possible ethical efficaciousness (in the person of Junior) for Diaspora education and manhood renewal of middle-class Black decency in the person of Romen. Junior, who is a first daughter of the Settlement, is also (as already discussed) *Love*'s paramount spokeswoman for the verbal demolition of male sexual violence. Her powers are those of the "wild"—that which actually violates the "natural" territory and memorially indicts "civilization." Her powers are spiritual and critical *regeneration*. Hence, only the lexicon of a unique Diaspora critical discourse can embrace her lavish excess.

The challenge to an adequate critique of *Love* is not only a certain brand of modernism's amnesia, but also the shifting narrative perspectives and dizzying proliferation of details in the novel. Morrison's modernism is not, after all, party to such overheated contemporary genres as Black-celebrity advice to young girls or "Black urban fiction." Confronted by Morrison's narrative complexity, harried reviewers scamper to find safe points of reference; they identify Morrison's expressive "borrowings." *Love* is, thus, reviewed as *Absalom, Absalom! Recidivus*. It is labeled Faulknerian fiction. William Cosey plays "the return of Thomas Sutpen." But how can *any* critical sortie into *Love* mistake William Cosey for Thomas Sutpen? Unlike Sutpen, Cosey understands from the youngest age precisely why his family history is anathema to Blacks and whites. Moral naiveté is not part of his makeup. He knows the blot and curse he inherits from his father. Called "Danny Boy" by seacoast whites but "Dark" by the Black community, his father is a race traitor, a penny-pinching courthouse snitch for white power. The father's treachery supports white discipline and punishment. "Dark" (and what a brilliant naming!) is by choice and design an agent of majority abjection. Cosey's legacy is racial-betrayal that cannot be overcome by a hundred acres, the services of a French architect, and the schadenfreude of a hundred "wild niggers" to wrestle.

William Cosey is pragmatic in the way of "New England pews." He does not strive to redeem a father's perfidy; he sets out to protect and transform it. If Dark was a miserly traitor to Black interests, his son will fashion a spendthrift, philanthropic, whoring hotelier-self who provides cash to ease Black trouble. Cosey is an ironic benefactor to the local Black majority. He keeps their sons and daughters out of handcuffs, pays their hospital bills, and sustains college educations for the chosen few. His charity, however, is Faustian. He absolutely refuses to grant local Blacks any access whatsoever to the amenities of his hotel and resort. Though he does small favors for the Black public sphere, his best labors, pleasures, and agendas are meant for his *private* satisfaction and profit. This is excessive mimicry of white masters in handsome Blackface.

The allure of Faulkner's Sutpen is a function of his ruthless, noble, and ultimately futile crusade to undo damaging exclusions of Southern class and racial hierarchies. By contrast, the smarmy charisma of Cosey is a legacy of ill-gotten Black wealth. Cosey boasts natural good looks and the services of younger Black women who are awed and shamed by his raw, pedophilic sexuality. In a shadowy upstairs hallway where Cosey's and his granddaughter Christine's bedrooms are located, "the handsome giant who owns the hotel" confronts the eleven-year-old Heed (190). Cosey then

touches . . . [Heed's] chin and then—casually, still smiling—her nipple,
or rather the place under her swimsuit where a nipple will be if the circled
dot on her chest ever changes. Heed stands there for what seems an hour
but is less than the time it takes to blow the perfect bubble. He watches
the pink ease from her mouth, then moves away still smiling. (191)

Within minutes, Cosey is exposing himself and masturbating out his
granddaughter's bedroom window.

How, in this entitled, male crudity, *does* Cosey differ from perpetrators of the Transatlantic? Though he defies everyday odds of Black
American survival, he possesses no nobility. He is not Sutpen, nor was
he meant to be. He is a vulture capitalist profiting from the Great Depression and creating a colored fairyland of middle-class mimicry dancing,
dining, flirting, and sudden death by drowning.

At its Diasporic foundation, Cosey's is a male, lazy, evil, and exclusionary life. His resort is afloat because sturdy Black women are at the
back of the clock of William Cosey's face. L says: "The two of us [L and
May] were like the back of a clock. Mr. Cosey was its face telling you the
time was now" (103). Cosey's "pleasure dome"—without impressionable
child-women, premenstrual adoration, wildly outlaw "sporting women,"
and a bribe-hungry White Law—would *never* have come into successful
being. Cosey is a "kept man." He is unredacted PTSS's avatar. Any criticism that reads him as a Faulknerian reappearance is color blind, and too
analytically shallow to matter. One might suggest that any "comparative
criticism" that attempts to yoke journalistically together *Sula* and *Love* is
equally blind.

In *Love,* Heed and Christine serve far more as carriers of class and
civil properties than as representatives of girlfriend egalitarianism shared
by Sula and Nell. True, we find Nell temporarily rebelling against her bourgeois colored family, especially her mother, who turns to light-skinned
"custard" before the rigors of Southern Jim Crow transportation. Heed,
by contrast, is a *permanent class rebel.* She possesses an incredible pen-
chant for numbers, is gifted with keen hearing, and holds remarkable
management skills. She is instinctively more gifted than those who mock
her. Hence, Cosey's portrait hangs above *her* bed. Heed is Erzulie sharing equal "fault" and deprivation with peasants, but possessed of a full
vault of accumulating assets. She relinquishes soft subtleties of romance

and matrimony to secure unyielding powers of ownership: "[Christine] who had attended private school kept house while . . . [Heed] who could barely read rules it" (86). "Heed" is an injunction to the Black majority.

Like Christine, Sula disappears for a number of years from the plot of her titular novel. When Sula returns, she does so with a plaque of robins. When Christine returns she carries a Wal-Mart shopping bag and a dozen diamond engagement rings. She is Erzulie eternally desirous. She does not depart *Love* of her own accord. She is sent away to protect her innocence, financial solvency, and potential class entitlements. She is partitioned from her class underling, Heed the Night, not by rituals of matrimony, but by *marital demons* conjured by Cosey's union with the pre-pubescent Heed. Entanglement par excellence. Cosey sets and pays Heed's "bride price" to the Johnson parents: two hundred dollars to the father, a new pocketbook for the mother. Christine and Heed's eventual hatred is a discoverable consequence of the resort owner's Black male perversion. This is a "chartered company" of partners in the post-trauma of the Transatlantic. Christine's absence from Silk transforms her into a woman with a "slut history" (72). Though not exactly a "sporting woman" like Celestial, Christine's knowable past is marked by "brawls, arrests, torching cars, and *prostitution*" (73).

At *Love's* conclusion, Christine and Heed are not nostalgically reconciled; they come together over the broken body of Heed, mutually facing the weight of trauma. They have been abused and victimized by gender-differentiated codes of female obedience and male sexual violence. They are betrayed by the Transatlantic. Their choral poem of betrayal and entanglement: "We could have been living our lives hand in hand instead of looking for Big Daddy everywhere" (189). There might have been a "working through" and not seven abortions for Christine and phantom miscarriage for Heed (171). It seems accurate to say that if Heed and Christine are revenants of Nell and Sula, they have suffered a sea change in *Love* and a monumental epistemological makeover.

In *Love*, agency belongs to L. Cosey drunkenly scrawls his will on a hotel menu one night, bequeathing his entire estate to an ambiguous "Sweet Cosey Child." L witnesses Cosey's act and suspects the hotelier means by "Sweet Cosey Child," the manifestation of Erzulie that is Celestial. L moves boldly to protect "family interests" against a man who, in L's view, has "lost his mind." She forges a substitute will on a substitute hotel menu and then poisons Bill Cosey with foxglove. Her actions lead "prudent men" and the "White Law" to read "Sweet Cosey Child" as a code for *Heed the Night*. Heed follows the law, believing fully that Cosey's portrait above her bed represents a "Daddy" who loved her. L knows better. Her protective regeneration of Cosey's drunken deceit ensures material and alchemical "re-writing" of Cosey's Black and maladaptive mimicry of white Atlantic treachery. L forges fortune for those women who have broken their backs at the back of Cosey's clock. Her inscription is, in effect, an instance of a Diasporically *different* and regenerative modernism. How many journalistic reviewers does it take adequately to explicate L's shrewd navigations of PTSS? There are not enough.

Ghost though she is (having "dropped dead at the stove" while cooking at Maceo's [189]), L is our only access to truth, judgment, and narrative closure. She hums along in the cemetery at the close of the novel with the formidable Celestial, who is perched atop Cosey's tombstone that bears a lie: "Ideal Husband. Perfect Father." The two women are characters who signify and endure in a traumatized and violent world that can produce such an inscription. Celestial sings the down home blues while unfurling folds of her red dress to cover the epitaph's "insult."

As observers and listeners at the conclusion of *Love,* we recognize the effect and affect of L and Celestial's spirit song. If we have tuned a Diaspora acumen to Black moans of Transatlantic passage, we recognize what precisely is occurring. L and Celestial's cemetery harmonies are acts of memory, mourning, and ambivalent exorcism. They are sounds in motion, confrontational rituals in the face of bizarre figurations of manhood and misshapen economies of love birthed by the Transatlantic. There is no more compelling trope for the regenerative ethics and memory of *Love* than Black women's magical hair dragging the clouds along like the moon.

From their first sighting of Celestial in her red sunback dress by the sea, marked with a faint scar running from cheek to ear, and hailed by William Cosey with the words "Hey, Celestial," Christine and Heed are possessed by new spiritual discourse: "And from then on, to say 'Amen,' or acknowledge a particularly bold, smart, risky thing, they mimicked the male voice crying 'Hey Celestial'" (188). "Amen" . . . "Hey Celestial." Atop William Cosey's tombstone in red-dress sassiness, Celestial *is* a woman who cosmically moves the moon, conquers the rhythms of the sea, and, surely, hints of Diasporic returns. She is—in "inclination," at the very least—a manifestation of Erzulie: Vodoun goddess of love, and much more.

In her essay "Erzulie: A Women's History of Haiti," Colin (Joan) Dayan makes clear the importance of Diaspora critique:

> For if the colonizer exercised privilege by distorting or annihilating the African past, Vodoun—the religion that kept alive the lives and deaths of the ancestors—re-imagined a unique relation to a brutal institution; Gods [such as Erzulie] were born in the memories of those who served, and then not only took on traits or dispositions of their servitors, but those attitudes and languages of the masters and mistresses from long ago, tough revenants carried in the memories of the descendants of slaves.[45]

Dayan thus signals the "entanglement" of domination and dominated, master and slave, possessor and possessed. Through multiple sources, she reprises the complexities of race, love, luxury, sexuality, cruelty, and eroticism in colonized and enslaved provinces.

The complexity of the admixture is scarcely captured by the binary "need/fulfillment." Rather, it is represented only by creolized *desire*. Erzulie is paramount as such *desire*, governing its rituals and presentations of combat, eroticism, torment, and beneficence. Dayan observes: "She [Erzulie] is called the loa of 'love,' but she forces us to enter a world where the word is undone, where certain tenants of affection or attachment undergo some strange, instructive metamorphoses . . . her incarnations de-idealize purity . . . the experience of possession itself become[s] a proof of memory, a something gained by those who were thought to have no story worth telling."[46] *Love*, clearly, is just such a story.

NOTES

This chapter was first published as "The Point of Entanglement: Modernism, Diaspora, and Toni Morrison's *Love*" by Houston A. Baker, Jr. *African and Black Diaspora* Vol.4:1 pp.1–18. New York: Taylor and Francis. Reprinted by permission of Taylor & Francis Ltd, www.tandfonline.com.

1. Morrison, *Love*. All citations refer to the Knopf (2003) edition.
2. Kakutani, Review of *Love*.
3. Ibid.
4. Showalter, Review of *Love*.

5. Ibid.

6. Ibid.

7. Simpson, Review of Gwendolyn Brooks's *Selected Poems.*

8. Miller, Review of *Love.*

9. "Diaspora Studies," as it appears in the present essay, is considered in the explanatory terms offered by Vanderbilt University's African American and Diaspora Studies' website (http://www.vanderbilt.edu/aframst/) as follows: "The program in African American and Diaspora [Studies] offers an interdisciplinary cross-cultural, and comparative study of the lived experiences of Blacks dispersed throughout the world from the continent of Africa, a dispersion (and its causes) referred to as the African Diaspora." What is to be stressed is the global, interdisciplinary cast of such study. At the same instant, the present essay suggests that access to comprehensive definitions of "Modernism," "U.S. History," "Economics of the Slave Trade and Their Consequences," and "Symbolic Action and Semantic Resonances of African American Expressive Culture" always need rigorously to be subjected to Diaspora Studies analyses. Helpful scholarship in the articulation of Diaspora Studies includes Colin A. Palmer, "Defining and Studying the Modern African Diaspora," *Journal of Negro History* (vol. 85, 2000); Sandra Adell, "Contemporary Literature in the African Diaspora," *African American Review* (vol. 35, 2001); Alexis Brooks De Vita and Ralph J. Hexter, *Methatypes: Signature and Signs of African/Diaspora and Black Goddesses;* Khalid Koser, *New African Diaspora;* Joseph Harris, *Global Dimensions of the African Diaspora;* Thomas Bender, *Rethinking American History in a Global Age* (especially chapter 5: "How the West Was One: The African Diaspora and the Re-Mapping of U.S. History"). "Diaspora Studies" can be taken as a sign for intellectual hybridity of encyclopedic dimensions, or it may be conceived of as an oceanic necessity for those who want to pay adequate analytical attention to a historical black "dispersion" (a term to which this essay shall have recourse) that continues to shape every aspect of the world as we think we know it. Certainly the term "Diaspora Studies" modified by "Black" may be of relatively recent academic vintage, but its genealogy is long, and its present analytical efforts in works such as Paul Gilroy's *The Black Atlantic* and Heather Russell's *Legba's Crossing* are profound.

10. Anecdote of willed *amnesia* and *critical refusal:* I recall the response of a tenured and academically well-respected colleague of mine who asked to borrow my copy of Ralph Ellison's *Invisible Man.* Two months later when I needed the book to prepare for class, I requested it from my colleague with the query: "So what did you think?" Her response: "I couldn't read it. It was too painful." My colleague was not of color. One wonders about "pain ratios." The charismatic and brilliant Professor Lemuel Johnson who died too early, spoke often of what he called the "intellectual terrorism" that black students in the academy endure daily as professors instruct them in the labors of Western thinkers who believed (and thinkers who still do believe) that Africa and dispersed Africans have no history and are impervious to reason, insult, and pain.

11. Rediker, *The Slave Ship,* 10, 40. All citations refer to the Penguin (2007) edition.

12. Ibid., 41.

13. Elkins, *Slavery.*

14. Rediker, *The Slave Ship,* 8.

15. Césaire, *Discourse on Colonialism,* 43. All citations refer to the Monthly Review Press (2000) edition, which has a first-rate introduction by Robin D. G. Kelley.

16. Ibid., 40.

17. Hayden, "The Middle Passage," 501. All citations refer to *The Norton Anthology of African American Literature* (1997) rendering of Hayden's classic poem.

18. "Post-Traumatic Stress Disorder (PTSD)," National Institute of Mental Health, http://www.nimh.nih.gov/health/topics/post-traumatic-stress-disorder-ptsd/index.shtml.

19. Leary, *Post Traumatic Slave Syndrome.* All citations to Leary's work refer to the Uptone Press (2005) edition.

20. Ibid., 50.

21. Marable, "Incarceration vs. Education."

22. Eckholm, "Plight Deepens for Black Men, Studies Warn."

23. Gilmore, *Golden Gulag.* All citations to Gilmore's work refer to the University of California Press (2007) edition.

24. Ibid., 21.

25. Oshinsky, *Worse Than Slavery.*

26. From *Life and Debt,* the brilliant documentary film directed by Stephanie Black.

27. O'Hehir, Review of *Love.* All citations of O'Hehir refer to the *Salon.com* (November 28, 2003) rendition. The finer contours of Diaspora critique already possess a sturdy history. Paul Gilroy turns astute critical attention to Morrison's place in "countercultures of modernity" in *The Black Atlantic,* noting: "Her work points to and celebrates some of the strategies for summoning up the past devised by black writers whose minority modernism can be defined precisely through its imaginative proximity to forms of terror that surpass understanding and lead back from contemporary racial violence, through lynching, towards the temporal and ontological rupture of the middle passage." Scholar Donna Weir-Soley in her powerful study *Eroticism, Spirituality, and Resistance in Black Women's Writings* suggests that the genealogy of Morrison's black modernist valorization of New World African belief systems such as Voudoun, Pukumina, Kumina, and other traces black womanist canon back to Zora Neale Hurston's *Their Eyes Were Watching God:* "Hurston evokes, through specific signs and symbols, the presence of the Haitian Voudoun goddess of love and sexuality, Erzulie as the leitmotif that introduces and sustains the synthesis of spirituality, and sexuality in the portrayal of Janie's character." Professor Weir-Soley not only offers a thoroughly persuasive analysis of the regenerative powers of the loas or orishas in the life of Hurston's protagonist, Janie Crawford but moves on to a reading of Morrison's *Beloved* under the signs of Erzulie and New World innovation and spiritual syncretism that is a model of Diaspora Critique. Both Gilroy and Weir-Soley would seem to join scholar Heather Russell, author of the commanding study *Legba's Crossing: Narratology in the African Atlantic,* under the productive sign and powers of *àshe.* Invoking the sign *àshe* as guiding concept and energy for her labors of Diaspora Studies, Russell writes as follows:

> In West African philosophy, the highest achievement of art is àshe, and when ascribed to a composition or performance, the resultant creation is held to have transcended all prescribed boundaries of form. As a consequence, art that achieves àshe would naturally defy conventional dictates; it would break down familiar/conventional/generic constructs, such as those governing fact, fiction, truth, reality, myth, history, national, imagination, and

narratology. . . . The power of àshe, then, lies in its transcendent ability to cross the borders and boundaries of fixed constructs regarding knowledge, interpretation, and apprehension as well as the form structures framing such hermeneutical engagement.

In the productive vein of Weir-Soley, Russell provides innovative readings of Caribbean and African American narratives that serve as hermeneutical guides—creolized "crossing signs," as it were—to carry us to a more sophisticated understanding of what Middle Passage, oceanic perils have yielded.

28. One of the Spanish painter Goya's masterpieces is titled *The Sleep of Reason Produces Monsters*. I realize this judgment is not one certified by all art historians. It is a motivated matter of my personal preference.

29. Quoted from Gilroy, *The Black Atlantic*, 221.

30. Quoted from Schwartz, "Toni Morrison and William Faulkner."

31. Glissant, *Caribbean Discourse*, 15. All citations are to the University of Virginia Press (1999) edition, translated and with an introduction by J. Michael Dash.

32. Quoted from Gilroy, *The Black Atlantic*, 221.

33. Ibid.

34. Morrison, Interview, *Oprah Magazine*.

35. A comprehensive bibliographic view suggests, of course, that as early as the eighteenth century, New World Africans (as Dorothy Porter's splendid anthology *Early Negro Writing, 1760–1837* demonstrates) aspired to escape the "White Gaze." Certainly, Morrison's creative compeers during her formative years—writers such as Larry Neal, Nikki Giovanni, Gwendolyn Brooks, Amiri Baraka, Jayne Cortez, Sonia Sanchez, Haki Madhubuti, Toni Cade Bambara, and others—were as successfully dedicated to rejecting the white gaze as the author of *The Bluest Eye*.

36. Morrison, Interview, *Oprah Magazine*.

37. Allen-Agostini, Review of *John Crow's Devil*.

38. Hayden, "The Middle Passage," 501.

39. Morrison, *Love*, 113.

40. Ibid., 114–115.

41. Ibid., 106.

42. Morrison, *Song of Solomon*. All citations to Morrison's novel refer to the New American Library (1977) edition.

43. http://www.megaessays.com/viewpaper/7442.html. A compelling combination of classical and popular culture references illustrates the "tragic flaw."

44. A salient feature of Diaspora Critique is its provision of access and analysis to New World African loas like Erzulie and syncretic religious practices such as Voudon.

45. Dayan, "Erzulie."

46. Ibid.

WORKS CITED

Allen-Agostini, Lisa. Review of *John Crow's Devil*. *The Caribbean Review of Books*, 2008. http://www.mepublishers.com/online/crb/issues/index/php?pid=1026/.

Black, Stephanie. *Life and Debt*. Video. New York: New Yorker Video, 2001, 2003. DVD.

Césaire, Aime. *Discourse on Colonialism.* Introduction by Robin D. G. Kelley. New York: Monthly Review Press, 2000.

Dayan, Colin (Joan). "Erzulie: A Women's History of Haiti." *Research in African Literature,* 25.2 (1994): 5–31.

Eckholm, Erik. "Plight Deepens for Black Men, Studies Warn." *New York Times,* March 20, 2006. Accessed April 25, 2011. http://www.nytimes.com/2006/03/20/national /20blackmen.html.

Elkins, Stanley. *Slavery: A Problem in American Institutional and Intellectual Life.* Chicago: University of Chicago Press, 1987.

Gilmore, Ruth Wilson. *Golden Gulag: Prisons, Surplus, Crisis, and Opposition in Globalizing California.* Berkeley: University of California Press, 2007.

Gilroy, Paul. *The Black Atlantic.* Cambridge, Mass.: Harvard University Press.

Glissant, Edouard. *Caribbean Discourse: Selected Essays.* Translated and with an introduction by J. Michael Dash. Charlottesville: University of Virginia Press, 1999.

Hayden, Robert. "The Middle Passage." *The Norton Anthology of African American Literature.* Edited by Henry Louis Gates Jr. and Nellie McKay. New York: W.W. Norton, 1997.

Kakutani, Michiko. Review of *Love. New York Times Book Review,* October 10, 2003.

Leary, Joy Degruy. *Post Traumatic Slave Syndrome.* Milwaukee, Ore.: Uptone Press, 2005.

Marable, Manning. "Incarceration vs. Education: Reproducing Racism and Poverty in America." *Race and Regionalism.* Accessed April 25, 2011. http://www.urbanhabitat .org/node/2808.

Miller, Laura. Review of *Love. New York Times,* November 2, 2003.

Morrison, Toni. *Love.* New York: Alfred A. Knopf, 2003.

———. Interview. *Oprah Magazine,* 2003.

———. *Song of Solomon.* New York: New American Library, 1977.

O'Hehir, Andrew. Review of *Love. Salon,* November 28, 2003.

Oshinsky, David. *Worse Than Slavery: Parchman Farm and the Ordeal of Jim Crow Justice.* New York: Free Press, 1996.

"Post-Traumatic Stress Disorder (PTSD)." National Institute of Mental Health. Accessed April 25, 2011. http://www.nimh.nih.gov/health/topics/post-traumatic-stress -disorder-ptsd/index.shtml.

Rediker, Eugene. *The Slave Ship: A Human History.* New York: Penguin, 2007.

Schwartz, Larry. "Toni Morrison and William Faulkner: The Necessity of a Great American Novelist." *Cultural Logic* 5 (2002). Accessed April 25, 2011. http://clogic .eserver.org/2002/Schwartz.html.

Showalter, Elaine. Review of *Love. The Guardian,* November 29, 2003.

Simpson, Louis. Review of Gwendolyn Brooks's *Selected Poems. New York Herald Tribune,* 1963.

TWO

"THE HISTORICAL BURDEN THAT ONLY OPRAH CAN BEAR": AFRICAN AMERICAN SATIRISTS AND THE STATE OF THE LITERATURE

DARRYL DICKSON-CARR

Deep within Paul Beatty's most recent novel, *Slumberland* (2008), the reader will find tucked neatly but auspiciously in a footnote the narrator's droll comment that around the time of the Berlin Wall's fall, Oprah Winfrey was "in the process of buying the rights to the life story of every black American born between 1642 and 1968 as a way of staking claim to being the legal and sole embodiment of the black experience from slavery to civil rights. Thus carrying the historical burden that only she has the strength to bear."[1] While we certainly have no proof that Ms. Winfrey has attempted to acquire any such rights, Beatty's footnote betrays two anxieties. The first regards Oprah Winfrey's real acquisition of film rights to or involvement in the adaptations of many revered or well-known African American literary texts, including Gloria Naylor's *The Women of Brewster Place* (1982), Sapphire's *Push* (1996), Toni Morrison's *Beloved* (1987), and Zora Neale Hurston's *Their Eyes Were Watching God* (1937). Garnering mixed reviews, each of these productions has caused no small amount of controversy. The televised film of *The Women of Brewster Place* (broadcast in 1989), in which Winfrey played a starring role and for which she served as executive producer, simultaneously achieved considerable success and generated widespread criticism within African American communities for its depiction of black males in arguably limited or simplistic roles. Winfrey's production of the Jonathan Demme–directed *Beloved* (1998) suffered negative reviews for its more literal interpretation of the source material, while the televised *Their Eyes Were Watching God* (2005) shared the same fate for Winfrey's considerable deviances from the film's textual source. Beatty's novel emerged, of course, well before the production and release of *Precious* (2009), the adaptation of *Push* that Winfrey also coproduced, so he clearly could not anticipate that film's runaway critical and commercial success. Nevertheless, his novel reflects an apprehension that Oprah Winfrey tends to compromise the artistry of the works she adapts well beyond the necessary changes that television and media demand.

Beatty's footnote, however, is less concerned with the amount of popular success of Winfrey's endeavors than it is with the depth of her involvement in shaping African American popular culture. Whether it is through the massive success of *The Oprah Winfrey Show* (1986–2011), the economic clout of "Oprah's Book Club," which has repeatedly catapulted books by a myriad of well-known and obscure authors into the commercial stratosphere, or Winfrey's film production efforts, her cultural cachet is undeniable. She recently purchased her aptly named television network, OWN (Oprah Winfrey Network). Beatty's concern links directly to a second anxiety regarding the state of African American popular cultural forms today or, to be more specific, the way "blackness" finds representation through literature and music. "Blackness is over," says *Slumberland*'s Ferguson W. Sowell, aka "DJ Darky": "[W]e blacks, the once eternally hip, the people who were as right now as Greenwich Mean Time, are, as of today, as yesterday as stone tools, the velocipede, and the paper straw all rolled into one[; t]he Negro is now officially human."[2] Blackness is therefore "passé," according to DJ Darky, which means that "colored folk will be looked upon with blithe indifference, not eroticized pity or the disgust of Freudian projection."[3] The "blackness" that Darky declares après-garde has its specific foundations in definitions of African American cultural forms that were anterior to the Black Arts movement of the 1960s and 1970s, but found their greatest articulation in that epoch. In the novel, blackness is a category that the work of jazz musician Charles Stone, aka Charles Schwa, or "The Schwa" has transcended, a performance of "indeterminate blackness and funkier than a motherfucker," at once possessing the "soul" at the heart of black identities, yet able to let it go, to cast it aside at any moment. The music thus cannot be categorized or reduced to a marketable trope. To a different extent, this is true for the beat miner DJ Darky, or at least what he wishes to achieve. It means, in effect, that The Schwa and DJ Darky had to leave the United

States for Cold War Berlin, where they might find appreciation not so much for their music as for the desire to achieve the sense of wonder that comes from the new and unknown, rather than the trite and cynical. Late in the novel, DJ Darky explains that the key to Charles Stone's music is the "semitone, that tiny musical interval that's a half step between harmony and noise," as the Schwa

> wants to show us that the best parts of life are temporal semitone, those nanoseconds between ecstasy and panic that if we could we'd string together in sensate harmony. If only we could be Wile E. Coyote walking on air for those precious few moments before the bittersweet realization he's walking on air. Before falling to earth with a pitiful wave of the hand and a puff of smoke.[4]

The semitone, in fact, is the most dissonant musical interval (one often used to denote surprise in cartoons). In dissonance, then, may be found a freedom in art, as harmony would be eschewed in favor of a painful but necessary creative tension.

For Beatty and other contemporary novelists, the fact that Oprah Winfrey or any large, powerful corporation would have the means to buy the rights to black lives and creativity—in essence, blackness itself—and reduce them to a vision that jibes with the sensibility of the corporation, to an endlessly reproducible commodity is an anathema. It removes the creative tension and turns the semitone into a banal scale, one that is serviceable, but has no lasting musical impact. Thus, when Ferguson encounters the music of trumpeter Wynton Marsalis, the "middle-aged child prodigy to whom everyone gives plaudits, but no one plays," he has found another embodiment of all he fears. Marsalis's "pretentious narcissistic nigrescence [sic] couldn't fool [him; t]he pentatonic scaling and the repetition of the ninth through twelfth bars belied an underlying skittishness, and the song flitted aimlessly about like a flock of canaries that have flown into a room and can't find their way out."[5] Marsalis has generated considerable controversy as a musician and critic of the jazz scene over more than thirty years as a renowned musician. For our purposes, though, we should note that it is Marsalis's cofounding of the Jazz at Lincoln Center program—for which he is currently the Artistic Director, and which Ferguson calls an "Auschwitz of free thought"—that links him to such a personage as Oprah Winfrey (Beatty 97). Like Ms.

Winfrey, Marsalis's position gives him a powerful and virtually unprecedented degree of influence within his cultural sphere, as demonstrated
by his central role in Ken Burns's *Jazz* (2001) documentary series. Put
simply, Marsalis and Winfrey, as two African Americans most known
and revered by the white mainstream in the United States in their respective professions, are among the most prominent faces of black popular culture. While it is certainly quite possible to be a successful artist
without the blessing of either personage, their opinions of and dealings
within artistic circles cannot be entirely ignored.

More damning to Ferguson is that Marsalis "reminds me that I was
born wearing the wrong uniform. That I'm a Negro-Nazi who, being only
a DJ and not a general, politician, or movie director, is at best a function-
ary or house-party gauleiter."[6] Ferguson reveals a deeply buried concern
at the heart of the texts at hand here, one echoed in Beatty's own debut
novel, *The White Boy Shuffle* (1996): Where are the "generals" in African
American culture who might be able to steer it away from the banal or
the corporate, and toward an appeal that challenges the status quo? In
Slumberland's ethos, Marsalis and Winfrey's greatest offenses are that
they are trapped by an imagined *status quo ante,* a tendency to play "in
the past tense" leading to "black conformity . . . devoid of funk, devoid of
mystery," in which Marsalis's "trumpet doesn't even change your mood,
much less your mind."[7] By contrast, the Schwa's music "is anarchy. It's
Somalia. It's the Department of Motor Vehicles. It's Albert Einstein's
hair."[8] It is, in short, defiant of most rules of decorum and order. It is free
of the United States's tendency toward conformity and consensus, opting for a rugged individualism that hearkens back to Ralph Waldo Emerson's "Self-Reliance" or better, Henry David Thoreau's "Civil Disobedience" (originally published as "Resistance to Civil Government"): "I
was not born to be forced. I will breathe after my own fashion. Let us see
who is the strongest."[9] Unlike Thoreau's United States, though, the rul-
ing government in Ferguson's world does not possess a "great and unen-
durable" inefficiency; it is altogether too efficient, streamlined, and intol-
erant of dissent and dissonance.[10] Nearly all but the Schwa are breathing
after the fashion of their neighbors, or at least after the fashion of Oprah
Winfrey and Wynton Marsalis's audiences.

Thus it is no accident that in Percival Everett's *Erasure* (2001), popular fiction writer Juanita Mae Jenkins, author of *We's Lives In Da Ghetto,*

appears on the book club segment of Kenya Dunston's show—a barely veiled clone of *The Oprah Winfrey Show*—to plug her novel, whose paperback rights had sold for $500,000.[11] As a minor character, Jenkins comprises elements from the lives and careers of several contemporary African American women authors: Toni Morrison's past employment at a major publishing house, Sapphire's time working with troubled youth in New York City, and Terry McMillan's enormous publishing advances. Although she shares little else with Morrison, Dunston's biography allows Everett to lampoon the link between contemporary black women authors and mass media. Although Random House was not the corporate behemoth it is today—Random House, U.S.A. alone comprises twenty-five imprints—Morrison was once an influential editor, responsible in part for aiding the careers of numerous African American authors, including Gayl Jones, Gloria Naylor, Toni Cade Bambara, Henry Dumas, Muhammad Ali, Angela Davis, and several others.[12]

In contrast, *Erasure*'s protagonist, Thelonious "Monk" Ellison, writes novels that show "a brilliant intellect" that are "challenging and masterfully written and constructed," but, according to one press's editor, are "too difficult for the market," as Ellison is interested in exploring mythology, rather than creating or perpetuating popular myths or stereotypes.[13] Ellison's surname and nickname come from Thelonious Monk, the pianist known for his dissonant compositions and performances, in which pleasure comes from the sublime, from what is *not* played, rather than the notes themselves. Little wonder that one of the historical Monk's most famous compositions is "Ugly Beauty," the essence of dissonance. For our Monk Ellison, though, the work that the Juanita Mae Jenkinses of the literary world issue has no beauty; they provide only an exploitative ugliness, one that offers no meaning, no way to comprehend the complexities of black lives. Their danger is not their appeal to popular sensibilities so much as their reification of all the expectations that white and black readers have for African American literature. In other words, Jenkins plays every note she can in the scale of authorial ambition, rather than holding fire. The sublimity of "ugly beauty" is lost upon Jenkins; to her, per Monk Ellison, all ugliness is beautiful, simply because it exists and may be reconfigured for the consumption of an audience that mistakes the presence of dissonance as the absence of beauty. To prove this argument, Monk Ellison later pens under the pseudonym Stagg R. Leigh (compare the "bad nigger" Stagolee/Staggerlee of black folklore) *My Pafology*, later retitled *Fuck*, as a parody of several texts: Sapphire's *Push*, Richard Wright's *Native Son*, and the black "gangsta" film trend of the late 1980s and early 1990s. More pointedly, the parody riffs on a popular fascination with all things black and urban that has its roots in the New Negro Renaissance of the 1910s–1930s, but found its greatest flowering in the naturalism and social realism of Richard Wright, Chester Himes, Frank Yerby, Ann Petry, and William Attaway. Monk Ellison's purpose is to reproduce all of the clichés with which white and black audiences have become familiar in popular black fiction: the pathologically twisted and undereducated youth born into a naturalistic world and an urban environment he can neither control nor understand; an urban underclass; sexual promiscuity; jarring violence; misogyny and misanthropy; parallels with biblical figures; adoration of popular culture; and so on. When Monk submits the typescript to his editor, predictably it is acquired by Random House for an advance of $600,000, is featured on Kenya Dunston's show, becomes the toast of the literary critical establishment— including the *New York Times*, no less—for its authenticity and "natural, right" depiction of black depravity and ignorance, and wins the National Book Award.[14] Monk, who is himself on the National Book Association's prize jury and votes against his own work, points out that it is not "art," but to no avail. American readers expect no art from black male authors, only pathology and "grittiness": ugliness, sans beauty.

Juanita Mae Jenkins and the pseudonymous Stagg R. Leigh, moreover, bear more than a passing resemblance to Bo Shareef of Mat Johnson's *Hunting in Harlem*. In that novel's literary scene, popular author Shareef is the nemesis of Bobby Finley, author of *The Great Work* and *The Tome*, whose sales figures are virtually zero. Shareef, the author of *Now That's What I'm Talkin' 'Bout!*, clearly resembles contemporary novelist Omar Tyree; both authors market and promote their works feverishly. Shareef enjoys nearly rabid popularity, especially among African American women, who flock to his readings and purchase every volume he produces at a rapid, nearly continuous clip. Bobby Finley finds himself hosting a reading and signing at the same bookstore as Shareef, where the patrons and staff duly ignore him. This leads to his assessment of the state of the art for "male writer[s] of African descent":

> There were only two roads to success. . . . The first was to write a romance
> novel with an illustration of three or fewer attractive black people on
> the cover, preferably done in a comic book style so as not to scare off the
> illiterati. One written in flat descriptions of every action so that the prose
> was completely subservient to the plot, even though that plot was invari-
> ably predictable, as close to the readers' expectations as possible so as not
> to scare them. This type of book was basically for a readership looking for
> melaninized, low-tech versions of their afternoon soaps.[15]

The other path, Finley continues, is "to create a work in the vein of Richard
Wright or the great Ralph Ellison, not in the sense that the works be
original and energetic, but that they focus on inner-city strife and racism.
Whites, who made up the majority of sales in the literary category, felt
their own writers could handle the other issues in the universe just fine,
they just wanted the black guys to clarify the Negro stuff."[16]

Unfortunately, the alternative that Finley offers is about as palatable as Monk Ellison's "retellings of Euripides and parodies of French
poststructuralists," his attempts to find literary respectability prior to
My Pafology/Fuck.[17] Finley's *The Great Work* is a novel that "refuses sum-
marization, defiantly," yet may be reduced to a single man's existential
sojourn in a closet at a work camp in Alaska, written almost without any
dialogue.[18] Finley's second novel, *The Tome*, is 478 pages written "for no
one" as a response to his resentment and alienation. In contrast to Bo
Shareef, Finley has created works of sheer beauty—or a semblance of
it—but without any connection to a single element that would make
them human, or even humane to a reader. Instead of examining how his
novels fail to connect, or how they "suck," as his friend Snowden puts it,
he opts instead to lambaste the African American literary scene, which
lies between the Scylla of formulaic popular fiction and the Charybdis
of equally formulaic urban realistic, social document fiction, neither of
which addresses craft, much less the tension that ugly beauty suggests.[19]

My citation of the myth of Scylla and Charybdis is deliberate. Those
mythical creatures not only attempt to destroy all who attempt to pass
between them, but they are also female, as are many of the writers and
likely readers of the genres lampooned in his present texts. Bobby Finley
reveals quickly his distrust of these (women) readers, whom he describes
generally as "dung beetles," as they "didn't just consume crap, they liked

it," and the critics who dismissed or ignored his work "were much less than that."[20] The largely female audience of Kenya Dunston's show in *Erasure* gives its "applause, approval, endorsement, blessing" to an extremely explicit and misogynistic passage from Monk Ellison's parody.[21] Throughout *Slumberland,* Ferguson Sowell, who is also an erstwhile scorer of pornographic films, notes during his quest how Berlin's sexual and racial politics threaten to destroy those who engage them. In Cold War Germany, "men of the diaspora [would] smile meekly while libertine frauleins debated as to who was the 'true black': the haughty African with his tribal scars, gender chauvinism, and piercing eyes, or the cocksure black American, he of the emotional scars, political chauvinism, and physical grace."[22] In all of these formulations, women become emasculating forces that deprive the writer of his ability to be his true self or to create what *he* will. In the case of Beatty's invocation of Oprah Winfrey and German women, the forces at hand threaten totalizing control of African or African American experiences, reducing them to "historical burdens" that need to be processed through other media to be palatable to a greater—and presumably whiter—audience.

What does this gendering of artistic control mean? While it is tempting to argue that these black male authored texts are identifying women, including black women as the primary or sole cause of contemporary authors' woes, it would be fallacious on a few grounds. First, in all three texts, the other debilitating force at work is the literary critical establishment, which seeks an absurd authenticity in African American literature and lives that is at least as insidious as the public's demands. Thus Bobby Finley names his commode "Irving Howe," after the famed critic who favored Richard Wright over Ralph Ellison; it affords Finley the opportunity to "take pleasure in shitting on it daily."[23] In Monk Ellison's words, he often argues with agents, artists, critics, and readers of both genders, black and white, who "tell me I am not *black* enough. . . . I have heard this mainly about my novels, from editors who have rejected me and reviewers whom I have apparently confused and, on a couple of occasions, on a basketball court when upon missing a shot I muttered *Egads.*"[24] We would also have to assume that the personae Johnson, Beatty, and Everett invent are direct representations of the authors, that Bobby Finley and Monk Ellison's assessments of contemporary African American writing are Mat Johnson's and Percival Everett's, unmediated. It would require ignoring the fact that each of these personae is deeply disturbed. Gulliver, in other words, would have to be Swift, rather than his creation.

It would be more productive instead to examine the abstract culprit that consistently torments these personae: the marketplace. In its December 10, 2007, issue, *Publishers Weekly* focused upon the black book market, specifically what African American readers will buy. The magazine consulted several prominent black booksellers, all of whom confirmed that "'[f]ar more commercial fiction [aimed at African American readers] is being published by mainstream publishers than ever'... Most of the buyers agreed that bestselling black novelists like Zane, Noire, Nikki Turner, Mary B. Morrison and Eric Jerome Dickey still command attention," and that "[u]rban fiction, or street lit, continues to sell well and seems to still be growing," with conglomerates such as Random House, Hachette, and Simon & Schuster established in the market. One book buyer said that "95% of titles" from small presses are urban fiction.[25] The buyers also indicated that Christian fiction and fiction aimed at young, black males were also growing in popularity.[26] At no point does this particular article indicate that black *literary* fiction from more established authors was gaining in popularity; in fact, it is not mentioned at all. Lack of attention, of course, does not necessarily equal lack of sales. Nevertheless, the article's silence on the question is deafening, perhaps damning. If the rule holds that commercial fiction sells nearly twice the copies that literary fiction does, and no impetus exists for reading audiences to find a stronger interest in the latter, then the relatively bleak picture that these novels paint holds true.

It should come as little surprise that African American literature has been here before, perhaps for much of its history in the twentieth century. During the New Negro Renaissance, new publishers—Alfred A. Knopf, Harcourt Brace, and Boni & Liveright chief among them—began publishing black literature when established mainstream publishing houses generally would not. These publishers broke through with works and authors that African American literary studies have now canonized— Nella Larsen, Claude McKay, Rudolph Fisher, Langston Hughes, Jean Toomer—all we now consider "literary." Also during that time, such luminaries as W. E. B. Du Bois cautioned against and bemoaned the tendency of McKay, the white author and patron Carl Van Vechten, and some of the younger authors to eschew "sincerity or art, deep thought, or truthful industry." "It seems to me," Du Bois writes, that in his novel *Nigger Heaven* "Mr. Van Vechten tried to do something bizarre and he certainly succeeded," but the scholar ultimately advises his readers to drop Van Vechten's book into the gutter "grate" where it implicitly belongs, and pick up the *Police Gazette* instead.[27] Ishmael Reed's *Reckless Eyeballing* (1985), Trey Ellis' *Platitudes* (1988), and Beatty's *The White Boy Shuffle* (1996)—all spiritual predecessors to Johnson's *Hunting in Harlem,* his earlier *Drop* (2000), or Percival Everett's more recent works—argue that African American literature and art have become subject to market forces in ways that they were not in the past.

In Ellis's *Platitudes,* for example, author Dewayne Wellington jousts with rival author Isshee Ayam about the markedly different, gender-based approaches each takes toward African American subjects. Whereas Dewayne focuses upon which characters he should kill, and which "characters, witticisms, grammatical devices, etc."[28] he should retain or reject, Isshee Ayam instead argues that he should open his novel thusly:

> Earle awakened to a day as new and as fresh as Mama's handstarched
> and sun-dried petticoat, a huge, plain garment as large and as fresh-
> smelling as the revival tents that bloomed every summer along Route 49
> in Lowndes County, Georgia. Yes, from out of those wide Baptist thighs,
> thighs that shook with the centuries of injustice and degradation, thighs
> that twitched with the hope of generations yet unplanted, thighs that
> quivered with the friction of jubilant, bed-thumping, and funky-smelling
> lovemaking, emerged Earle.[29]

This hilariously overwritten paragraph contains most of the platitudes that inspires Ellis's title: the pastoral Southern setting; the folk/blues-based culture; the earthy sexuality. Most significant is the omnipotent and omnipresent matriarchal figure that could just as easily be the "Mama" in "The Last Mama-on-the-Couch Play" in George Wolfe's *The Colored Museum* (1988), who reposes on the eponymous sofa, reading her Bible and spouting folksy wisdom.[30] Wellington, predictably, rejects this opening, opting instead for his oversexed bildungsroman until he and Ayam eventually come to a literary détente.

The rural setting seems to trouble all of the authors under scrutiny here. Beatty opens *The White Boy Shuffle* with his protagonist, Gunnar Kaufman, defiantly asserting that "[u]nlike the typical bluesy earthy folksy denim-overalls noble-in-the-face-of-cracker-racism aw shucks Pulitzer-

Prize-winning protagonist mojo magic black man, I am not the seventh son of a seventh son of a seventh son. I wish I were, but fate shorted me by six brothers and three uncles."[31] Compare as well Monk Ellison, who "graduated *summa cum laude* from Harvard, hating every minute of it," is "good at math . . . cannot dance," and "did not grow up in any inner city or the rural south."[32] Gunnar and Monk's declarations underscore the clichés that have become commonplace in African American literature. If thematic and marketing trends are any indication, then the only "black" experiences are to be found in urban areas and the enslaving or segregated South, whether old or new. Suburbs do not exist, except as sites to be disdained for sucking away blackness, with the latter term implying a black community alternately constructed as romantic, tragic, or unstintingly bleak. People in other parts of the African Diaspora do not exist except as Others that delineate the black Self. History ended after the Civil Rights movement.

Perhaps needless to say, African American literature has frequently extended beyond these overdetermined sites and the boundaries that circumscribe them, policed by publishers and critics. Whereas the publishers of the New Negro Renaissance took risks with African American authors writing both traditional literature and more popular forms, the novels at hand insist that the contemporary mainstream publishing industry no longer takes any risks, inasmuch as it is dominated by but a few conglomerates. Eight of the most popular African American–oriented imprints, for example, are under the aegis of only five major conglomerates: Amistad (HarperCollins); One World (Ballantine/Random House); Harper Trophy (HarperCollins); Jump at the Sun (Hyperion/Disney); Dafina (Kensington); Walk Worthy (Warner); Strivers Row (Villard/Random House); Harlem Moon (Broadway/Random House).[33] Experimentation is to be eschewed for social document fiction and urban sensationalism.

But does this narrative ring entirely true? It is worth noting that all of the authors discussed here publish with one of the major houses listed above, and all have received positive reviews for these works. The recognition for and success of Colson Whitehead's *Sag Harbor* or Edward Jones's *The Known World*—helped by a Pulitzer Prize—suggest that urban realism and tragic, bluesy tales of woe are not the only alternatives to street lit. *Publishers Weekly* has also confirmed that "street lit," as popular as it is, along with self-published titles, is but enjoying a cycle of popularity that may very well wane as they "get backlash against urban fiction from the community."[34] While this does not necessarily favor the notion that literary fiction will ever equal commercial fiction in sales, it does suggest that the final word has not been written on the subject. Reed's *Reckless Eyeballing,* like Ellis's later *Platitudes,* casts playwright Tremonisha Smarts—Alice Walker in all but name—as an author of *Wrong-Headed Man,* from which "critics and the people who praised [her] took some. . . characters and made them out to be *all* black men," a response that "hurt" Smarts.[35] Reed's *Japanese by Spring* (1993) follows suit, constructing a world in which intellectuals and writers of all ethnic and political backgrounds write to follow current trends, rather than their true beliefs and experiences. As critiques of their times, and portents of the future, they simultaneously provoke and damn. Yet it is far more likely—and pernicious—that African American fiction will suffer the same fate that may befall the publishing industry in general as a result of the current crisis in print publishing: obsolescence. That is, if certain expressions of black lives are no longer commodities worth reproducing, buying, and selling in an industry that is already distressed, will this lead to a general demise for representations of this history and these experiences? Will authors and publishers alike be able to give these lives meaning that rise above commodification, randomness, and entropy?

An answer may be found in Johnson's *Hunting in Harlem,* in which Cedric Snowden asks Bobby Finley to consider whether "it ain't the other way around? Like, oh, I don't know, maybe every other human being in the world is right and you're the one that's wrong. Maybe *The Great Work* just sucks. You ever think of that?" Finley responds, "Yeah, I thought about that for a minute. But then I reread it. It's brilliant, they're dung beetles, trust me on this one."[36] Finley's arrogance comes from a failure to recognize not only his own clear flaws, but also the fact that the question regarding the creation and marketing of African American literature has never had a pat answer. Even when we include the New Negro Renaissance and the Black Arts movement of the 1960s and 1970s, we cannot find a single era in which literary fiction received its just due from publishers, readers, or critics. At no time have black authors been able to ignore or minimize the perils of the publishing market, to consider whether their lives and experiences will be reduced to bits of easily digestible categories. The works before us recognize this fact, even if the characters within them do not. Their goal is not to return to a utopian marketplace, but instead to place the limits of that marketplace in the foreground, where we as readers may ensure that talented authors do not die from neglect or find themselves punished for caring about their art. At the end of *Hunting in Harlem,* Bobby Finley *has* moved beyond his earlier position by finding love, by giving human feeling to his writing. As he declares his unfulfilled love and reveals his third manuscript, he immolates himself in front of a crowd of New York onlookers who rush to get copies of his novel.[37] This is the fate that the art must avoid: a Pyrrhic (or pyromaniacal) victory that comes only after authors have exhausted and destroyed their talents. To do so is to become part of an industry which, through its own conglomeration and perilous reluctance to adjust to new technologies, may have inadvertently taken a cue from Bobby Finley long ago.

NOTES

1. Paul Beatty, *Slumberland,* 162.
2. Beatty, 3.
3. Beatty, 16.
4. Beatty, 180.
5. Beatty, 95–96.
6. Beatty, 96.
7. Beatty, 97.
8. Ibid.
9. Henry David Thoreau, "Civil Disobediance," 217.
10. Thoreau, 206.
11. Percival Everett, *Erasure,* 53.
12. Marilyn Sanders Mobley, "Toni Morrison," 296.
13. Everett, 4.
14. Everett, 136, 259–261.
15. Mat Johnson, *Hunting in Harlem,* 49.
16. Johnson, 50.
17. Everett, 2.
18. Johnson, 167–168.
19. Johnson, 49.
20. Johnson, 48.
21. Everett, 251.
22. Beatty, 62.
23. Johnson, 50.
24. Everett, 2; emphasis in the original.

25. Felicia Pride, "Buyers Beware," 24–25.
26. Pride, 25.
27. W. E. B. Du Bois, "Books," 81.
28. Trey Ellis, *Platitudes*, 14.
29. Ellis, 16.
30. George C. Wolfe, *The Colored Museum*, 24–32.
31. Paul Beatty, *The White Boy Shuffle*, 5.
32. Everett, 2.
33. Paul D. Colford, "Publishers Find It Pays to Do Write Thing," 34.
34. Pride, 25.
35. Ishmael Reed, *Reckless Eyeballing*, 129–130.
36. Johnson, 49.
37. Johnson, 282–283.

WORKS CITED

Beatty, Paul. *The White Boy Shuffle*. New York: Holt, 1996.
———. *Slumberland*. New York: Bloomsbury, 2008.
Colford, Paul D. "Publishers Find It Pays to Do Write Thing." *New York Daily News*, December 11, 2000.
Du Bois, W. E. B. "Books," *Crisis* 18 (December 1926).
Ellis, Trey. *Platitudes*. New York: Vintage, 1988.
Everett, Percival. *Erasure*. New York: Hyperion, 2001.
Johnson, Mat. *Hunting in Harlem*. New York: Bloomsbury, 2003.
Mobley, Marilyn Sanders. "Toni Morrison." In *The Concise Oxford Companion to African American Literature*. Edited by William L. Andrews, Frances Smith Foster, and Trudier Harris, 295–297. Oxford: Oxford University Press, 2001.
Pride, Felicia. "Buyers Beware: Inside the Black Book Market: *PW* Talks with Seven Booksellers about African American Book Buying." *Publishers Weekly*, December 10, 2007.
Reed, Ishmael. *Japanese by Spring*. New York: Atheneum, 1993.
———. *Reckless Eyeballing*. New York: Atheneum, 1985.
Thoreau, Henry David. "Civil Disobedience." 1849. *Collected Essays and Poems*. Edited by Elizabeth Hall Witherell. New York: Library of America, 2001.
Wolfe, George C. *The Colored Museum*. New York: Grove, 1988.

THREE

BLACK IS GOLD: AFRICAN AMERICAN LITERATURE, CRITICAL LITERACY, AND TWENTY-FIRST-CENTURY PEDAGOGIES

MARYEMMA GRAHAM

I want to draw a map, so to speak, of a critical geography and use that map to open as much space for discovery . . . as did the original charting of the New World—without the mandate for conquest.

—TONI MORRISON, *PLAYING IN THE DARK*

I. INTRODUCTION

The two operative phrases from the Morrison epigraph that serve as a point of departure for the discussion that follows are "critical geography" and "space for discovery." Morrison, by her own example, demonstrates the capacity of language to move beyond the limitations of geography and social predicament, to give the imagination full reign. In the second decade of the twenty-first century we take this as an invitation to map another type of critical space that leads to a different, but no less influential, set of discoveries in a global context. Shifting our attention from writer to reader, and mapping the developments that feed the explosion in print culture—and the extraordinary diversity now reflected within black and other ethnic writing—immediately forces our attention to a broader spectrum of cultural and intellectual practices. No discussion, therefore, of contemporary theory and pedagogy in African American written expression is complete without considering the implications and consequence of the radical shifts occurring in the creation, production, and distribution of literature in particular and the consumption of knowledge in general.

These shifts, in turn, point us to larger questions of literacy, or more precisely *critical literacy,*[1] the conscious and unconscious framing one employs to read and interpret texts, and its corollary, *critical pedagogy,* which focuses more specifically on teaching and learning practices. While raising such matters may be a byproduct of the post–Civil Rights era— which is very much present in today's social justice movement and readily aligns itself with Bakhtinian and Foucauldian theories of discourse, language, and power—digital technology significantly extends and redefines them all. If the global circulation of mass-produced print and media texts produces "divisions and dislikes, instead of opportunities to negotiate shared meaning and value,"[2] as one study reports, then in our reluctance to question accepted models and boundaries of scholarly engagement, we widen the gap between our own academic literacy and the critical literacies of our students. Books take their meaning and sustain their existence through their circulation among readers as much as they do from the criticism that scholars themselves produce and circulate. We who study literature have learned to read and interpret through those theoretical constructs that have informed our training and reaffirm our academic investments.

Our students, on the other hand, have learned to construct meaning and indeed develop critical practices that rarely find space for discussion, let alone recognition inside the classrooms that they enter. What emerges then is a widening gap in an intellectual landscape that historically privileges a particular brand of print literacy ignoring the critical geographies—that is, physical and social spaces—that our students occupy. Without a doubt, what is historically called African American literature (works by self-identified African American authors or those that constitute a specific canon) together with an extensive body of criticism is "in print" more than ever before. Few, at least in the field of black literary and cultural studies, would have it otherwise since it is today a highly marketable academic and commercial enterprise. And yet, a reassessment of our academic and scholarly practices is in order if we are to fully understand how specific gaps in our contemporary media culture help or hinder these practices.

The foremost challenge we face in our critical and pedagogical practice is the ability of our current frameworks to capture the changing definition of what African American literature is and whom it serves. Technology disrupts the conventions of African American literary study by promoting greater facility with literacies that operate beyond the classroom. How do we conceptualize what we do when questions about research and practice are placed in the larger context of societal and institutional transformations: new graduate and undergraduate programs, new journals and associations, new comparative and cross regional or diaspora studies, as well as wider social networks and spheres of influence? What do we do when the classroom functions less as the place for developing traditional intellectual competencies than it does for ensuring greater access to sustainable employment? The two are not mutually exclusive, but the shift in focus is significant. Widespread exposure to media cultures gives us greater proficiency in negotiating and appropriating technology's meaning and uses.

What drives this dialogue is the reality, whether we like it or not, that our students are forming their own types of critical literacy that are at once beyond our preferred scope of analysis and generated through newer forms of cultural production and communication. Moreover, the explanation cannot entirely be attributed to technology but must take into account the intellectual and social transformations within the mainstream academy with regard to institutional structure, individual and collective agency, and access. All three are critical for understanding how the field of African American literature came to occupy a particular space within the academy. Mapping that history is important for us to consider before we proceed.

II. THE INTELLECTUAL SPACE OF AFRICAN AMERICAN LITERATURE

In some ways, the post–Civil Rights era has become a victim of its own success. Admittedly, the Civil Rights and Black Power movements did NOT meet many essential objectives or go as far as they should have gone in addressing sustained economic inequities and dismantling the more obvious forms of racism, for example. Yet these movements have had a visible and lasting impact on the academy and educational reform. As a preeminent example of the transformation within the academy, black studies, according to Abdul Alkalimat and Ronald Bailey, represents

a "paradigm challenge to the white supremacist framework that dominated the media, schooling and public policy at all levels . . . segregat-
ing the intellectual life of the black community into its own black public
sphere."[3] Reminding us that the birth of black studies was part of a world-
wide trend for radical change between 1967 and 1969, the authors point
to the importance of the quantitative shift that lay behind the qualitative
one: the overall increase in student enrollment between 1967 and 1974
was 30 percent, but the black student enrollment in Northern white institutions during those same years increased 160 percent.[4]

Generally, we identify black studies with those ideological, political, and physical confrontations that occurred as first-generation college
students and others from vastly different backgrounds came together in
closer proximity. Correspondingly and subsequently, black studies sustained a distinct set of intellectual, curricular, and institutional changes
in U.S. higher education. Thus, nearly fifty years after its birth, responses
to the role and function of black studies within the academy continue
to be multiple and varied. Moreover, as each new generation of black
intellectuals attaches new uses and meanings to the intellectual space
that their forebears "earned," these uses and meanings can easily subvert, challenge, or otherwise resist what many once held in high regard.

In a 2004 essay, Farah Jasmine Griffin focuses on the changes in African American literature and literary studies, a field that accounts for
the largest visible increase in black intellectual production within the
academy today. Griffin refers to the "explosion of literary production by
people of African descent . . . [as] an era of institutionalizing and diver-
sifying literature, identifying and creating a market for it, and formal-
izing its study, all resulting from the civil rights, Black Power and black
arts movements, as well as a profound response to the latter."[5] We need
not limit these observations to the field of literary studies alone. While
other disciplines might have been slow to change at first—the sciences,
for example—targeted efforts to diversify the academy and challenge the
underrepresentation of people of color have had a decisive effect in providing access and opportunities for an African American working class
at an unparalleled rate. From the perspective of institutional change and
class privilege, the era of desegregation—beginning with *Brown vs. Board
of Education*—can record its success in terms of the rise and growth of
black educational advancement and achievement, all leading to an expansion of a black intellectual class.[6]

While the transformation of academic culture has both a complicated and gendered history, a discussion of which the present space does
not allow, most scholars are generally in agreement today that the paradigm shift that occurred within the academy went against many of the
more activist, antiestablishment goals of the black studies foundational
era.[7] It was one thing to gain access to the academy but quite another to
shake loose the conventional hierarchies that restrict the potential for a
level playing field. The larger movement for economic and social justice
and equality and the movement for educational reform specific to United
States institutions of higher learning may have derived from the same
source, but the two approaches to reform did not embody the same goals
or outcomes. In this case, it would not be an exaggeration to say that the
presence of black people in the academy has not necessarily meant any
fundamental change for black people *as a whole* in terms of their historical relationship to society. Rather, it has meant a significant increase in
the number of professionally trained black intellectuals.

As the preceding discussion suggests, mapping changes and shifts in
our current literary and cultural landscape is not simply a matter of publishing more books, a flourishing body of literary criticism and theory,
and having intellectual space within the academy. Equally as fundamental to the map that we draw is an understanding of the dynamics of production and its beneficiaries. Recent trends suggest that a sizeable entrepreneurial market for independent black publishing is the largest it
has ever been, even larger than during the Black Arts Movement, when
black publishing houses flourished.[8] Moreover, this new market creates its
own systems of valuation that are not dependent on academic approval
or its protocol. If we acknowledge that the impact of literary theory and
desire for intellectual capital might well have been a failure to question
high-culture critiques, then we must also accept the subsequent class implications. In other words, it does matter whether one is operating inside
or outside the academy or, more importantly, writing for one audience
or another, where social and political contexts, experiences and forms of
self-representation can vary widely.

One such implication is fairly obvious: most of the reading public
(nonacademics) refuses to accept fixed and rigid notions of art or literature, and given the venues for production and distribution that technology now makes possible, the terms of the discourse are quickly shifting. For example, while many of us uphold the distinctions between

"literary fiction" on the one hand, and "popular" or "genre fiction" on the other, much writing today crosses these boundaries just as distinctions between and among genres are collapsing. This realignment serves to destabilize established hierarchies of high and low culture, exploiting those dynamics that challenge a dominant white culture. The result is an increased emphasis on subject matter variously identified with "the black underclass" or "the culture of poverty." This realignment is especially visible in the rise of a black music and entertainment industry as a global phenomenon, which many critics welcome as a mixed blessing. Academic critics express widely divergent opinions about these developments associated with postmodernism. Terms such as "New Black Aesthetic" (NBA) emerge as a marker for the paradigm shift that took place for those who came of age in the generation after the Civil Rights era. Although they maintain the moral imperative of the black aesthetic, a newer generation resists its "propagandistic positivism" and the notion of a racial community bound together through cultural nationalist ideals. Their revisionist thinking derives from what Trey Ellis calls their "cultural mulatto" status (raised in a multiracial mix of cultures) and shows little if any concern with the history of racism. In acknowledging a sea change, the participants in the NBA movement pay due respect to their avant-garde elders while fully exploring their own individualism, hybrid identities, and different cultural/aesthetic combinations, which middle-class access and opportunity enabled.[9]

Another expression of the paradigm shift is especially troubling for many: the proliferation of contemporary black urban fiction, most of which enters our classrooms tucked away in student backpacks, rather than on the pages of assigned syllabi. This new kind of cognitive dissonance impairs our ability to understand the shifting terrain in the modes and enactment of literacy. While it would be unfair to attribute the source of this dissonance to one moment or event in particular, it is possible to isolate certain developments in the institutionalization of literary study that may have contributed significantly to this division.

In their enthusiasm to claim a space to teach and appropriately critique black literature, one group of early black critics engaged, however unintentionally, in certain deliberate acts of exclusion and separation. Their motivation, both honest and sincere, came from a need to draw distinct boundaries that could produce an appropriate body of critical discourse and to diffuse the heated political debates that the Black Arts Movement (BAM) had generated. Since BAM was on the wane, in the late 1970s, linking art to activism and privileging cultural practices grounded in community transformation was too much a reminder of the spirit of rebellion and revolution that had wrecked the nation, too much a reminder of the "unfinished business" of the Civil Rights movement and the tragedies that it entailed. Noticeable signs of progress and change were essential as a new generation of black scholars took their first posts in mainstream, frequently Ivy League, institutions. For them, newer, more pressing concerns replaced the politicized space of the classroom where "education for liberation" had become a mantra. Moreover, eliminating the possibility of valuations of the literature easily available to the general black reading public—as much black writing in the 1960s and 1970s was—also ensured the development of a certain homogeneity of tastes. Because a large percentage of those black students who entered colleges beginning in the 1970s were urban working class, the purpose of their school re-socialization was unlearning if not devaluing what they brought with them.

In the field of literature, perhaps much less so in the social sciences, the role of education and pedagogy during the era did not serve the purpose of growing organic intellectuals, to borrow from Gramsci,[10] by helping students to make sense of their own social reality, but rather to embrace a new reality altogether. Furthermore, the distinction between criticism and scholarship on the one hand, pedagogy and teaching, on the other, something with which all academics are familiar, has a long and important history as an academic practice. Maria Regina Kecht's summation is useful for understanding the discourse of professional legitimacy:

> By the end of the 19th century, criticism gained professional legitimacy primarily through increased specialization and withdrawal from politically "contaminated" social reality. Criticism thus acquired esthetic idealism, moral superiority, and ostensibly redemptive power by relinquishing social relevance. The following years have shown no fundamental change for the better.[11]

A similar process of professional legitimacy occurred in the field of African American literature and literary study in an effort to establish a new paradigm. One example provides a portal for understanding how the threads of cognitive dissonance systematically came together.

In 1977, during and following a two-week institute on "Afro-American Literature: From Critical Approach to Course Design," young Robert Stepto began thinking about a way to continue the conversation. He took the institute's lessons—and its message—to the larger academic community in *African American Literature: The Reconstruction of Instruction* (1978), which he edited with Dexter Fisher, and published through the Modern Language Association (MLA). The desire for legitimacy was visible in the volume's intent: to refine critical approaches to teaching so as to yield a "literary" (quotes in the original) understanding of Afro-American literature.[12] To ensure this kind of professional legitimacy within the academy meant drawing boundaries for the field and often redefining for its practitioners the meaning of social relevance and community engagement.

The book was not the customary proceedings of a conference, but a charge and a pronouncement. MLA's connection to the book seemed strangely ironic, perhaps even a concerted effort to correct past oversights. With its known history of professional segregation, which Darwin Turner had detailed in a 1971 essay,[13] MLA seemed to have missed an opportunity to form a critical bridge between themselves and the all-black College Language Association. They saw instead a new breed of academics more ready to align with the era's newfound politics of inclusion. From our vantage point today, the book's subtitle "reconstruction of instruction" provided a striking metaphor recalling the complicated nature of the first Reconstruction: its promise of progress, its certain accomplishments, and its failures. The memory of that Reconstruction might well have been a sign to do things a bit differently, but such understanding can only come with hindsight.

In their introduction, the editors presented a deficit model of African American literary instruction, arguing that earlier critical and pedagogical practices were lacking in a consistent application of approaches derived from the discipline of literature. "Even a cursory look . . . reveals this deficiency. Many schools still do not teach Afro-American literature, while other institutions offering courses seem caught in a lockstep of stale critical and pedagogical ideas, many of which are tattered hand-me-downs from disciplines other than literature . . . entrapped in a hermeneutical web of race and superstructure."[14] The suggested academic models were Northrop Frye, Geoffrey Hartman, and Octavio Paz; Langston Hughes's literary importance was associated with his "international vision" rather than his status as a "North American writer." The value of black literature, according to the editors, lay in its use as a "functional model for further comparativist scholarship and teaching."[15] The volume put the Black Arts Movement on notice by identifying new formations and modalities that made it easier to dismiss the previous period of community-based, black radical politics and those writers associated with such activity.

With the exception of essays on Ralph Ellison, those diasporic movements like Negritude and the prescriptive essays on course design, the subject of Frederick Douglass dominated the volume. The work of only a few scholars appeared in the volume, but nothing by the twenty-four institute participants. The volume signaled the theoretical debut of Henry Louis Gates, then at Yale; he and Stepto authored five of the volume's ten essays, which added to the seeming exclusiveness of the collection. The single essay by Sherley Anne Williams did little to break the overall focus of the volume. She outlined a vernacular theory of Afro-American poetry and the blues aesthetic, taking key ideas from Stephen Henderson's previously published *Understanding the New Black Poetry* (1973) and introducing her own term, "ethnopoetics." It would have been impossible for Williams not to reference *some* poets of the 1960s, in an essay entitled "The Blues Roots of Contemporary Afro-American Literature," and she chose her examples carefully. Extensive commentary on Hughes, Michael Harper, and a lesser-known poet at the time, Lucille Clifton, counters a passing reference to Marvin X. Jackman, one of the most innovative and forgotten poets of the 1960s,[16] and the better-known Nikki Giovanni. Giovanni's "Great Pax Whitey," Williams tells us, is "a rather pedestrian and undigested patchwork of folk and personal legends and black nationalist philosophy, [that] becomes, when viewed (or better yet, read) as a poem in which a congregation of voices speaks, a brilliant literary approximation of the collective dialogue . . . of which the blues was an important part."[17]

The volume gave no space to the "furious flowering," as Gwendolyn Brooks called the Black Arts generation. Not surprisingly, *Understanding the New Black Poetry* would remain the only sustained examination of the poetry of the 1960s until the appearance of *The Black Arts Enterprise* thirty-five years later.[18] *Reconstruction* prophesied a bright future for the institutionalization and professionalization of black literature and literary studies, even as it rendered the Black Arts Movement invisible.

The absence of any reference to the work of the preceding generation of African American scholar/critics is equally glaring. The classic anthologies *Negro Caravan* (1941), by Arthur P. Davis, Ulysses Lee, and Sterling Brown, and *Cavalcade: Negro American Writing from 1760 to the Present* (1971), by Arthur P. Davis and J. Saunders Redding, were two of many important interventions in the discourse on the creation and construction of a black literary tradition. While the approaches and goals were different from *Reconstruction,* the editors of *Caravan* and *Cavalcade* were just as concerned about the need for more critical discussions about black literature. Stepto and Fisher, however, believed it was no longer necessary to prove the existence of black literature, "[that] fills bookstore shelves, the stacks of libraries . . . Symposia and seminars are regularly held . . . prominent contemporary black writers give scores of readings. The need is for an advanced volume that presupposes an awareness of the literature," they argued.[19]

Yet, in all honesty, they did more than "presuppose the awareness of a literature." The volume imposed, as if by imperial design, its own particular theoretical perspective through the erasure of others. As a result, a particular method of critical study replaced a more democratic form of critical engagement and its social sphere of influence. The ongoing failure to grasp the range and complexity of literary politics of the three decades before the 1960s and the precariousness of an entire movement of black writers, critics, and poets, which would become the focus of Lawrence Jackson's excellent study,[20] endorsed certain historical practices but also privileged certain forms of academic scholarship that followed. Nevertheless, an affinity did exist between the *Reconstruction* school and their predecessors: a shared concern with developing a critical literature that could compete on the world stage. Both generations saw themselves as custodians of black literature and sought to prepare the way for the future, if not the path to mainstream acceptance. The difference, however, is that the generation of critics and scholars between 1934 and 1960 felt the necessity to redeem the historical past "that enabled [them] to challenge more fully the prominence of western artistic tradition . . . [and]

prepare the ground for the militant writers' aggressive rejection of America's liberal ideas."[21] The younger generation of scholars saw rupture rather than continuity.

These actions were certainly understandable, given who the members of the *Reconstruction* project were and what they represented. They were newly trained as academics, hailing mostly from elite graduate institutions, and had neither the social base of Black Arts/Black Aesthetic nor the legacy of historically black institutions as was the case for the earlier generation of scholars and critics. This younger generation wanted and needed its own intellectual space in the academy, and sensing a void, they accepted the prevailing intellectual hierarchies that reinforced normative ideas about literary value and valuation, even in the face of growing dissension. By contrast, practitioners and proponents of the Black Arts Movement, without the mainstream institutional support or any recognized academic legitimacy, continued to operate primarily outside the academy.[22] BAM artists continued to define themselves primarily by their politics that governed their art and aesthetics and took pride in their opposition to the black middle class.

During this period, African American scholarly discourse moved in concert with contemporary critical theories, the most prominent of which was deconstruction. In addition to being a suitable topic for examination, the focus on Frederick Douglass offered sufficient distance from ideological debates of the 1960s. It became fairly easy to separate their views, both in theory and practice, from those of their predecessors, with some exceptions.[23] Focusing attention on the slave narrative and on slavery in general was also a logical way to readily identify with peers who were experiencing similar shifts in the discourse in other fields, especially history, where, "new history studies" had opened up new areas of critical inquiry. And yet, as more gendered critiques of Douglass' *Narrative of the Life of Frederick Douglass* began to surface, a most notable one by Deborah McDowell,[24] *Reconstruction* seemed to participate in another kind of reconstruction: the uncritical acceptance of representations of slavery that privileged male slave authority and independence at the expense of female exploitation, brutality, and humiliation.

A more concrete sign of this cognitive dissonance, as acts of separation and exclusion, lies in the history of black literary journals. The premier journal in black literature today, *African American Review,* founded in 1967 as *Negro American Literature Forum,* bore the subtitle "For School and University Teachers" and received its support from Indiana State University's School of Education. The first change occurred in the title: *Negro* to *Black* when the journal moved to the College of Liberal Arts. *African American Review,* like many early black journals, followed the conventional practice of subordinating pedagogy to literary criticism, as the need to validate and "credential" black literature increased. A similar case holds for the *College Language Association Journal,* founded ten years earlier in 1957. While the name did not change, a review of the contents over more than five decades shows the progression from discussions of teaching practice, to major essays on traditional British and American literature, to today's focus almost exclusively on African American literary criticism.[25]

This institutional legacy has its parallel in our general understanding of artistic and cultural practice. The distinction between high and low art remains, even when a major objective of postmodern culture is to collapse these boundaries. We blame the publishing industry for implementing the distinctions between "literary" and "genre fictions," but we consistently reinforce these classifications by privileging certain kinds of texts over others in our teaching and our research. More difficult still is the differential value we place on orality versus written literacy. Students will receive less praise for their mastery of oral communication skills and literacies than for the preferred academic writing they may or may not master. We do not welcome the "other" kind of writing even when it comes with passion and focus. The distinctions we make between types of writers, speakers, and readers encourage exclusion and invisibility. The preference for the ideal academic student reader or writer can blind us to the student aiming for a career as a writer in a non-academic environment.

Stepto and Fisher's belief in the necessary *divestment* of the more "elementary" functions associated with academic practice calls to mind Barbara Herrnstein Smith's discussion of "critical problematics." Literary value and evaluation are different for those inside the class and the "reading public," according to Smith, but because we have no record of the latter, we are left with the "social parochialism of academic critics" and rarely question "the social, cultural and political functions that [their] evaluative statements perform."[26]

Arguably, the urgency to transform and consolidate a particular "brand" of literary criticism in order to gain credibility and authority within an elitist-driven academy was ambitious, if not radical in its own right. In the twenty-first century it is impossible to fully comprehend the range, intensity, and impact of the battles to counter a history of racist neglect by and within the academy. Indeed, entrenched societal attitudes, persistent exclusionary practices, and multiple forms of emotional and psychological, if not physical violence were responsible for many of the cultural wars in which African Americans were engaged as they became a critical mass in U.S. universities.

The institutionalization of literary study in the academy in the post-1960s era, however, is not the only explanation for the cognitive dissonance that exists. The absence of a more homogeneous racial identity, recalling a time when blacks suffered as a whole from racial discrimination, makes even more apparent certain polarizing tendencies. African American social and economic mobility beyond the academy is visible in expanded employment opportunities, increased political participation, and notable achievements in the corporate and government sectors, all of which disrupts a social and spatial process generally associated with a perceived earlier black community cohesiveness. Recent cultural and class formations, displaying an authority that is rarely compatible with self-critique, likewise exists without the incentive for rigorous examination of relevant ideological, social, or cultural contexts. When a growing elite no longer identifies with the commonality of interests and shared social values of the "traditional" black community, it becomes both victim and perpetuator of increasing intraracial class divisions.

Perhaps none of these formations is more problematic than the public intellectual phenomenon. Those who have taken on this role, according to Madhu Dubey, tend to give uncritical acceptance to the media's "panic-stricken attention to an allegedly growing black 'underclass,' thereby reinforcing [William] Wilson's picture of post–Civil Rights black America as more divided than ever before along the lines of class." Dubey's conclusion is that "African American intellectuals seeking to speak for the race as a whole occupy a position of extreme contradiction in the postmodern era." The central challenge is the need for a "collective racial politics that gives due weight to intra-racial differences."[27] Yet, explanations and contemporary panaceas are extensive, ranging from the call for an idealized return to a transclass racial community to bell hooks's "Post-modern Blackness."[28]

More to the point of this discussion, however, is Kenneth Warren's *What Was African American Literature?*, which puts the contradictory impulses among black intellectuals in sharp relief. Warren's work looks back to the *Reconstruction* school in efforts to clarify the terms of black literary discourse by establishing boundaries of meaning and interpretation. At the same time, however, Warren is reminiscent of an even earlier generation of scholars, who had contradictory impulses of their own.[29] Sixty years and many careers later, in a crucial turn, Warren's proposal that African American literature is a "post-emancipation phenomenon that gained coherence as an undertaking in the social world defined by the system of Jim Crow segregation"[30] sets forth a narrowly circumscribed vision, defining the practitioners rather than the practice. If J. Saunders Redding's generation had feelings of anguish at their racial obligations and the Reconstruction school wanted to ensure the field's academic legitimacy, Warren wishes to draw a line of demarcation, privileging one or maybe two generations, a distinct body of knowledge and a closed curriculum. The limitations he imposes flies in the face of much contemporary scholarship on the origins and development of African American and diaspora literature, as much as it welcomes the forces of marginalization and new forms of essentialism.[31] His view replaces resilience, organicism, and dynamism as fundamental features of cultural change with stasis; it obliterates the relationship between the past and the present; and any future literature becomes culturally insignificant and socially inconsequential.

In a real sense, however, Warren brings us back to the very question that this essay seeks to address: what should be the appropriate response to the changing landscape of African American literature in a technology rich and globally aware world. What lies beneath Warren's provocative claim that "African American literature is over" is a failure to see intellectual opportunities in the current moment that reexamine African American studies more broadly. Warren's proposal suggests the fear of losing authority as we pry African American literature loose from those intellectual assumptions underscoring a more or less uniform field of inquiry, which, by the mid-1980s, had established its own set of hierarchies and controls, and is largely responsible for shaping the careers of a significant number of late twentieth-century scholars, not only within the United States but abroad.

The real and present danger has more to do with the paradigm shift that is likely to evoke questions, engaging in the kind of work that takes us out of our intellectual or political comfort zones, transcending the class divisions from which many of us have benefitted. Moving beyond Warren's vision that, in effect, sees racial matters "banished as the relic of a bygone era," means recognizing instead "racial politics in the post-modern period can no longer be premised on the models of unmediated racial representation or of a monolithic black community."[32] The choice to expand definitions, inviting different, more collective visions, means placing urgent intellectual questions in the larger matrix of cultural influences that can better shape future research, scholarship, and pedagogy. Warren has done us a real service in foregrounding the challenges and opportunities that the field confronts.

III. BLACK PRINT CULTURE AND ITS DISCONTENTS

Few would argue that our critical frameworks are inadequate for understanding the form and function of contemporary African American writing. Foremost among these challenges is the inability of our current frameworks to capture the radical changes in what African American literature is and whom it serves. Technology empowers, gains momentum, expands and redefines literature, creating a contested space where older more traditional paradigms cannot expect to persist unchanged. The most frequently taught canon of African American literature is but one part of our larger print culture,[33] whose driving force today is technology. Students who operate within this larger print culture trouble our understanding of literature *as well as* literacy, which we have typically understood as a specific set of autonomous cognitive skills to be taught rather than as a socially constructed and dynamic practice. The resulting disconnect between our expectations and those of our students may look like racial, gender, class, or generational differences but might be better explained as differences in the meaning of literacy.

The shift from literature to literacy here suggests that understanding today's black print culture cannot be based solely on the ability to read and write. More critical to this changing definition of literacy are the distinct characteristics of media saturation that are multisensory, and employ image, sight, sound, and kinetic and tactile modes. The most sophisticated users have learned to manipulate the tools of technology for communication, self-expression, and creation. They are, in essence, highly print literate and display a type of competence that is no less cognitive or intellectual but derives from different types of intelligence that these forms embody. Early scholars like Geneva Smitherman, and more recently Keith Gilyard and Adam Banks, have pointed out the existence of language diversity and varieties of linguistic competence as other bases for understanding black literacy, arguing vehemently against the kinds of valuation systems we employ, systems that privilege standard English writers and speakers to the exclusion of all others. That "different" did or does not mean "inferior" has seldom been an easy sell. Banks makes the bridge from print literacy to technology and the potential for eliminating racism and exclusion.[34] The expansion of literacy that has spurred the growth of African American literature, exhibits the same potential for creating a more democratic society, according to Doug Kellner, who proposes that we invest more fully in "the cultivation of print literacy . . . [that] can promote democratic self-expression . . . invigorating debate and participation."[35] The democratizing of self-expression has led to new contestations of intellectual and cultural space as different sites of cultural production become more visible. Despite the perception that technology has been largely responsible for disabling print culture, black print culture is larger than ever and remains the place where discussions of literacy, culture, and democratic access collide and connect.

The evolution of a new print culture has other social and intellectual implications, reflecting a process of literary production markedly different from and in direct competition with the traditional corporate publishing world. The repositioning in the publishing industry has meant that mainstream publishers no longer dominate the market as they once did. Many have consolidated or closed as the independent publishing sector continues to expand. The publishing "empire" is toppling because the multitier system is not needed to move a book from manuscript to published form. The large editorial staffs, marketing departments, art and design teams, and financial units that once comprised distinct entities in the successful publishing houses have become obsolete. Less-expensive publishing options have replaced the hardcover blockbuster, and distribution mechanisms are easier to access. Books circulate and re-circulate through Amazon, Google, and eBay, allowing readers to have more control over their choices and to exercise their purchasing power.

These changes are linked with a critique of assorted new types of literature in circulation and the culture that produces it. The growth of popular culture has forced a rethinking of many of the analytical categories for organizing print culture. Terms such as "literary," in contrast to "popular" or "commercial," have little bearing on what people read. Moreover, that these distinctions reinforce an implicit hierarchy serving publishers rather than readers has become increasingly clear. In this context, we do well to remember that African American literature and cultural production have rarely "played by the rules." The need and ability to cross various linguistic and structural boundaries accounts in large part for the distinctive utilitarian and aesthetic qualities in African American literature.

Thus, despite the efforts to prevent the further spread of "extraliterary values, ideas and pedagogical constructions that have plagued literature," the major concern expressed by the *Reconstruction* school,[36] mass distribution of print and media texts has followed its own course. Well-established boundaries become less visible and viable when we move from inside the space of the classroom to the outside. We, like our students, impart and exchange views representing different tastes as we participate in different media practices. Assuming that print literacy does not bind these practices or that students are constructing their identities exclusively through various forms of social networking would be a mistake.

The question to ask then is not about the meaning of communicating and accessing information through the internet but about the relationship between the various forms of literacy to which we have access. Even if the expansion of media culture presents a challenge to traditional print culture, it has not brought about a declining interest in the black book per se. One of the major contributions of the Black Arts Movement publishers like Detroit-based Broadside Press, founded by Dudley Randall, and Chicago-based Third World Press, founded by Haki Madhubuti, is the expansion of the market of readers and writers committed to black literature. Although the goals of Black Arts authors and publishers were different from those of the white owners of Holloway House, who entered the market of black popular fiction early, the latter coined the phrase

"Black Is Gold" for its marketing campaign, predicting the commercial potential in black literary production.[37]

Returning to Griffin's 2004 review of African American literature, of the ten trends she notes, three of them are far more relevant now than when the review appeared:

- the rise in the production of black commercial fiction;
- the creation of new literary and artistic institutions outside of the academy, such as Art Sanctuary, founded by Lorene Cary, and the Before Columbus Foundation, founded by Ishmael Reed;
- the emergence of the internet as a site of publication, distribution, and discussion.[38]

The major complaint and prediction in 2004 was that while the number of authors and readers was rapidly increasing, these writers continued to experience marginalization by a mainly white publishing industry. The signs in the larger print culture, however, were pointing in a different direction.

Publishing Trends (currently part of Content Licensing), an online review that provides "news and opinion on the changing world of book publishing," has followed the growth of independent book publishing in 1994. Its lead article for April 2003 reported the explosion in independent publishing, in comparison to the larger publishing conglomerates. According to *Publishing Trends,* Barnes and Noble, for example, saw purchases from the ten largest publishers decline from 74 percent in 1994 to 46 percent in 1997.[39] A little more than a decade later, Borders would file for bankruptcy, following a trend that *Newsweek* and other news media had already begun to predict. As these conglomerates try to adjust and create new strategies to bring themselves out of a deep slump, smaller presses began to pick up the slack, doing precisely what Hyperion's Bob Miller proposed in 2003: "cultivate specialties, pounce on trends quickly to beat out the sluggish large houses."[40] As a result, their sales for the Independent Publishers Group are soaring, with the figures to back it up: more than 30 percent annual revenue increase in nearly two decades, owing to such factors as "desktop publishing, internet ubiquity, come-one-come-all chain bookselling . . . grooming niche markets with direct special sale tactics."[41] Thus while Griffin was correct in her assessment that major publishers were likely less interested in publishing more black authors, what she did not consider was the ability of a rapidly growing independent press to aggressively pursue new voices that, according to *Publishing Trends*, "push the envelope."

It is not insignificant that some academic scholars have successfully navigated what many still see as troubled waters. They work across the class and digital divide as they embrace the broader meaning of intellectual and cultural work. For example, Elizabeth Nunez, a provost at Medgar Evers College, publishes academic books and is an award-winning Random House novelist as well. Readers know her, however, through the largest site for commercial black literature AALBC (African American Literature Book Club), where one finds Nunez's seven novels: *When Rocks Dance* (1992), *Beyond the Limbo Silence* (2003), *Bruised Hibiscus* (2003), *Discretion* (2003), *Grace* (2006), *Prospero's Daughter* (2006), and her latest, *Anna In-Between* (2009). With its own search engine (http://thebestblackbooksearch.com), AALBC has an impressive author listing, including books by Barack Obama. Logging on to Nunez's books, one can view a podcast of Nunez reading as well as brief descriptions and excerpts from each of the books. The site approaches black print culture holistically, refusing to distinguish between author "types." AALBC markets *all* black authors; they are nonhierarchical. Ben Okra, winner of the Booker Prize, is featured alongside Frank Matthews, a recent discovery of Karen Hunter Publishing, one of the fastest growing contemporary producers of black fiction. Matthews' life behind bars provided the solitude and the motivation for his transformation, extending the long tradition of prison literature, while simultaneously expanding on it for increased accessibility. The power of words and images combined to make *Respect the Jux* successful: a four-minute music video, starring Matthews himself, was undoubtedly a big factor in the book's successful advance promotion. *Twenty thousand* copies sold immediately on the book's 2010 release.

Many authors do well without such a distribution network, however. Gwendolyn Pough, who is not on AALBC's list, is a professor of women's and gender studies, writing and rhetoric at Syracuse University. Pough wrote *Check It While I Wreck It: Black Womanhood, Hip-Hop Culture and the Public Sphere* (2004), a major contribution to cultural studies and feminist scholarship but elected to write her romance novels under a pseudonym, Gwyneth Bolton. Her access to the romance tradition, historically the domain of women readers, came through her background. Having grown up in a working-class community in Paterson, New Jersey, Pough speaks warmly of an attentive mother who was an avid reader of Harlequin romances, the most continuously successful series for women readers. Prolific in the genre, Pough releases a book almost bimonthly through Kimani Books, Harlequin's black romance fiction imprint. According to Pough, by the beginning of the twenty-first century, romance publishers had begun to look for writers and were willing to provide one-on-one editorial attention, which made it relatively easy to get through the publication process: the exact opposite of the conglomerates. Moreover, a separate reward system and support networks provide the necessary incentive to improve and master the craft. Although E. Jerome Dickey takes the lead in black romance fiction sales, Bolton has acquired a name for herself along with a sizeable number of honors. Her independent website announces her awards such as the 2010 Emma Author of the Year Award and provides an intimate space for her readers to communicate directly with her. The social networking phenomenon updates a much older strategy in women's fiction, the art of familiarity, going back to the epistolary novels of the nineteenth century. One thinks of Harriet Jacobs in *Incidents in the Life of a Slave Girl,* for example, who used the language of sentiment to gain her women readers' approval for exercising unauthorized agency as a black woman. Bolton actively builds her network by communicating by email with her readers, sharing personal information on the website, posting questions and answering them publicly. She knows her audience and rarely fails to give what she promises on her site: "sexy romance with an urban flair."

The potential of information technologies as a tool for writing and publishing has its megastar, of course, in Zane, the pen name of the Baltimore-based author, who founded Strebor Books in 1999, a one-woman publishing enterprise. The "Zane phenomena" began with the distribution of her first stories to paid subscribers through her electronic newsletter. The entrepreneurial venture was an immediate success, filling a huge void in books for black women, a market that had exploded following the success of Terri McMillan's *Waiting to Exhale* (novel, 1992; film, 1995). Zane quickly began to write longer works, watching the sales figures for her books reportedly reach more than 250,000 for early titles such as *Addicted* (2001) and the ever-popular *The Sex Chronicles: Shattering the Myth* (2002). The innovative use of digital space would become the standard among small independent publishers, the category that includes *all* black publishers without exception.[42] Zane's success did not go unnoticed by mainstream publishers, and Simon and Schuster, which had already begun to distribute her books, acquired Strebor in 2005. By then, Zane had written nine books, published more than 100 titles by other authors, and sold more than three million copies combined, with annual sales of $15 million. In an effort to stabilize their own declining markets, Simon and Schuster acknowledged that Zane represented a "new publishing category for African American readers" and through her, wanted desperately to "grow [their] share of this increasingly vibrant market." Zane was exactly what they needed, "that self-generated gem," the company's spokesman was quoted as saying.[43] The "new publishing category," was of course black erotica. Zane, however, was in good company. A report of best-sellers for September 2004 listed Zane's *Nervous* as number one in the hardcover fiction category, alongside Bill Clinton's *My Life* and Rick Warren's *The Purpose Driven Life,* the top-selling books among hardcover nonfiction. The same issue reported Zane's anthology of black erotica, *Chocolate Flavor,* as the #4 best-selling paperback, ranking above Edward Jones's Pulitzer Prize-–winning *The Known World.*[44] While Strebor Books carried a highly diverse line, including mysteries, police dramas, science fiction, historical fiction, urban fiction, gay and lesbian themes, and religious-themed books, Zane chose to write about sex, she said, "because we freed our bodies from slavery a long time ago, and now it is time to free our minds."[45]

Undoubtedly, an improved print-on-demand technology, e-books, e-marketing, and guerilla marketing (a popular Black Arts Movement strategy), and black distributors like AALBC and Black Books Direct enable black publishers to find and deliver to their audiences. Black print culture today includes books of all kinds: romance novels, mysteries, speculative fiction, historical fiction, nonfiction essays, memoirs, letters, experimental writing, spoken word, graphic novels, self-help books, and Christian fiction. It has also embraced the reader's culture through the cultivation of black book clubs, a longstanding African American tradition, one that did not begin with Oprah, as many have assumed. While we have always known that black people *read* more than the data suggested, today they are claiming an increasingly larger share of the book-*buying* public.

As best-selling authors Terry McMillan, E. Lynn Harris, and Zane learned—all three self-published their first books—becoming a force in today's print culture is a bottom-up process. This, too, is not new in the history of black writing; many early black authors, the wildly popular nineteenth-century poet Frances E. W. Harper as well as turn-of-the-century authors E. Sutton Griggs and Pauline Hopkins published their first books independently. Hopkins and Griggs, unable to find a publisher, created their own companies and continued to successfully publish and distribute their own books and those of others. They were among the best-selling authors of their times, and their relative invisibility says more about their exclusion from the mainstream discourses than it does about their importance in the history of black writing and publishing.

Within print culture, the fastest growing market is urban fiction, with an assortment of ever-shifting and expanding categories: street lit/hip-hop/gangsta lit, urban fantasy, urban romance, erotica, and Christian or inspirational fiction. Authors of these fictions recognize the particular geography of social relations as well as the reluctance of the academic establishment to incorporate or seriously examine their work. What criticism exists falls within the purview of "popular culture studies." Writers of urban fiction comprehend and claim a space as gendered—male, female, lesbian, gay, bisexual—and black by exploring the particularities of contemporary life. At times they use essentialized discourses that establish a racial, cultural connection with the reader and acknowledge the commodity culture of our postmodern world as their characters navigate complex lives and multiple identities. These authors make themselves known to their readers through a wide array of social networking communication.

Despite the high visibility of contemporary black print culture, we have limited informational resources and even less aggregate or reliable data on which to base our analysis. While short, pithy essays on Zane are available, almost all appeared *after* Simon and Schuster acquired her line of books in 2004/2005, suggesting that she gained a different kind of mainstream access at that point. AALBC and BlackbooksDirect have done extremely well through e-marketing and sales, but even most of that information is anecdotal. Directories of publishers and writers are even more difficult. The Project on the History of Black Writing (http://www.hbw.ku.edu) maintains an electronic database, one that is far more comprehensive up to 1980s, but the growth of independent publishing and self-publishing has made this increasingly more difficult. Grace Adams's *Black Authors and Publishers International Directory,* an invaluable compendium of information published annually since 2006, is also very uneven, since it relies heavily on individual submissions, rather than a systematic search. Nor does it provide composite data. A few case studies exist such as the brief one quoted earlier on Holloway House, but traditional scholarly studies are emerging slowly, although the work of Candice Love Jackson[46] shows much promise.

The lack of "hard" data notwithstanding,[47] enough evidence suggests that African Americans are and will remain wedded to print culture. As the demand for books increases, we expect to see continued growth in black distribution outlets and the number of black authors, as well as more black book clubs, book fairs, and festivals. A technology-rich society levels the playing field, making access less dependent on academic privilege, and more dependent on the utilization of information resources.

IV. CREATING NEW SPATIAL GEOGRAPHIES

This final section of the essay argues for a different kind of discursive space that looks at a multivalent print culture without excising the literacy and literary practices that such a culture implies. The chasm that separates the reality of black print culture from the academic discourses in which most of us are engaged sends mixed if not conflicting messages to those who participate at some level in both. It is this population—especially the students we encounter in our classes—who deserve a space where dialogue and discussion can thrive independent of the dictates of exclusionary critical theories.

Thadious Davis suggests that social/spatial geographies are indeed narratives where issues of power and privilege collide.[48] Using Southern literature as a point of departure, she considers what happens when exclusion becomes an intellectual and cultural practice within the social geography of segregation, focusing on the works of Richard Wright, Ernest Gaines, Alice Walker, and others as specific cases in point. Following Davis's lead, we might say that postracial culture as having created its own social/spatial geography, one in which black literary production has moved from a constrictive spatial reality to a spatial imaginary. Like other sites of black cultural production, this shift challenges our pedagogical practices and our theoretical assumptions as well. Readers figure prominently in this new spatial geography, pushing against the limits of our current academic knowledge, as well as the power and privilege that it presumes. Using the tools of technology, we extend the range of intellectual and literary production and simultaneously extend the audiences and groups that particular products can reach.

The growing use and application of digital technologies further complicate issues of power and privilege in the field of black studies, however. To fully engage the digital is to have access to independent windows into past and current knowledge, lessening the dependence on the views of any single group. As a key point of continuity within the black experience, the creation of new spatial geographies replicates the push and pull factor identified with the earlier transformation from the rural agricultural South to an urban industrial North. In this instance, the inadequacies of our current pedagogical practices push people away from engagement, while the dynamism and transformative potential of technology pulls people into an awareness of new possibilities. The *eBlack*[49] studies group at the University of Illinois, who have been providing in-depth analysis of black studies for the last four decades, concludes that "everything is being invented and reconnected, as we move from an industrial society to an informational, networked one in a new global system,"[50] confirming the belief in digital technology as a new form of grounding with the capacity to guide the future.

Nevertheless, myths about "the poverty of black print culture," according to Dubey, come frequently from black (postmodern) intellectuals who "aspire to broad-based racial representation but cannot overtly sanction the modern idea of acculturating the lower classes into a print literate tradition."[51] Cornel West draws an even sharper distinction when proposing "the ur-text of black culture is neither a word nor a book . . . [but] the 'guttural cry' and the 'wrenching moan'."[52] Dubey correctly points out that this kind of essentialism "re-enacts all the founding moves of 1960s black cultural nationalism" in its "attachment to . . . outmoded definitions of racial authenticity . . . [that] reproduces the nationalist hierarchy of (elite, inauthentic) print and (popular, authentic) vernacular culture."[53] These hierarchies, whether intentional or not, reveal a not-so-thinly-veiled class bias that prohibits self-critique, a thoroughgoing analysis of contemporary black print culture—or black culture in general—and renders most scholars incapable of understanding the pivotal role that technology can and does play in redefining, if not expanding, social and intellectual space. This may well be, as Eric Lott suggests, "a defensive posture . . . symptomatic of a situation in which black critics function inside left and intellectual subcultures without enough institutional support from inside the race."[54] In the end, these feed our failure to generate a new critical thinking practice.

At best, most contemporary black writers acknowledge the existence of a double standard, even if academics don't call it that. Reading and writing are valuable enterprises, but not all reading and writing have the same value—something we implicitly accept. A canon of accepted literary texts exists, some popular texts cross over, and other texts exist purely for commercial reasons and do not deserve our attention. Octavia Butler and Tananarive Due as writers of speculative fiction have gained increasing acceptability as crossover authors; they frequently appear on class reading lists and in theses and dissertations. Butler's *Kindred* is now accepted as an important neo-slave narrative. Due's work is linked to discourses on the post-human and Afrofuturism as a literary and cultural aesthetic. Both authors fall into the "popular" category, a contested term, says Candice Jackson, since it is "linked not with time but with taste."[55] This reminder that tastes are cultivated, class specific, and socially conditioned brings us back to the classroom as a critical space, or as Mary Louise Pratt has told us, a "cultural contact zone," the place to allow dialogue between the different tastes, especially as they relate to power.[56] Pratt proposes that we have a decided advantage when we consider the classroom a site of engagement for socially transformative practice. Teaching without awareness of those issues of class and power that underlie the pedagogical choices limits opportunities for any real engagement.

If contemporary black fiction in every genre imaginable disturbs the pedagogical *and* personal comfort zones for many of us, our students find them compelling because of the ways in which these texts engage the actualities of their lives, real or imagined. These are reader-identified books. Zane argues, for example, that her books help "shatter the myth of sexual dysfunction between black men and women." She hopes that she is imparting "moral lessons in each of her stories, with liberation as the underlying premise." Readers, many of whom are young women, see "strong, take-no-prisoner-type women who learn hard lessons by the end of the book," she tells us.[57] The reader as a subject of analysis is not new; it has given rise to more than one variety of reader response theories and a host of key texts such as Janice Radway's *Reading the Romance,* Shirley Samuels's *The Culture of Sentiment,* and more recently Elizabeth McHenry's *Forgotten Readers: Recovering the Lost History of African American Literature Societies.* Still the pedagogical implications of focusing on readers rather than writers escape us.

Do these writers *deserve* the space we might give them in the classroom, we ask? How seriously do they take themselves as writers? Harlequin author Artist (A. C.) Arthur, with nearly two dozen novels in seven years, specializes in paranormal romances, a popular genre within romance fiction that combines elements of science fiction. Arthur rises at 4:00 AM to exercise and begin her writing routine; writing is for her hard work, and she prepares for it. The challenge is in the development of different characters for her novels that have brought her success, including *Full House Seduction* (2009), *Guarding His Body* (2008), *A Cinderella Affair* (2007), and *Object of Desire* (2003). Several years ago, when her creative energies shifted, she confronted a new challenge, as she began to write multicultural paranormal young adult fiction. This, she argues, is a different kind of story creation, and it has to cross many boundaries. She has written two novels in her new Myxtix series, which stresses greater diversity than her earlier fiction: teenagers facing more than puberty, differences among them, small towns in which they live, and the supernatural. She remains with Harlequin, writing under their young adult imprint, Kimani TRU. The scholarly potential is high as these science fiction works treat young adult themes and cultural conflict. Her response to the question of academic criticism about her work is gracious: after a dozen books, she knows of no articles in academic journals and has only given a few interviews for online magazines.[58]

Arthur's story is not unusual. Like many authors, success with adult fiction is sufficient motivation to test their talents in another genre, often for younger readers. Thus, we must challenge the view that these are not "serious writers of literature" who consistently work at their craft. Some publishers are fighting back, fully aware of their exclusion from academic discourses. The growing interest in romance fiction in particular has encouraged the Romantic Writers of America to initiate a research grant competition to advance academic research.

Writers, too, are fighting back. Marita Golden (*Migrations of the Heart, Long Distance Life, And Do Remember Me*) founded the Hurston/Wright Foundation in 1990 as an independent space to train and cultivate writers of color at early stages of their career. The foundation has held regular summer workshops and gives annual awards for the most promising work in poetry and fiction. In 2002, Golden coauthored, with E. Lynn Harris, *Gumbo: An Anthology of African American Writing.* As the title suggests, this book is a collection of all varieties of black print culture. Literary novelists such as Edwidge Danticat, John Edgar Wideman, and Gloria Naylor appear in the collection alongside Eric Jerome Dickey, Terry McMillan, J. California Cooper, as well as more experimental authors such as Mat Johnson. His works include *Incognegro, Drop, Dark Rain, Hunting in Harlem,* and *Pym.* The volume includes lesser-known but prolific writers such as David Anthony Durham (*Gabriel's Song, Walk Through Darkness, Pride of Carthage*) and Bertice Berry (*Redemption, The Haunting of Hip Hop*). The book's goal is to teach us by its example, challenging boundaries that exist and divide writers, boundaries we reinforce in our classroom practice. Golden, a writer and teacher, understood that anthologies by definition exclude. Just as the Hurston/Wright Foundation created an independent organization to meet the needs of developing writers, so too does *Gumbo* move toward a purposeful unity within the writing community, intentionally moving beyond genre classifications.

Greater receptivity to the crossing of boundaries exists within contemporary black texts that bear the labels "experimental" or "postmodern." The graphic novel, as a case in point, offers unlimited possibilities for reinvention as a sequential art form, using thematically coherent narrative and comic book design. Contemporary black graphic novelists have used the genre to examine the politics of race and representation just as early black cartoonists did. The work of Melvin Van Peebles does this and more. Van Peebles made history in 1971 when he wrote, produced, scored, and starred in the independent film *Sweet Sweetback's Baadasssss Song*. Blaxploitation films thus made their appearance, and Van Peebles faced a critical environment that deplored his reliance on hypervisibility and stereotype, although his subsequent work, such as *Ain't Supposed to Die a Natural Death*, confirmed him as one of our most innovative and experimental artists. In his first graphic novel *Confessions of a Ex-Doofus-Itchy-Footed Mutha* (2009), Van Peebles extends his reputation for crossing boundaries, disciplines, and traditions and for his skillful blending of literary and visual culture. The story is a coming-of-age narrative in the picaresque tradition; the protagonist experiences black culture through its various modalities (blues, jazz) together with ritualized initiations. He learns the lessons of history that he must take with him to manhood. The story is told through visual frames that include illustrations and photography and uses a narrative style that alternates between poetry and prose. As with all of his work, Van Peebles presents countervisions in complex and contradictory ways that demand a keen critical eye to unpack.[59]

Other blended forms show the potential of contemporary black writing to respond in inventive ways, using both print and digital literacies. J. T. Kemp calls his new genre "prolyretry" and has produced four e-novels thus far: *b'n'b* (beauties and bitchwhores), *Infinite Love, Living Lyrics,* and *Tripolar*. What does it mean for a book to "look like poetry, read like prose, sound like music," he asks? Colleen Dixon has coined the phrase "quadrilogy" as a framing device for her connected fictions (*Simon Says, Every Shut Eye, Behind Closed Doors,* and *Relative Secrets*.) These works push the boundaries of textual form and meaning—whether we use the terms "literary" or "popular" to categorize them—and thus require new pedagogies and critical tools to give them proper attention.

The most important place to begin our dialogue about this new writing is to acknowledge the chasm between our teaching canon and the vast domain of black print culture. Print literacy historically identifies one's status as educated and middle class, but the digital revolution plays a democratizing role by giving greater information freedom, connectivity, and global access.[60] How does understanding this contradiction play itself out in the classroom? What authors do our students know that we do not? How do our reading choices reflect our interpretations and identities, values, and beliefs that we bring to/take away from the text? What shapes the characters in the stories? How might they act differently depending on the circumstances that they face? What criteria do we use in determining what is good or bad about a text? These dialogues can easily extend beyond the classroom through web-based discussion forums that increase the investment in a process. Such discussions invite not only reflection but also moral and ethical choices. An objective is to get students to see the classroom as a space for "negotiating shared meaning and value through cultural differences."[61] Using pedagogy to achieve critical literacy means risking "safe" answers and allowing more inclusive dialogue and debate to heighten everyone's awareness of those views that others hold and share.

When *Black Issues in Higher Education* did a cover story on "New Literary Lights" in its January 2000 issue, Colson Whitehead, Calvin Baker, John Keane, Danzy Senna, and Natasha Tarpley all appeared on the cover. Since then, many of these authors' books have made it into classrooms, notably Colson Whitehead's *Intuitionist* (1999), Danzy Senna's *Caucasia* (2000), and Natasha Tarpley's *Girl in the Mirror: Three Generations of Black Women in Motion* (1999). The selection of this particular group of novelists for the issue's cover generated controversy because it appeared to support the myth that literary achievement presumes middle-class privilege, guaranteeing access. A story intended to introduce the future "stars" seemed to say nothing new: Whitehead, Tarpley, and Senna—graduates of Harvard (Whitehead, Tarpley) and Stanford (Senna)—have received the most attention. Whitehead added to his reputational capital by earning a prestigious Macarthur "genius" Award even before his career was in full swing. If we are to challenge these myths, we must begin to question the different frames of interpretation among students who already know well how to make careful distinctions between what is possible for whom.

If the standards that we use today continue to give scant attention to the full spectrum that is today's black print culture, we unknowingly compromise the very history that we have worked so hard to recover, running the risk of leaving a thin or incomplete record of what may well be the last stage of print culture as we know it. More importantly, addressing the disconnect between our students' reading practices and our teaching canon can ensure that our critical literacy practice transcends the boundaries that reinforce differential power relations. Acknowledging and allowing the cultural, generational, and class differences that may surface provides a useful context for interpreting texts from multiple perspectives, just as shifting our focus from writer to reader can elicit a new critical pedagogy. Challenging traditional conceptions of the domains of literature puts texts and our students in conversation with each other, and our students in conversation with us.

While research and teaching are complementary functions, they do not necessarily share the same social or intellectual space. If we are to restore the unity between them, creating a larger critical space for dialogue could be one of the most important contributions we can make. Rather than a call for an uncritical unity, this is a call for making our intellectual production the guide to our work, without privileging one component over the other, and allowing for their substantive reintegration.

V. CONCLUSION

Critical literacy is a dialogue that reeducates and reinvents as we enter new cultural contact zones. It comes into being when there is a shift in the space occupied by those ideas we have routinely advanced, ideas that may exclude and marginalize. Critical literacy derives from the employment of effective pedagogies that take us beneath the surface of those texts that collectively may tell us how different cultural beliefs, values, and practices mediate interpretations. The recognition that we were readers before we were writers, scholars, or critics requires us to respect this trajectory in our students, placing it at the center of our debates. We must deplore and condemn those discourses that pathologize our students and what they read—even if *we* aren't actively participating in them. Such discourses a pathology, according to Dubey, that "fuels disturbing assumptions that a group's cultural practices should have some bearing on the question of its right to public resources and social justice."[62] Such assumptions are likely to further discourage any trust in our authority.

Because our students can engage in online discussion groups, post reviews on Amazon.com, or find a willing publisher for that romance novel they have been dying to write, they have agency, independent of what we teach. Our acceptance that "Black Is Gold" should not be a disparaging comment on the rise in black commercial fiction but a way to engage more sophisticated forms of literary and pedagogical practice through the active use of technology.

We want to enter this new space of learning and critique—the new cultural contact zone—fully aware of the forms of social stratification that accompanied a highly successful hierarchical compartmentalization within the academy. When and if we do, we can prepare our students and ourselves to comprehend a different social geography that does not normalize exclusion in order to support a viable print culture. Making the classroom a real place of learning and critique and not another stage in the culture wars can restore our faith in the kind of social transformation that brought most of us to the academy in the first place. We can indeed chart the map of a new world "without the mandate for conquest."

NOTES

1. Various definitions for the term "critical literacy" abound, from Freire (1987), Lanksheer and McLaren (1993), Shannon (1992), Morgan (1997), Furstenburg (2005). Two specialized journals *Literacy* and *Language Learning and Technology,* as well as Phipps and Guilherme's 2004 *Critical Pedagogy: Political Approaches to Language and Intercultural Communication,* provide useful surveys of the topic.

2. Jamie Myers and Fredrick Eberfors, "Globalizing English through Intercultural Critical Literacy, *English Education* (January 2010): 149 [148–168].

3. Abdul Alkalimat and Ronald Bailey, "From Black to eBlack: The Digital Transformation of Black Studies Pedagogy," *Fire!!! The Multiple Media Journal of Black Studies* 1:2 (2012):10.

4. Christopher Lucas, *American Higher Education: A History* (New York: St. Martin's Press: 1994), 241 ff.

5. Farah Jasmine Griffin, "Thirty Years of Black American Literature Studies: A Review," *Journal of Black Studies* 35:2 (November 2004): 165–166.

6. Derrick Darby provides an important intervention in the dialogue about ongoing educational inequality in his article "Educational Inequality and the Science of Diversity," *University of Kansas Law Review* 57 (2009): 755–793.

7. I use the term "black studies" here in its broadest sense, i.e., the reformation of the academy, however reluctant, in response to the presence of black students in its midst. Numerous contemporary examples remind us how sharply drawn some of these ideological battles were and continue to be, obscured perhaps by the changing social landscape of the academy. Decisions at Cornell University and Medgar Evers College over the disposition and dismantling of black studies and related programs have generated acrimonious debate among various sectors.

8. See James Smethurst and Howard Rambsy, "Reform and Revolution, 1965–1976: The Black Aesthetic at Work," in *The Cambridge History of African American Litera-*

ture, Maryemma Graham and Jerry W. Ward, eds. (Cambridge: Cambridge University Press, 2011), 405–451.

9. Trey Ellis, "The New Black Aesthetic," *Callaloo* 38 (Winter 1989): 235 ff.

10. See Antonio Gramsci, *Selections from the Prison Notebooks,* ed. and trans. Quinton Hoare and Geoffrey N. Smith (New York: International Publishers, 1971).

11. Maria Regina Kecht, *Politics Is Pedagogy: Literary Theory and Critical Teaching* (Urbana: University of Illinois Press, 1992), 1.

12. Robert Stepto and Dexter Fisher, eds., *African American Literature: The Reconstruction of Instruction* (New York: MLA, 1978), vii.

13. In his essay "Afro-American Literature Critics: An Introduction," *Dictionary of Literary Biography* 33, Trudier Harris and Thadious Davis, eds. (Detroit: Cengale Gale, 1984), Darwin Turner tells us that "no more than two or three black scholars read papers at the annual meeting of the Modern Language Association between 1949 and 1965," and that "as early as 1939 black scholars felt that they had so little opportunity to present papers at the regional or national MLA meetings that they formed an organization for black teachers of language and literature—the College Language Association," (310).

14. Stepto and Fisher, *Reconstruction,* 1, 2.

15. Stepto and Fisher, *Reconstruction,* 2.

16. Marvin X. Jackman, former associate editor of *Black Theatre,* was a seminal member of the Black Arts Movement with publications beginning in 1967: *Sudan Rajuli Samia,* 1967; *Sudan Rajuli Samia, Fly to Allah,* 1969; *Son of Man,* proverbs, 1969; *Flowers for the Trashman,* a play, 1965, and *Parable of the Black Bird,* 1968. He is credited with having created new genres of American literature. In 1969, he was refused a teaching position at Fresno State College.

17. Sherley Anne Williams, "The Blues Roots of Contemporary Afro-American Poetry," in *Reconstruction,* Stepto and Fisher, eds. 81.

18. Howard Rambsy, II, *The Black Arts Enterprise and the Production of African American Poetry* (Ann Arbor: University of Michigan Press, 2011).

19. Stepto and Fisher, *Reconstruction,* 1.

20. Lawrence P. Jackson, The Indignant Generation: A Narrative History of African American Writers and Critics, 1934–1960 (Princeton: Princeton University Press, 2011).

21. Jackson, *Indignant Generation,* 9.

22. Rarely did Black Arts poets receive invitations to teach at mainstream universities. An exception was Haki Madhubuti, still Don L. Lee at the time, who became writer-in-residence at Cornell following the highly publicized student takeover there in 1968. His main base of operation remained Third World Press.

23. I note here that scholars such as Charles Davis, J. Saunders Redding, Arna Bontemps, and Darwin Turner ended their careers in white institutions while others like Sterling Brown, William Leo Hansberry, Nick Aaron Ford, and Therman O'Daniel remained at HBCUs. I do not intend to suggest, therefore, that there was no contact or intellectual exchange between the younger scholars and their predecessors, either in the course of their graduate education or early in their careers.

24. McDowell contends that part of the popularity of Douglass lies not only in its condemnation of slavery but also in its ubiquitous image of the brutal beating of (naked) slave women (Douglass's Aunt Hester), which Douglass observes and on which he comments. Douglass, as both "witness and participant," according to McDowell,

suggests a "voyeuristic relation to the violence against slave women" (192) in his depiction of these events. Deborah McDowell, "In the first place: Making Frederick Douglass and the Afro-American Narrative Tradition," in *Critical Essays on Frederick Douglass*, ed. William Andrews (Boston: G.K. Hall, 1991), 192–214. The argument is extended by Hartman who elected not to include the Aunt Hester scene in her book, arguing that these kinds of representations allow the slave narrative to serve as pornography of the period. Saidiya Hartman, *Scenes of Subjection: Terror, Slavery, and Self-Making in Nineteenth-Century America* (New York: Oxford University Press, 1997).

25. These trends are not peculiar to black literature but reflect the divisions in broader professional practice. One does literature, literary studies, and the modern languages at MLA but focuses on teaching of English at the National Council of Teachers of English (NCTE) and the Conference on College Composition and Communication (4 Cs). English departments have made little progress in altering these standard practices. Traditional divisions between the teaching of writing and literature call for graduate students and nontenured faculty to be almost exclusively tied to the former.

26. Barbara Herrnstein Smith, *Contingencies of Value: Alternative Perspectives for Critical Theory* (Cambridge, MA.: Harvard University Press, 1988), 9.

27. Dubey, "Postmodernism," 4.

28. bell hooks, "Postmodern Blackness, Yearning: Race, Gender, and Cultural Politics" (Boston: South End Press, 1990).

29. J. Saunders Redding, for example, one of the most eloquent critics of African American literature, had said near the end of his publishing career that he no longer wished "to live with the race problem . . . It has itself been an imperative, channelizing more of my energies than I wished to spare through the narrow gorge of race interest." He, like those of his generation, had produced a body of work dedicated to the "race question" not because he wanted to, he had said, "but because, driven by a daemonic force, I had to." Saunders Redding, *On Being Negro in America* (New York: Harper and Row: 1969 [1951]), 18.

30. Kenneth Warren, *What Was African American Literature* (Cambridge, MA: Harvard University Press, 2011), 1.

31. See "Introduction," Graham and Ward, *The Cambridge History*.

32. Dubey, "Postmodernism," 5.

33. Print culture generally refers to the process for interpreting, producing, circulating, and consuming texts and images that create a connected community.

34. See Adam J. Banks, *Race, Rhetoric and Technology: Searching for Higher Ground* (Mahwah, NJ: Lawrence Erlbaum and NCTE, 2006).

35. Douglas Kellner, *Media Culture: Cultural Studies, Identity and Politics between the Modern and the Postmodern* (New York: Routledge, 2003 [c1995]), 336.

36. Stepto and Fisher, *Reconstruction*, 1.

37. Justin Gifford, "'Harvard in Hell': Holloway House Publishing Company, *Players Magazine* and the Invention of Black Mass-Market Erotica," *Melus* 35: 4 (Winter 2010): 111. Holloway House, founded in 1959 by two Hollywood publicists, Ralph Weinstock and Bentley Morriss, originally published an eclectic mix of Hollywood biographies, skin magazines, and the literature of Casanova and the Marquis de Sade. Following the 1965 Watts rebellion, says Gifford, "the white owners, Morriss and Weinstock, recognized the uprisings across the country as a crisis of representation, and they capitalized on this crisis by creating a culture industry that catered to a large-scale black

readership." The first mass marketed "black experience fiction," complemented the blaxploitation films of the period. Among their most successful authors were Iceberg Slim
(David Beck) and Donald Goines.

38. Griffin, "Thirty Years,"166.

39. *Publishing Trends* X: 3 (March 2003): 3

40. *Ibid.*

41. *Publishing Trends* X: 4 (April 2003), 1, 6. I wish to thank Elisabeth Watson for
combing through a decade of non-indexed back issues of the review for this valuable data.

42. Traditional black independent publishers like Third World Press, unable to
meet the needs of newer readers, continue to find their sales declining.

43. Wayne Dawkins, "Buying Zane," *Black Issues Book Review* (September/
October 2005): 10.

44. *Black Issues Book Review,* accessed March 23, 2011. http://www.thefreelibrary
.com/Flying+off+the+shelves.-a0121572362

45. Lynette L. Holloway, *Ebony* (March 2005): 104.

46. See Candice Love Jackson, "From Writer to Reader, Black Popular Fiction," in
Cambridge History ed. Graham and Ward, 655 ff.

47. *Behind Those Books,* a new documentary by Mills Miller and Kaven Brown, was
released in 2011. The film takes a critical look at urban fiction as a genre and the industry
it has spawned, and features Cornel West, Teri Woods, Zane, Terry McMillan, Kwan,
and Michael Eric Dyson, along with representative book publishers.

48. Thadious Davis, *Southscapes: Geographies of Race, Region and Literature*
(Chapel Hill: University of North Carolina Press, 2011).

49. eBlack Studies formed from a group that began working together in 1971, producing one of the major introductory textbooks in the field of black studies, *Introduction
to African American Studies, A Peoples College Primer,* now in its fifth edition. *Introduction*
models the transformation of technologies from print to digital and is now available online as a series of free ninety-minute lectures.

50. Abdul Alkalimat and Ronald W. Bailey, "From Black to eBlack: The Digital
Transformation of Black Studies Pedagogy" (Unpublished essay, 2011).

51. Dubey, "Postmodernism," 11.

52. Henry Louis Gates Jr., and Cornel West, *The Future of the Race* (New York:
Vintage, 1997), 81.

53. Dubey, "Postmodernism," 11.

54. Eric Lott, "Response to Trey Ellis' 'The New Black Aesthetic,' *Callaloo 38*
(Winter1989): 246.

55. Jackson, *Indignant Generation,* 655.

56. Mary Louise Pratt, *Profession 91* (New York: MLA, 1991): 34.

57. Holloway, *Ebony,* 104.

58. Telephone interview with the author, September 2009.

59. I wish to thank Deborah Whaley, University of Iowa, for bringing to my attention the role of comic art as launching pads for thinking through the politics of race and
representation that both prefigured and extended to film and television.

60. eBlack Studies, "Draft Manifesto" (2008).

61. Jamie Myers and Fredrik Eberfors, "Globalizing English through Intercultural
Critical Literacy," *English Education* (January 2010): 149.

62. Dubey's essay provides an excellent overview of these debates and discourses.

WORKS CITED

Alkalimat, Abdul, and Ronald Bailey. "From Black to eBlack: The Digital Transformation of Black Studies Pedagogy," *FIRE!!! The Multimedia Journal of Black Studies* 1: 1 (2012): 9–24.

Banks, Adam J. *Race, Rhetoric and Technology: Searching for Higher Ground.* Mahwah, NJ: Lawrence Erlbaum and NCTE, 2006.

Darby, Derrick. "Educational Inequality and the Science of Diversity," *University of Kansas Law Review* 57 (2009): 755–793.

Davis, Thadious. *Southscapes: Geographies of Race, Region and Literature.* Chapel Hill: University of North Carolina Press, 2011.

Dawkins, Wayne. "Buying Zane: Strebor Books founder says her new deal with Simon & Schuster frees her to write more." *The Free Library:* September 1, 2005. Accessed March 23, 2011. http://www.thefreelibrary.com/Buying Zane: Strebor Books founder says her new deal with Simon & . . . -a0138056103.

Dubey, Madhu. "Postmodernism as Postnationalism? Racial Representation in U.S. Black Cultural Studies," *The Black Scholar* 33, no.1 (2003): 2–18.

Ellis, Trey. "The New Black Aesthetic," *Callaloo* 38 (Winter 1989): 233–243.

Gates, Henry Louis, Jr., and Cornel West. *The Future of the Race.* New York: Vintage, 1997.

Gifford, Justin. "Harvard in Hell: Holloway House Publishing Company, Players Magazine and the Invention of Black Mass-Market Erotica," MELUS 35, no. 4 (2010): 111–137.

Graham, Maryemma, and Jerry Ward, eds. *The Cambridge History of African American Literature.* Cambridge: Cambridge University Press, 2011.

Gramsci, Antonio. *Selections from the Prison Notebooks,* ed. and trans. Quinton Hoare and Geoffrey N. Smith. New York: International Publishers, 1971.

Griffin, Farah Jasmine. "Thirty Years of Black American Literature Studies: A Review," *Journal of Black Studies* 35, no. 2 (2004): 165–174.

Hartman, Saidiya. *Scenes of Subjection: Terror, Slavery and Self-Making in 19th Century America.* New York: Oxford University Press, 1997.

Holloway, Lynette R. "ZANE: Up Close and Personal," *Ebony* 60 (March 2005): 100, 102, 104.

hooks, bell. "Postmodern Blackness," *Yearning: Race, Gender, and Cultural Politics.* Boston: South End Press, 1990.

Jackson, Candice Love. "'From Writer to Reader,' Black Popular Fiction." In *The Cambridge History of African American Literature,* edited by Maryemma Graham and Jerry Ward, 655–679. Cambridge: Cambridge University Press, 2011.

Jackson, Lawrence P. *The Indignant Generation: A Narrative History of African American Writers and Critics, 1934–1960.* Princeton, NJ: Princeton University Press, 2011.

Kecht, Maria Regina. *Politics Is Pedagogy: Literary Theory and Critical Teaching.* Urbana: University of Illinois Press, 1992.

Kellner, Douglas. *Media Culture: Cultural Studies, Identity and Politics between the Modern and the Postmodern.* New York: Routledge, 2003 [1995].

Lott, Eric. "Response to Trey Ellis' 'The New Black Aesthetic,'" *Callaloo,* 38 (Winter 1989): 244–246.

Lucas, Christopher. *American Higher Education: A History.* New York: St. Martin's Press: 1994.

McDowell, Deborah. "In the first place: Making Frederic Douglass and the Afro-American Narrative Tradition," in *Critical Essays on Frederick Douglass,* edited by William Andrews, 192–214. Boston: G. K. Hall, 1991.

Myers, Jamie, and Fredrick Eberfors. "Globalizing English through Intercultural Critical Literacy," *English Education* (January2010), 148–168.

Pratt, Mary Louise. *Profession* 91. New York: MLA, 1991, 33–40.

Rambsy, Howard II. *The Black Arts Enterprise and the Production of African American Poetry.* Ann Arbor: University of Michigan Press, 2011.

Redding, J. Saunders. *On Being Negro in America.* New York: Harper and Row, 1969 [1951].

Smethurst, James, and Howard Rambsy. "Reform and Revolution, 1965–1976: The Black Aesthetic at Work." In *The Cambridge History of African American Literature,* edited by Maryemma Graham and Jerry W. Ward, 405–451. Cambridge: Cambridge University Press, 2011.

Smith, Barbara Herrnstein. *Contingencies of Value: Alternative Perspectives for Critical Theory.* Cambridge, MA: Harvard University Press, 1988.

Stepto, Robert and Dexter Fisher, eds. *The Reconstruction of Instruction.* New York: MLA, 1978.

Turner, Darwin. "Afro-American Literary Critics: An Introduction," *Dictionary of Literary Biography* 33, edited by Trudier Harris and Thadious Davis, 309–316. Detroit: Cengale Gale, 1984.

Warren, Kenneth. *What Was African American Literature.* Cambridge, Massachusetts: Harvard University Press, 2011.

Williams, Sherley Anne. "The Blues Roots of Contemporary Afro-American Poetry." In *Afro-American Literature: The Reconstruction of Instruction,* edited by Dexter Fisher and Robert B. Stepto, 72–88. Urbana: University of Illinois Press, 1979.

FOUR

HIP HOP (FEAT. WOMEN WRITERS): REIMAGINING BLACK WOMEN AND AGENCY THROUGH HIP HOP FICTION

EVE DUNBAR

INTRODUCTION: WOMEN AND HIP HOP

"It's bigger than religion / Hip Hop / It's bigger than my niggas / Hip Hop," chants Erykah Badu on "The Healer" off her 2008 release, *New Amerykah, Part One: 4th World War.* While Badu is typically considered a neo-soul artist, she is deeply enmeshed in the Hip Hop music world, occupying roles that range from singing hooks on popular rap songs to engaging in highly publicized romantic relationships with male artists. In this range of possibilities, female emcee does not rank highly. Still, "The Healer" speaks not only to Badu's claims on Hip Hop but also to her vision of what the music might be and become. In no uncertain words, Badu simultaneously raises Hip Hop to religious significance, while claiming it away from black men. Either rhetorical shift might be a form of sacrilege to some, but I begin with Badu's mantra in order to provide a historical perspective for understanding black popular cultural production during the first decade of the twenty first century and the role of women within the spheres of Hip Hop and black popular fiction. Sandwiched between the legal and personal troubles that dogged many female rappers[1] and the interstellar rise of female rapper Nicki Minaj,[2] Badu's chant speaks to the possibilities for the black female imagination in Hip Hop.

In 2008, Badu sent her chant out into an ether heavy with the laments of unsigned female rap artists, bygone female rappers, and various feminist Hip Hop scholars who were pondering Hip Hop's historic sexism and aching to know where all the female emcees had gone. Many supposed this blight on women rappers could be attributed to Hip Hop's sexist origins, coupled with the misogyny of a global music industry. Gwendolyn Pough's *Check It While I Wreck it* (2004), Imani Perry's *Prophets of the Hood* (2004), Patricia Hill Collins' *From Black Power to Hip Hop* (2006), Denean Sharpley-Whiting's *Pimps Up, Ho's Down* (2007), Tricia Rose's *The Hip Hop Wars* (2008) and the 2008 special issue of the feminist journal *Meridians* dedicated to women, Hip Hop, and popular music all signify an increase in extended scholarly attention to the role of women in Hip Hop. In their respective texts, these feminist scholars grapple with the question of women's place within Hip Hop's public sphere, each coming up with arguments running the gamut between the belief that Hip Hop simply perpetuates the patriarchal sexual objectification of black and Latina women and the notion that women have changed the very cultural fabric within which Hip Hop is both created and consumed. While these may appear to be dichotomous descriptions of women in Hip Hop, they actually point to the multiple avenues from which critics have approached and engaged Hip Hop's "woman question." In fact, with regard to gender, the Hip Hop wars, as Tricia Rose dubs America's conversation on Hip Hop, often require that one be either "for" or "against" Hip Hop. But the music and some of the more thoughtful scholarship that explores Hip Hop cultural production proves that binaries don't hold for very long. Not only are binaries unable to take into account the capacity for artists to develop over time, but restrictive binaries also fail to fully encapsulate the questions of agency that have to be encountered when one explores the role of women. That is to say, the moment one begins to argue that Hip Hop, especially in its musical form, is a black male space, and thus doomed by its sexism, one must also be aware of the women who continue to make claims on the musical form and culture. As Denean Sharpley-Whiting notes, "Hip Hop is an obvious land mine of contradictions that we as women painstakingly negotiate and renegotiate."[3] If Hip Hop is a land mine, then it is one in which women are neither absent nor completely destroyed, although they may be socially and psychologically maimed. As the self-described Hip Hop feminist, Joan Morgan, reminds us, when it comes to thinking about women and Hip Hop, "there is a much greater story being told," one greater than "a narrative of women who are oppressed."[4]

Morgan's interest in the female "story" of Hip Hop, coupled with Badu's chant, compel us to think more critically about what is lost when one declares Hip Hop a masculine space or limits his or her understanding of Hip Hop to musical production exclusively. This essay, then, explores alternative sites of Hip Hop cultural production and centralizes women as creators and consumers within those sites. I establish Hip Hop fiction as a productive literary genre for black women writers and readers; I do this while also establishing it as a genre maligned by perceptions that it both lacks an aesthetic-consciousness and benefits from a publishing industry that prefers to perpetuate racial stereotypes. Additionally, referencing the lyrics of two of the most canonical Hip Hop artists of the late twentieth century, Nas and Mos Def, I examine the relationship between the written word and the spoken word within the musical tradition, arguing that while many of us consider Hip Hop a mainly musical form, the act of writing is central to the form. Finally, I establish the relationship between the music and the early twenty first century publishing phenomenon that is commonly referred to as "Hip Hop fiction,"[5] in order to argue that it is within its written form that Hip Hop opens up to reveal a creative space for women during a period when the mainstream Hip Hop music scene seemed vacant of female voices. Using as a case study the *Girls From Da Hood* book series, originally published in 2004 by the Kensington Press imprint Urban Books, I tell an alternate story of black female production and consumption that will augment our understanding of black women in Hip Hop.

HIP HOP + FICTION ≠ HIP HOP FICTION?

Publishing houses and theatrical promoters are in the business to make money. They will sponsor anything they believe will sell.

—ZORA NEALE HURSTON[6]

In order to begin positing Hip Hop fiction as a possible site for locating a female voice within Hip Hop cultural production, one must do the hard work of first locating the place of Hip Hop within the world of literature. I say this because Hip Hop and literature are strange bedfellows for many due to longstanding hierarchical debates regarding "high" and "low" art, especially as they relate to the African American literature within the publishing landscape. While Hip Hop music has historically suffered through and come out victorious from early debates regarding its legitimacy as a musical form, much of Hip Hop fiction remains at the margins of literary studies and critical engagement. As Maryemma Graham suggests in "Black Is Gold," scholars of African American literature "blame the publishing industry with coming up with the distinctions 'literary' and 'genre fictions,' but we consistently reinforce these classifications by privileging certain kinds of texts over others in our teaching and research."[7] Thus, undergirding the framework of this essay is a desire to remediate the very high-low distinctions that negate the critical value of Hip Hop fiction and to provide a mode of feminist critique that might allow us to re-imagine the role of women within Hip Hop cultural production.[8]

Couple the lack of inclusion within the framework of African American literary studies with a tense debate among writers regarding the quality, nature, and validity of Hip Hop fiction, and one begins to see more clearly the vexed landscape of the genre. For instance, in his essay, "On Lit Hop," writer Adam Mansbach argues for the importance and power of Hip Hop literature. In the essay he suggests that the capacity of a Hip Hop aesthetic lies in its layering of "reference and meaning and plot and dialogue and character, which tweaks the levels of the mix for smooth reading but still allows you to dissect the individual elements and analyze them."[9] This vision of a Hip Hop literary aesthetic is one in which both the writer and reader are engaged in a quest for deep meaning and further exploration of what is on the page. Flowing from an understanding of Hip Hop music's use of sonic and lyrical collage, Mansbach is invested in establishing a Hip Hop literary aesthetic uses collage to help the form supersede the content of the narrative. In other words, he imagines a Hip Hop literary aesthetic by which one might not have to write *about* Hip Hop but could instead *write Hip Hop*[10] in order to deliver what many trained literary scholars and critics expect from canonical literature: aesthetic integrity.

Hip Hop literature has the capacity and the integrity to be treated as literature, on par with any canonical text, but only if one manages to separate *true* Hip Hop literature, that which is created with aesthetic integrity, from that *other* Hip Hop literature. "As it stands," Mansbach laments, "a Hip Hop novel denotes any book in which words usually ending in '-er' instead terminate in '-a'; any book containing characters who are young, urban, and black or at least two out of the three; any book aimed at a demographic group more notorious for purchasing CDs."[11] It becomes clear that Hip Hop literature, in Mansbach's view, is diluted by the influx of what he interchangeably describes as "street lit" and garbage.[12] The damning qualities of this faux Hip Hop fiction are that it is "chocked with brand names, populated by blinged-out thugs and video-vixen-style women, and plagued by shallow characters and bad storytelling."[13] Mansbach's commitment to aesthetic integrity, even within the maligned genre of Hip Hop fiction, might seem fairly compelling since he's arguing that Hip Hop literature, done well, has the capacity to reach the status of literary fiction. But one need only consider the faulty logic upon which his argument rests because he assumes all Hip Hop is "quality" Hip Hop—that the musical form itself does not have representatives plagued by conspicuous consumption, shallow characters and storytelling. Instead, the true sweep of his essay results in the creation of a dichotomy between "high" and "low" Hip Hop literature. This dichotomy maintains distinctions that legitimize claims to the sacred status of "literature" and reinforce the notion that a particular mode of being—one invested in capitalist desire and heteronormative aspirations—is less valid than others. The form and content of Hip Hop fiction come under fire in ways that legitimize only the trained writer and renders as garbage the work of writers who fail to produce "literary fiction." Because Mansbach's essay appears in the anthology *Total Chaos: The Art and Aesthetics of Hip-Hop* (2007) and is one of the only essays in the anthology to tackle the topic of fiction and Hip Hop, it is becoming a fairly authoritative articulation of what might constitute aesthetic integrity in the realm of Hip Hop literary production.

But Mansbach is not the only writer interested in gatekeeping the imagined boundary between Hip Hop fiction and literary fiction. In fact, the outrage of some critics and writers when they describe the impossible hoops one must jump through if they are a black literary writer attempting to get literary fiction published by major publishing houses in the United States versus the relative ease with which authors publishing black urban/Hip Hop fiction has a well-documented history. In 2006, Nick Chiles, in a *New York Times* op-ed condemned "street lit" for being "almost exclusively pornography for black women" that had effectually rendered very little of "import" for the future of African American literature.[14] Chiles's oft-cited opinion piece, coupled with Terry McMillan's 2007 email tirade against Simon and Schuster editors regarding that particular publisher's tendency to publish "exploitative, destructive, racist, egregious, sexist, base, tacky, poorly-written, unedited, degrading" books, speak to a sentiment among some African American literary writers regarding Hip Hop, urban, street, or ghetto fiction. And one must not forget Percival Everett's novel *Erasure* (2003), which features the character Thelonious Ellison, a black college professor who is so fed up with the reading public's lack of interest in his own esoteric writings that he pens an urban-inspired novel entitled *We's Lives in Da Ghetto* in order to protest the stupidity of the genre. Much to Ellison's chagrin, he's offered a six-figure advance and his "honesty" is praised by Random House. At the core of Everett's *Erasure* is a meta-critique of the publishing industry's fascination with urban black fiction that lacks the integrity of literary fiction. Like Everett, Mansbach, Chiles, and McMillan are keen on separating the so-called literary fiction from the more quotidian genre fiction produced by less skilled black writers and published by profit-driven publishers under the umbrella of urban fiction.

But the African American literary writer's disdain for the capitalist impulse among publishers is far from a new phenomenon. In 1950, Zora Neale Hurston issued a critique similar to Chiles's, McMillan's, and Everett's, in which she argued that the multitude of black possibilities were denied by the publishing world, which believed readers would be unwilling to buy art that evidenced the fact that black people were capable of "high and complicated emotions."[15] Feeling pressure from publishing houses to produce racial hyperbole, Hurston said she longed for a day when "the best kept secret in America," the "average, struggling, non-morbid Negro" might be portrayed on the page.[16] In many ways, Hurston's mid-twentieth-century criticism of publishing houses' tendency to let the imagined market limit the types of black narratives continues to lie at the crux of what many black literary writers perceive to be the contemporary injustice of black publishing. As writer and critic Kiese Laymon points out in an entry on his blog, *Cold Drank,* "'Hip Hop Fiction' is some corporate simpleness conjured up to sell books and make some other American writers [sic] who wish s/he was a rapper feel better about being a writer."[17] Like Hurston, Everett, McMillan, and many literary writers and critics before him, Laymon is suspicious of the integrity of those texts that purport to be Hip Hop fiction because he believes that "Hip Hop fiction" is merely a generic nomenclature invented to capitalize on the lucrative global commodity that Hip Hop music has become over the past three decades. Their suspicions may be warranted.

Hip Hop fiction is no small business: in 2009, approximately twenty-five new urban titles were released every month for each literary title released.[18] In a recent *Elle* magazine feature on Hip Hop novelist Miasha, writer Bliss Broyard interviews a fiction buyer for Barnes and Noble who estimates that in about 125 of 700 stores around the country, "urban fiction not only outsells classics by black authors such as Richard Wright, Ralph Ellison, Zora Neale Hurston, Toni Morrison, and Alice Walker, but also popular genre fiction like *The Da Vinci Code*."[19] This increase in the consumption of Hip Hop fiction and the prevalence of female writers and readers of the fiction has multiple origins. One should not assume that an increase in consumption of urban fiction is necessarily indicative of an increase in the utility of the form to female readers' lives. Likewise, the genre's popularity cannot necessarily be considered solely a reaction to cultural shifts. Rather than simply a function of the consumptive desires and needs of the readership, book buying is "an event" that is "affected and partially controlled by the material availability as well as a socially organized technology of production and distribution."[20] Much like the romance novel before it and the state of black publishing historically,[21] one must acknowledge the reality that publishers hold a great deal of the responsibility for gatekeeping and the influx of Hip Hop fiction consumers.

There is no need to deny the reality that mainstream publishers are most interested in the genre because it promises a relatively untapped niche market: young, black, urban readers. Arguably, Hip Hop's aesthetic and political significance cannot be considered without some attention to its market-driven global proliferation. As Mireille Miller-Young, whose research is most interested in the fluidity between pornography and Hip Hop music culture, notes, "Hip Hop is the main form of legibility for black American culture in this contemporary moment, one that has diasporic and global effects."[22] Although Miller-Young acknowledges that the history of Hip Hop–inspired pornography coincides with the rise of the musical form's growing global significance in the last decades of the twentieth century and signals pornography's realization that a niche market of black consumers (and white consumers of black bodies) might be tapped for its benefit, she is also aware that the genre produces a "sexual economy of illicit eroticism" that might be able "to refigure the racial logic of sexual respectability and normativity."[23] In light of Chiles's disparaging critique cited earlier in this essay, which centers on the pornographic imperative of Hip Hop fiction, it might be unwise to discursively link my own generative critique of the fiction to any argument that might further tie Hip Hop fiction to the porn industry. Yet, Hip Hop, and the other artistic mediums it inspires, continues to provide a lucrative and culturally significant space within which black artists are able to work. So, in addition to being a byproduct of increasingly streamlined book production mechanisms and consumer manipulation by publishers, the success of Hip Hop fiction must also be considered in light of the deep cultural shifts taking place within the world of Hip Hop. The links between niche markets that capitalize on non-normative narratives and progressive cultural interventions made by these same narratives open up particular possibilities as we consider women writers within the sphere of Hip Hop cultural production.

HIP HOP, FICTION, AND THE FEMALE WRITER

Returning for a moment to Erykah Badu's 2008 lyrical statement regarding Hip Hop, we are reminded of the expressed necessity to create a recognized space for people other than black men within Hip Hop because it is more inclusive than it appears. Considering the link between Hip Hop music and Hip Hop fiction forces us to reconsider the gender breakdown and dynamics that exist between the two forms, and thus illustrates the reality that such a dichotomy only serves the function of occulting the role of women, particularly women cultural producers, within the Hip Hop narrative sphere.

In arguing for the important place within African American literary criticism of Donald Goines, author of sixteen original 1970s street lit classics, LaMonda Horton-Stallings critiques the valorizing of the oral over the written word in African American literary criticism. She admonishes the reader to, "Forget that everything we know about Hip Hop is based on this romanticized notion of the folk not being able to read, and to pay attention to the producers of the culture. When Nas raps about Goines, it is because he reads."[24] She goes on to argue that she does not seek to "fetishize the written word, but to fully investigate black folk culture, even if it means going to a written text. Every oral art form isn't for the masses. Every written piece isn't simply for the bourgeoisie."[25] Seeing the resonance between Goines's 1970s urban fiction and contemporary rap lyrics, we are reminded that fiction bears an important role in Hip Hop music's production. The age-old "oral-versus-written culture" dichotomy has less relevance.

I would put even more stress on the dichotomy's breakdown by highlighting that the rapper also writes—the form borrows as much from the written as it is does from an African American oral tradition. Take for instance Nas, who begins *Illmatic*'s (1994) "N.Y. State of Mind" by revealing writing's necessity to the creation of his Hip Hop persona: "Rappers I monkey flip 'em with the funky rhythm I be kickin' / Musician, inflictin' *composition* / of pain I'm like Scarface sniffin' cocaine / Holdin' a M-16, *see with the pen I'm extreme*" (italics my emphasis). Nas's hyperbolic boast is both made possible only with his extreme pen, thereby exposing the role of writing in the creation of one of Hip Hop's most celebrated narrative compositions. Nas goes on to recount not only dreams of champagne, guns, and being another iconic gangster, Al Capone, but also the reality of himself as an urban scribe awaiting the stories of his neighborhood: "In the P.J.'s, my blend tape plays, bullets are strays / Young bitches is grazed each block is like a maze / full of black rats trapped, plus the Island is packed / From what *I hear in all the stories* when my peoples come back, black / I'm livin' where the nights is jet black." In a moment that should remind readers of the close-quarter living that marks the opening scene to Richard Wright's *Native Son*, Nas offers a vision of authorship that allows for Hip Hop music's production based not upon his own experiences but upon his ability to listen and translate the experiences of others from his community. Nas hears "all the stories" from his community and gives these stories back to his listeners in verse. He boasts that the "stuff [he] write[s] is even tougher than dice."

Similarly, on his track entitled "Hip Hop," which is featured on his album *Black on Both Sides* (1999), Mos Def rhymes:

My restlessness is my nemesis
It's hard to really chill and sit still
Committed to page, I write rhymes
Sometimes won't finish for days
Scrutinize my literature, from the large to the miniature

I mathematically add-minister
Subtract the wack
Selector, wheel it back, I'm feeling that

Mos Def peppers "Hip Hop" with references to masculinist canonical African American titles such as Richard Wright's *Native Son,* Ralph Ellison's *Invisible Man,* and Amiri Baraka's *Blues People* thereby proving that he can read—he "scrutinizes" his literature. Yet, more telling is that Mos Def represents himself as a troubled and deliberate writer, who takes days to finish a rhyme, which he overtly identifies as literature. The double entendre behind his evocation of the phrase "my literature" points to both his own literary production and his understanding of the African American literary tradition as illustrated by his intra-rhyme citations. Mos Def is a writer who edits to perfection so that his art might please his soul: "I'm feeling that," he coos.

I use Nas and Mos Def not to detract from Hip Hop fiction as a mode of literary expression in and of itself, but to highlight the already present importance of writing/composition to Hip Hop music's creation. The *word* links Hip Hop music to Hip Hop fiction in ways that the dichotomy between the written and oral tradition seems to obscure. I am by no means suggesting that works of Hip Hop fiction are necessarily on par with the music of Nas and Mos Def—which are the musical equivalent of "classic" narratives within the African American literary tradition. Instead, I am insisting on two things: first, that Hip Hop music and Hip Hop fiction both share the word as a site of connection and composition as a mode of expression; and second, that Hip Hop fiction can offer women writers access to the male-dominated world of Hip Hop cultural production. Just as Hip Hop music is often the dream of many young black men in the United States, Hip Hop fiction might be the female version of that dream. Or as Bliss Broyard suggests, "Just as the rap album contract used to be the golden ticket out of Compton (or Queens), writing has become the [black urban female's] unlikely conduit to fame and fortune."

In the face of deep similarities, I'd like to return briefly to words of Mos Def in order to now issue a point of departure between the two mediums and, thus, the two genders that produce each most predominantly. In the lyrics from Mos Def's "Hip Hop," cited previously, Mos ends the verse stating, "Selector, wheel it back, I'm feeling that." This line marks the departure and difference between Hip Hop music and Hip Hop fiction, it marks the seamless transition between the written composition and the recorded voice. "Wheel it back," Mos tells the imagined producer, calling the listener's attention to the fact that while he may be a writer, Mos ultimately aims to speak his words out loud and to have his imagined world brought into being and immortalized on disc by being set to music. Moreover, even before he tells us he is a writer, he tells us "Speech is [the] hammer" with which he bangs "his world into shape."

The seamless transition between the written and the rapped word that is the hallmark of great mainstream male rappers, and it seems to have been unavailable to women rappers if one takes seriously much of the public discourse regarding Hip Hop and women. For example, in a 2007 NPR roundtable discussion between the scholar Tricia Rose and rappers Monie Love and MC Lyte, each of the women articulates a sense of sadness concerning the state of female emcees. Rose laments:

> I mean, it's not that I think rapping about sexuality is a problem, it's about the kind of sexuality and the oppressive limited way that women's expression is being contained. So that young women, who are the next generation of Monie Love and MC Lyte, are not likely to imagine themselves as people who can participate in these much more meaningful and serious ways as artists and as community members, because they think their avenues of participation are related to what's profitable.
>
> And once they believe that that's the track for them, then they pretty much have to figure out how to sell themselves physically. They're not interested in advancing their art because it doesn't really get them anywhere. And the women who don't fit this model, either for a variety of reasons, they don't see themselves in the culture as well.
>
> And this is a tragedy both for the communities, for young people who need creative ways to deal with their life, but also for women in general and for black women in particular who have distinctive stories to tell. We desperately need to hear what these artists have to say and we need to create more space for them.[26]

Rose's comments speak to the perceived limits of access that black women have within the sphere of Hip Hop if they seek to be cultural producers. Not content with the expectation that women might be managed and contained by the Hip Hop music industry to occupy roles that require them to sell their bodies, Rose's understanding of the "art" of Hip Hop is at once insightful and limited. In a sense, while the reality of black female rappers may or may not have been one of extinction, Rose's observations are in line with a discursive tendency during the early twenty-first century to speak of a "golden age" of female rappers that had passed and possibly would never return. That is to say, she is right to push for the importance of creativity in the narratives of women within Hip Hop, but she is limited by an assumption that women's only options rest either between being a hyper-sexualized emcee or a hyper-sexualized video vixen. These two are pitted as the only viable options in which women could cultivate creative narratives (for profit) within the Hip Hop sphere. But as late as 2008 a look at the author list of the most successful Hip Hop fiction publisher, Triple Crown, would reveal that of its twenty-five authors, fifteen were women and all of them were African American.[27] At the moment when the fate of women rappers seemed dimmest, some would-be rappers found their golden goose in Hip Hop fiction.

GIRLS FROM DA HOOD: A CASE STUDY IN HIP HOP FICTION

At some level, my interest in *Girls From Da Hood* marks a shift in emphasis from the oral to the written in order to locate a form of working-class black female agency that goes against a long-standing conceptualization of music being the preferred mode of cultural intervention and self-representation for working class women. As Hazel Carby has argued in her canonical essay, "It Jus Be's Dat Way Sometimes: The Sexual Politics of Women's Blues," historically, black feminists have placed too much emphasis on written representations of black women and, thereby, placed too much emphasis on black middle-class women and notions of sexual propriety.[28] Carby calls for an exploration of early twentieth-century black female blues singers in order to create a richer understanding of black female sexuality and identity not necessarily constrained by patriarchal expectations. Likewise, in *Domestic Allegories of Political Desire*, Claudia Tate argues that during the post–Reconstruction era the domestic novel became a form that "kept the distressed ambitions of African Americans for racial justice alive, not as abstract desires but as courtship stories in which the might of true love, like vigilant self-will, frees the individual from dominant racist construction and conventions."[29] Tate's work explores how these women use the domestic novel to imagine and cultivate a black bourgeois sensibility to combat the emotional, psychological, and social effects of state-sanctioned racism at play in the late nineteenth century. Although Carby and Tate frame writing and lyric orality as oppositional forms of self-expression among black women, I believe this binary does not account for the capacity of the novel, in both form and composition, to hold the aspirations of working black women. Thus, a series like *Girls From Da Hood* bridges writing and orality in order to advance a particular black working class female sensibility.

Published between 2004 and 2009, the *Girls From Da Hood* book series perfected an innovative method for creating and introducing new Hip Hop urban fiction writers to its readership. Using the writing of self-described "Queen of Hip Hop Fiction," Nikki Turner[30] as the series's hook, the first installment of *Girls From Da Hood* earned its distinction as a vehicle to introduce new writers into the Hip Hop fiction fold. The series originally paired a novella-length story by Turner with novellas written by two relatively unknown urban writers. Authors of the novellas featured in the series include Chunichi, Roy Glenn, Joy, Kashamba Williams, Mark Anthony, MadameK, and others who have gone on to have fairly fruitful careers publishing solo novels for the Urban Books imprint.[31] But the pairings done in the originating book of the series delivered Turner's well-established reading audience to these new writers, while providing the authors a space to develop their own voices and storylines. The marketing method used by the *Girls From Da Hood* series is not necessarily unique because it does, in fact, make use of established marketing strategies utilized by paperback publishers. Since "it's much easier to introduce a new author by fitting his or her work into a previously formalized chain of communication than it is to establish its uniqueness by locating a special audience" for that author, paperback publishers have relied on new writers predictably writing into a form for an established audience.[32] In other words, Urban Books makes use of the reputation of an established author (i.e., Nikki Turner) and is able to develop its new talent without having to take too much of a financial risk. While this marketing ploy is an established practice for paperback fiction, the *Girls From Da Hood* series also benefits from its imagined audience's familiarity with the "featuring" practice used in Hip Hop music. This featuring practice is used throughout the rap music industry to create opportunities for all artists involved. In many cases, "featuring" describes the collaboration between two or more Hip Hop artists, and relies on a more established Hip Hop artist rapping with a lesser-known artist in the attempt to validate and usher this new artist to an established fan base. If a newer artist becomes a success, then the more established artist reaps the benefits of seeming current and relevant while also having the opportunity to increase his fan base with any audience members that the newer artist may attract. Like Hip Hop music, the *Girls From Da Hood* series may do little to counter notions of black sexual ferocity or innate black violence, but it does attempt to create a rich and dynamic imaginary space for new and more established writers of urban fiction to co-create.

The success of the original *Girls From Da Hood* spawned four more installments in the series. The series was, in fact, so successful that Turner, after lending her second novella to the second installment of *Girls From Da Hood,* branched out to produce her own series-based projects published by Random House: *Street Chronicles Volume I and II* and another novella series listed under Turner's own imprint with Random House: "Nikki Turner Presents." Said to have netted a six-figure, two-book deal with One World/Ballantine in 2004, Turner's writing and publishing careers is marked by success unheard of by many of the most well-established black literary writers. By 2007, even rapper 50 Cent had entered into the Hip Hop literary fold by establishing his G-Unit Books imprint at MTV/Pocket Books (a division of Simon and Schuster). 50 Cent's imprint further fuses the relationship between Hip Hop fiction and Hip Hop music, demonstrating how both the Hip Hop music and Hip Hop fiction industries attempt to balance a quest to increase profits, develop established artists' profiles, and cultivate new artists.

In addition to tapping into their imagined audience's cultural knowledge of mainstream Hip Hop music's "featuring" practice, *Girls From Da Hood,* features protagonists whose ages and racial identities mirror those of the intended audience of the series: young, black women between 15 and 25 years of age. Like the imagined readership of Hip Hop fiction, the authors are also often black women who share geographic, social, and economic origins of the readership, which contributes to the perceived "authenticity" of such texts.[33] As with much of the fiction of its genre, the young protagonists of this series are urban dwelling and find themselves caught up in various scenarios that may combine one or more of the following plot lines: embarking on an ill-fated love affair with a drug dealer or hustler, becoming a drug dealer, developing a self-destructive drug habit, entering the world of stripping and/or prostitution, committing murder, and, finally, doing a bid in the state penitentiary. While the original book in the series featured three novellas set in the Richmond area of Virginia, later books in the series feature urban settings ranging from Brooklyn, New York, to Miami, Florida. All of the novellas are complete within themselves; however, over the course of the series, locations, events, and even characters are cross-referenced to create intertextuality between the stories. For instance, Turner reprised her character Unique for the second volume of the series, offering readers a more comprehensive story of her character's progress. Nearly all the stories are open-ended, which allows characters to be reintroduced in future issues. Thus, each story has the potential to become a serial, rather than a finished product.

Like most urban fiction, the *Girls From Da Hood* series uses sex and violence to propel forward the storylines of its novellas. This coupling is done not only to titillate but also to instruct its young readers in the vices of lives lived as indiscreetly as they are lived by the protagonists of these stories. As Nikki Turner notes, she is interested not only in entertaining her readership but also in showing them how destructive a life riddled with crime, sex, and drugs can be. On her website, Turner says that a book like *A Hustler's Wife* is "not just about drugs—it's about a girl and her struggle. I wanted to warn young girls about street life. They never know the risks that come with it. They listen to the music and see the bling-bling. But nobody ever says what can happen to you— that you can go to jail. . . . I try not to reinforce stereotypes, I try to show a different light."[34] In this sense, these urban imprints often take cues from earlier popular forms, such as the domestic or sentimental novel of the eighteenth or nineteenth centuries. For example, the novellas from *Girls From Da Hood* have protagonists that may be more akin to Daniel Defoe's namesake protagonist in *Moll Flanders* than they are to the female protagonists of racially conscious texts produced by black female writers like Frances Harper or Pauline Hopkins. Yet, Turner functions as a sort of Harriet Jacobs authorial voice that is able to sentimentalize and moralize the character of her protagonists, even if these protagonists seem themselves unburdened by the politics of respectability expected of black women and their literary representatives in nineteenth- and early twentieth-century black fiction. The protagonists of the *Girls*

From Da Hood series engage in premarital sex, partake in drugs, engage in low-order forms of prostitution, and generally behave in ways that are non-normative when compared to our perceptions of mainstream American culture. And while there are major thematic divergences between contemporary and earlier novels, the writers of the *Girls From Da Hood* series create narratives with the intention to both entertain and instruct the reader on the morality of the times through the immorality of their female protagonists.

Still, I would not venture to call these female-authored Hip Hop tales feminist narratives within a traditional framework of liberatory agency. Although close readings might be made that run against the grain of misogyny, conspicuous consumption, and violence that mark these tales written by women, the texts in the *Girls From Da Hood* series fail at a deep level to free their female protagonists from the bondage of what Michael Eric Dyson has termed, "femiphobia,"[35] and which Imani Perry further develops to describe the tendency within Hip Hop music to create hypermasculine personas at the expense of black women and their bodies. For Perry, this femiphobia is in some ways a reaction to deeper "gender/racial oppression" and "powerlessness experienced by black men in relation to white men" in the United States.[36] Much like their masculine counterparts in Hip Hop music, the writers in the series make use of imagery, relationships, consumptive patterns, life stances, violence, and sex in ways that mirror—be it with a slight difference—the narratives assigned to women in Hip Hop music. Take, for instance, Nikki Turner's description of her protagonist, Unique, in the premiere story of the book series:

> This was game she had falling out of her mouth. Unique wasn't really thinking about getting any job to hold the bills down. As far as she was concerned she shouldn't be paying any bills anyway. *She knew there were plenty of suckers dying for a lick, and with so many suckers on the streets of Richmond, her bills would get paid one way or another* (emphasis mine). Still, she had to fake like she was so responsible, holding the fort down while Took [her boyfriend in lockdown] was gone, so she could keep him under control.[37]

From the inception of the series, Turner, with the other writers of the series following in line, creates female leads that fall into the typical hustling "ho," who uses sex to control men and who refuses to make a "legitimate living," preferring instead to barter sex and/or sell drugs for money. Unique becomes for Turner and her readers an occasion to "take [her narrative] straight to the gutter."[38] In a note to her readers she tells us that she's going to the "gutter" in order to instruct us how to "spot a hoodrat a mile way."[39] Much like traditional Hip Hop musical narratives, Turner expects that her readers won't value the female hustle, especially when it is had at the expense of a black masculinity that subscribes to traditional patriarchal norms of mastery and authority.

Yet, the lack of confidence in the female hustle as it is often represented in the stories collected in the *Girls From Da Hood* series speaks to the larger conundrum of Hip Hop fiction, and Hip Hop more generally: the perceived need to make the unsavory representations serve some larger social goals. In the face of critics such as Chiles and McMillan, Turner's note to her readers serves as a warning that one might enjoy going to the gutter via her protagonists, but staying in the gutter is unrighteous. So even as these narratives recognize the female hustle by representing it, the author's expressed intention is to create morality tales meant to show readers, via the ill-fated ends met by many of these female protagonists, that such salacious behavior is unsavory at best and punishable by death at worst. Although these authors argue that their texts function as morality tales, meant to instruct young female readers away from using sex and deceit to hustle men, the stories they create not only reinscribe the narratives about black women prevalent in Hip Hop music but also undermine the hustle of their protagonists.

Seemingly taking cues from the eighteenth- or nineteenth-century novel's concern for moral purpose, these writers of Hip Hop fiction would have us believe that they are producing the narratives that young women will find exciting, but will ultimately leave them implicitly instructed in the politics of respectability.[40] In other words, critics are to believe that the young women of these narratives suffer under femiphobia so that their readers might live.

This dissonance between these narratives as possible sites of black female creative production within Hip Hop and the reality that these same narratives inevitably re-inscribe a politics of racial-gender oppression common to Hip Hop may strike some as confounding. It is. There is no way to deny the femiphobia that blemishes much of Hip Hop culture. Moreover, couple this femiphobia with the mask that many black female writers have to don in order to make their narratives of drugs, sex, and violence palatable to a critically concerned reading public intent on policing and enforcing the politics of respectability, and one can begin to see the conundrum of the genre and/or any female engagement with an "anti-establishment, outlaw aesthetic" that defines itself as a "masculinist, commodified terrain of cultural production."[41] Rather than focusing on the inherent lack of liberation politics within a more commercialized type of Hip Hop narrative, it is more fruitful to imagine a different modality for understanding the work done by black women who choose to create Hip Hop fiction. As Saba Mahmood suggests, "the capacity for agency is entailed not only in acts that resist norms but also in the multiple ways in which one inhabits norms."[42] In other words, we must be able to imagine the ways in which writing within a masculinist form might produce new forms of agency, albeit unrecognizable to most contemporary Western feminists, who are committed to a model of liberatory agency. Mahmood's understanding of nonliberatory agency provides the time and space for us to begin imagining anew the ways women, particularly black women, find space to create and tell their stories through embodying the very forms that seek to oppress them. And if we were able to embrace multiple modalities of agency, writers like Turner might not have to issue reading instructions meant to dichotomize respectable women from "hoodrats." This understanding of agency is at odds with much of feminist discourse, but without such an understanding of agency, feminists are left with few options for critically engaging and appreciating black, female-authored Hip Hop fiction on its own terms.

CONCLUSION: THE WRITTEN TEXT BECOMES THE FORM

As I close this essay, I'd like to go back to Horton-Stallings's reading of Donald Goines for a moment. In her creation of Goines as a proto–Hip Hop writer, Stallings argues that Goines lived under the same urban social and economic turmoil that birthed the four elements of early Hip Hop, but lived therein as an incarcerated man. "Deprived of body and technology," Horton-Stallings's reading of Goines offers a way to think about the devalued and vexed position of black women's bodies within American culture at large and in Hip Hop culture in particular. Much like Goines, who is forced to turn to the printing press when denied access to the mic, the works of women Hip Hop writers might represent not only a viable but also a lucrative avenue into Hip Hop culture in the early twenty-first century. Again, rather than merely offer a critique of the femiphobia and possible lack of aesthetic quality inherent in these tales, it is more telling to explore what the written text might reveal about the new and varied gender relations formed in the intersection between Hip Hop music and Hip Hop fiction, between black male and female artists. To take Badu's chant a step further, Hip Hop is bigger than rap music. It is only when we recognize that fact we can begin to see that even in what is described as the darkest hours for female rappers, Hip Hop always had women present ... we need only look for their narratives in unexpected places.

NOTES

1. From 2005–2006 Lil' Kim served a jail sentence for perjury, Lauryn Hill's post–*Miseducation of Lauryn Hill* career faded into non-relevance due to her prolonged personal removal from the scene, Missy Elliot was plagued by rumors of male ghost writing, and various other female emcees were unable or unwilling to be signed to major record labels.

2. Writer Mesfin Fekadu describes Minaj as rising out of the ashes of demised female emcees in "Nicki Minaj Revives Female Voice in Rap," Associated Press, accessed August 18, 2010, http://abcnews.go.com/Entertainment/wireStory?id=11426081.

3. Denean Sharpley-Whiting, *Pimps Up, Ho's Down: Hip Hop's Hold on Young Black Women* (New York: New York University Press, 2007), 149.

4. Faedra Chatard Carpenter, "An Interview with Joan Morgan," *Callaloo* 29:3 (2006): 766.

5. "Hip Hop fiction," "street lit," "ghetto lit," "gangsta lit," and "urban fiction" are often used interchangeably to describe the genre of literature featuring the narratives of urban, working-class, black characters. In keeping with this essay's overarching argument regarding the role of women within Hip Hop cultural production, I will use the term "Hip Hop fiction" to describe the genre. However, when citing the writings of others, I will use their preferred nomenclature.

6. Zora Neale Hurston, "What White Publishers Won't Print," *Zora Neale Hurston: Folklore, Memoirs, and Other Writings* (New York: The Library of America, 1995), 951.

7. Maryemma Graham, "Black Is Gold: African American Literature, Critical Literacy, and Twenty-First-Century Pedagogies," chapter 3 in this volume.

8. While I suggest this critical intervention because fiction is a fruitful space to imagine alternative spaces of women's roles in Hip Hop, I do so with awareness that Hip Hop in its musical form is more far-reaching than literature. Even the most unpopular rap album will likely outsell the most popular novel, let alone Hip Hop novel. Moreover, I do not intend to suggest that we do not continue to interrogate the absence of

female emcees, but rather that we might find other productive spaces to interrogate, as well.

9. Adam Mansbach, "On Lit Hop," in *Total Chaos: The Art and Aesthetics of Hip Hop,* ed. Jeff Chang (New York: Basic Civitas Books, 2006), 94.

10. Ibid., 95.

11. Ibid., 96.

12. Ibid., 101.

13. Ibid.

14. Nick Chiles, "Their Eyes Were Reading Smut," *New York Times,* January 4, 2006.

15. Hurston, 953.

16. Ibid., 954.

17. Kiese Laymon, "Ether for Hip Hop Fiction, American Literary Writing and Dexter—Part 2," (Cold Drink, 2009), accessed August 1, 2010, http://kieselaymon.com /?p=16.

18. Bliss Broyard, "Pulp Princess." *Elle,* accessed June 17, 2009, http://www.elle .com/Pop-Culture/Movies-TV-Music-Books/Pulp-Princess.

19. Ibid.

20. Janice Radway, *Reading the Romance: Women, Patriarchy, and Popular Litera-ture* (New York: Verso, 1987), 20.

21. See M. Genevieve West's *Zora Neale Hurston: American Literary Culture* (Gainesville: University Press of Florida, 2005) and John Young's *Black Writers, White Publishers: Marketplace Politics in Twentieth-Century African American Literature* (Jackson: University of Mississippi Press, 2006) for more on the way Hurston's career was circumscribed by a fickle publishing world.

22. Mireille Miller-Young, "Hip-Hop Honeys and Da Hustlaz: Black Sexualities in the New Hip-Hop Pornography," *Meridians: Feminism, Race, Transnationalism* 8.1 (2008): 271–272.

23. Miller-Young, 264.

24. Horton-Stallings, 180.

25. Ibid.

26. Chideya, Farai, *News & Notes,* National Public Radio. June 11, 2007. Accessed May 30, 2012. http://www.npr.org/2007/06/11/10948084/hip-hops-herstory.

27. Marc Lamont Hill, et al., "Street Fiction: What Is It and What Does It Mean for English Teachers," *English Journal* 97.3 (2008): 77.

28. Hazel Carby, "It Jus Be's dat Way Sometime: The Sexual Politics of Women's Blues," *Radical America* 20.4 (1986):12.

29. Claudia Tate, *Domestic Allegories of Political Desire: The Black Heroine's Text at the Turn of the Century* (New York: Oxford University Press, 1992), 14.

30. Nikki Turner earned her notoriety as the author of Hip Hop fiction titles *A Hustler's Wife, The Glamorous Life, A Project Chick,* and others. She was one of the most name-recognized writers of the genre during the early twenty-first century.

31. The fifth book in the series is published by Urban Trade Paper.

32. Radway, 36.

33. Elizabeth Marshal, et al., "Ghetto Fabulous: Reading Black Adolescent Femi-ninity in Contemporary Urban Street Fiction," *Journal of Adolescent and Adult Literacy* 53.1 (2009): 31.

34. Malcolm Venable, et al., "It's Urban, It's Real, But Is This Literature?," *Black Is-sues Book Review* (Sep–Oct. 2004): 25.

35. Michael Eric Dyson, *Holler If You Hear Me: Searching for Tupac Shakur* (New York: Basic Civitas Books, 2001), 182.

36. Imani Perry, *Prophets of the Hood: Politics and Poetics in Hip Hop* (Durham, NC: Duke University Press, 2004), 127–28.

37. Nikki Turner, "Unique," in *Girls From Da Hood* (New York: Urban Books, 2004), 15 (emphasis mine).

38. Ibid., 8.

39. Ibid.

40. See Evelyn Brooks Higginbotham's *Righteous Discontent: The Women's Movement in the Black Baptist Church, 1880–1920* (Cambridge, MA: Harvard University Press, 1993) for more on this subject; Deborah Gray White's *Ar'n't I a Woman?: Female Slaves in the Plantation South* (New York: W. W. Norton, 1999); E. Frances White's *Dark Continent of Our Bodies: Black Feminism and the Politics of Respectability* (Philadelphia: Temple University Press, 2001); and Katie Canon's *Womanism and the Soul of the Black Community* (New York: Continuum, 1995).

41. Miller-Young, 271–272.

42. Saba Mahmood, "Feminist Theory, Agency, and the Liberatory Subject" in *On Shifting Ground: Muslim Women in the Global Era* (New York: The Feminist Press at CUNY, 2008), 119.

WORKS CITED

Broyard, Bliss. "Pulp Princess." *Elle*. http://www.elle.com/Pop-Culture/Movies-TV -Music-Books/Pulp-Princess. Accessed June 17, 2009.

Carby, Hazel. "It Jus Be's dat Way Sometime: The Sexual Politics of Women's Blues," *Radical America* 20.4 (1986): 12.

Carpenter, Faedra Chatard. "An Interview with Joan Morgan." *Callaloo* 29:3 (2006): 766.

Chideya, Farai. *News & Notes*. National Public Radio. 11 June 2007. Accessed May 30, 2012. http://www.npr.org/2007/06/11/10948084/hip-hops-herstory.

Chiles, Nick. "Their Eyes Were Reading Smut." *New York Times*, January 4, 2006.

Dyson, Michael Eric. *Holler If You Hear Me: Searching for Tupac Shakur*. New York: Basic Civitas Books, 2001.

Fekadu, Mesfin. "Nicki Minaj Revives Female Voice in Rap." Associated Press. http:// abcnews.go.com/Entertainment/wireStory?id=11426081. Accessed August 18, 2010.

Graham, Maryemma. "Black Is Gold: African American Literature, Literacy and Pedagogical Studies." In *Contemporary African American Literature: The Living Canon*, edited by Lovalerie King and Shirley Moody-Turner, 55–90. Bloomington: Indiana University Press, 2012.

Hill, Marc Lamont, et al. "Street Fiction: What Is It and What Does It Mean for English Teachers," *English Journal* 97.3 (2008): 77.

Hurston, Zora Neale. "What White Publishers Won't Print." *Zora Neale Hurston: Folklore, Memoirs, and Other Writings* New York: The Library of America, 1995.

Laymon, Kiese. "Ether for Hip Hop Fiction: American Literary Writing and Dexter— Part 2." Cold Drink, 2009. http://kieselaymon.com /?p=16. Accessed August 1, 2010.

Mansbach, Adam. "On Lit Hop." *Total Chaos: The Art and Aesthetics of Hip Hop*. Ed. Jeff Chang. New York: Basic Civitas Books, 2006).

Mahmood, Saba. "Feminist Theory, Agency, and the Liberatory Subject." *On Shifting Ground: Muslim Women in the Global Era.* New York: The Feminist Press at CUNY, 2008.

Marshal, Elizabeth, et al. "Ghetto Fabulous: Reading Black Adolescent Femininity in Contemporary Urban Street Fiction," *Journal of Adolescent and Adult Literacy* 53.1 (2009): 31.

Miller-Young, Mireille. "Hip-Hop Honeys and Da Hustlaz: Black Sexualities in the New Hip-Hop Pornography." *Meridians: Feminism, Race, Transnationalism* 8.1 (2008): 271–272.

Perry, Imani. *Prophets of the Hood: Politics and Poetics in Hip Hop.* Durham, NC: Duke University Press, 2004.

Radway, Janice. *Reading the Romance: Women, Patriarchy, and Popular Literature.* New York: Verso, 1987.

Sharpley-Whiting, Denean. *Pimps Up, Ho's Down: Hip Hop's Hold on Young Black Women.* New York: New York University Press, 2007.

Tate, Claudia. *Domestic Allegories of Political Desire: The Black Heroine's Text at the Turn of the Century* New York: Oxford University Press, 1992.

Turner, Nikki. "Unique." *Girls From Da Hood.* New York: Urban Books, 2004.

Venable, Malcolm, et al. "It's Urban, It's Real, But Is This Literature?" *Black Issues Book Review* (Sep–Oct. 2004): 25.West, M. Genevieve. *Zora Neale Hurston: American Literary Culture.* Gainesville: University Press of Florida, 2005.

FIVE

STREET LITERATURE AND THE MODE OF SPECTACULAR WRITING: POPULAR FICTION BETWEEN SENSATIONALISM, EDUCATION, POLITICS, AND ENTERTAINMENT

KRISTINA GRAAFF

During the past decade a new form of black popular fiction emerged in the nation's inner-urban areas—spaces that the publishing industry and book distribution networks never imagined would be commercially viable. Known as Street Literature or Urban Fiction, the novels are often written by first-time authors—some of them former or current prisoners—and deal with street violence, prison experiences, and the drug business, especially the crack trade since the 1980s. Mainly circulated through the practices of self-publishing and street vending, these books reach a broad audience, particularly in black working-class communities, and have forced major publishers and book outlets to take notice. Since the genre's commercialization, large presses also aim to attract nonurban and nonblack audiences.[1] Although exact sales numbers are difficult to determine, bestseller lists of the *African American Literature Book Club* (AALBC), *Essence Magazine* and the African American book announcement website, *Books of Soul,* indicate that Street Literature is currently one of the most widely read subgenres of African American fiction.[2]

Street Literature can indeed be read in the tradition of authors such as Donald Goines or Iceberg Slim, whose novels from the late 1960s and 1970s are known as "pulp" or "ghetto realistic fiction."[3] Like Street Literature, novels in this subgenre were mostly set in urban low-income neighborhoods and portrayed the inescapable fates of black hustlers, gangsters, or drug addicts through the use of graphically explicit street slang.[4] Primarily, however, Street Literature grew out of a Hip Hop culture, sharing with rap music not only language styles but also, since the 1980s, the narrative location of "the hood" and topics such as black mass incarceration, police violence, and postindustrial inner-urban decay. The two cultural expressions are also comparable in generating a wide variety of entrepreneurial practices that, in the case of Street Literature, range from the formation of small independent publishing and printing companies to street vending stands. Like certain aspects of Hip Hop culture, popular urban novels have been the subject of controversy, due in particular to graphic cover art and explicit language. This chapter elaborates on such explicitness by linking it to the novels' dramatic content, structure, and style in order to illustrate how Street Literature can be read beyond a simple good/bad binary. Utilizing the concept of "spectacular writing," which comprises the novels' visibility, immediacy, and externalization of conflicts, I show how works of Street Literature are instead characterized by multiple interpretational layers that serve simultaneously sensationalist, didactic, political, and entertaining functions.

THE CONTROVERSY AROUND STREET LITERATURE

Despite the genre's economic success, Street Literature remains controversial. One of the advocates for Street Literature is author and former editor-in-chief of *Vibe* magazine Danyel Smith, who praises Street Literature authors for raising sensitive issues—such as crime and drugs, or the impact of incarceration on many black communities—and for daring to tell these stories "boldly, without nuance, and with pride."[5] For Smith, Street Literature's venture lies in its confrontational expressivity that *"put[s] it all out there*—the stuff many African Americans spend their lives trying to get past, move away from, or talk about only among themselves."[6] She opposes controlling access to the literary scene, an "unless-you-can-act-proper-don't-come-outside dictum,"[7] and instead pleads for a side-by-side relationship between Street Literature and black "literary" fiction.

Her call for the coexistence of popular Street Literature with more "literary" titles, however, is criticized harshly by author and journalist Nick Chiles, who fears that works like his own cannot compete with "these purveyors of crassness."[8] Chiles disapproves of Street Literature for its "glorification and exploitation of sex, violence, greed—the worst aspects of our nature, the things that we all must fight to tame, rather than to celebrate."[9] He also objects to the fact that visual appropriation emanating from Street Literature, with "lurid book jackets displaying all forms of brown flesh,"[10] would represent the majority images within the African American literature sections of many bookstore chains. Notably, both camps base their judgments on the novels' outward and externalized forms of expression, by either valuing the bold storytelling and "busty, trigger-happy covers"[11] as daring, or by dismissing the novels' explicit engagements with criminal life as a "degradation of black fiction."[12] Whereas this externalized style of storytelling is discussed abundantly in academic research on Hip Hop music and performances—ranging from the examination of explicit lyrics[13] and conspicuous consumption[14] to the objectifying display of black female bodies,[15] thus far no literary analysis has been made that specifies, deconstructs and challenges Street Literature's narrative mechanisms that create the impression of "putting it all out there." Indeed the novels' graphic covers speak to the readers' visual senses, but what are the structural and stylistic devices, as well as topical foci, that evoke the label of "crassness?"

THE MODE OF SPECTACULAR WRITING

In order to specify and distinguish the different narrative modes that are used to produce such an externalized style of storytelling, this essay introduces the interpretative tool of spectacular writing. Spectacular writing is suggested here to signify a writing style marked by the attributes of visibility, immediacy and the externalization of conflicts. The notion of spectacular writing draws upon literary techniques of novels written in the tradition of American realism that aim to achieve verisimilitude by deploying a matter-of-fact tone, short sentences, direct discourse, fast-paced storylines, and close and detailed depictions of conditions and practices of daily life. Equally important for the analysis of Street Literature, however, is the connection of spectacular writing to the notion of drama, understood not only as a structural and stylistic component but also as a topic, practice, and character trait.

Working from an interpretation that links Street Literature and drama, I elaborate on four different modes and functions of spectacular writing as sensationalist, didactic, political, and entertaining. The aim of this essay is to illustrate that spectacular writing can serve as an instrument not only to interpret Street Literature beyond a binary judgment of "good" versus "bad" but also to reveal how most of the popular novels possess multiple, often coexisting, interpretational layers. Further, in my analysis of the notion of spectacular writing, I propose an interpretative framework that can be linked to the few ongoing research projects on Street Literature, especially those studies that focus on the novels as didactic tools, their potential to promote literacy,[16] and their gender constructions.[17]

SPECTACULAR WRITING AS SENSATIONALISM

An elaboration of the novels' dramatic components is essential to understanding how spectacular writing enacts a sensationalist reading of Street Literature. Dramatic elements can be found not only on a structural and stylistic level but also on a topical level; such elements contribute centrally to the novels' visuality, immediacy, and externalization of conflicts.

The relevance of drama to many stories is often indicated initially by the novels' titles, such as *No More Drama* by La Jill Hunt, *Drama Is her Middle Name* by Wendy Williams, *St. Louis Drama* by Bilal S., or simply *Drama!* by Tia Hines. Beyond the references made in the various titles, the narrative structure of most novels follow the formal features of drama, in particular, the tragedy in the Aristotelian tradition. A typical Street Literature story starts out with an introduction to the location, usually inner-urban boroughs like East Atlanta, North Philadelphia, or Harlem. The circle of protagonists is also initially introduced, normally a male or female kingpin and his or her entourage, with rival gang members representing the antagonists, and minor characters such as drug addicts or "legit" working-class people rounding out the cast. The story then proceeds to the main conflict, frequently the battle for supremacy in the drug trade that usually peaks in the confrontation of two opposing drug dealers or gangs. After reaching the turning point, for example, a fatal homicide of a member of the main character's gang, the conflict between protagonist and antagonist unravels, mostly driven by the motives of revenge, wounded respect, or reputation. The drama's falling action includes moments of final suspense, such as the kidnapping of the kingpin's wife or a shootout between the two main characters. Most stories end with a tragic solution to the conflict, either with the protagonist's failure—frequently in the form of arrest—or with his or her death.

Thus due to their already dramatic narrative structure, most Street Literature novels are characterized by antagonistic storylines resulting in externalized conflicts between the opponents. The fact that the multitude of actions takes place within a very brief timeframe—sometimes only a few weeks—guarantees fast-paced developments and a rapid culmination of the conflicts. Spectacular writing's immediacy, visuality, and extroverted conflicts are hence already inherent to most novels' basic narrative structure. Drama, however, not only plays a central role in Street Literature as a generic convention but is also used on the topical level to describe conditions, interactions, and character traits.

First of all, the daily conditions in the hood are associated with drama as can be seen in Shannon Holmes's novel *Never Go Home Again*.[18] The third-person narrative is set in the Bronx of the 1980s and depicts how Corey, despite his parents' attempts to keep him away from the streets, immerses himself in the lucrative drug trade. Corey's mother, in her concern about her son's illegal street activities, assigns drama to their daily living conditions: "Who needs to go to the movies these days? You got killings, rape, and drug dealing. A lifetime full of drama for fifty cent."[19] Not knowing that her son will indeed turn into the tragic hero when eventually shot by a police officer, she is aware that the tragedy's rise-and-fall structure parallels the "what goes around comes around" moral of the inner-urban hustle. With the activity of street life, which stands at the center of most novels and is itself considered as drama-based, conflictual, and externalized actions are also guaranteed on the topical level. In particular, the street activities contain a performance element that can be considered dramatic. Defending a corner, showing off a weapon, and cruising the streets in a car are all practices that possess a theatrical component and indicate how one's position in the illicit business has to be constantly maintained, negotiated and made visible through public performances.

Secondly, the notion of drama is used to visualize conflictual interactions between couples. As "drama" in this context designates an an-
tagonism between attraction and repulsion, externalized verbal or physical altercations between partners turn into an inevitable part of Street
Literature. This conflictive activity is well illustrated in Freeze's novel
Against the Grain.[20] The story revolves around the protagonist Kay, who,
after doing a nine-year prison stint for bank robbery, returns to Baltimore to establish a soon flourishing heroin business with his crew. Com-
motion is produced not only through the need to permanently defend his
drug empire but also through Kay's relationship with Sonia, triggering
extroverted conflicts catered to the reader's visual senses:

> She was crazy about him and one time stabbed a girl that she had caught
> Kay with. Another time, she cut Kay while she was in a jealous rage. They
> both loved the drama and when it came right down to it, they were made for
> each other. A lot of the times they acted as if they couldn't stand each other,
> but neither of them could stand to be away from the other very long.[21]

When deployed in relation to interpersonal relationships, "drama"
is clearly situated in the tension between appeal and avoidance, simultaneously expressing a disruption and connection between characters.
With intimacy being externalized into impulsive and body-centered exchanges, the reader is placed in the perspective of an observer who can
gaze freely at the characters' physical interaction. This omnipresence of
drama in the characters' daily activities recalls Zora Neale Hurston's con-
tention that African American "life is highly dramatized," that "[e]very-
thing is acted out."[22] Although displaying essentialist ideas and maintaining the binary of primitive and civilized, a variation on Hurston's
assumptions could be applied to the analysis of the popular novels. Among
them are the entertaining function of acting out and its usage to openly
display power relations, the absence of privacy as well as the claim expressed by both Hurston and various Street Literature authors to represent "authentic" black life "realistically." Hurston's examination of drama,
however, focuses on its performative potential by defining all verbal or
physical expressions as creative mimetic acts of reinvention—an attribute that she also assigns to all African American art.[23] Reading Street
Literature narratives as performative acts—in content, structure, and

speech but also in regard to character practices—could thus represent another interpretative approach to work out the novels' multiple layers.

As the above quote also indicates, dramatic behavior is primarily assigned to female characters, which becomes particularly clear in the naming of women as "drama queens," turning impulsive behavior into an embodied *character trait*. Sandra, a minor character in Freeze's novel who is a girlfriend of one of Kay's crew members, is thus reduced to her uncontrollable behavior, being known as the "drama queen . . . who didn't mind busting [a] nigga in the head or cutting him when they got in an argument."[24] Assigning to females a lack of control over their alleged externalized emotions provokes a more general pathologizing of women by associating their supposed emotional excess with the disorder of female hysteria. Even more so, it inscribes the gender cliché of the acting out or the angry black woman who is usually portrayed as unpredictable, overbearing, and melodramatic and as belonging to a lower-class community. The figure of the drama queen especially perpetuates this stereotype of the black working-class woman as "aggressive, loud, rude, and pushy"[25] and continues a long tradition of denigrating outspoken women by portraying them as Sapphire caricatures. As Patricia Hill Collins has pointed out, these gender- and class-specific attributes became particularly prominent in black popular culture in the post–Civil Rights era and promote a distinction between an interiorized and respectable black middle-class behavior and an outwardly acting, "authentic" African American lower class.[26] Viewed in this light, it is the dramatic component of the novels—that are themselves already marked as working-class fiction—that reinforces the class-specific stereotyping of women by placing visible appearances and acting-out behavior at the center of the reader's gaze.[27]

The focus on the characters' outward appearances and externalized actions is, finally, also achieved through the notion of drama on the *stylistic* level. Many authors use a narrative form that the literary theorist Gérard Genette terms dramatic mode, in reference to the mimetic technique of the drama.[28] Written in a perspective that Genette defines as external focalization,[29] Street Literature novels often focus on the characters' actions, direct speech, and surroundings rather than on their inner thoughts. Using a perspective that refrains from comments on the characters' activities and appears to follow them from the outside without knowing their interior life, most novels give the impression of an absent narrator. The effect is well illustrated in Wahida Clark's *Thugs and the Women Who Love Them.*[30] The novel narrates the stories of three young college-educated women who fall in love with criminals. One of the women, Angel, gets caught up in an abusive love-hate relationship with Snake, a pimp with whom she is involved regularly in physical confrontations. As the following passage reveals, the couple's already externalized conflict gains even more immediacy through Clark's use of the dramatic mode:

> Angel, still propped on the floor, kicked him in the stomach and called him a punk bitch as she reached for her 9mm. She held it with both hands and aimed at his face. Snake just stood there and looked at those sexy hazel eyes, perky nose, and smooth, sensual lips, which were now in a pout. "Put down the gun, baby." She didn't move an inch. Blood was slowly dripping down her forehead. . . . Angel was still lying there with the 9mm cocked, pointing it at him. She was drenched in sweat and her nipples were protruding through the tight, see-through blouse she had on.[31]

Applying the controversial distinction between showing and telling to *Thugs and the Women Who Love Them,* the fight between Angel and Snake is depicted in a mode of showing that seemingly omits the narrator's mediation. Restricted to the visible and audible, the narrative perspective gives the impression of having direct access to the scene. As the case of Angel also exemplifies, the literary staging of characters—which primarily focuses on outwardness and immediacy—becomes particularly problematic in the uncommented upon display of female figures. Even in her resistant action, Angel is thus primarily portrayed as a body and perceived as acting through a male gaze. Comparable to women in Hip Hop videos, who frequently function as "visually appealing props,"[32] female characters in Street Literature are often reduced to dramatized objects.

As the first examination of Street Literature in the framework of drama illustrates, spectacular writing can be interpreted as a sensationalist mode. In this reading, the achieved effects of visibility, immediacy, and externalization of conflicts allow neither a critical distance on the reader's side nor an insight into the characters' inner lives. Instead, the novels' characters are propped up on the urban stage, where they are exhibited and perform for the reader.[33] Engrossed in the extroverted and immediate action, the reader assumes the role of the gazing voyeur, who, in a mixture of repulsion and attraction, devours the presented spectacle. Being comfortably located behind the protective shield of the book, she or he can safely observe the often dangerous or even deadly interactions—a form of "literary slumming" that allows the reader to observe unseen a feared and "fascinating" urban space from an allegedly safe location. Especially those readers who are not familiar with the depicted urban settings may turn the narrative locations into spaces of exoticization, by believing they observe "the other" in authentic city scenery.

Even more so, however, in its sensationalist mode, Street Literature's spectacular writing evokes the legacy of black bodies as spectacles. Putting black bodies on visual display for public consumption by the gaze of white audiences has been an American practice for centuries. Black performances, ranging from music, dance, and speech have long been constructed as "'spectacles of primitivism' to justify the colonial and racist gaze";[34] the racial enactments of nineteenth-century theater culture, especially minstrel shows and racial melodramas, also objectified the black body as a spectacle and "restaged [its] seizure and possession . . . for the other's use and enjoyment."[35] The most violent exhibition of black bodies, however, is found in the practice of lynching, "a tool of domination meant to coerce (and not rough-handedly correct), to deny (and not merely restrict), and to subjugate (not only banish or dispatch) black people."[36] Technical advancements, especially the snapshot camera, enforced the visual consumption, reproduction, and commodification of black bodies in pain. Engrossing the viewer in the mere visual surface of the bodies, lynching photographs hypervisualized their victims, and, providing no background about the murder, made them invisible at the same time.

The same "anticognitive dimension"[37] of the spectacle can be applied to Street Literature when spectacular writing is interpreted as a sensationalist device. Being portrayed as acting-out black bodies without an inner life, the hypervisualized characters thus perform under the readers' gaze. Considering that characters are often involved in criminal activities, Street Literature also contributes to a white racist imaginary of unruly blacks and—depicting their usually failing attempts to leave the inner-urban neighborhoods—"legitimize[s] the spatial confinement of the black urban poor."[38] As a sensationalist mode, spectacular writing thus confirms Nick Chile's criticism that the novels' hypervisuality, vulgarity, and lack of subtlety lead to a degradation of black literary fiction and the reinscription of racist stereotypes.

SPECTACULAR WRITING AS EDUCATION AND POLITICS

Street Literature's externalized narrative modes, however, cannot merely be reduced to exhibitionist qualities and voyeuristic gazes. A different understanding of spectacular writing's visuality, immediacy, and externalized conflicts can be gained, especially when considering the prologues and epilogues that often frame the narratives. The introductory and concluding remarks serve comparable functions as in ancient drama, where prologues were used to introduce the play, comment on its topics and characters, provide a bridge between the performance and the outside world, and dedicate the play to a particular audience or defend it against critics. Epilogues, on the other hand, usually summarized the play, elaborating on the moral, and expressing the thoughts of the playwright.

Street Literature's framing devices and those of classical drama parallel each other especially in regard to their didactic intentions, as Shannon Holmes's *Never Go Home Again* exemplifies.[39] With the protagonist Corey being incarcerated several times and finally shot by a police officer, the story clearly represents a cautionary tale. Holmes's educative intentions, however, are additionally expressed in his introductory remarks, entitled "Word from the Author." Aware of the educative responsibility that comes with having his "voice heard and influenc[ing] people's thoughts and opinions,"[40] he uses the prologue to provide reading directions, instructing the audience that his novels are not to be read as "guidebooks on lawlessness"[41] but as warning examples of "the flip side of the game."[42] Essential for the credibility of his didactic mission is Holmes's connection of the fictional narrative to the "real" world by citing his own participation in the described illegal activities. Holmes thus admits to his own wrongdoings—"I've turned too many people on to 'hustles' in the past when I was doing dirt"[43]—but nevertheless deploys his inside knowledge to strengthen the novel's didactic underpinning: "I was in the streets seven days a week and three hundred sixty-five days a year . . . [selling] drugs in more cities and towns than most people have relatives."[44] Finally, elaborating on one of the main aspects of *Never Go Home Again,* Holmes uses the novel's epilogue to take up the politically charged issue of mass incarceration, again with the intention of educating his audience. While accepting his own prison experience as justified, Holmes points to the disproportionate numbers of incarcerated African Americans, noting that African Americans represent only 12 percent of the United States population "but over 50 percent of its prison population."[45] Revealing "the corrections department . . . [as] the biggest-growing industry in America" and concluding with the call to "do your own research,"[46] Holmes deploys the epilogue as a tool to reinforce a politicized reading of the preceding fictional narrative and to thereby create critical awareness among his audience.

Even Street Literature narratives like the *True to the Game* trilogy by Teri Woods[47] that are not overt cautionary tales are didactically framed. Indeed, the series rather uncritically revolves around the illegal activities and conspicuous consumption of the couple Gena and Quadir, a drug kingpin in Philadelphia. After Quadir is purportedly killed by a rival drug gang member, Gena is persecuted by various enemies, all of whom are interested in her several million dollars of inherited drug money. Ending with Quadir's reappearance and the couple's reunion, the trilogy leaves the protagonists unpunished. Woods, however, uses the epilogue to the first part of *True to the Game* to critically position herself against the characters' behavior. Linking the fictional world to that of her readers, she addresses "those caught in the trap of temporary pleasures," warning them that "the root of all evil, which is the love of money and the next man's pain, will surely come back to haunt you."[48] In an explicit message, she calls upon her readers to not follow the path of her protagonists: "We have a choice. . . . Give yourself time to grow and open your minds to education, because it is a key to the way out."[49] Even more blatant are Woods's didactic intentions in *True to the Game* 2 and 3, which end with a list of questions challenging the protagonists' faulty behavior that are comparable to textbook instructions: "Do you think Gena could have done more to prevent her pregnancy?"[50] or "Do you think it was good that Quadir and Gena got away with the money?"[51] Given that her characters get away with their questionable behavior, Woods's reading guidance aims not only at avoiding a misinterpretation of the story as a glorifying tale, but it also represents an attempt to shape the moral values of the primarily adolescent readership.[52]

Taking into account the didactic orientation that becomes particularly clear in light of the framing through prologues and epilogues, the visuality, immediacy, and externalized conflicts can provide for a second reading of spectacular writing. Instead of simply exhibiting the characters, externalized conflicts between clear opponents may thus be used to better exemplify and clarify the story's moral. The characters' immediate and visible acting out does not necessarily need to produce merely a lack of critical distance or a gazing reader; it may likewise serve to evoke the reader's participation by facilitating involvement. Hence, the explicit enactment of street life can also be interpreted as a strategy to induce the readers' empathy. Potentially, identifying and empathizing with the protagonists' fates may even have a cathartic or deterrent effect on the reader. Moral instruction would thus also be achieved through the reader's emotional and mental "cleansing." Considering that the majority of readers, like the characters, are in their teens and twenties, spectacular writing can also be defined as a didactic device, chosen with the intention that the audience might not commit the same errors as the gangsters, dealers, or addicts in the narratives.

Inextricably linked to the didactic function of spectacular writing is its usage as a political tool, which has already been illustrated here by the prologues and epilogues of Shannon Holmes and Teri Woods, who connect their didactic intentions with political messages. Apart from being mediated through the novels' framing, political awareness is also raised within the stories. Genette's dramatic mode, cited earlier to illustrate the characters' voyeuristic display, can hereby also be deployed as a tool to create awareness for politically charged topics. Its usage is well exemplified in one of the classics of Street Literature, *The Coldest Winter Ever*, which was written by the rapper and activist Sister Souljah.[53] The novel tells the story of the spoiled protagonist Winter, who attempts to continue her lifestyle of conspicuous consumption even after her father Ricky Santiaga, a former drug kingpin who at one time had all of Brooklyn "locked down," has been sentenced to life in prison. Describing one of the prison visits during which Winter and her mother go to see Santiaga, the following sequence utilizes external focalization not to expose sensationally the characters but to narrate laconically the processing of prison visitors:

> They patted us down, frisked us, and escorted us to a bus that took us to the prison waiting room. We signed in a big book, learnt my father's prison number, were told never to forget it, and we sat. The room was filled with all kinds of women, all ages, and some children . . . There was one big-mouth guard coming in from the corridor that led to where the prisons are. He would come into the room yelling the last name of the prisoner, escort the visitor to the back, and signal when your time is up.[54]

Here, the dramatic mode—understood as a sober and detached perspective—stresses the formal and humiliating practices of the prison system. The impression of immediacy and lack of inner thoughts are deployed to underline the objectifying processing procedures that place the visitor in the same position as the prisoner, both being equally subjected to the prison authority. In this case, the mode of showing, which emphasizes direct actions and speech, evokes the effect of what Danyel Smith has positively described as "put[ting] it all out there" by immediately visualizing controversial issues—seemingly without a mediating instance and circumlocution. In such a way, spectacular writing can also be understood as a political tool, used to direct the view to neglected figures and to raise underrepresented topics, like that of mass incarceration. In the case of *The Coldest Winter Ever,* descriptions of the humiliating treatment of visitors address the underlying issue of relatives being discouraged from frequent visits, leading to an increasing social dislocation and disconnection of the inmate from the 'outside' world, an effect already achieved through the placing of prisoners in remote facilities. Applying again the metaphor of the stage to Street Literature's narrative locations of inner-urban streets or prison, spectacular writing does not solely turn them into spaces of exposure. Instead, they can also be seen as spaces of revelation, in other words necessary platforms to illustrate social hierarchies and visualize them in spatial parameters.

SPECTACULAR WRITING AS ENTERTAINMENT

Finally, Street Literature's mode of spectacular writing undoubtedly also serves an entertaining function. Whereas the dramatic structure and its antagonistic figures guarantee a fast-escalating conflict, within the narratives, clear-cut characters and their detailed depictions are important elements to draw the readers into the storylines. Immediacy, visuality, and extroverted interactions between the characters are thus essential entertaining attributes of the popular novels. They guarantee a page-turning read and fulfill a demand for distraction and escapism that can be considered as a central function of popular literature in general.[55] A central requirement for the novels' entertaining consumption is also the creation of an atmosphere of realism, which is achieved in two ways.

First, the novels' prologues and epilogues, apart from providing a didactic and political framing, are also essential in laying ground for an entertaining read not only by marking the difference between the "real" and the fictional world but also by precisely concealing the distinction between them. In the aforementioned prologue to *Never Go Home Again,* Shannon Holmes, on the one hand, stresses his imaginative skills by emphasizing how he "paint[s] [his] characters into a corner with words."[56] On the other hand, however, he introduces his novel as an eyewitness testimony:

> I invite the readers to journey with me into the streets. Come see what I've seen; go where I went, in your mind, from the safety of your living room, bedroom, or office. If you have never been to Baltimore, Philadelphia, or whatever other urban community I choose to write about, let me take you there. Let me show the gritty and grimy undercarriage of society.[57]

Holmes consciously plays with realism as a means of representation by simultaneously situating his novel between an informative impulse and the intention to entertain. While announcing his ability to make a social world legible especially to those readers who are unfamiliar with the depicted urban terrain, Holmes at the same time places emphasis on how the "gritty and grimy" life of "the other half" can be consumed from a safe spot. The secure position of the reader, earlier described as the location behind the protective shield of the book, not only leads to a voyeuristic gaze but also allows for the entertaining consumption of the narrative. With Shannon Holmes inviting the gaze, sensationalism to a certain degree becomes a prerequisite for the reader's experience of suspense.

The play with verisimilitude is also well encapsulated in the prologue to Freeze's novel *Against the Grain,* in which the editor, Nikki Turner, remarks: "[This story] is a certified three-point game-winning shot that puts you so close to the streets you'd have to be careful not to be indicted on conspiracy charges just by reading it."[58] On the one hand, the impression of participating in a real-life enactment is clearly intended for the reader's entertaining thrill and pleasure. On the other hand, in its hyperbole, Turner's statement also indicates that the novel's exaggerated criminal acts are precisely *not* to be taken literally. The entertaining effect is hereby generated through the permanent shift between a style of witnessing and narrating, chronicling and fantasizing. In contrast to the assumed audience that gazes at putative "real" living conditions, this type of spectacular writing expects readers who draw their pleasure exactly out of the two inextricably linked narrative stances.

Secondly, the impression of a correspondence with a social reality is evoked through a textual device that Roland Barthes has termed "reality effect."[59] It is generated by the description of apparently superfluous details that have no function for the progress of the plot, yet are indispensable for the novel's sensually produced atmosphere of realism.[60] The precise descriptions aiming to denote a "concrete reality" can be comprised of "insignificant gestures, transitory attitudes, insignificant objects, redundant words"[61] and suggest an immediate witnessing of the narrated accounts. In the following random dream sequence from Freeze's novel *Against the Grain,* the incarcerated protagonist Kay reminisces about his former crew back home. It is the visualization of every single gesture, leaving nothing to the reader's imagination, which produces the feeling of witnessing first-hand a daily exchange on the street:

> [Scatter] turned back to Kay and pointed at him with both hands. Then he made two fists and crossed his hands like an X and patted his chest twice. He turned and tapped Big Duke on the arm as if to say, "Come on." And in a fast pimp strut, he caught up with Apache and Kahdijah. Big Duke put both hands in the big pocket on the front of his hoodie, showed Kay that he still had his burner, turned and followed them. [62]

While not necessary to the plot, the wordless exchange between the men contributes to the novel's realist atmosphere by drawing upon a repertoire of male gestures and postures that can be considered an inherent part of street culture and in particular Hip Hop culture. By displaying a detailed knowledge of street-specific practices from the nonfictional world, the author gives his work not only credibility but also evokes a reading pleasure, either through the effect of recognition or the imparting of knowledge for those readers not familiar with the urban practices.

CONCLUSION

Street Literature's characteristic mode of spectacular writing, marked by its immediacy, visuality, and externalized conflicts, can be interpreted in at least four ways. It might generate a sensationalist reader, who passively gazes at exoticized bodies and urban spaces. It might didactically educate its audience by judging questionable behavior and suggesting moral standards. As a political device it might raise awareness for politically charged issues, and finally, as an entertaining tool, it might lead to escaping into a conflictual and apparently realistic, but also comic and pleasurable, fictional world.

Essential for such a multiple reading of spectacular writing are the novels' various dramatic components that permeate not only their structural and stylistic levels but also their topical levels when used to describe conditions, interactions, or character traits. While in a sensationalist reading the characters' acting out brings about their exposure, the theatrical staging also serves as an attention-getting tool by giving voice and presence to neglected figures, spaces and themes. From a didactic point of view, following the characters' tragic rise and fall helps to clarify the story's moral, whereas the impression of witnessing a real-life enactment also enhances the novels' entertaining thrill.

Without doubt, it is possible to read the popular novels as promoting the "sexualization and degradation" of black fiction, although only when analyzed on one level of spectacular writing. The same holds true for a reading that endorses how Street Literature deals with issues like crime or incarceration "boldly, without nuance, and with pride."[63] The challenge that Street Literature presents to us, however, is to accept and to allow for the coexistence of complex levels of reading and interpretation—not only within the genre but also within a single work of fiction. Accepting Street Literature's multiple interpretational layers will also acknowledge that the genre eludes a binary categorization of "good" or "bad" fiction. Instead Street Literature is ambiguously situated between these oppositions and can therefore not be judged as easily as it may seem at first sight.

NOTES

1. So far, no research on Street Literature has dealt specifically with the genre's range of readership. According to different scholars, the main readership is generally defined as black women and girls, ranging in age from 13 to 40. See Shanita Jones, "Street Lit Novels and Triangle-Area Public Libraries: A Search through the OPACS" (Master's thesis, University of North Carolina at Chapel Hill, 2006), 5. However, interviews with street vendors, especially with Sidibe Ibrahima, who owns several Street Literature book stands throughout New York City, have shown the continuous rise in the number of white readers. See Sidibe Ibrahima, interview by author, New York City, January 10, 2009.

2. Street Literature titles also regularly make the *New York Times* bestseller list, such as 50 Cent's novel *From Pieces to Weight* (*New York Times* bestseller list, August 28, 2005) and *True to the Game II* by Teri Woods (*NYT* bestseller list, November 18, 2007).

3. Kermit E. Campbell, *Gettin' Our Groove On: Rhetoric, Language, and Literacy for the Hip Hop Generation* (Detroit: Wayne State University Press, 2005), 92.

4. Among the most prominent works of these authors are Iceberg Slim's *Pimp: The Story of My Life* and *Trick Baby* as well as Donald Goines's *Dopefiend, Whoreson, Inner City Hoodlum,* and *Black Gangster.*

5. Danyel Smith, "Black Talk and Hot Sex: Why 'Street Lit' Is Literature," in *Total Chaos: The Art and Aesthetics of Hip-Hop,* ed. Jeff Chang (New York: Basic Civitas Books, 2006), 192.

6. Ibid., 189.

7. Ibid., 193.

8. Nick Chiles, "Their Eyes Were Reading Smut," *New York Times,* 4 January 2006, 15.

9. Taylor Nix, "Nick Chiles: A Critical Look at Street Lit," *The Urban Book Source* (2009), http://www.theurbanbooksource.com/interviews/nick-chiles.php.

10. Chiles, "Their Eyes Were Reading Smut," 15.

11. Smith, "Black Talk and Hot Sex: Why 'Street Lit' Is Literature," 189.

12. Chiles, "Their Eyes Were Reading Smut," 15.

13. Michael Eric Dyson, *Holler If You Hear Me: Searching for Tupac Shakur* (New York: Basic Civitas Books, 2001); Michael Eric Dyson. *Know What I Mean?: Reflections on Hip-Hop* (New York: Basic Civitas Books, 2007); bell hooks, *Outlaw Culture: Resisting Representations* (New York: Routledge, 1994); Crispin Sartwell, *Act Like You Know: African American Autobiography and White Identity* (Chicago: University of Chicago Press, 1998); Robin D. G. Kelley, *Race Rebels: Culture, Politics, and the Black Working Class* (New York: The Free Press, 1994).

14. Imani Perry, *Prophets of the Hood: Politics and Poetics in Hip Hop* (Durham, NC: Duke University Press, 2004); Davarian L. Baldwin, "Black Empires, White De-

sires": The Spatial Politics of Identity in the Age of Hip-Hop," in *That's the Joint: The Hip-Hop Studies Reader,* ed. Mark Anthony Neal and Murray Forman (New York: Routledge, 2004).

15. Patricia Hill Collins, *Black Sexual Politics: African Americans, Gender, and the New Racism,* 2nd ed. (New York: Routledge, 2004); Tricia Rose, *Black Noise: Rap Music and Black Culture in Contemporary America* (Hanover, NH: University Press of New England, 1994); T. Denean Sharpley-Whiting, *Pimps up, Ho's Down: Hip Hop's Hold on Young Black Women* (New York: New York University Press, 2007).

16. Simone Cade Gibson, "Critical Readings: Adolescent African American Girls and Urban Fiction" (Doctoral thesis, University of Maryland, 2009); Marc Lamont Hill, "(Re)Negotiating Knowledge, Power, and Identities in Hip-Hop Lit" (Doctoral thesis, University of Pennsylvania, 2005); Vanessa Morris, "Inner City Teens Do Read" (2007), http://www.jahreinaresearch.info/urbanfiction/Inner%20City%20Teens%20Do%20Read.rtf.

17. Biany Perez, "The Politics of Gender in Hip-Hop Fiction" (Master's thesis, Temple University, 2007); Jeana Morrison, "Sex, Violence, and Female Representation in Hip-Hop Fiction" (Master's thesis, Temple University, 2007).

18. Shannon Holmes, *Never Go Home Again* (New York: Atria Books, 2004).

19. Ibid., 296f.

20. Freeze, *Against the Grain* (New York: One World, 2008).

21. Ibid., 37.

22. Zora Neale Hurston, "Characteristics of Negro Expression," in *Within the Circle: An Anthology of African American Literary Criticism from the Harlem Renaissance to the Present,* ed. Angelyn Mitchell (Durham, NC: Duke University Press, 1994), 79.

23. Ibid., 86f.

24. Freeze, *Against the Grain,* 203.

25. Hill Collins, *Black Sexual Politics,* 123.

26. Ibid., 122f.

27. Although the essay focuses on the stereotyping of women, the same applies to male Street Literature characters, whose portrayals often perpetuate the stereotype of the violent and hyper-sexualized black man. Even though the female acting out is more typically associated with drama, both character groups are equally determined by their externalized actions.

28. Gérard Genette, *Die Erzählung,* 2nd ed. (München: Wilhelm Fink Verlag, 1998), 116, 222.

29. Ibid., 135f.

30. Wahida Clark, *Thugs and the Women Who Love Them* (New York: Dafina Books, 2004).

31. Ibid., 10.

32. Hill Collins, *Black Sexual Politics,* 128.

33. When following a sensationalist interpretation of *spectacular writing,* the characters' visual display shows parallels to Guy Debord's analysis of the "*society of the spectacle.*" For Debord, the spectacle represents the fulcrum of modern capitalist society, in which all social relations are conditioned by consumer culture and commodity fetishism. In this world of the spectacle, which according to Debord only represents a precise reflection of an alleged, no longer accessible "reality," human beings reduce themselves to an assigned role and, geared towards appearance, act out their daily lives on display (Guy Debord, *The Society of the Spectacle* [Detroit: Black & Red, 1983], theses 1

and 10 and chapter 2). A sensationalist reading of Street Literature therefore shares with Debord's spectacular a privileging of the visual as the main medium of representation and perception.

34. E. Patrick Johnson: *Appropriating Blackness: Performance and the Politics of Authenticity* (Durham, NC: Duke University Press, 2003), 7.

35. Saidiya Hartman: *Scenes of Subjection: Terror, Slavery, and Self-Making in Nineteenth-Century America* (New York: Oxford University Press, 1997), 31f.

36. Jacqueline Goldsby: *A Spectacular Secret. Lynching in American Life and Literature* (Chicago: University of Chicago Press, 2006), 18.

37. Ibid., 218.

38. Madhu Dubey, *Signs and Cities: Black Literary Postmodernism* (Chicago: University of Chicago Press, 2003), 116.

39. When questioned about their reading habits, most Street Literature authors state that they read bestsellers, other Street Literature novels, nonfiction titles, and self-help books (J. M. Benjamin, interview by author, Plainfield, NJ, July 3, 2010; Wahida Clark, interview by author, East Orange, NJ, December 15, 2009; Jihad, personal interview by author, New York City, December 2, 2009). Since none of the authors mention plays or other dramatic works, it can be assumed that the didactic dramatic patterns within Street Literature are deployed rather intuitively and do not result from a study of classical drama. Further, the usage of didactic components can probably also be ascribed to many authors' familiarity with the narrative patterns of self-help books.

40. Holmes, *Never Go Home Again*, 1.

41. Ibid.

42. Ibid., 4.

43. Ibid., 1.

44. Ibid., 3f.

45. Ibid., 319.

46. Ibid., 320.

47. Teri Woods, *True to the Game* (New York: Teri Woods Publishing, 1999); Teri Woods, *True to the Game 2* (New York: Grand Central Publishing, 2007); Teri Woods, *True to the Game 3* (New York: Grand Central Publishing, 2008). As various online discussion forums reveal, the authorship of the *True to the Game* series as well as that of other novels written in Teri Woods's name (such as the *Deadly Reigns* trilogy and *Dutch* series) is controversial. According to exchanges on Allreaders.Com and Thumperscorner.com, Teri Woods heavily relied on material written by various male prisoners that she gave out as having produced herself (http://www.allreaders.com /Board.asp?listpage=2&BoardID=31769, http://www.thumperscorner.com/discus /messages/36042/33032.html). However, as no final proof of the actual authorship exists, Teri Woods will in the following be cited as the author of the three *True to the Game* volumes.

48. Woods, *True to the Game*, 239.

49. Ibid.

50. Woods. *True to the Game 2*, 224.

51. Woods. *True to the Game 3*, 212.

52. Due to the scope of this essay, the aspect of Street Literature's moral values cannot be detailed. It should, however, be remarked that they oscillate between traditional US–American middle-class values, such as hard work, education, and persever-

ance and a "code of the street" that focuses on the maintenance of respect, defense of honor, loyalty, and revenge. See Elijah Anderson, *Code of the Street: Decency, Violence, and the Moral Life of the Inner City,* 1st ed. (New York: W. W. Norton, 1999). Although some minor critical comments can be found within Woods's trilogy (such as on the neglected children of the "crack generation" and on racial conflicts between the usually white police officers and local drug dealers), there is a noticeable discrepancy between the novels' rather uncritical content and their critical framing that is rarely found in other Street Literature narratives. Apart from providing guidance for adolescent readers, citing conventional values in the novels' prologues and epilogues could possibly be understood as a carte blanche, used strategically to justify the characters' ruthless behavior within the narratives. The fact that the most obvious didactic tool—the discussion questions at the end of *True to the Game* parts 2 and 3—have only been inserted when the trilogy was taken up by the mainstream press Grand Central Publishing (the first part of *True to the Game* was published by her own company, Teri Woods Publishing), might indicate that the framing has taken place at the behest of the publisher.

53. Sister Souljah, *The Coldest Winter Ever* (New York: Pocket Books, 1999).

54. Ibid., 127f.

55. As especially Janice Radway's study on female romance readers illustrates, the escapist function of the act of reading popular novels is not only linked to a justification for withdrawal from daily duties but also central to the maintenance of a personal space. See Janice A. Radway, *Reading the Romance: Women, Patriarchy, and Popular Literature* (Chapel Hill: University of North Carolina Press, 1991), 90f.

56. Holmes, *Never Go Home Again,* 1.

57. Ibid., 4.

58. Freeze, *Against the Grain,* vi.

59. Roland Barthes, *The Rustle of Language* (Oxford: Basil Blackwell, 1986), 141f.

60. Ibid., 141, 146.

61. Ibid., 146.

62. Freeze, *Against the Grain,* 255.

63. Smith, "Black Talk and Hot Sex: Why 'Street Lit' Is Literature," 192.

WORKS CITED

50 Cent. *From Pieces to Weight: Once Upon a Time in Southside Queens.* New York: Pocket Books, 2005.

Anderson, Elijah. *Code of the Street: Decency, Violence, and the Moral Life of the Inner City.* New York: W. W. Norton, 1999.

Aristotle. *Poetics.* New York: Penguin Books, 1996.

Baldwin, Davarian L. "Black Empires, White Desires": The Spatial Politics of Identity in the Age of Hip-Hop." In *That's the Joint. The Hip-Hop Studies Reader,* edited by Mark Anthony Neal and Murray Forman. 159–176. New York: Routledge, 2004.

Barthes, Roland. *The Rustle of Language.* Oxford: Basil Blackwell, 1986.

Benjamin, J. M. Interview by the author Plainfield, NJ. July 3, 2010.

Booth, Wayne C. *The Rhetoric of Fiction.* 2nd ed. London: Penguin Books, 1991.

Cade Gibson, Simone. "Critical Readings: Adolescent African American Girls & Urban Fiction." Doctoral thesis, University of Maryland, 2009.

Campbell, Kermit E. *Gettin' Our Groove On: Rhetoric, Language, and Literacy for the Hip Hop Generation.* Detroit: Wayne State University Press, 2005.

Chiles, Nick. "Their Eyes Were Reading Smut." *New York Times,* January 4, 2006.

Clark, Wahida. Interview by the author. East Orange, NJ. December 15, 2009.

———. *Thugs and the Women Who Love Them.* New York: Dafina Books, 2004.

Debord, Guy. *The Society of the Spectacle.* Detroit: Black & Red, 1983.

Dubey, Madhu. *Signs and Cities: Black Literary Postmodernism.* Chicago: University of Chicago Press, 2003.

Dyson, Michael Eric. *Holler If You Hear Me: Searching for Tupac Shakur.* New York: Basic Civitas Books, 2001.

———. *Know What I Mean?: Reflections on Hip-Hop.* New York: Basic Civitas Books, 2007.

Freeze. *Against the Grain.* New York: One World, 2008.

Genette, Gérard. *Die Erzählung.* 2nd ed. München: Wilhelm Fink Verlag, 1998.

Goines, Donald. *Dopefiend.* Los Angeles: Holloway House, 2007 (1971).

———. *Whoreson.* Los Angeles: Holloway House, 2007 (1972).

———. *Inner City Hoodlum.* Los Angeles: Holloway House, 1992 (1975).

———. *Black Gangster.* Los Angeles: Holloway House, 2006 (1977).

Goldsby, Jacqueline: *A Spectacular Secret: Lynching in American Life and Literature.* Chicago: University of Chicago Press, 2006.

Hartman, Saidiya. *Scenes of Subjection: Terror, Slavery, and Self-Making in Nineteenth-Century America.* New York: Oxford University Press, 1997.

Hill Collins, Patricia. *Black Sexual Politics: African Americans, Gender, and the New Racism.* 2nd ed. New York: Routledge, 2004.

Holmes, Shannon. *Never Go Home Again.* New York: Atria Books, 2004.

hooks, bell. *Outlaw Culture: Resisting Representations.* New York: Routledge, 1994.

Hurston, Zora Neale. "Characteristics of Negro Expression." In *Within the Circle: An Anthology of African American Literary Criticism from the Harlem Renaissance to the Present,* Angelyn Mitchell, ed. 79–94. Durham, NC: Duke University Press, 1994.

Ibrahima, Sidibe. Interview by the author. New York City. January 10, 2009.

Jihad. Interview by the author. New York City. December 2, 2009.

Johnson, E. Patrick. *Appropriating Blackness. Performance and the Politics of Authenticity.* Durham, NC: Duke University Press, 2003.

Jones, Shanita. "Street Lit Novels and Triangle-Area Public Libraries: A Search through the Opacs (Online Public Access Catalogs)." Master's thesis, University of North Carolina at Chapel Hill, 2006.

Kelley, D. G. Robin. *Race Rebels: Culture, Politics, and the Black Working Class.* New York: The Free Press, 1996.

Lamont Hill, Marc. "(Re)Negotiating Knowledge, Power, and Identities in Hip-Hop Lit." Doctoral thesis, University of Pennsylvania, 2005.

Lubbock, Percy. *The Craft of Fiction.* London: Jonathan Cape, 1963.

Morris, Vanessa. "Inner City Teens Do Read." 2007. http://www.jahreinaresearch.info/urbanfiction/Inner%20City%20Teens%20Do%20Read.rtf.

Morrison, Jeana. "Sex, Violence, and Female Representation in Hip-Hop Fiction." Master's thesis, Temple University, 2007.

Nix, Taylor. "Nick Chiles: A Critical Look at Street Lit." *The Urban Book Source.* http://theubs.com/interviews/nick-chiles.php. 2009.

Perez, Biany. "The Politics of Gender in Hip-Hop Fiction." Master's thesis, Temple University, 2007.

Perry, Imani. *Prophets of the Hood: Politics and Poetics in Hip Hop.* Durham, NC: Duke University Press, 2004.

Plato. *Republic.* Indianapolis: Hackett, 1992.

Radway, Janice A. *Reading the Romance: Women, Patriarchy, and Popular Literature.* Chapel Hill: University of North Carolina Press, 1991.

Rose, Tricia. *Black Noise: Rap Music and Black Culture in Contemporary America.* Hanover, NH: University Press of New England, 1994.

Sartwell, Crispin. *Act Like You Know: African-American Autobiography and White Identity.* Chicago: University of Chicago Press, 1998.

Sharpley-Whiting, T. Denean. *Pimps up, Ho's Down: Hip Hop's Hold on Young Black Women.* New York: New York University Press, 2007.

Slim, Iceberg. *Trick Baby.* Los Angeles: Holloway House, 2004 (1967).

———. *Pimp: The Story of My Life.* Los Angeles: Holloway House, 2004 (1969).

Smith, Danyel. "Black Talk and Hot Sex: Why 'Street Lit' Is Literature." In *Total Chaos. The Art and Aesthetics of Hip-Hop,* edited by Jeff Chang, 188–197. New York: Basic Civitas Books, 2006.

Souljah, Sister. *The Coldest Winter Ever.* New York: Pocket Books, 1999.

Woods, Teri. *True to the Game* New York: Teri Woods Publishing, 1999.

———. *True to the Game 2.* New York: Grand Central Publishing, 2007.

———. *True to the Game 3.* New York: Grand Central Publishing, 2008.

PART TWO

ALTERNATIVE GENEALOGIES

SIX

PORTRAIT OF THE ARTIST AS A YOUNG SLAVE: VISUAL ARTISTRY AS AGENCY IN THE CONTEMPORARY NARRATIVE OF SLAVERY

EVIE SHOCKLEY

I

Among the illustrations appended to Harriet Jacobs's *Incidents in the Life of a Slave Girl. Written by Herself,* in the volume edited by Jean Fagan Yellin, is a copy of the advertisement placed in the papers by Jacobs's owner when she escaped from his control. It describes the twenty-one-year-old Jacobs and provides would-be apprehenders with a set of characteristics by which to identify her. Along with a description of her skin color, hair texture, and general manner, the ad sketches her apparel as follows: "Being a good seamstress, she has been accustomed to dress well, has a variety of very fine clothes, made in the prevailing fashion, and will probably appear, if abroad, tricked out in gay and fashionable finery."[1] Jacobs does not describe herself in her text as fashionably dressed—in part, I suspect, because her sense of modesty would have prevented her doing so. She dispenses with modesty in her narrative only to the degree necessary to achieve the primary end to which all of the "slave narratives" were written and published: to increase support for the abolition of slavery.[2] To this end, she permits—or we might say *forces*—herself to describe her sexuality as a young enslaved woman, particularly the chronic sexual harassment inflicted by her "master," his refusal to allow her to marry the (free black) man she loved, and her decision that rather than become the unwilling concubine of a man she despised, she would become the lover of a man of her own choosing. Thus, her narrative re-counts a dilemma—and a corresponding exercise of agency on the part of the enslaved—that might be understood to be "feminine," as opposed to the more "masculine" forms of resistance to bondage exemplified by the lives of Nat Turner and Frederick Douglass. Rather than plotting armed rebellion or physically fighting with her tormentor, Jacobs seeks freedom by allowing and encouraging the attentions of a wealthy, young white man who is kind to her. That is, she exercises a degree of freedom of choice, for one thing, and, moreover, secures the possibility that her lover, if as kind and enamored of her as he seemed, might purchase and free her outright.[3] One reason why *Incidents* is so important to the African American literary tradition, particularly the (ex-)slave narrative genre, is that the text's incorporation into the canon participated in expanding how we think about resistance to slavery—that it frequently took far less visible (but not invisible) forms than physical combat and overt rebellion.

Indeed, to return to the advertisement of Jacobs's escape and the reward for her capture, we might consider the extent to which Jacobs's attire was itself a visible form of resistance. Though Jacobs neither gives us an account of the dresses she sewed for herself nor assigns much significance to her talent for sewing, her narrative provides us with evidence of the social meaning of clothing in the small North Carolina town where she lived and beyond. In describing her childhood, she recalls "the scanty wardrobe" her mistress provided her, noting specifically "the linsey-woolsey dress given me every winter . . . How I hated it! It was one of the badges of slavery" (11). By setting aside the annual dress of coarse fabric that identified her as enslaved and making for herself "a variety of very fine clothes" (215), Jacobs used her sewing skills *creatively* in two senses. To make clothes not simply serviceable, but *fashionable*, is to make art; and to make art that enables one to replace "one of the badges of slavery" with clothes one can feel good about wearing is to resist subjugation. Though foregrounding her enjoyment of fine apparel within slavery probably would not have served Jacobs's purpose of creating pro-abolition sympathy, she could express her satisfaction at dressing her children well by cloaking that expression within the discourse of motherhood.[4] Thus she tells her reader that, while in hiding from her master, and unable to make her presence known to her son and daughter, she occupied herself with "making some new garments and little play-things" for their Christmas gifts and "had the pleasure of peeping at them [from her cramped, miserable hiding place] as they went into the street with their new suits on" (118). They may have been the "property" of their own father, but Jacobs's skill with the needle and textiles meant that they did not have to dress the part.

2

> "African religion . . . appeared in a form and a place in which whites would least expect African religious expression of any kind—in the quilts of slave women. Fashioned from throw-away cloth, slave quilts were used to clothe mysteries, to enfold those baptized with reinforcing symbols of their faith." . . . In the quilts themselves, textile approaches textuality.[5]
>
> —HARRYETTE MULLEN, "AFRICAN SIGNS AND SPIRIT WRITING"

I would like this discussion of artistry as agency in Jacobs's 1861 (ex-) slave narrative to serve as a backdrop for considering the same issue in two contemporary narratives of slavery: specifically, Thylias Moss's *Slave Moth: A Narrative in Verse*, published in 2004, and Edward P. Jones's novel, *The Known World*, winner of the 2004 Pulitzer Prize for Fiction. These texts have in common not only their slavery-era settings, but also the representation of enslaved characters as, among other things, visual artists. As such, they offer valuable support for the argument of this essay: that the significance of visual arts within African American literature, particularly as a means of communicating ideas about black subjectivity, has been underestimated and understudied.

I am using Arlene Keizer's term—"contemporary narratives of slavery"—to describe these texts, rather than the more commonly used "neo-slave narrative," for two reasons, the second of which relates directly to my discussion of *Incidents*. First, the latter term, as defined in Ashraf Rushdy's influential study of the genre, would exclude Jones' novel on the grounds that it fails to make the requisite formal gesture toward the (ex-)slave narratives—that is, *The Known World*, with its strikingly omniscient narrator, diverges from the first-person accounts that link the neo-slave narrative to the historical genre.[6] Keizer's term, while admittedly less compact, deliberately encompasses a broader range of works than either Bernard Bell's original classification or Rushdy's reinterpretation of it, which have in common an emphasis on the formal legacy of the (ex-)slave narratives. Keizer's "contemporary narratives of slavery" formulation embraces the works that might rightly be called neo-slave narratives, but uses a much more inclusive rubric. Her understanding of the genre divides it into three categories based largely on temporal, rather than formal, considerations: (1) texts in which slavery functions as setting for an antebellum or immediately postbellum historical tale, (2) those in which it emerges as a haunting presence in lives lived long after emancipation, and (3) texts that combine those two approaches through multiple narrators, time travel, or other such devices.[7] *Slave Moth* falls squarely into the first group, as does *The Known World,* with the exception of a few brief passages that cast the scope of the narrative into the mid-twentieth century.

The second reason I use Keizer's term is to signal my engagement herein with her articulation of the genre's defining preoccupation, reflected in the title of her compelling study: *Black Subjects: Identity Formation in the Contemporary Narrative of Slavery.* Her work concerns the tendency of African American writers to take up the era or institution of slavery in order to interrogate and theorize the development of black subjectivity. Building on the insights of scholars like Rushdy and Deborah McDowell, Keizer justifies her temporal conceptualization of the genre by arguing that the bridges these works repeatedly produce between past and present insist upon a relationship between the era of slavery and our contemporary moment that is grounded in "the necessity of resistance" to oppressive "physical, social, and psychological forces" confronting African Americans in both.[8] She concedes the validity of the question Saidiya Hartman poses in *Scenes of Subjection:* "How is it possible to think 'agency' when the slave's very condition of being or social existence is defined as a state of determinate negation . . . and [her] personhood refigured in the fetishized and fungible terms of object of property?"[9] Yet, according to Keizer, the writers of contemporary narratives of slavery collectively argue that we must not only think it, but *assume it.* She writes: "These [creative] writers seem to be telling us that denying the possibility of agency to the enslaved and recently freed constrains our own sense of agency in the late-twentieth and early twenty-first centuries."[10] In an era when the existence and significance of black subjectivity is regularly called into question by the popular notion that the U.S. has or should become (with the election of President Barack Obama) a "post-racial society," we may be particularly interested in what we can learn from an earlier period in which black subjectivity, indeed black humanity, was negated.

As already noted, we have learned to look for agency not only in such large-scale efforts as the armed rebellion but also in much more subtle forms of resistance; those expressions of agency that did not necessarily or immediately jeopardize one's survival. What fascinates me about *Slave Moth* and *The Known World* is that one of the central ways they figure black subjectivity and resistance to the social meaning of "slave" is through representations of enslaved characters as artists. Particularly striking is that, rather than casting their artist figures primarily as singers, musicians, or storytellers, as one might expect, Moss and Jones instead give us characters who create visual art—work that blends conceptual art, textile art, and writing, in the case of *Slave Moth,* and, in *The Known World,* blends plastic arts with performance art. This turn is unexpected insofar as it flies in the face of the logic that structures so much of African American literary theory and criticism (and, thus, structures the literary tradition itself), a logic that privileges the oral and the aural as sites of black expression and cultural memory.

Although it neither begins nor ends with Amiri Baraka (then LeRoi Jones), his assertion of the primacy of African American popular music over African American literature and other art forms, in his 1966 essay "The Myth of a 'Negro Literature,'" is certainly one of the most uncompromising articulations of that stance. It serves well as a particularly bracing and informative introduction to this cultural hierarchy. The essay opens:

From Phyllis [*sic*] Wheatley to Charles Chesnutt, to the present generation of American Negro writers, the only recognizable accretion of tradition readily attributable to the black producer of a formal literature in this country, with a few notable exceptions, has been of an almost agonizing mediocrity. In most other fields of "high art" in America, with the same few notable exceptions, the Negro contribution has been, when one existed at all, one of impressive mediocrity. Only in music, and most notably in blues, jazz, and spirituals, i.e., "Negro Music," has there been a significantly profound contribution by American Negroes.[11]

My point here is not to make a straw man of Baraka, who has long since revised his positions on this and many other things. But the logic that underwrites his still startling pronouncement has for decades continued to hold sway in theories of and critical approaches to African American literature. We might think of Houston Baker's *Blues, Ideology, and Afro-American Literature* or Tony Bolden's *Afro-Blue: Improvisation in African American Poetry and Culture,* as regards the aural, and Henry Louis Gates's *The Signifying Monkey* or Fahamisha Patricia Brown's *Performing the Word: African American Poetry as Vernacular Culture,* with regard to the oral, just for example. These studies have made potent and compelling arguments about the ways that African American music and African American vernacular speech patterns and forms have furnished material for the content and structure of a distinctive, or "authentic," African American literary tradition. On the other hand, without denying the importance of the aural and the oral to African American culture, some critics—such as Harryette Mullen, Nathaniel Mackey, and Aldon Nielsen—have argued that the privileged conceptual position accorded to those forms of expression overdetermines and impoverishes the African American literary tradition.[12] To the extent that "black music and black speech" begin to be more than rich cultural resources, and are constructed instead as tropes and tools that are deemed *essential* (in both senses of the word) to "authentic" or "relevant" work by African American artists, they participate in a problematic whittling down of the universe of our art.

Admittedly, to suggest that music and vernacular speech are more distinctively "black" than other forms of African American cultural production is to recognize, as Baraka argued, that there have been formidable material obstacles to the practice of other types of artistry, including writing, during slavery and beyond, insofar as African Americans were systematically denied education, often challenged by poverty (a bar to obtaining the equipment and media required for many art forms), and vulnerable to having the "artifacts" of cultural production deliberately destroyed.[13] But Mullen reminds us that constructions of African American literature that privilege orality obscure African traditions of writing that research has shown *did* survive the Middle Passage and the conditions of enslavement. These are traditions in which "writing" is understood to include literacy (in Arabic, for example), but not exclusively; rather, they also signify "indigenous script systems used for various religious purposes in their own cultural contexts."[14] This second type of writing, she argues, may productively be seen as linked to a tradition of African American writing other than the one beginning with the (ex-)slave narratives: namely, "African-American spirit writing."[15] African American spirit writing, like the (ex-)slave narrative, is a genre of early autobiographies by black writers; but where the latter describes a social transformation from enslaved to free, the former recounts a spiritual transformation or conversion, as in *The Life and Religious Experience of Jarena Lee.*[16] Importantly, Mullen connects both the African traditions of religious script and the related tradition of African American spirit writing to *visual arts* traditions. In doing so, she makes visible the points of convergence between work by such contemporary visual and performance artists as Romare Beardon, Alison Saar, and Robbie McCauley and such "visionary" writers as Toni Cade Bambara, Toni Morrison, and Gloria Naylor (among many others).[17] These mid to late twentieth century creators are generating work, she argues, that reconnects the spiritual and secular aspects of African culture that African American spirit writing represented as fused but which have developed over the years of African-descended people's presence in America into separate (or at least separable) elements of African American culture.[18]

This point brings us back to Moss and Jones, whose work demonstrates the relevance of this visual/visionary tradition to the ongoing, post-essentialist, poststructuralist conversations about forms of "authentic" black cultural production, by engaging the generic preoccupation of contemporary narratives of slavery with black subjectivity in their texts. Their texts encourage us to understand artistic imagination—expressed largely as writerly, visual, and conceptual art—as a form of resistance to limiting definitions of black identity, whether the objectifying status of "slave" imposed by (white) law during slavery, the legally and socially constructed concept of black "inferiority" that continues to color dominant culture to this day, or the restrictive notion of "authentic blackness" proposed by late-twentieth-century, black nationalist–inflected conceptions of race. In the second half of this essay, I begin to trace how each of these contemporary narratives of slavery represents artistic creativity, particularly in visual art forms, as critical expressions of the desire of enslaved African Americans for freedom *and* as a means of nurturing the desire for, or even moving towards, freedom.

3

"You are not what comes to mind when I think of slaves."

"I'm what comes to my mind when I think of slaves."[19]

—EXCHANGE BETWEEN RALLS JANET AND VARL IN *SLAVE MOTH*

Thylias Moss's narrative in verse, *Slave Moth,* functions fairly straightforwardly as a *künstlerroman,* a portrayal of its protagonist, the young enslaved girl, Varl, as a budding artist. Born into slavery, but literate from her early childhood, she has long been of interest to her "master," Peter Perry, for her "deformity": his word for her capacity to occupy the social status of "slave" without exhibiting most of the qualities commonly associated with (or attributed to) that condition (3, 5). Not only is she literate, but she has long been aware that his wife, Ralls Janet, who cannot read, is jealous of her knowledge and obvious intelligence—a jealousy that only increases as Varl, at 14, reaches puberty and becomes potentially of a different kind of interest to Perry. Leslie Hankins, discussing the implications of gender for our understanding of the *künstlerroman,* notes that the question for the developing (white) male artist is one of vocation— "'Will I be an artist or a banker?'"—whereas the (white) female artist confronts a question of identity: "'Will I be an artist or a woman?'"[20] Varl might well be expected to have a question of *order*—"Can I be an artist and a slave?"—if we take as evidence what Ralls Janet says to Varl in the passage that serves as the epigraph to this section. But Varl's response makes clear that Ralls Janet's question would not be her own; instead, Varl (and Moss) might ask: "*How* can I be an artist and a slave? And to what purpose?" *Slave Moth* attempts to answer these questions by linking Varl's development as an artist to her development of a free— or potentially free—subjectivity, even while she remains enslaved as a physical and social matter.

Moss takes great care to construct Varl not simply as smart, but also as *imaginative,* artistic. Varl's first-person narrative is vivid, highly visual, often lyrical, and full of delightful wordplay. Importantly, within the first pages of the book, we learn that we are not "overhearing" a speaker, as the conventions of lyric poetry would normally have it; rather, we are reading a text written by Varl—written, and yet not written. She explains:

> Starting tonight
> I won't write any more of my thoughts on paper
> though I did like to steal it from the master,
> Ralls Janet especially perturbed by that
> to the amusement of her husband;
> starting tonight
>
> on cloth I stitch my words,
> the larva drawing its silk back and forth
> through squares of cloth
>
> that will be luna wings . . . (7)

This passage makes clear that Varl *could* have written her narrative in the usual way, with pen and paper, if she wanted. Instead, she puts her time and energy into physically and artistically realizing a metaphor.

Her decision to sew her words, rather than simply write them, is her creative response to what she understands as an unspoken challenge from her master. He has left one of his books open to a page describing (and picturing) the luna moth, knowing—Varl insists—that she will come upon it during her work and feel compelled to read and learn. She goes him one better: not only does she absorb the information about the luna moth, she transforms it, first, into a metaphor for the process of becoming free, and then, into a work-of-art-in-progress that visually represents that metaphor *and* conceptually enacts her own transformation from enslaved to free:

> You can fit all of my name *Varl* into larva. You can fit all of my name into something that undergoes complete metamorphosis. (6)

Moss's genius is in simultaneously representing Varl's anagrammatic linguistic creativity and her visual imagination, which seizes on the idea of the cocoon and reworks it as squares of cloth that she can layer around her body under her clothes. In this way she figures Varl's resistance to enslavement (and, particularly, to the threat of sexual violation by Perry) as an exercising of artistic agency, an aesthetic process which requires both intellectual acumen and the talent to execute it. Significantly, Moss enlarges the implications of this proposition—artistry as agency—in two ways.

First, she focuses the reader on the essentially human characteristic of imagination, through Varl's repeated references to and demonstration of the mental work that goes into artistry. One chapter, "Sweet Enough Ocean, Cotton," seems to serve no purpose but that of allowing us to see Varl's imagination in action. Noting that she's never seen the sea, Varl imaginatively develops a description of the cotton field in contrast to such a body:

> It's not that the cotton seems watery
> or that each cotton seed hair is like
> a separate one of the sparkles the sun makes
> when light bounces in moving water,
>
> —though it is like that
> now that I think about it. (40)

Moss reenergizes the idiom "now that I think about it," making it work not simply as a constative statement, to mark the act of (re)thinking, but also as part of a performative statement, an enactment of the creative power the poet exercises in generating metaphor. That is, the second stanza of this passage does more than simply *report* a subjective, imaginative act, one in which Varl (on second thought, so to speak) conceives of one thing (cotton) in terms of another quite different thing (ocean); it actually *creates* the likeness between two (heretofore) unlike things. Now that she thinks of cotton as "watery," now that she reenvisions the "cotton seed hair" as "the sparkles the sun makes / . . . in moving water," "it *is* like that"—and henceforth she (and her readers) cannot help but see the watery-ness of something that had until then been firmly associated with the opposite of water (40, my emphasis). Moss thus insists that imagination is a powerful form of agency, whereby the enslaved subject can, in a sense, alter her world by perceiving it differently.

And, second, while the artistry Varl practices with her sewing makes this agency visible in a unique way, Moss enlarges the possibilities of artistry as agency by suggesting that such artistry is, in the first instance, a matter of intellect and thus within reach of large numbers of the enslaved, even those without access to literacy or the material resources available to Varl. As Varl explains in this same chapter, she can exercise her imagination even while laboring in the cotton field:

> I've been thinking about this.
> While I'm working, I think
> about this. My mind is the part of me
> that gets the least rest. (41)

In this passage, Moss takes particular advantage of the *other* genre in which she writes; this is a "narrative in verse," after all. Thus, she can employ the fundamentally poetic device of the line break to invite the reader to pause briefly and understand the second line of this stanza *as a line* (i.e., as a distinct unit of meaning)—"While I'm working, I think"—before turning to the subsequent line and the conclusion of the *sentence*. Using metaphor, line break, and repetition, then, Moss underscores the conceptual, intellectual aspect of Varl's artistry—a direct challenge to the received image of the "slave" as impossibly befogged by mind-numbing drudgery and educational deprivation.

Moss further precludes our considering Varl the anomaly that Peter Perry makes her out to be, by describing Varl's artistic practice in a way that revises a moment in Toni Morrison's *Beloved*. Varl's cocoon of cloth squares is made of material that "[s]hould . . . have gone to some new curtains, / tablecloths, sheets, new clothes" for the Perry household, material that Varl has stolen, along with the buttons she uses to fasten them to each other (Moss, 93, 8). This practice recalls for Morrison's readers the then-14-year-old Sethe's determination to celebrate her marriage to Halle with, if not a wedding, at least a wedding dress. Like Varl, Sethe sews together pieces of fabric—"two pillow cases," "a dresser scarf," and an "old sash"—borrowed without permission from here and there around her owners' house.[21] Telling the story twenty years later, Sethe represents her effort as an aesthetic failure, unlike Varl, who at one point writes of her cocoon: "The only grace there is, is in the beauty of these / intricate stitches" (61). Still, Moss asks us to re-read Sethe's insistence upon a material marker of her marriage as a projection of artistic imagination that also serves as a rejection of the supposed difference between her and her mistress. The resonance between the two narratives undercuts the false

equation of illiteracy—forcibly the condition of most of the enslaved—
with unintelligence; in light of Varl's cocoon, Sethe's dress becomes all
the more clearly a text that reads as resistance.[22] By the same token, the
dress's function as a "ritual object," conferring a spiritual or sacred significance to Sethe and Halle's marital union that their owners refused to
recognize, redounds to the sense in which the text on Varl's cocoon offers
the kind of "protective power" for which African "spirit-script" was valued.[23] Within the space marked off by her stitched script, Varl is "Free"
to imagine freedom.

4

> As he took up the knife, Alice ... danced down the lane and stood before
> him with her hands on her hips. They had rarely spoken because nothing
> she said ever made sense. "Whatcha makin now?" she said, surprising
> him. "Somethin for my boy." "Well, you just make it good, make it to last,"
> Alice said.[24]
>
> —EDWARD P. JONES, "THE KNOWN WORLD"

Edward P. Jones offers no suggestion in *The Known World* that field work
and creative practice go hand-in-hand. His two primary artist figures,
Elias and Alice, wait until the workday is done to take up their respective nocturnal artistic practices. *The Known World* is set in Manchester County, Virginia, where not just one, but a handful of black families
participate in the "Peculiar Institution" as members of the slaveholding
class. Elias, a man whose love of freedom is matched only by his love for
his family, does not bother to be shocked by the fact that his "master,"
Henry Townsend, is African American. While another man enslaved to
Townsend wonders what this unusual situation suggested about God,
Jones's narrator tells us that Elias found the whole world order illogical:
"Elias had never believed in a sane God and so had never questioned a
world in which colored people could be the owners of slaves, and if at
that moment, in the near dark, he had sprouted wings, he would not have
questioned that either. He would simply have gone on making the doll"
(9). The doll referred to here is to be a gift for his eldest daughter, whittled
from a piece of pinewood and adorned with corn silk for hair. His artistry

is challenged by the dim light available, but luckily his knife seems to rely upon his inner vision, rather than his eyes. In contrast to Varl's explicit, stitched meditations on freedom, the connection between Elias's artistry and freedom is only implied, but with masterful subtlety: "The right leg of the doll was giving him trouble: He wanted the figure to be running but he had not been able to get the knee to bend just right. Someone seeing it might think it was just a doll standing still, and he didn't want that" (9). That Elias was thrice a runaway before falling in love and starting his family illuminates the significance of the running doll he carves for his daughter, as well as the horse, the boat, and the bird he later carves for his sons: they all represent resistance, his aesthetic rendering of the love of freedom, the capacity for flight, that he has not given up and hopes to pass on to them. His daughter, freed as a very young woman by the termination of American slavery, kept the doll to the end of her ninety-seven years, which suggests, among other things, that in 1947 she still had call for a talisman of freedom (67).

Another significant artist figure in Jones' novel is Alice, who—as the story goes—was kicked in the head by a mule on her previous "owner's" farm, which knocked all the sense out of her. "A good worker," but seemingly unable to put two coherent sentences together, Alice is just crazy enough to go wandering at night—out of her cabin, around the Townsend plantation, and all over the county—all the while chanting and singing "nonsense" at the top of her lungs (269, 75). The first few times, the patrollers, who are more than a little spooked by her (pun intended), haul her back to the plantation for Henry Townsend to deal with, but when it becomes clear that nothing short of tying her up will keep her home nights, her nocturnal rambles become part of the landscape. When she encounters the patrollers, her madness kicks into high gear: she dances around, accuses their horses of telling lies on her, urges the men to dance with her, tells their morbid fortunes, flashes them a view beneath her dress. "Sometimes," Jones writes:

> when the patrollers had tired of their own banter . . . they would sit their horses and make fun of her as she sang darky songs in the road. *This show* was best when the moon was at its brightest, shining down on them and easing their fear of the night and of a mad slave woman and lighting up Alice as she danced to the songs (13, emphasis added).

Jones portrays Alice as a minstrel without blackface, whose nightly "show" of "darky songs" and dances, comedy routines, and other entertaining acts passes for black insanity because of the way it simultaneously confirms and defies the patrollers' stereotypes about the enslaved people.

Obviously, Alice's "show" is composed largely of oral and aural elements; however, I would argue that she is not engaged in the *performing* arts as much as *performance* art, in which the emphasis is on the concept or ideas being explored in the piece, rather than the act and quality of the performing. Over the course of the novel, we come to realize that Alice's "madness" is wholly subterfuge: she is not a madwoman giving free reign to an urge to make a joyful noise; she is crazy like a fox, giving a tightly controlled performance of madness in order to obtain a mobility normally denied to the enslaved. The concepts her performance explores are freedom and knowledge. She gains an unusual freedom to move about at night, letting the loudness and persistence of her mesmerizing act assure her audience that she has no plans of escape, then uses her mobility to help fugitives move through the county toward a greater freedom. In the process, Alice learns every inch of Manchester County, which she proves in the final act of her performance. By "final act" I do not mean the last time she sings and dances for the patrollers, but rather her production and display of two works of visual art in Washington, D.C., the city to which she escapes when she herself ultimately flees. As Calvin, her former owner's brother-in-law, describes them, the first work is "an enormous wall hanging, a grand piece of art that is part tapestry, part painting, and part clay structure—all in one exquisite Creation," "a wondrous thing," "a map of life" that depicts "what God sees when He looks down on Manchester" (384). The second, made of the same combination of mixed media, "may well be even more miraculous" than the first: a God's-eye view of the Townsend plantation and all of the people who lived there when Alice did, with "nothing missing, not a cabin, not a barn, not a chicken, not a horse" (385). He affirms that "every single person is there, standing and waiting as if for a painter and his easel to come along and capture them in the glory of the day" (385).

The culmination of Alice's performance and the culmination of the novel converge in these two magnificent works of art. By calling them "maps," Jones invites a comparison between the precise knowledge Alice gained during her enslavement in Manchester County and the decidedly imperfect knowledge obtained by the European "explorers" of North and South America, as represented on the map that gives the book its title. This map, which hangs in the county jail, symbolizes the collective achievement of Europe, insofar as the narrator takes pains to note that it was created by a German, who was living in France, and sold to the sheriff of Manchester County by a Russian (174). The map's legend is headed with the ironic phrase "The Known World"—ironic because "the land of North America on the map was smaller than it was in actuality, and where Florida should have been, there was nothing" (174). The European cartographer uses flawed, secondhand information acquired in the quest to exploit the land and peoples of the two continents called "America," and produces a "hideous," misrendered map that arrogantly announces its own erroneous authority (174). The contrast between this map and the gorgeous, exquisitely accurate tapestries created by Alice Night could not be more dramatic. The beauty and detail of Alice's artwork underscores her creative process, which is grounded in firsthand experience and an intimate knowledge of the landscape acquired for the selfless purpose of helping others flee from slavery. Calvin calls her first work a "vision," identifying Alice as one of the "African-American visionary folk artists" Mullen describes in her essay, who understood their divinely inspired art to "superced[e] human authority" (174).[25]

Such an understanding of the power of, and their relationship to, the divine must have been a part of what kept African American subjects focused on the goal of freedom through the long era of slavery in the U.S. While the importance of black speech and black music to African American literature and culture should not be diminished, the role of the visual arts in representing black subjectivity and expressing the enslaved black subject's desire for freedom needs to be more fully accounted for, as contemporary narratives of slavery like *Slave Moth* and *The Known World* clearly suggest. The small wood sculptures Elias carves, no less than the majestic mixed media hangings created by Alice, demonstrate the eloquence of the uneducated and remind us of the interconnection of visual art with the everyday lives of even the poorest people. And the transformative narrative produced by Varl, deliberately sewn onto a wearable cloth "cocoon" rather than inscribed on paper, reminds us of the protective, nurturing function served by African American visionary writing, like the noncommunicative African script systems to which it hearkens back.

NOTES

1. Jacobs, 215. Hereinafter cited in text.

2. The name of this genre has been criticized for being inaccurate in relation to the identity of the genre's writers and for unintentionally reifying the system its writers were fighting against. On the former point, see Harryette Mullen's "African Signs and Spirit Writing," in which she uses the alternative term "the ex-slave narratives." On the latter point, Sonia Sanchez has noted: "Some people call them slave narratives but I like to call them Freedom narratives," specifically because they document "this whole idea" that an enslaved person "could free himself"—the longing for and journey towards freedom being key to her understanding of the genre (56).

3. As Jacobs writes, poignantly and insightfully: "It seems less degrading to give one's self, than to submit to compulsion. There is something akin to freedom in having a lover who has no control over you, except that which he gains by kindness and attachment" (55).

4. This gesture might be seen as an additional way that Jacobs's narrative, in Stephanie Li's terms, "presents motherhood as a force that resists slavery and its supporters," using the powerful social significance of motherhood to gain readers' sympathy for acts of resistance that would otherwise have been perceived as unmitigatedly shocking and damning. Li, "Motherhood as Resistance," 15.

5. Mullen, "African Signs and Spirit Writing," 676, 677.

6. I make this distinction not as a criticism of Rushdy, but in order to preserve the specificity of his term, which is often used more broadly to refer to any twentieth-century fictional treatment of slavery. Specifically, Rushdy defines "Neo-slave narratives" as "contemporary novels that assume the form, adopt the conventions, and take on the first-person voice of the antebellum slave narrative." Rushdy, *Neo-slave Narratives*, 3. His study takes off from Bernard Bell's initial identification of the genre using the term "neoslave narrative" (without the capitalization or the hyphen), which Bell described as "a residually oral, modern narrative of escape from bondage to freedom." Bell, *Contemporary African American Novel*, 199. Except when quoting these scholars, I use the now-standard spelling "neo-slave narrative" to refer to the genre.

7. Keizer, *Black Subjects*, 2.

8. Keizer, *Black Subjects*, 8.

9. Hartman, *Scenes of Subjection*, 52. For Keizer's discussion of Hartman's question, see *Black Subjects*, 16.

10. Keizer, *Black Subjects*, 17.

11. Jones, "Myth," 105–106.

12. See, e.g., Mullen's essays "African Signs and Spirit Writing" and "'Incessant Elusives': The Oppositional Poetics of Erica Hunt and Will Alexander"; Mackey's *Discrepant Engagement: Dissonance, Cross-Culturality, and Experimental Writing;* and Nielsen's *Black Chant: Languages of African-American Postmodernism.*

13. Jones, "Myth," 110–11.

14. Mullen, "African Signs and Spirit Writing," 671.

15. Ibid.

16. Lee's book, published in 1836, was the first extended autobiography by an African American woman.

17. Mullen, "African Signs and Spirit Writing," 686–87.

18. As Mullen describes it, "African-American culture [is] marked by a productive tension between individuality and collectivity, and between the sacred and the secular, aspects of everyday life that African cultures had worked to integrate seamlessly through communal rituals that forged collective identities and assured human beings of their significance in the universe." She argues that this African cultural perspective was more substantially preserved in the African American spirit writing tradition than in the (ex-)slave narrative tradition. "African Signs and Spirit Writing," 686.

19. Moss, *Slave Moth*, 136. Hereinafter cited in text.

20. Hankins, "Alas, Alack! or A Lass, A Lack?," 394.

21. Morrison, *Beloved*, 58–59.

22. See Keizer, *Black Subjects*, 28, for a brief discussion of another way of conceiving of Sethe's improvisational dress-making as resistant agency.

23. Mullen, "African Signs and Spirit Writing," 686, 672.

24. Jones, *Known World*, 78. Hereinafter cited in text.

25. Mullen, "African Signs and Spirit Writing," 674.

WORKS CITED

Baker, Houston A., Jr. *Blues, Ideology, and Afro-American Literature: A Vernacular Theory.* Chicago: University of Chicago Press, 1984.

Bell, Bernard W. *The Contemporary African American Novel: Its Folk Roots and Modern Literary Branches.* Amherst: University of Massachusetts Press, 1987.

Bolden, Tony. *Afro-Blue: Improvisations in African American Poetry and Culture.* Urbana: University of Illinois Press, 2004.

Brown, Fahamisha Patricia. *Performing the Word: African American Poetry as Vernacular Culture.* New Brunswick, NJ: Rutgers University Press, 1999.

Gates, Henry Louis, Jr. *The Signifying Monkey: A Theory of African-American Literary Criticism.* New York: Oxford University Press, 1988.

Hankins, Leslie Kathleen. "Alas, Alack! or A Lass, A Lack? Quarrels of Gender and Genre in the Revisionist *Künstlerroman:* Eudora Welty's *The Golden Apples.*" *Mississippi Quarterly* 44, no. 4 (1991): 391–409.

Hartman, Saidiya V. *Scenes of Subjection: Terror, Slavery, and Self-Making in Nineteenth-Century America.* New York: Oxford University Press, 1997.

Jacobs, Harriet A. *Incidents in the Life of a Slave Girl. Written by Herself.* Jean Fagan Yellin, ed. Cambridge, MA: Harvard University Press, 1987.

Jones, Edward P. *The Known World.* New York: Amistad/HarperCollins, 2004.

Jones, LeRoi. "The Myth of a 'Negro Literature.'" In *Home: Social Essays,* 105–115. New York: Morrow, 1966.

Keizer, Arlene. *Black Subjects: Identity Formation in the Contemporary Narrative of Slavery.* Ithaca: Cornell University Press, 2004.

Lee, Jarena. *The Life and Religious Experience of Jarena Lee*. 1836. Reprinted in *Sisters of the Spirit: Three Black Women's Autobiographies of the Nineteenth Century*. Edited by William L. Andrews, ed. Bloomington: Indiana University Press, 1986.

Li, Stephanie. "Motherhood as Resistance in Harriet Jacobs' *Incidents in the Life of a Slave Girl*." *Legacy* 23, no. 1 (2006): 14–29.

Mackey, Nathaniel. *Discrepant Engagement: Dissonance, Cross-Culturality, and Experimental Writing*. Tuscaloosa: University of Alabama Press, 1993.

Morrison, Toni. *Beloved*. New York: Plume/Penguin, 1987.

Moss, Thylias. *Slave Moth: A Narrative in Verse*. New York: Persea, 2004.

Mullen, Harryette. "African Signs and Spirit Writing." *Callaloo* 19, no. 3 (1996): 670–689.

———. "'Incessant Elusives': The Oppositional Poetics of Erica Hunt and Will Alexander." In *Holding Their Own: Perspectives on the Multi-Ethnic Literatures of the United States*, Dorothea Fischer-Hornung and Heike Raphael-Hernandez, eds., 207–216. Tübigngen: Stauffenburg Verlag, 2000.

Nielsen, Aldon Lynn. *Black Chant: Languages of African American Postmodernism*. New York: Cambridge University Press, 1997.

Rushdy, Ashraf H. A. *Neo-slave Narratives: Studies in the Social Logic of a Literary Form*. New York: Oxford University Press, 1999.

Sanchez, Sonia. "Interview with Sonia Sanchez." By Larvester Gaither. In *Conversations with Sonia Sanchez*, edited by Joyce A. Joyce, 47–61. Jackson: University of Mississippi Press, 2007.

SEVEN

VARIATIONS ON THE THEME: BLACK FAMILY, NATIONHOOD, LESBIANISM, AND SADOMASOCHISTIC DESIRE IN MARCI BLACKMAN'S PO MAN'S CHILD

CARMEN PHELPS

"... we can stop this train. White man may have put us on it, but we're the ones who stayed on board. And we're the ones who can step off, any time we please."

—"PO," FROM MARCI BLACKMAN'S *PO MAN'S CHILD*

In the novel *Po Man's Child*, Marci Blackman's character Po deliberately and secretly cuts herself. In such moments of extreme pain and escapism, through fantasy and role playing, Po asserts an authority that violates heterosexist expectations of the broader black community. Yet even through Po's own admission, her engagement in sadomasochistic practices is linked to her attempts to render herself visible within the black community. Thus, Po's immersion in what is conventionally believed to be alternative, radical, and indeed threatening approaches to achieving such legitimacy is in fact consistent with the broader, collective desires among black Americans to achieve racial, social, and political visibility within mainstream American culture.

Readers may be resistant to accept Blackman's character as exemplary of the cultural ideals explicated within the heteronormative conventions of the black vernacular tradition, which perpetuate and reflect patterns of cultural kinship through various mediums of expression and performance. However, as I will demonstrate in this essay, Po's lesbianism and sadomasochistic practices serve as more than what readers might (and indeed Po's family and community *do*) determine to be "problematic" and/or disruptive behavior patterns, and are instead viable means through which it becomes possible and indeed necessary to consider what Hortense Spillers refers to as the "discursive and iconic fortunes and misfortunes, facilities, abuses, or plain absences that tend to travel from one generation of [black] kinswomen to another" (152–153). Spillers's insights provide a rationale for my evaluation of Po's lesbian character alongside two of her female literary predecessors or "kinswomen"—Renay from Ann Allen Shockley's *Loving Her* (1974), and Dana from Octavia Butler's *Kindred* (1979). Furthermore, I argue that Blackman's character, Po, represents the author's experimentation with specific conventions of the black vernacular tradition via the treatment of sexual performance in ways that consequently belie the assumption of Po's deviancy and confirm her deeply rooted kinship ties to her immediate and broader cultural community. As Samuel Delaney points out, even as sadomasochism is perceived as a socially deviant act, it is "just an appetite. . . . It needs to exist—and always-already has—in a *social* world," and can be understood as both an expression of difference and/or deviancy just as it is capable of mimicking mainstream or "missionary" sexual and political paradigms of expression.[1] Ultimately, such experimentation can be useful to our thinking about the placement of LGBTQI perspectives within the black vernacular tradition.

When Po chooses to have her partner Mary inflict pain upon her, she is doing so to avoid the effects of a family curse, referred to as the "Curse of Uncle George," which is believed to be the source of every member of her family's dysfunctionality, including her own. Simply put, each member of Po's family suffers from what can be interpreted as depression—a diagnosis which carries with it its own set of stigmas within the black community. According to Po's Aunt Florida,

> What made folks look at Uncle George sideways was that every time he ran and got caught, the lashing he gave himself was worse than any the overseer could have imagined. All told, he ran five times through entanglements of birches, poplars, and chokeberries, looking for something called freedom. And each time, after the overseer brought him

back and made an example of him, Uncle George found some way to mutilate himself even further. The fifth time he ran was his last. The overseer was nearly doubled over in hysterics when he brought him back, like he couldn't wait to see what new castigation Uncle George had in store for himself. He wouldn't wait long. As soon as he cut him loose, before he could gather his wits to stop him, Uncle George reached for the overseer's rifle, stuck the barrel inside his mouth and blew his head off. Rushing death or not, if being was truly the same as dying, Uncle George had finally found freedom. (Blackman, 54)

While Aunt Florida's interpretation of Uncle George's fate and its haunting legacy for Po's family may justify Po's self-destructive behavior and depression, in creating a black lesbian character who willingly engages in sadomasochism as a means of combating emotional "numbness," Blackman is in no way playing it safe. As scholar Alycee Lane notes,

> Nella Larsen's *Quicksand* (1925) and *Passing* (1929); the poetry of Harlem Renaissance writers Angelina Weld Grimke, Alice Dunbar-Nelson, and Georgia Douglass Johnson; the early poetry of Audre Lorde—all of these works are to some degree marked by an unmistakably and yet concealed homoerotics, "lesbian themes" played out, perhaps in as safe a way as possible. The times in which these writers were writing did not provide the space for them to tell explicitly—if, in fact, they desired to do so—a black lesbian story. (v)

Lane goes on to cite how Civil Rights, Black Power, Women's Liberation, New Left, and gay liberation movements, for example, helped to create literary spaces in which GLBTQ- themed works found increasing marketability and earned more critical attention. Yet despite such progress, scholars remain resistant to engage texts like *Po Man's Child,* which not only challenge the canonical edifice of the black literary tradition but also progressively advance the conventions of the black lesbian literary tradition. Po's lifestyle is defined as much by episodes of violence and self-inflicted pain within the scope of her lesbian relationship as it is by her cultural kinship with her immediate family and her mindfulness of a traumatized ancestral past. Thus, through its courageous treatment of social stigmas, the novel effectively highlights the intertwined cultural fates of black mainstream and black LGBTQI communities.

Po's engagement in sadomasochistic acts is a response to the curse and meant to arouse her ability to experience depth of emotion and feeling. Such episodes are painful yet effective reminders of her emotional and physical presence:

> Before I know it, for a while anyway, the numbness is nowhere to be found . . . I rarely flinch or falter. The real reason Mary stops is because she's had enough. She only stops me because she knows I want her to . . . She's never truly understood the numbness that stalks me. Truth is, the levels of pain I endure frighten her. And the thought that I might enjoy the pain is something she doesn't want to think about . . . (Blackman, 11)

Po's ability to come to terms with the painful realities of her life, as well as the trauma of witnessing the self-destructive behavior of other members of her family is contingent upon her ability to combat her emotional numbness through extreme and convincing pain. Her efforts to do so are futile if she is incapable of feeling, which compels her to do what she must to convince herself that she is indeed alive and breathing, hence the physical punishment. Ironically, her lover Mary's enactment of an abusive "master" to that of Po's "slave" in one of their sadomasochistic role-playing moments serves as the ultimate symbolic and physical act that propels Po into a tortured yet life affirming state that forces her to confront her demons.

As both a demonized figure that complicates ideals of black empowerment and community, as well as a symbol of racial and sexual visibility and legitimacy, Po's character is indeed discursively complex. Her own description of what ensues between herself and her lover, Mary, during their S/M episodes is in fact more technical than it is erotic or emotional:

> "it's an act," she says. ". . . a game we play. Mary picks a spot on my body, any spot; tests how hard she can pinch or bite it, how deep she can cut it, or how long she can burn it. While I recount—without flinching—a story that's never happened. Mary got the idea from a book one of her fag friends loaned her called *Intellectual S/M*. I was curious to see how long my imagination would hold out. How long I could keep the story going . . . (Blackman, 11)

Certainly, Po's character epitomizes some of the most complicated yet interlinked taboos regarding race, sexuality, and sexual practice. As theorist Patricia Hill Collins reminds us, "Reducing Black lesbians to their sexuality, one that chooses women over men, reconfigures Black lesbians as enemies of Black men" (69). Collins's assessment is relevant to the way in which Po's brother, Bobby, comments on her interracial lesbian relationship with her white lover, referring to it as that which is tantamount to a "sickness," a "white man's disease"—a sentiment that cripples Po's ability to participate in the fulfillment of a black family and/or ideal concept of black nationhood. When Bobby asks Po, "What, you don't think you sick?" and Po responds, "No, Bobby, I don't. No sicker than you and the rest of the world" (Blackman, 206), her comment simultaneously confirms her identification with the historical roots of social alienation and exclusion that traumatize the black community, as well as her resistance to her brother's attempts to exclude her.

Such trends to "silence" these populations exist within academic discourses as well, particularly those that focus on black literary expression as a medium for evaluating black vernacular traditions. Generally speaking, these discourses assume the marginality and "outsider" status of LGBTQI or gay, lesbian, bisexual, transgender, and "questioning" writers and/or communities while policing and preserving an ostensibly heterosexual, exclusive, and *palatable* version of the black vernacular tradition. Indeed, texts such as *Po Man's Child* rightfully occupy spaces within the black American writing experience as part of the broader vernacular tradition that continues to be integral to identity construction for black Americans and remains essential to the preservation of cultural, artistic, and political legacies.

For some readers, it may seem ironic that Blackman's courageous exploration of racial and sexual taboos, including suicide, S/M practices, interracial desire, and lesbianism actually engages universal aspects of the black American vernacular tradition, Therefore, the novel can be evaluated as exemplary of rather than as a threat to this cultural tradition and its import. Consider Po's conversation with her brother Bobby, a converted Muslim who's fighting a drug addiction, but who continues to judge Po for her response to the trauma of a troubling family history rooted in patterns of self-inflicted punishment and abuse as a way of avoiding pain. When Bobby tries to explain his addiction to Po, he says:

"What, you think I'm just runnin' away?"
"We all are," I said without looking up.
"Then why you still here?," he asked.

"Oh, I'm gone," I said quietly. "Just chose a different path, that's all."

"Uh-huh. You be runnin' to them knives." When I looked up he was smiling, like he was holding something sinister just above my head. I just stared at him.

"Yeah, I know," he said, still smiling. "May look all fucked up in the head, but I know what's goin on. That's why you wearin' all them clothes . . ."

"Better than sticking needles in my veins." Now it was my turn to smile.

"Oh yeah? Do it work?," he asked, feeling a little too smug.

"What do you mean?" . . .

"Do it get rid of the numbness, girl?" He mouthed the words slowly, as if he'd read my mind. "You know what I mean."

I was stunned. I knew exactly what he was going to say, and it still caught me off guard. The numbness. Out loud, it sounded so airy, so light, so . . . phony. Yet there it was, night and day, as real as I was, wreaking havoc in our lives. (Blackman, 194–195)

Not only is the mutual awareness between Po and her brother regarding their individual afflictions made clear in this scene, but the exchange also confirms that they are each responding to an acknowledged and shared pain. While Bobby sees her sexuality as deviant, Po reminds him that he is guilty of his own form of social deviancy, rendering them both susceptible to the moral scrutiny of the black community. As this scene affirms their psychological connectedness as siblings, readers also see the extent to which they are both afflicted by the same source—a painful, oppressive past—and each character recognizes the other's struggle to overcome their demons. Although they remain combative toward one another throughout the novel, the foundation of their trauma is discussed openly in this conversation as each of them identify with the other's psychological "numbness." In this way, Blackman aligns Po with Bobby, and her otherwise alienated status is reconfigured within the boundaries of her family's fate.

In his ambitious project *The Contemporary African American Novel: Its Folk Roots and Modern Literary Branches,* published in 2004, scholar Bernard Bell calls for "a reinvigorated discourse on the liberating impact of vernacular and literary cultural production by African American novelists and on continuity and change in the tradition of the African American novel" (xiv). He continues by saying that he is "committed to an aesthetic that imaginatively seeks to challenge and change insidious contemporary language and other institutional manifestations of the system of anti-black racism in the U.S." (xvi). Unfortunately, the black American folk vernacular tradition is often explored in ways that mute the perspectives of LGBTQI writers and their characters, even though these perspectives have progressively shaped our collective black vernacular, aesthetic, and novel traditions. In Bell's project, LGBTQI literature is discussed alongside other "fringe" genres, including science and detective fiction, while more popular genres and writers that he discusses within the context of the black American folk vernacular tradition are organized in lengthier, separate chapters. This is but one example of the ways in which "alternative" and less commercial works continue to be perceived on the margins and perhaps on the outside of the black American vernacular and writing traditions. Although I hesitate to go so far as to suggest that Bell's critique is "essentialist," I think that projects such as his run the risk of conforming to a problem that bell hooks identifies within the context of her critique of postmodernism.

> [Black folks] are empowered to recognize multiple experiences of black identity that are the lived conditions which make diverse cultural production possible. When this diversity is ignored, it is easy to see black folks as falling into two categories: nationalist or assimilationist, black-identified or white-identified . . .
>
> Given the various crises facing African Americans (economic, spiritual, escalating racial violence, etc.), we are compelled by circumstance to reassess our relationship to popular culture and resistance struggle. Many of us are as reluctant to face this task as many non-black postmodern thinkers who focus theoretically on the issue of "difference" are to confront the issue of race and racism. (*Feminist Literary Theory*, 706)

Indeed, as hooks suggests, unless black scholars in particular see the urgency of recognizing the ways in which the black vernacular tradition has been perpetuated by and indeed survives through diverse rather than monolithic responses to oppression—including those responses that expose the experiences of an increasingly visible LGBTQI community—we run the risk of imitating white, racist paradigms that continue to deny the legitimacy of black artistic and cultural expression as a whole.

Blackman's novel reflects a fairly recent exploration of the theme of sexual difference in the form of sadomasochistic practices as a radical but nonetheless conceivable approach to asserting visibility; however, Ann

Allen Shockley's *Loving Her,* published in 1974, also addresses a version of sexual deviancy in the form of domestic violence as it relates to the construction of a black lesbian character. The protagonist, Renay, suffers emotional and physical abuse at the hands of Jerome Lee, her abusive and controlling husband, who becomes violent when he finds out that Renay intends to divorce him and becomes especially hostile when he learns that she has been involved in a sexual relationship with Terry, an affluent white woman. The "numbing" sensation that Blackman's character Po refers to as part of her sadomasochistic experience has partial roots in Shockley's earlier fiction, where we see Renay, Po's literary predecessor, suffer the consequences of her decision to leave Jerome Lee:

> The blow came swiftly, knocking her against the wall. She felt the others following like a rain of shocks, fists pounding, hitting her face, breasts, stomach. She fell to the floor, tasting the bile rising to her lips. His foot kicked her side and pain streaked white slivers of heat throughout her body. . . . She rolled onto her stomach, throwing her arms around her head to protect her face. She tried to scream over the pain, the horror, and in her *numbness* thought something had come out, but it was only the blood trickling down the corners of her mouth. (132, emphasis mine)

Renay's ability to feel anything in this scene—even pain—is denied by Jerome Lee. His attack on her is a literal and symbolic attempt to eradicate her existence, which he perceives as a threat to his black manhood. As the narrator states, "He had married her, but in the long run, wouldn't it have been better if he hadn't? Marriage isn't always the best solution. He would forever feel the arrogant black knight-errant who had done the right thing by a black maiden in distress—a noble deed performed in the name of honor" (Shockley, 129).

Jerome Lee's suggestion that Renay's relationship with Terry undermines his authority and privilege as a black man implicates her disruption of the black family heteronormative ideal. "Have you loved *me*?" he asks (Shockley, 129). Yet it is his own hurtful behavior that leads to the demise of the family, when his attempt to kidnap their daughter, Denise, results in a fatal accident. In the wake of losing her only child, Renay realizes that the only way to preserve herself and move forward is to liberate herself from Jerome Lee's toxic version of normalcy, projecting a conventional, mythologized concept of black manhood in particular and the black family, that is, black nationhood in general.

Like Po, Renay must give herself permission to "feel" and be awakened to her own potential as a necessary step in claiming authority over her body, refusing to be resigned to the margins. She allows herself to experience "that which was stronger than words" with her white lover, Terry, in the form of "touches, kisses, and movements." In addition, both Po and Renay allude to a reinvention of themselves characterized by contrasting images of darkness and light. Compare Renay's experiences of "waiting for the morning, which promised to be even better than the night" after making love to Terry, with Po's "I never understood that the shadows' tales, by nature, were false. Had to be. That the real story, the one worth telling, was buried deep beneath the fabric of suggestion, the interception of light" (Shockley, 187; Blackman, 234). In each instance, the characters express an enlightened state of being achievable only through physical suffering and as a consequence of allowing themselves to be reborn despite the painful process of psychological rebirth.

The conscious act of combating "numbness" for black female heroines is also reminiscent of the experiences of Octavia Butler's character Dana in the novel *Kindred*, published in 1979. Like Po, Dana exhibits a penetrating, alienating "numbness" that dissolves only after she is fantastically transported two hundred years back in time to pre-emancipation Maryland, where she must ensure the birth of her ancestor and preserve her family lineage. Dana is also involved in an interracial, though heterosexual, relationship with her white fiancé, Kevin, who comments on Dana's apathetic, zombie-like demeanor when meeting her, an implication of Dana's alienation from her family and past (Butler, 53).

The first few lines of *Kindred* read like a confession by Dana, as she makes a seemingly illogical statement that she has somehow lost her left arm on the last occasion during which she's summoned back in time by her white slaveholding ancestor, Rufus Weylin (Butler, 9). Indeed, such an opening foretells the extent to which Dana's life as a modern black woman living in post–Civil Rights California will be threatened both physically and psychologically in light of her journeys back to the antebellum period, where she finds herself having to protect her white, racist ancestor if she is to preserve her family's past and assure its future.

Thus, it is Dana's ability to endure the physical trauma of slavery that leads to her heightened sense of consciousness about her place in her family's past and which motivates her to ensure its preservation. Similarly, Dana's literary sister and successor, Po, tests her own ability to survive and endure physical pain in the process of realizing her place in her family's history as well. Like Butler's *Kindred*, Blackman's *Po Man's Child* also opens with a scene of physical violence, depicting a physically compromising S/M scene between Po and Mary, which ends in Po's being admitted to the emergency room.

After the publication of *Kindred*, Butler expressed the following in an interview: "I wasn't trying to work out my own ancestry. I was trying to get people to *feel* slavery. I was trying to get across the kind of emotional and psychological stones that slavery threw at people."[2] Butler's expressed interest in rendering the experiences of her protagonist, Dana, believable through harsh and oftentimes disturbing references to the physical stress and trauma of her circumstances is noteworthy. It is important to keep in mind that Dana shares a fate with the women and men she encounters on the antebellum Weylin plantation, where the laws of the slaveocracy are imposed upon blacks and ensure the simultaneous prosperity of white slave masters and the dehumanization of black slaves as their legal property. Dana, like the slaves she befriends, has no choice but to endure such stresses if she is to survive and ensure the birth of her great, great grandmother, Hagar. As part of her self-preservation, she must emotionally disconnect herself from situations when she is whipped or beaten into submission, just like her ancestors, which further perpetuates their ancestral and experiential kinship.

Contrastingly, in Blackman's novel, Po's physical pain and abuse are self-inflicted, even narcissistic. Still, Butler's characterization of her protagonist, Dana, is useful when interpreting Blackman's character, Po. Like Dana, Po's desire to indulge in sadomasochistic rituals is rooted in her attempts to affirm a connectedness with her family. Ultimately, her acts lead to a renewed sense of purpose and investment in her life, and she is compelled to preserve herself and her family's past. Just as Dana is jarred by force from her zombie-like or "numbed" status (before the experience of being transported or summoned back in time), Po's attempt to combat her own psychological numbness, though self-inflicted, awakens her to her own sense of place in her family's history.

Furthermore, Blackman, Shockley, and Butler all rely upon themes such as fantasy and psychological and physical transgression as means of elucidating their characters' life experiences, and all three of their main characters—Po, Renay, and Dana, respectively—must exercise complete authority, self-awareness, and a heightened sense of individual significance *within* their families and communities if they are to evolve and survive (emphasis mine). In this way, as Spillers suggests, "they do not live out their destiny on the periphery of American race and gender magic, but in the center of its Manichean darkness" (174). My hope is that audiences—whether mainstream or academic—will begin to look beyond what have conveniently been marginalized as "alternative" novels and characters to explore the implications of such constructs more routinely.

In *Queer in Black and White,* Stefanie K. Dunning argues that the function of interracial relationships in texts authored by gay, lesbian, and bisexual writers is to provide a context for the *assertion* of blackness rather than a *denial* of it. In one of the most powerful moments in *Po Man's Child,* Po expresses her intentions to sever ties with Mary, and this decision signals Po's racialized black consciousness. Po *needs* their sadomasochistic rituals in order to authenticate the trauma of her family's history of racial oppression and alienation as well as the toxicity of the psychological and social impact of such burdens. At one point in the novel, Po admits that "Mary could have whipped [her] silly if she'd wanted to . . . then cut off my feet to keep me from running away. As long as she didn't freak out or grovel later, everything would have been fine. As long as she'd meant it. And if she hadn't, as long as she made me believe every ounce of her being had meant it, we could have gone on" (Blackman, 61).

Although Dunning's argument regarding interracial sex and its potential to affirm the racial identity of black characters is useful in this particular critique, I am equally interested in the extent to which modern and contemporary black LGBTQI writers such as Blackman construct characters whose "deviancy" is framed within the expressive conventions of the black vernacular tradition. Black LGBTQI writers are willing to challenge and complicate our collective impulse as black people to market a particular brand of blackness that conveniently speaks to the industry needs of academic as well as mainstream cultures. Such artistic activism assures them a much deserved place within the African Diasporic literary and vernacular traditions, despite cultural resistance to their inclusion. Ultimately, these works can be interpreted as creative endeavors that arise out of writers' desires to respond to the shared traumas and triumphs of being black as they seek new methods of decolonizing our collective oppression.

In the introduction to *Does Your Mama Know?: An Anthology of Black Lesbian Coming Out Stories*, editor Lisa C. Moore writes,

> I think by making these stories available, black lesbians will become aware of their history, and feel comfort and strength from that knowledge.... These women have gone out on a limb to share their voices, coming out in a most public way. It is my hope that this book will get black people talking, and remembering that we are yet another layer of richness in the black community.... We *are* out here. (iv, emphasis in original)

It should be noted that Moore is also the founder of Redbone Press, which is dedicated to the publication of writing by black lesbians, whose narratives not only address the subject of sexuality and/or sexual orientation, but whose voices also articulate the life experiences of black America. Yet the existence of a press dedicated to this particular market implicates the degree to which it remains necessary to provide such outlets for the publication of LGBTQI literature of the black experience. The cultural experiences of black lesbians are being marginalized as are other representative voices of the black LGBTQI community, who continue to be dismissed as fringe or countercultural rogue cultures that are perceived as threats to the social, cultural, and political aspirations of the "heterosexual" black community. Until such time as scholars, readers, editors, and publishers become collectively committed to ensuring that every black voice within the African Diaspora be provided a space on the proverbial literary platform from which to express that which has often been discredited as deviant, our study of the black vernacular tradition will be incomplete.

As Po mumbles at the finale of her narrative, "It [is] time to let the shadows walk silent and embrace the narrative of the whole" (234).

Indeed.

NOTES

1. For the complete Delaney interview with Josh Lukin, entitled "The Wiggle Room Theory: An Interview with Samuel Delaney," see the online publication of the

Minnesota Review (Spring 2006), at http://www.theminnesotareview.org/journal
/ns6566/iae_ns6566_wiggleroomoftheory.shtml.

    2. See John C. Snider's "An Interview with Octavia Butler," conducted in 2004,
available online at http://www.scifidimensions.com/Jun04/octaviaebutler.htm.

WORKS CITED

Bell, Bernard. *The Contemporary African American Novel: Its Folk Roots and Modern Literary Branches.* Amherst: University of Massachusetts Press, 2004.

Blackman, Marci. *Po Man's Child.* San Francisco: Manic D Press, 1999.

Butler, Octavia. *Kindred.* Boston: Beacon Press, 1979.

Collins, Patricia Hill. *Fighting Words: Black Women and the Search for Justice.* Minneapolis: University of Minnesota Press, 1998.

Dunning, Stefanie K. Introduction. *Queer in Black and White,* edited by Stefanie K. Dunning, 3–22. Bloomington: Indiana University Press, 2009.

hooks, bell. "Postmodern Blackness." *Feminist Literary Theory and Criticism,* edited by Sandra M. Gilbert and Susan Gubar, 701–708. New York: W. W. Norton, 2007.

Lane, Alycee J. Foreword. *Loving Her,* by Ann Allen Shockley, v–xvi. Boston: Northeastern University Press, 1997.

Moore, Lisa C. Introduction. *Does Your Mama Know?: An Anthology of Black Lesbian Coming Out Stories,* edited by Lisa C. Moore, i–iv. Austin, TX: Redbone Press, 1997.

Shockley, Ann Allen. *Loving Her.* Boston: Northeastern University Press, 1997.

Spillers, Hortense. *Black, White, and in Color: Essays on American Literature and Culture.* Chicago: University of Chicago Press, 2003.

EIGHT

BAD BROTHER MAN: BLACK FOLK FIGURE NARRATIVES IN COMICS

JAMES BRAXTON PETERSON

A LITANY OF BADMEN

Recent scholarship in Africana Studies has revisited the "badman" folk figure in African American culture. Much of this scholarship (Perry 2004, Cobb 2006, and Ogbar 2007) has reengaged this classic black folk figure in order to explicate similar characters emerging in the lyrics and music videos of Hip Hop culture. In this essay I will extend these new theoretical analyses to interpret the figure of the "badman" in comics and graphic novels. Mat Johnson and Warren Pleece's *Incognegro: A Graphic Mystery,* Derek McCulloch and Shepherd Hendrix's *Stagger Lee,* and Kyle Baker's *Nat Turner* all depict either fictional or historical outlaw figures derived directly from the rich reservoir of African American oral and folk culture. *Incognegro, Stagger Lee,* and *Nat Turner* each have intriguing and integral relationships with history, mythology, and the legendary narratives of black "badmen," but also of interest here is the interstitial relationship between these comic (anti)heroes and the American justice system. Each of them is either an outlaw, a fugitive, or a vigilante at specific points in their narratives and each in turn emerges from a narratological set of experiences that embolden them as culturally aspirational outlaws.[1] These Bad-Brother-Men narratives depict a complex twenty-first-century portrait of the black heroic outlaw; visually dense and verbally articulated as historic essays, each of these narratives suggest the untapped potential for comics to engage American history and the politics of identity.

Scholarly writing about Hip Hop culture and new scholarship centered on the graphic narrative form are both emerging genres of study in the academy. As such, we might expect that there will be challenges, miscues, and possibly even errors as each of these subjects of inquiry continue to garner the academic attention they so richly deserve. While there are multiple points of intersection between Hip Hop culture and graphic novels/narratives or comics, the lynchpin of the discussion in this essay is the African American (black) folk figure commonly known as the "badman." For various (and maybe some seemingly obvious) reasons, Hip Hop figures/artists and the narratives they record have been consistently connected to and contextualized via the folkloric history of the black badman. While some of these connections are warranted and productive, at times the connections are facsimiles of previous attempts to connect the badman to the rapper, and unfortunately certain nuances of this important folkloric and historical interconnectivity are lost in the balance. The recent publication of three powerful graphic novels (*Nat Turner* in 2008, *Stagger Lee* in 2006, and *Incognegro* in 2008)—centered on what I am calling the Bad-Brother-Man figure—will unveil some of the complexities lost in the oversimplified connections regularly made between rappers and badmen or "bad niggers."

As an oral (and often folk) form derived from African American expressive culture, rap music has oracular roots in spirituals, the black sermonic tradition, the blues, jazz (especially scat—or vocalized improvisation), and the tradition known as toasting.[2] As Quinn points out, there are "striking continuities" between gangsta rap and the toasts in both "form and function" (94). "Toasting," Quinn explains, "is a black working-class oral practice, involving the recitation of extended and partially improvised narrative poems. These toasts were most typically performed and exchanged by men in street corner conversations, barbershops, and prisons" (94). Listening to a Stackolee toast and a rhymed excerpt from nearly any N.W.A. tune will bear this out clearly.[3] The toast was the vehicle through which the black badman's exploits were often narrated, lionized, and identified with on the part of the teller/toaster and the audience/listener. In the opening verse of "I Ain't Tha 1" a generally catchy albeit misogynistic rap/toast on N.W.A.'s debut album, Ice Cube drops the following lines: "I ain't the one, the one to get played like a pooh butt / See I'm from the street, so I know what's up / On these silly games that's played by the women / I'm only happy when I'm goin up in 'em / But you know, I'm a menace to society . . ."[4] Note that N.W.A.'s badman, exemplified via Ice Cube's powerful persona, tethers his derogatory, chauvinistic themes to his menacing presence in American society. This particularly telling example underscores the notion that the more current vehicle for the cultural processes associated with the traditional toast is so-called gangsta rap and/or popular rap music itself.

This aspect of the connection between badman and rapper (made by Quinn, but also taken up by Ogbar, Perry, Pinn, Cobb, and others) is fairly accurate. The issue or query rests in a subtle distinction that many of these scholars either fail or find unnecessary to make in their respective arguments and discussions. For example, in the essay "How Ya Livin?: Notes on Rap Music and Social Transformation," Anthony Pinn states, "Badmen emerge during the early 20th century and receive the mixed praise of many Black Americans. . . . Badmen struck out at any time and at any one. Although they defied social norms and the power structures created by White Americans, they also wreaked havoc within the Black community" (5). Pinn then goes on to quote Labov who says that "the heroes [in black vernacular culture] are all 'bad'" (6). First, folklorists and other scholars will quibble with Pinn on the historical emergence of the badman. John Roberts cites several badman narratives, including Railroad Bill and Stagger Lee, from the nineteenth century. And although Labov is regularly referenced and well respected by linguists, sociolinguists, and scholars from various disciplines, clearly not all of black culture's heroes are 'bad', not even bad meaning cool or bad in a good way. Pinn goes on to quote several versions of Stagger Lee's narrative both in lyrical/song and toast form. Eventually he parallels the "violent behavior" of Stagger Lee with Dr. Dre and points out the "self-destructive life of defiance exhibited by badmen" in the lyrical work of the Geto Boys (Pinn 6–7). Again, some of these comparisons hold up but certain inaccuracies—here in the form of a limited definition of the badman—seep into Pinn's analysis.

In *Hip Hop Revolution*, Jeff Ogbar dedicates a section of a chapter entitled "Badman" to this comparative discussion. Ogbar lists the core components of male authenticity for the badman thusly: "1) willful ability to inflict violent harm on adversaries, 2) willful ability to have sex with many women, [and] 3) access to material resources that are largely inaccessible to others" (75). Ogbar suggests that these components are "grounded in the tales of Stagolee" and after some discussion of how Muhammad Ali bridges a historical gap, he proceeds to draw various connections between his iteration of the badman and the machismo present in some rap music. Again, Ogbar's comparative assessment (not unlike Pinn's) is fairly accurate in the point-to-point examples he constructs based on the components of the badman figure he details in *Hip Hop Revolution*. However, certain preferences shape his analysis. First, prioritizing violence as a core component is a deliberate and consequential course of his argument. That is, by locating violence in the primary position of his analysis of the badman, Ogbar brings to the fore an element of this folkloric narrative that incisively reflects the violent narratives of too many gangsta rap lyrics. As important as this connection may be (to Pinn and Ogbar), other scholars suggest otherwise. According to Imani Perry: "The badman does not remain within the realms of acceptable black behavior established through community norms, but he is heroic by virtue of his very lawlessness in a society where law has often proven the definitive sign of African American inequity, either by means of legal or judicial injustice" (129). Perry follows John W. Roberts here, whom I will return to shortly, and begins to deconstruct the seemingly fixed notion of the badman as the precursor to the violent misogynistic and materialistic progenitor of the so-called gangsta rapper.

In *To the Break of Dawn*, Jelani Cobb begins to unveil the crux of the misunderstood matter in his comparison of the blues folk figure known as the "Baaad Nigger" and the "thug life" ethos so well publicized and popularized by Tupac Shakur. It is worth noting that thug life is an acronym for The Hate U Gave Little Infants Fucks Everybody. Often misunderstood and robbed of its acronymic complexity, T.H.U.G. L.I.F.E was Tupac's way of capturing some of the complexity of the badman figure among his generational cohort. According to Cobb, "The lauded Thug Icon is nothing if not the remix version of the blues' Baaad Nigger archetype. Whereas the Baaad Nigger and the trickster exist as parallel types in the blues, the thug alone has become the patron deity of hip hop: St. Roughneck" (30). Cobb's assertion that the blues underwrites the aesthetics of rap music is powerful, accurate, and, although rarely mentioned, is also borne out in the musicological research—consider Portia Maultsby's model of African American musical developments[5]— but his comparative analysis of the blues' Baaad Nigger and the Thug Icon in Hip Hop is merely the opposite/other side of the badman discussions detailed by both Pinn and Ogbar. Cobb's Baaad Nigger cannot and should not be thought of or used interchangeably with Pinn's or Ogbar's bad-man. These terms (Baaad Nigger and badman) represent distinct folk fig-urations with divergent folkloric narratives.

Fortunately, John W. Roberts cogently parsed the distinctions be-tween the bad nigger archetype and the badman in 1989. *From Trickster to Badman: The Black Folk Hero in Slavery and Freedom* explores and ex-plicates African American folk culture from Bre'er Rabbit to Stagolee and the badman/bad nigger figure(s). In order to suggest and demon-strate the complexity of the badman/bad nigger figure, Roberts uses the example of Railroad Bill. In 1893, Railroad Bill (née Morris Slater), had a run-in with the law. History suggests that Slater refused to give up his firearm and in the ensuing struggle the policeman was killed—shades of Mumia Abu Jamal.[6] He jumped on a train and through various stra-tegic robberies and evasive maneuvers was able to avoid the police until he was set up and killed in 1896 (Roberts 171–72). Roberts seamlessly in-tegrates the black folk narrative that complements and enhances the his-torical narrative: "Railroad Bill's success in eluding his would-be captors was due to the fact that he was a conjure man who could transform him-self into almost any shape at will. Some African Americans told stories of how Bill on different occasions eluded policemen and railroad detec-tives by turning himself into various animals including a black sheep, a fox and a bloodhound" (172). Railroad Bill's narrative gestures toward the visual narrativity that the graphic novel or comic narrative forms render. The shape-shifting Railroad Bill is both an indicative example of the fluid identity in badman/bad nigger figures—what I refer to here as the Bad Brother Man—and the visual narratives (both folkloric and graphic) that so poignantly construct this popular black folk narrative.

Roberts explains that an overreliance on the badman narratives pro-duced by the toast tradition ignores other earlier folk expressions of the figures: "A consequence of ignoring the earlier manifestations of the bad-man tradition in black culture is evident in folklorist discussions of the tradition where there is a constant emphasis on the destructive and un-productive nature of badman heroes" (174). In the aforementioned ex-amples of discussions regarding the badman in Hip Hop this tendency maintains. According to Roberts this oversight positions the bad nigger as the archetypal example of badman folklore. A generally "uncritical acceptance" of the (more negative) bad nigger as the figure representing the badman has obscured the research investigating the influences on the production of black folk heroes, particularly the badman (Roberts 174–75). This insightful analysis has interesting valence with much of the Hip Hop scholarship that seeks to draw sundry connections between rappers' personas and the badman and/or between rap lyrics and the badman/bad nigger folk narratives. Pinn, Ogbar, and Cobb take a more reductive turn in establishing the relationship between rappers (usually gangsta) and (I'm assuming here) the narrators of badman/bad nigger folktales. Thus they are, like some of the folklore scholars Roberts takes to task, swift in their presentation of the badman figure as the bad nigger. For Pinn and Ogbar, they use the badman term/figure, with the bad nigger meaning, exclusively as the folkloric touchstone from which certain rap narratives take their cues. Cobb employs the Baaad Nigger blues configuration with the bad nigger meaning exclusive of the more fleshed-out definitions of the figure detailed by Roberts and others including Imani Perry. Perry's emphasis on the law as well as the confrontations with and evasion of the law is consistent with Roberts's suggestion that "an act of lawlessness constitutes the central event in the folklore of badmen" (174). What Roberts ultimately concludes is that "[t]o understand the folklore of the black badman as a normative model of heroic action in black culture, it is essential that we view the black badman not only within the tradition of black folk heroic creation begun during slavery but also as an outlaw folk hero" (184).

Eithne Quinn's contribution to this discourse in *Nothing But a "G" Thang* does an exceptional job of presenting this fleshed out version of the badman/bad nigger figure.[7] At the onset, Quinn situates her argument squarely within one of the longstanding and ongoing debates in cultural studies. In this sense, oppression like that resulting from the social invisibility, unchecked globalization, and the postindustrialism plaguing the US West Coast urban environs (where gangsta rap developed in the late 1980s) can create a critical consciousness; consider here the kind of social critique found in powerful rap lyrics like N.W.A.'s anti-police brutality anthem "Fuck tha Police" or Tupac's redemptive "Dear Mama." Yet more often than not, for Quinn, gangsta rap also reflects a pervasive false consciousness in the Marxist sense where ideology is posited as "a kind of 'veil' over the eyes of the oppressed" (15). False consciousness is reflected in much of the misogyny that runs rampant through the lyrics of gangsta rap, where women have become the local (and easy) targets of choice for too many rappers and in too many songs to name here.[8]

Quinn identifies the forefathers of gangsta rap such as Stackolee (or Stagolee) and other bad nigger figures that precede the Tupacs and Ice Cubes of the genre. Quinn's objective handling of African American folk and cultural history further underscores the nuanced meanings of the badman figure and the range of discussions to be had regarding its impact on current or popular culture. Quinn, Roberts, and Perry work to render complicated accurate portraits of the badman figure in black culture. Pinn, Ogbar, Cobb, and others tap into the "bad nigger" aspects of the badman figure particularly as they relate to or reflect certain gangsta rap personas in Hip Hop culture. The sheer volume of the critical discourse suggests the badman's luminous influence on black masculinity, broadly conceived.

GRAPHING THE BAD BROTHER MAN

Utilizing this more nuanced understanding of the badman figure, I explore several graphic novels that in their engagement with certain historical incidents and themes require a fully fleshed-out conceptualization of this oft-referenced black folk figure. The term "Bad Brother Man" is a somewhat limited attempt to capture the aforementioned discussions and to aptly reconsider the possibility of multiple meanings attaching to recent depictions of the bad man figure. I suggest that this fleshed out understanding is realized in the three recently published graphic novels considered in this essay. While the preponderance of my argument here—that a more nuanced term for this traditional folk figure, that is, the Bad Brother Man, accurately reflects the graphic novel's iteration of the badman/bad nigger figure—relies largely on focalization in visual narrativity; the term itself also attempts to reflect other forms of narrativity pertinent to the badman discourse. Each component of the term then carries with it significant narratological value that can be applied to each of the examples discussed in the remainder of this chapter. 1) The term "bad" engenders the sociolinguistic force of the badman folk narrative. Consider the sociolinguistic (i.e., contextual) meaning of the word "bad." Run-DMC make this point succinctly: "not bad meaning bad, but bad meaning good." This is the simplest example of sociolinguistic variation, but its socially contextualized meaning underscores an historic narrative of the black outlaw whose badness was goodness from the perspective of the African American folk audience. Perry and Roberts both make this point clear in their respective discussions. 2) "Brother" reflects the arc of yet another African American folk-oriented narrative through which the term engenders social, political, and communal meanings beyond its standard meaning of sibling. Thus "brother" becomes a communally inflected modifier of solidarity, signaling a history of social movements and common experiences within certain social institutions. 3) "Man," at least in this particular sketch, represents the ongoing narratives regarding masculinity throughout the African American experience. Consider this aspect of the term as a "shout out" to the ongoing literary narrative in black male writing that so often gestures toward and wrestles with manhood especially via the challenges faced by protagonists in texts such as Native Son, Black Boy, Invisible Man, "Dutchman," and Manchild in the Promised Land.

As a term, Bad-Brother-Man also affords me the opportunity of mitigating our usage of the "n-word" particularly in this interpretive situation where the conflation of "nigger" and "man" in the badman—bad nigger paradigm functions as a source of critical confusion among so many of the aforementioned scholars of African American culture. The n-word's force, historical baggage, and sociolinguistic variance confound our understanding of this figure and its erasure in my formulation is a deliberate attempt to generate a more productive and nuanced means with which we can envision those black folk figures that operate outside the law in systems and in historical moments in which the law works against the interests of black people. These sociolinguistic, communal, political, and masculinist narratives (sans the n-word complexities) outline the content of the Bad-Brother-Man narratives, while the form of these narratives take many shapes, most especially here that of focalization in the graphic novel's capacity for visual narrativity.[9]

Through powerful visual narrative and black folk themes, Baker's Nat Turner, McCulloch and Hendrix's Stagger Lee, and Johnson and Pleece's Incognegro remix the various versions and takes on the badman/bad nigger figure in both folklore and Hip Hop scholarship. Each graphic novel centers on an historical Bad-Brother-Man figure. Each accomplishes this via the form of the graphic narrative/novel steeped in the black folk narrative tradition specifically here of the badman/bad nigger figure. Generally speaking, visual narrativity has two components: 1) reading the narratives of written images, including orthography and 2) reading/viewing the narratives of graphic images (Bal 629). I am primarily concerned with the narrativity of the visual here, which relies heavily on the concept of focalization. Manfred states that "focalization theory covers the various means of regulating, selecting, and channeling narrative information, particularly of seeing events from somebody's point of view, no matter how subjective or fallible this point of view might turn out to be" (175).[10] According to cognitive theorist David Herman, "to say that an event or object or participant (in the storyworld) is focalized in a certain manner is to say that it is perspectivally indexed, structured so that it has to be interpreted as refracted through a specific viewpoint and anchored in a particular set of contextual coordinates" (303). Focalization, then, is a primary tool for reading and interpretive analysis of the graphic narratives of the badman/bad nigger figure or what I will henceforth refer to as the Bad-Brother-Man (figure).

The vast majority of narrative content in Kyle Baker's *Nat Turner* is conveyed via visual imagery in smudgy black/greyscale/brown tones in discreet four-sided panels. The paucity of orthographic narrative puts into bold/stark relief the vivid psychological and experiential depth of the graphic narrative. In fact there are no words uttered at all in chapter one of the novel, entitled "Home."[11] The only orthographic narrative, aside from the boom of the enslavers' shotguns, appears at the end of the chapter directly adjacent to one of the most compelling images of the entire narrative. The caption is an announced excerpt from *The Confessions of Nat Turner.* In part it reads: "I was telling them something which my mother, overhearing, said it had happened before I was born—I stuck to my story, however, and related some things which went, in her opinion, to confirm it" (Baker 57). According to Gray, Turner goes on to say that this incident lead the community to deem him a prophet able to narrate scenes that happened before he was born. The story that initiates Turner's Bad-Brother-Man narrative is a retelling of his parents' experience during the middle passage. The story rendered powerfully and exclusively via Baker's pictorial imagery, details the awful conditions and underscores a moment where an African tries to commit infanticide. He attempts to throw his child overboard to the sharks that tracked slave ships throughout middle passage waiting to feed on dead human cargo matter-of-factly dispensed. At the moment he releases his child, a money-minded slave trader catches the child. The father then bites down on the slaver's arm and the child is mercifully released in the waiting jaws of a shark. There are multiple focal points or ways of seeing the scene depicted in this particular panel (Baker 57). The baby in the jaws of the shark is situated in what is in traditional comic/graphic narratives a dialogue bubble—hence indicating or channeling Turner's telling of the story via the visual.[12] This dialogic image is then focalized by the young children listening to the narrative and facing a young Nat Turner, even as it reflects the focal point of the father who bit the arm of the slaver so that his child might plummet to his/her death. The reader's focal points also include the dark and determined look on Nat Turner's face as well as the shocked and awed expressions of Nat's mother and the woman who stands adjacent to her. The bad or mean facial expression of Nat Turner, the attentive huddling of the young black (male) slaves, the awe in the expression of his mother and the historical and political narrative reflected in the dialogue bubble all contribute to the visual narrativity that in turn constructs the Bad-Brother-Man that Nat Turner will eventually become. In this one panel, Turner's Bad-Brother-Man narrative is at least partially visualized. His prophetic sensibilities are signaled both by the visual bubble of the infant being eaten by the shark during middle passage, prior to his own birth and his mother's shocked expression at this revelation. And those very same boys who huddle around him, looking to him for the powerful telling of this story will grow up to be his accomplices in the bloody rebellion. Thus prophecy, communal leadership, and a preview of Turner's outlaw exploits (and at least some of the reasoning behind these exploits) are depicted in this densely rendered image.

In two full-page images, a young Nat Turner screams for his father to "Run!" as he attempts to escape slavery (Baker 82–83). The father is not seen again, but the focal point of this panel is of the reader looking into Nat's anguished face, and also (possibly) of a fleeing father looking back at his son as he runs away. The reader/viewer is being compelled to adopt the perspective of Turner's father. While this particular instance of focalization indexes the anguish of both the father and the son, it also serves to elicit our emotions in response to the familial fragmentation that chattel slavery produces. In fact each of these images delineate the communal destruction upon which the institution of slavery was predicated. In opening pages of the first chapter, we see the villagers of Nat's homeland running frantically from the enslavers (Baker 17). Here too we are invited to experience the history and circumstances of Nat Turner's existence and again the frenzied anguish depicted in the image continues to trace the communal aspects of Turner's Bad-Brother-Man narrative.[13] Chapter 3 of the graphic novel presents images of the rebellion itself from the focal points of several of the more than sixty victims. The brutality of the Turner revolt, during which more than sixty white men, women, and children were brutally murdered with sticks, axes, clubs, tools, and so on, is as disturbing as the images Baker renders in order to express the enslavement scenes/panels. This range (and inversion) of racialized violence creates the space for graphic narrative audiences to visually and literally appreciate the distinct perspectives of the Bad-Brother-Man figure. The subtle symmetry of these images (that of the capture of the slaves and middle passage vis-à-vis the rebellious murder of the white slave master families) suggests retributive balance as well as the arbitrary nature of socially constructed legal and/or social rules and laws.

McCulloch and Hendrix's *Stagger Lee* takes the form of a historically based folkloric essay. Rarely, but with increased frequency in recent years, is the comic or graphic narrative form put to this purpose. The graphic novel version of Stagger Lee is in debt to the scholarship and painstaking research of various thinkers including: John David, Cecil Brown, author of *Stag Shot Billy,* and various other scholars, performers, folklorists and ethnographers. In some ways the text, both visually and literally, is a stunning achievement as it collects much of the folklore, mythology, musicality and versification of the Stagger Lee/Stagolee/Stack-o-Lee narrative. That being said, most if not all of the scholars and cultural critics discussed in this essay would agree that Stagger Lee's narrative rests at the heart of the folklore surrounding the badman/bad nigger figures in African American culture. A brief return to focalization theory underscores the various decisions behind and (in fact) the organizing principles of the visual narrativity of the Stagger Lee graphic novel. To wit: McCulloch and Hendrix must depict and indeed acknowledge the multiple points of view from which the Stagger Lee folk narrative is and has been told throughout history. In this context the graphic narrative be-

FIGURE 8.1.

comes a catalogue of the folk history so readily transposed, refigured, and re-imagined. Even with a couple hundred pages of words and dense visual imagery—*Stagger Lee* must wrestle with the limitations of myth-making and the variation of vernacular culture as it is transmitted—mostly through song, but also through toasts and storytelling.

Figure 8.1 provides one example of how McCulloch and Hendrix exploit the graphic narrative form in order to focalize the narrative and present multiple points of view, in this case on one page. Although the written narrative is in third person—"He fought John Henry, drew down on Jesse James"—the visual narrative assumes distinct perspectives. The battle with legendary folk hero John Henry visually echoes the third-person narrative. Stag's "draw down" on Jesse James a traditional Ameri-

One noted scholar of Stagger Lee – or, as he prefers, Stagolee – suggests that the creators of early Stag songs combined characteristics of killer and victim to arrive at a brand new archetype.

FIGURE 8.2

can badman, straddles the second and third person perspectives as we can see the canon-sized holes blown through Jesse James's body but the visage of Stagger Lee is directed at you/us—the reader. Many Hip Hop scholars will appreciate the gangsta-five-fingered-ring-wearing figure who gives us his best respect-pose. And although the image of Stag shooting Billy Lyons aims off panel he is still, again, facing you/us or the reader. There are too many of these multifocalized visuals throughout the narrative to catalogue them all here, but McCulloch and Hendrix summarily demonstrate the potential of visual narrativity in the graphic novel form. At times the work reads and views more like an essay then a comic book but the end result is a text dense with folkloric information about one of the most oft referenced Bad-Brother-Man figures. Of particular import here is the depiction of Stagger Lee as the modern-day gangsta with two five-finger rings that read: "gangsta" and "respect." This image is a direct allusion to Hip Hop culture and it helps to visually connect the Bad-Brother-Man narratives of Stagger Lee to his Hip Hop cultural progeny. McCulloch and Hendrix do not belabor this connection but the ways in which folk history coalesces around rappers and other figures within Hip Hop culture is an incisive suggestion for the development of innovative language (i.e., Bad-Brother-Man) that captures these sophisticated relationships among history, popular culture, and black artistic production.

Figure 8.2 provides a more direct example of how discreet visual narrativity makes powerful and historically far-reaching conclusions possible in the Stagger Lee graphic novel. Through a visual mathematic equation, the authors reflect one of the central effects of the Stagolee folk narratives in aggregate *and* point to the complexity of the badman/bad nigger figures and the possibilities for an introduction of the Bad-Brother-Man. The focalization inherent in the multiple tellings and retellings generate a new archetype (i.e., a Bad-Brother-Man) who has characteristics of both killer and victim. This newer archetype or what I am referring to as the Bad-Brother-Man (again at least in part to avoid the n-word but also to convey multiplicity and complexity of character over reduction and simplification) suggests interactive valence with various major figures in Hip Hop culture including: Tupac Shakur, Biggie Smalls, and 50 Cent—among many others. For all of the critical discourse that attempts to connect folk figures such as Stagger Lee to artisans of Hip Hop culture it is the visual imagery that most aptly and accurately captures these connections.

My final example for this essay adds Mat Johnson and Warren Pleece's *Incognegro* to this carefully selected list of examples from the graphic novel genre. In Figure 8.3, a full page that occurs fairly early in the text, the main character of the narrative, Zane Pinchback, prepares to make his transformation from "black" to "white" in order to continue his crusade to expose lynching in the South using his super powers to pass as the Incognegro. Even the name Incognegro suggests a certain black folkloric aesthetics but the visual narrativity of the panels produce an accretion of racial, gender, and historical identities. Although we might argue that each panel assumes a third-person point of view, the mirror-panels suggest the reflective nature of passing and force the reader to look at the Incognegro via his mirrored reflection as opposed to his actual face, which in all of the panels is turned away from us. In two of the panels the point of view or focalized visual narrative is superimposed with the forced miscegenation and rape of Zane's female ancestor (or mother) and the American flag—subtly suggesting that miscegenation and the systematic rape of black women is as American as, well, as American as the American flag. What readers might visually conclude in the "assimilation as revolution" panel is that Zane and Incognegro actually do not look much different from each other in their mirrored reflections. Even Madame CJ Walker's straightening comb doesn't seem to do much to Zane's hair. But this is precisely the point of the graphic novel— racial, and gender, identities are always already blurred in the world of *Incognegro*—for Zane race is a strategy. While this might sound or seem trite, the visual depiction of this thesis puts into bold relief the extent to which it is literally reflected in the world in which we live.

Inconegro's exploits as a Bad-Brother-Man figure allow readers/viewers to appreciate the significance of working outside the confines of the law in order to address systematic injustices committed against black

FIGURE 8.3

people. As a journalist, Zane Pinchback investigates and writes about the awful practice of lynching in the South during the Harlem Renaissance era. As Incognegro, Zane infiltrates lynch mobs and takes names and pictures by posing as a photographer who is selling postcards that commemorate the lynching practices that he is investigating. While Incognegro does not conduct himself in the same manner as certain Bad-Brother-Man figures such as Nat Turner or Stagger Lee, he is, in practice, an outlaw and his goals are wholly consistent with his other more historically authentic counterparts. The notion that assimilation might be a form of revolution, or that passing as white might be used for purposes beyond self-service, is an original contribution to this discourse and yet another reason or call for terminology that might capture this innovation and contextualize it amongst the discourses on black folk figures.

The graphic narratives of *Incognegro*, *Stagger Lee*, and *Nat Turner*— taken together—demonstrate an important development and revisitation in the African American and graphic novel genres. If we consider these three, among several others, as revisiting the badman figure in all of its complexities and nuances, then my suggestion for a new term— the Bad Brother Man becomes readily apparent. Thus the Bad-Brother-Man figure is an important place-holder in the versioning of the badman figure. The Bad Brother Man *links* Nat Turner, Stagger Lee, and Incognegro in graphic narratives and projects the fleshed-out sense of the badman/bad nigger figures that Roberts, Perry, and Quinn so eloquently delineate/detail. It also seeks to support the spaces provided by these texts to recover various folkloric expressions, to underwrite multiple points of view necessary for the development and transmission of black folk narrative. And finally these Bad-Brother-Man narratives serve as a corrective for certain (Hip Hop) scholars who may have been a bit too hasty and reductive in comparative analyses of the bad man and the rapper.

NOTES

1. In "The Glorious Outlaw: Hip Hop Narratives, American Law, and the Court of Public Opinion," chapter 4 of *Prophets of the Hood: Politics and Poetics in Hip Hop*, Professor Imani Perry delves into the cultural nuances of outlaw subjectivity in the African American community (102–116).

2. I am using the term "folk" here in its nontheoretical dictionary sense as referring to the "common" or working or poor class of people of a particular society—in this

case those constituents of Hip Hop culture—especially as those people are considered the originators and/or purveyors of art. Hip Hop is often produced or practiced by folk but not always.

3. N.W.A. is an acronym for Niggaz Wit Attitudes.

4. N.W.A., "I Ain't Tha 1," *Straight Outta Compton.* California, Ruthless/Priority/EMI: 1988.

5. Portia K. Maultsby, "Africanisms in African American Music," in *Africanisms in American Culture,* edited by Joseph E. Holloway (Bloomington: Indiana University Press, 1991), 186.

6. We should include Huey Newton, Assata Shakur, and countless others who have had convoluted confrontations with police involving shootings/shoot-outs with Mumia and Railroad Bill. That Railroad Bill's narrative resonates with so many incidents that follow it historically is a powerful suggestion of the myth itself and the extent to which the bad man figure—figures in African American folk culture.

7. Might there be some gendered insight that allows for the deconstructed version of the badman—i.e., the badman/bad nigger figure?

8. Quinn is also critical of the consumerism reflected in the "blinged-out'" era of gangsta rap music where spending hundreds of thousands of dollars on jewelry and cars is commonplace for artists who "represent" communities in desperate need of economic resources.

9. In a larger project of which this essay will be a part, I file these instances of narrativity under a rubric that I call "Black Graphix." Black Graphix relies heavily on Johanna Drucker's useful conceptualization of graphic devices and the ways in which said devices are manipulated and utilized in order to navigate narration (and narrative). Drucker's usage of the term *graphic* "includes all aspects of layout and composition by which elements are organized on a surface" while navigation "refers to the to the active manipulation of features on the level of discourse and presentation" (121). According to Drucker, graphic devices are ideological—in the strictest sense—because they "encode the values and beliefs in any historically specific cultural circumstance" (124). They also "constitute their own order of meaning-producing elements. Their syntactic *and semantic* qualities enact a powerful rhetoric of inter-textual connections and structures. This rhetoric is articulated through graphic means, *as* graphic means, creating relations among the familiar verbal-visual-pictorial narrative elements" (125). Simply put, Black Graphix are those graphic devices that signal racial identity and/or the social constructs that shape race, particularly here those devices that inform, shape, and articulate Black American identity in graphic narrative forms.

10. Note well here that I am bluntly synopsizing this discussion in the interest of time, and suffice it to say that Gérard Genette's concept of focalization, the abstract aspect of "point of view" that attempts to capture the "who sees?" of a given narrative, has proven to be one of the most contested (and discoursed) concepts in the history of narrative theory, which for me none too subtly suggests its extraordinary import to the discipline and provides sufficient reason for its continued use in applying narrative strategies to literary interpretation.

11. In one particularly potent panel, Turner's mother reenacts the classic scene from *Birth of a Nation* as she tries to escape her enslavers—who are of course African/Arab/Black—she even jumps from a bluff, choosing death over liberty, but she is lassoed by her captors in midair.

12. Consider here the reference to Nat Turner as a "semiotic" rebel based upon his revelatory visions from God.

13. Note here that these enslaver scenes are focally and visually symmetrical with the revolt/rebellion scenes nearer to the conclusion of the graphic novel.

WORKS CITED

Baker, Kyle. *Nat Turner.* New York: Abrams, 2008.

Bal, Mieke. "Visual Narrativity." In *The Routledge Encyclopedia of Narrative Theory,* edited by David Herman, Manfred Jahn, and Marie-Laure Ryan, 629–633. New York: Routledge Ltd., 2005.

Cobb, William Jelani. *To the Break of Dawn: A Freestyle on the Hip Hop Aesthetic.* New York: New York University Press, 2007.

Drucker, Johanna. "Graphic Devices: Narration and Navigation," *Narrative,* 16, no. 2 (May 2008): 121–139.

Herman, David. *Story Logic: Problems and Possibilities of Narrative.* Lincoln: University of Nebraska Press, 2002.

Jahn, Manfred. "Focalization." In *The Routledge Encyclopedia of Narrative Theory,* edited by David Herman, Manfred Jahn, and Marie-Laure Ryan, 173–177. New York: Routledge Ltd., 2005.

Johnson, Mat and Warren Pleece. *Incognegro.* New York: Vertigo, 2008.

Maultsby, Portia K. "Africanisms in African American Music." In *Africanisms in American Culture,* edited by Joseph E. Holloway, 326–355. Bloomington: Indiana University Press, 1991.

McCulloch, Derek and Shepherd Hendrix. *Stagger Lee.* California: Image Comics, 2006.

N.W.A. "I Ain't Tha 1" *Straight Outta Compton.* Compact Disc. Los Angeles: Ruthless Records, 1988.

Ogbar, Jeffrey. *Hip Hop Revolution: The Culture and Politics of Rap.* Lawrence: University of Kansas Press, 2009.

Perry, Imani. *Prophets of the Hood: Politics and Poetics in Hip Hop.* Durham, NC: Duke University Press, 2004.

Pinn, Anthony. "How Ya Livin?: Notes on Rap Music and Social Transformation." *Western Journal of Black Studies* 23 (1999): 10–21.

Quinn, Eithne. *Nuthin' But A 'G' Thang: The Culture and Commerce of Gangsta Rap.* New York: Columbia University Press, 2004.

Roberts, John W. *From Trickster to Badman: The Black Folk Hero in Slavery and Freedom.* Philadelphia: University of Pennsylvania Press, 1990.

Run-DMC. "Peter Piper." *Raising Hell.* Compact Disc. New York: Def Jam Records, 1986.

PART THREE

BEYOND AUTHENTICITY

NINE

SAMPLING THE SONICS OF SEX (FUNK) IN PAUL BEATTY'S *SLUMBERLAND*

L. H. STALLINGS

For the nigger, it niggereth everyday.

—CHARLES SCHWA

Afro-German identity emerged as a relational concept where the construction of race/blackness and identity are constituted through a sense of community and relation both to those positioned in similar ways, as well as to the discourses and categories of racial difference and identity through which this process of positioning is enacted. Black German identity is thus the product and process of importing individual, social, and cultural meanings to blackness as a strategic form of self-definition and identification.

—TINA CAMPT

Blackness. Even as historians and critics have attempted to articulate the historical beginning of blackness, as well as the modernity of it, who can say when or where this phenomenon of blackness, a force akin to the start of a world religion rather than the beginning of a racial identity, will end. Though in vastly different contexts, scholar Tina Campt and Charles Schwa—a minor but important character from Paul Beatty's novel *Slumberland*—provide insights as to how American and German black identity might be conceptualized, while also privileging the experience of being black over the debates that race is a false social construct. The question as to whether there is, in fact, an end to blackness is one of the major considerations of this essay, which examines how contemporary African American literary and cultural theories have grappled with and continue to grapple with this question. Through a close reading of Paul Beatty's *Slumberland,* and through an engagement with scholars' focus on periodizing African American literary and cultural traditions, I explore how black literary production and blackness itself resists moves to mark it. I suggest that critics must form new conceptualizations of time and space in order to change the trajectory of future discourses about race and racial identity. Standard, western, or straight time may be useful for charting the representations or performances of blackness, but they have often failed to fully delineate the experience of being black. In *Slumberland,* Beatty proposes that rhythmless constructs of time can never represent indeterminate blackness. Further, as he diagrams this blackness as the funkiest break beat[1] in the world, his novel implores people of the African Diaspora to form complex identities that elide restrictions of time and space imposed on black bodies and communities by tradition, nation, and modernity.

Slumberland tells the story of Ferguson W. Sowell aka DJ Darky, a DJ, jukebox sommelier, and porn musical scorer/composer. As a result of having a "phonographic memory," DJ Darky's livelihood and passion in life is his talent for reproducing sounds and creating sick beats. After receiving a video of a man having sex with a chicken accompanied by a musical masterpiece composed by an unnamed musician, DJ Darky decides that he knows who composed the porn score, a jazz musician by the name of Charles Schwa. He resolves himself to find "the Schwa" and have him bless his own magnificent beat. DJ Darky's quest takes him out of the United States and to Berlin where he works as a jukebox sommelier at Slumberland Bar, a cruising utopia for persons wanting to engage in interracial sex. Symbolically, though, DJ Darky's search for the Schwa ends up being a mission to explain the value of indeterminate blackness, made indeterminate by one's own individual experience and relationship to blackness, and its intersectionality with a collective identity. With *Slumberland* Beatty updates African American expatriate fiction that typically represented a black American's journey to resolve the conflict between blackness as it intersects with American identity and citizenship by moving to a purportedly more progressive country. Works such as Nella Larsen's *Quicksand* or John A. Williams's *The Man Who Cried I*

Am inevitably revealed that the process of attempting to resolve those conflicts could then produce a different sense of alienation even more difficult to overcome. Beatty's revision stems from his protagonist's interactions with and commentaries on other U.S. expatriates, Black Germans, and East Germans. In *Slumberland,* the misnomer of "the" black experience is contested by the way Beatty refuses to situate blackness as bound to the U.S. or connected to uncontested concepts of time. Beatty's novel experiments with fictionalizing the global and diasporic production of blackness and the importance of black consciousness as conceived in the U.S. to that global production. DJ Darky's journey implicitly symbolizes the desire to make room for indeterminate blackness in terms of cultural production and personal identity. As characters in the novel seek to define and redefine blackness based on their individual lives and experiences, readers can glean how important Beatty's notion of blackness as a beat for an incomplete song is to understanding the indeterminate nature of blackness for individual and collective identity, and the infinite evolution of blackness in cultural production across the African Diaspora.

BLACK IS, BLACK AIN'T: POST-BLACK, POST-SOUL

At the beginning of his important documentary about race, sexuality, gender, class, and disability Marlon Riggs uses an image of gumbo to signify his understanding of black experience and identity formation in the U.S. In *Slumberland,* music, beats, and breaks in sampling become metaphors for understanding blackness and black identity outside of a U.S. context. In the novel, sound can be equated with experience in the determination of where blackness ends and begins, while DJ Darky stands as the literal personification for the discourse of race. Hence what DJ Darky does for a living and what he is named are Beatty's clever artistry, presenting the alienation of essential blackness and the unstoppable force of indeterminate blackness. Beatty's configuration of Ferguson W. Sowell as linked to the social discourse of race is made evident by Sowell's professional name DJ Darky. The stereotypical connotations of "darky" as the blackest of the black, as well as its use as a pejorative term that might be as offensive to some as "nigger," also alludes to iconographic minstrel performance in blackface. The value of darky and its meaning is fabricated by social mores of a specific time. There is an end and a beginning to that fabrication. DJ Darky represents an image culled from the gaze of early twentieth-century white people. As we will learn later, DJ Darky must decipher that the marking of representations of blackness is very different from the experience of blackness. The falseness of representation becomes obvious in the lack of depth, texture, and feeling.

Sound, conversely, is one of the more affective senses and the reality of it is made obvious by the experience of feeling its absence or presence. Even if we had not named it, our bodies would still feel its presence or know its absence. As a person who has vast knowledge and skill on how to organize, break down, and reassemble beats, DJ Darky equivocates the potential to acknowledge affect or experience of indeterminate blackness in the absence of signs and markers called race (social or biological). When DJ Darky proclaims, "the sound of American rhetoric is one of the reasons that I left, it's the last remaining tie I have left to the country of my birth," he situates himself as a U.S. citizen not necessarily disenchanted with the nation, but rather the culture of a nation that produces phrases such as "keeping it real . . . as a way to disguise the emptiness and mundanity" (Beatty 13). DJ Darky's reference to sound highlights his gift and calling as a DJ with phonographic memory—the ability to remember any sound ever heard (Beatty 14). Because he is able to remember every sound he has ever heard, he can then comprehend the infinite possibilities of any sound based on numerous and varied combinations of the same sound or beat. He can create new sounds, as well as recognize new sounds. This gift makes him weary of the ways in which others cannot do the same. Thus, he ventures to another country to locate new sounds and recognize the possibilities for original sounds.

Professionally, DJ Darky's sampling ways do more than authenticate blackness. Music scholar Murray Forman indicates that digital sampling enacts specific tasks:

> Apart from constructing a bridge between musical antecedents and the present, digital sampling can imbue an element of authenticity on newer tracks as the patina of the past seeps into the new mix. The hiss and pop of old vinyl records provides a sonic link to the original recording by referencing its age and wear through what are, in most conventional recording contexts, deemed as imperfections. (Forman 390)

DJ Darky, then, an allegory for black identity in the U.S. and a figure who has the gift for sampling, must understand the construction and use of blackness outside of its U.S. minstrelsy context. During his search for the Schwa, he will learn that the creation of black identity is akin to digital sampling. Beatty's creative decision to focus on sound and the sampling of sound is more about taking up the temporal concerns of black people than essentializing blackness. At the beginning of the novel, DJ Darky proclaims, "Blackness is passé and I for one couldn't be happier, because now I am free to go to a tanning salon if I want to, and I want to" (Beatty 4). Such a statement sets the stage for a narrative meant to address concerns regarding the end of race or blackness. DJ Darky's words are meant to contextualize his experience as a black American in which current debates argue that the construct of race is false, and that the need to politically identify and claim blackness has passed in the U.S. Such arguments also impact theories about black culture. Because Beatty produces work that becomes a part of black culture, *Slumberland* stands as a novel that is meant to dismantle investment in such criticism.

CP TIME

Long before Judith Halberstam's *In a Queer Time and a Queer Place: Transgender Bodies, Subcultural Lives* took up "queer uses of time and space . . . in opposition to the institutions of family, heterosexuality, and reproduction" (1), black communities culturally developed African time, colored people's time, and other sacred and lewd names for its culturally coded context of temporalities that did much of the same prior to the civil and human rights movements of the late twentieth century. Its continued use to this day speaks volumes about its purpose. Spatially, a great deal of work has been conducted on black culture and identity in regard to dispersal and displacement based on geographical space and nation, notably in the massive amount of scholarship and theories on diasporas and transnationalism. However, little work has been done to examine the impetus to create the temporal placement and displacement of black identity and culture, as well as its intersections with diaspora and transnationalism.[2] This is not simply an act of canon making and periodization of culture, but elaborate labor done to conflate how people experience their bodies in the world with the language used to signify that experience. Any discursive model that combines race and time into a single entity is more than periodization, it is a "race-time continuum." Foundationally, race and time are basic social discourses that reverberate off each other. Based on the title of Clifton Taulbert's genteel novel title *Once Upon a Time When We Were Colored,* some folks know how to periodize culture and race and why they do it, but we have yet to fully delve into how our marking of culture and people through the language of time is based on one theory of time over another. Do we comprehend how the definition of time that we have chosen to live by privileges racial discourse over the experience of race in our current debates about race, racism, identity, and culture? In the case of black literature and culture, using a linear sense of time locks us into discourses that discount the experience of race. Because someone thought to chart when the discourse of race began, does that mean that we now have to mark where it ends? "It" has been connoted to be both the discourse and experience of race. This is a conundrum of time caused by the gap between experience and language, between doctrine and behavior, between perceived reality and unperceived reality. If we consider time divorced from the mission of keeping and writing history, outside of the BC/AD model, or away from the concerns for shaping the labor of community and nation, what models of time reveal themselves as relevant to black people in the diaspora, and do those vehicles provide more efficient ways of interpreting indeterminate blackness for community building and cultural production?

Before concepts of post-race, post-black, or post-soul were invented, black Americans showed an interesting relationship to time historically through the interchangeability of the affectionate moniker of CP time—colored people's time or conscious people's time. History operates on the basis that time and space are linear and flat, but how individuals experience the world proves that it is not. CP time has stood as a term to explain this. Before theorizing about colored people's time, I would like to explore the link between conscious people's time and the race-time continuum. As conscious people's time demonstrates, time need not only be conceptualized around material and labor to be produced for the world, but it can also be defined or based upon spiritual and psychological necessities of self. When Amiri Baraka proclaimed, "What time is it? It's Nation Time," he did more than issue a call for revolutionary action, he promoted the idea that somehow blackness might be marked by time: "Time to be one strong fast Black energy, / Space . . . / Future of the world / Black man is the future of the world."[3] Baraka later concludes, "Time to get, Time to be one, Time to get up, Time to become." In "Nation Time," listeners understand that the beginning of blackness occurs when one becomes conscious or wakes up. Hence, the insistence and repetitive nature of the active phrase "get up" in which Baraka can insert whatever he wishes: "Get up Santa Claus," "Get up muffet dragger, get up rasta for real to be rasta farari," "Get up Diana Ross" "Get Up Roy Wilkins." Get up serves as a wake-up call for African Americans to get up, get black, or you gone be late. The implied connection between racial identity and consciousness of what that racial identity entails for people in the U.S. has been marked by time as much as by origin. Given this preoccupation as to when black people become conscious of their racial identity, it makes sense that it would be important to note when such consciousness ends and what that means for the place, space, and status of those groups of people. Paul Taylor's eloquent "Post-Black, Old Black" describes the work of current literary and cultural theory as an endeavor to understand race and culture. Taylor remarks upon this impulse to note historical shifts in politics and culture as the motivation to "posterize" (626). Posterizing, he claims, "is a device for understanding divergent evolution, for clearing conceptual space, or for expressing skepticism and suspicion" (629). Blackness at the end of the twentieth century and going into the twenty-first century certainly needs those three things, but posterizing, while useful for the critic, seems to be a one-dimensional and flat device for the writer who sees time as non-linear and multi-dimensional.

In 2005, *African American Review* solicited essays for a special issue on the post-soul aesthetic to be published in 2007. By the time *African American Review* decided to do the issue, the post-soul aesthetic had been in effect for twenty years according to its own call:

> Recognized nearly 20 years ago primarily by Trey Ellis ("The New Black Aesthetic," 1989), Greg Tate ("Cult Nats Meet Freaky-Deke," 1986) and Nelson George (*Buppies, B-Boys, Baps and BoHos: Notes on Post-Soul Black Culture*, 1992), the Post-Soul aesthetic could be used to describe the work of Paul Beatty, Jean-Michel Basquiat, Danzy Senna, Mos-Def, Dave Chappelle, Me'Shell Ndege-Ocello, Colson Whitehead, Aaron McGruder, Ellen Gallagher, The Roots, Spike Lee, Saul Williams, Kara Walker, Living Colour, and Darius James, to name only a few. (609)

Like nation time, theories of post-soul aesthetic come with their own temporal markers based on a historical collective consciousness. According to the guest editor of the special issue, Bertram Ashe, it was envisioned as a way to

> establish a critical framework for the study of post–Civil Rights movement art in general and the post-soul aesthetic in particular. After all, at this point, there is little consensus on anything regarding the fledgling scholarship on the era: names, for instance, range from "The New Black Aesthetic" to "postliberated" to "post-soul" to "post-black" to "NewBlack"—and beyond. There is disagreement over whether the era should be restricted, as I believe it should be, to artists and writers who were born or came of age after the Civil Rights movement, and there is disagreement on when the era begins and whether or not it has ended [regrettably, some scholars already see sub-generational breaks such as the post-post-soul, for instance]. (Ashe 609)

In this case, post-soul with its inherent and explicit connection to cultural activity after a political movement, rather than the political movement itself, makes it easier to think of blackness outside of the black nationalist parameters seen in Baraka's "Nation Time," but still limited by the concept of nation since the Civil Rights movement remains a United States movement. As Paul Gilroy and Mark Anthony Neal have shown, soul transcends United States borders and the Civil Rights era. Still, the disagreement over naming, the shifts in blackness generated by individuality, and the aforementioned question about whether blackness ever ends has contributed to critics' and writers' discussion of the subject. While *African American Review* delved into the late-arrival moniker of post-soul, most of the would-be post-soul writers were unmaking the very classification that was being pressed upon them by either consciously rejecting labels or through creative slights and asides in their works. The most evident example occurs with Beatty's use of Wynton Marsalis as a fall guy for the NBA (New Black Aesthetic) or PSA (Post-Soul Aesthetic) throughout *Slumberland*. In the novel, DJ Darky's pointed barbs about Wynton Marsalis represent Beatty's rejection of the rhetoric found in Trey Ellis's now canonical essay, "The New Black Aesthetic":

> What I'm noticing most nowadays about the New Black Aesthetic Movement is its magnetism. Since anything (good) goes, almost every month a talented new black artist blows into town with a wild new cultural

combination. . . . A few years ago it seemed that no blacks were playing jazz anymore and that the legacy would default upon sympathetic white negroes. Now besides Wynton and Branford Marsalis, we have bluesman Robert Cray. Somehow these dry, neo-conservative Eighties, these horse latitudes for mainstream culture, are proving one of the most fertile periods black culture has ever known. (272)

Though Ellis's work covers a broad range of black culture, music, film, literature, and art, he inevitably sets parameters on blackness by privileging jazz as a black art form that might have gone extinct had it not been for, in the words of DJ Darky, "Wynton's pretentious narcissistic nigrescence" and his "tempo's self-important braggadocio" (Beatty 95). Beatty never has to say that he rejects the New Black Aesthetic/Post-Soul Aesthetic label. His novels often do it for him. Other writers have been more pointed while remaining diplomatic about the terms ascribed to their work or the work of their peers. This has been especially true of the term post-black. In responding to Toure's review of his novel *Sag Harbor*, Colson Whitehead broached the work of critics and scholars' fascination with labeling writers such as himself as post-black. He retorted, "Because someone wrote that review about my book, I'm now accountable for his theory of post-blackness."[4] Toure's foray into post-blackness is only the most recent use of the term to irritate a contemporary black writer, but the term's potential for causing controversy occured before Toure's review.

Thelma Golden, curator of the Studio Museum in Harlem, received negative criticism when she first introduced the post-blackness moniker and expanded on it during the *Freestyle* exhibition at the Studio Museum in Harlem. She explained it as "a clarifying term that had ideological and chronological dimensions and repercussions. It was characterized by artists who were adamant about not being labeled as 'black' artists, though their work was steeped, in fact deeply interested, in redefining complex notions of blackness" (14). Later, Golden's reflection on her artists' works seems less clear when she says of their work: "They are both post-Basquiat and post-Biggie" (15). Statements such as these, Taylor insists, are exactly why post-blackness must be properly explicated if it's going to be used. Assessing that contemporary racial conditions need comprehensive tools to engage them, Taylor critiques Thelma Golden's use and definition of the post-black.[5] However, if posterizing is, as Taylor claims, "a complex enterprise, enjoining those who would engage in it to embrace *and* to reject the past, while also embracing but remaining wary of the present" (629), then future writers and critics must remain wary of its inability to bridge the divide between discourse and experience. Indeed, the very term post-blackness assumes a linearity, a false assumption somehow that blackness is organized, cohesive, orderly, and stays put in one place or moves in one direction. In order to better understand the indeterminate nature of blackness, we need to reconsider the concept of time that we are employing in defining our blackness, as opposed to assuming the end of it by marking a period of time.

Rather than utilizing linear models of time, we could consider CP time—colored people's time in this instance. As opposed to reflecting on the negative connotations of colored people's time, that of black people consistently arriving late, we should think of it as an affective appropriation able to allude to different conceptions of time in which the measurement of time is not shaped by the rules and divisions of labor and duties of a Western workday.[6] Or that an individual's own spiritual, physical, psychic, intellectual, or emotional needs can be used to create a doctrine of time. In the same way that scholars have devised notions of origin, geography, and space to conceptualize the African Diaspora and theories about its people and their cultures, colored people's time acknowledges the simultaneous existence of various and divergent black experiences and blackness as a component of racial discourse at any given time. Like the M.W.I. (Multiple Worlds Interpretation) concept of temporal spatialization,[7] if critics of black literature and culture employed an alternative model of time, CP time, then the divide between the experience of blackness and the social construct of race that produces alienation and immobility lessens. It wouldn't be the first time. It is the reconfiguration of time and space by artists such as Sun-Ra and George Clinton that Beatty's *Slumberland* relies upon. Sun-Ra, at the beginning of the film *Space is the Place,* suggests that "the first thing to do is to consider time as officially ended" and that "we'll work on the other side of time." Creating new points of origins and myths, both Sun-Ra's space music and George Clinton's P-Funk easily disrupt the arguments of authentic and essential blackness derived from theories utilizing blues, jazz, soul, and hip-hop. Indeed, the Schwa is essentially Sun-Ra to DJ Darky's George Clinton.

For Beatty, that means conceptualizing his notion of CP time around things that can actually be experienced, like sound, as opposed to words or categories (measurement) that stand in for the actual experience of what they signify. Throughout *Slumberland,* Beatty attends to posterizing by having his characters signal a recognition of the limited ways in which time is conceptualized through language rather than the experience of it through senses. For example, while explaining the impact of the Schwa's music, DJ Darky provides an alternative measure of time: "The Schwa's music . . . shatters time. Stops time really" (Beatty 224). He continues, "Whenever I hear about a method of time travel that involves worm holes, flux capacitators, or cosmic strings and no music I am not impressed. If there is such a thing as a vehicle for time travel it's music . . ." (Beatty 224). Again, Beatty employs music as a way to re-imagine time and in doing so assigns significant value to indeterminate blackness.

In "Black Crisis Shuffle: Fiction, Race, and Simulation," Rolland Murray analyzes the work of Paul Beatty and Darius James and asks an important question for current African American literature. Murray inquires, "How do we interpret black literature that neither pines ambivalently for the nationalist past nor positions art as a proxy for a communal wholeness that is nationalism in another guise?" (215). Adapting the strategies from CP time, which directs how we interpret and understand our place in the world, is one way. For Ralph Ellison, it was jazz. Since Beatty rarely writes criticism, funk and sampling within his novel become symbolic time machines for blackness that resist the impulse for posterizing because they insist on understanding blackness via CP Time. With *Slumberland's* plot, settings, aesthetics, symbols, and metaphors Paul Beatty deflects any potential moves to posterize his work by sampling the sonics of sex (funk) and focusing it on Black German identity construction.

SONICS OF SEX—FUNK

As Beatty samples the sonics of sex for *Slumberland,* he directs close readers to return to Susan Willis's freakishly fantastic theoretical introspection on Toni Morrison, an essay entitled "Eruptions of Funk." Willis observed of Morrison and funk, "Morrison's aim in writing is very often to disrupt alienation with what she calls 'eruptions of funk'" (265). "At a sexual level, alienation is the denial of the body, produced when sensuality is redefined as indecent" (Willis 266). While Willis demonstrates that Morrison's eruptions of funk were in response to black alienation in terms of nation and gender for the 1970s, Beatty's sampling the sonics of sex (funk) has a much different agenda. Beatty's use of funk is psycho-cultural, and through it, he explores the interiority of self as opposed to attending to exterior expression or performance. Funk is easily noted as an aesthetic that challenges ideologies of the mind and body. Such re-flexivity explains why it can also be felt as a mood. Funk also exists as an object that engages the sensory experiences of smell and sight. However, funk also touches and can be touched. The key to comprehending this sensory variation of funk means that an individual or group must act out-side of traditional temporal and dimensional boxes in order to sense the interior shift that happens when confronted with exterior limitations.

Using the ethos of funk, Beatty avoids the inclination to posterize while constructing a character who pontificates on posterizing. *Slumber-land* begins with DJ Darky railing against the white Germans' disbelief at his wish to tan at a local tanning salon. The tirade addresses the when of blackness, and it also serves as Beatty's official rejection of NBA and post-soul:

> You would think they'd be used to me by now. I mean, don't they know that after fourteen hundred years the charade of blackness is over. That we blacks, the once eternally hip, the people who were right now as of Greenwich Mean time, are, as of today, as yesterday as stone tools, the velocipede, and the paper straw rolled into one. The Negro is now offi-cially human. Everyone, even the British, says so . . . we are as mediocre and mundane as the rest of the species . . . (Beatty 34)

The satire imposed on the end of blackness should not be taken as an ac-ceptance of post-black rhetoric; to the contrary it critiques and makes fun of the rhetoric by first renegotiating the measurement of time with "Greenwich Mean time." Beatty then utilizes a major trope from slave narratives (white authority authentication, in this case the British are meant to authenticate the validity of the slave's experience and words) to buttress DJ Darky's claim that blackness is passé. DJ Darky laments the loss of any exciting black cultural production. Though he never mentions literature, the broadness of black culture, including music and literature, is implied. The charade of blackness that DJ Darky mentions occurs at a young age for Ferguson W. Sowell, aka DJ Darky.

As a failed product of the Winthrop School of Music, DJ Darky formed pivotal questions early on about sound and music that inform and shape his quest to complete his perfect beat. During his time at Winthrop, he ponders the school's initial placement of him in certain classes based on his blackness, without really addressing the purpose of art: "Why? Why was I playing? Why was music so powerful? What can I do with music? Can it heal? Can it kill?" (Beatty 21). Thus the knowledge that he has, either about blackness or music, means nothing without purpose. He later figures out that purpose and asserts of his quest to find,

> a beat so perfect as to render musical labels null and void. A melody so transcendental that blackness has officially been declared passé . . . It's what we've claimed we always wanted, isn't it? To be judged 'not by the color of our skins, but by the content of our character?' Dude, but what we threw down was the content not of character, but out of character. It just happened to be of indeterminate blackness and funkier than a motherfucker. (Beatty 16)

DJ Darky's quest is a search for indeterminate blackness carried out through funk. Even DJ Darky's comrades, the Beard Scratchers, observe DJ Darky's collision course with funk: "Look, dude, you've sampled your life, mixed those sounds with a funk precedent, and established a sixteen-bar system of government for the entire rhythm nation. Set the DJ up as executive, the legislative, and the judicial branches . . ." (Beatty 35). Though this ideology seems more like Janet Jackson's "Rhythm Nation," music aficionados know that Funkadelic was the first to boldly articulate the vision of one nation under a groove. Further, P-Funk's vision exceeded traditional tropes of nation and moved into interstellar frequencies that understood the value of both the individual and the community.

Beatty's attention to beats and sampling via DJ Darky reflects this condition and serves as the perfect metaphor, while the embedded philosophy and ethos of funk guides the protagonist's journey and situates Beatty's characters as invested in representing indeterminate blackness. Willis pointed out twenty-five years ago that "'funk' is really no more than the intrusion of the past in the present" (280). Perhaps this is why Beatty samples the ethos and philosophy of funk to construct a desired indeterminate blackness that moves beyond authenticity and essential blackness that scholars of jazz and hip-hop have produced time and again. Throughout *Slumberland,* Beatty continues to work on CP time. He has DJ Darky redefine time so that it is relevant to his life and needs: "I'd worked most of the clubs in West Berlin and had long since stopped measuring time in days of the week. Tomorrow was the day after South African pop night at Abraxas. Yesterday was jazz brunch at the Paris Café" (Beatty 121). If black people, as human products of Western imperialism, insist on keeping track of time, we should at least be able to establish how to do so (according to Beatty). Further, DJ Darky's sommelier duties enable him to occupy multiple spaces of the party DJ and the rap DJ, which means that he serves a dual purpose in the novel that hints at tradition, invention, and modernity. According to Russell Potter's *Spectacular Vernaculars: Hip-hop and the Politics of Postmodernism,* the rap DJ should be seen as an evolution of the party DJ:

> The rap DJ evolved from the party DJ, whose ostensible role was merely to play pre-recorded music for dance parties; like their audiences, these DJs were consumers of pop music. Yet by taking these musical sounds, packaged for consumption, and remaking them into new sounds through scratching, cutting, and sampling, what had been consumption was transformed into production (36).

DJ Darky works as the facilitator for the white Germans' consumption of blackness, while also producing music that will aid in the fabrication of Black German identity. DJ Darky's quest for the perfect beat becomes an introspective journey, where funk and indeterminate blackness operate as one and the same. Funk simultaneously produces many worlds of blackness and so there is no need for posterizing. Beatty explores how alienating the struggle for individual identity and autonomy can be for persons who hunger for collective identity in order to survive. He presents this not simply through DJ Darky's musings on American and black American culture, but also through the divisions between Germans before and after the Berlin Wall comes down, and the psychological displacement and alienation of Black Germans in Berlin.

Once DJ Darky leaves the U.S. and is in Berlin, we learn when and where he enters. Beatty's use of German history and culture as the temporal and geographical location forces readers to contemplate discourses of race and blackness outside of a U.S. context that might lend itself to posterizing blackness. Beatty replaces the Civil Rights Movement with the Berlin Wall, but he avoids the mistake of marking time by introducing readers to Slumberland Bar, a place where the wall disappears. Beatty's fictional representation of Germans in Berlin and the formation of a contemporary national identity are highlighted when DJ Darky discovers Slumberland Bar: "The Slumberland Bar was a repressed white supremacist's fantasy. At almost every table sat one or two black men sandwiched by fawning white women" (Beatty 62). Slumberland Bar serves as an interzone haven where interracial sex and desire occur outside the imperatives to form a national identity. DJ Darky's musical selections are meant to create a sonic barrier that protects the zone and enhances the mood for interracial sex. Beatty's irony is evident since the history of Hitler and Nazi Germany lingers over present day Germany, but it is also complicated by the more recent history of the Berlin Wall. Slumberland Bar exists as a way to explore the national conflicts Germans were dealing with outside of its guilt over Nazism. In the words of DJ Darky, "This was Berlin before the Wall came down. State-supported hedonism. Every one-night stand a propaganda poster for democratic freedom and third world empowerment . . ." (Beatty 62). Beatty's satire hints at a truth that the movement may have also served as a way for Germans to release their psychological guilt over Nazism and pursue interracial sex, or to experience eruptions of funk.

What East Germans learn about themselves before the wall comes down, and what they will know of themselves after it has been demolished, may be the same thing. Although DJ Darky first describes the bar as propaganda for a democratic movement, the truth is revealed in its unspoken policy of admittance: "These men of the diaspora who smiled meekly while libertine frauleins debated as to who was the 'true Black': the haughty African . . . or the cocksure Black American" (Beatty 62). As readers learn, Slumberland is a place for white German women to go slumming for sex with foreign black men. The Black German man or woman is not valued as much as the exotic non-natives. After the wall has come down, DJ Darky remarks that this time period reminds him of "the Reconstruction period of American history, complete with scalawags, carpetbaggers, lynch mobs, and the woefully lynched. There were the requisite whining editorials warning . . . that the inherently lazy and shiftless East Germans would never be productive citizens. There were East Germans passing for West Germans" (Beatty 134). Because Beatty establishes German people as very much like post-emancipated or post-segregated Negroes, they might also share some similarities with Morrison's take on the black middle class of whom she proclaims, "They learn how to behave. The careful development of thrift and manners. In short, how to get rid of the funkiness. The dreadful funkiness of passion, the funkiness of nature, the funkiness of the wide range of human emotions" (Morrison 68). Indeed, the German history of exterminating funky races by erecting concentration camps or building walls were deadly and successful attempts to preserve German purity. Slumberland Bar, at least its depiction by Beatty, is an eruption of funk for Germans. Funk in the sense of body odor, as opposed to aesthetics and style. This eruption of funk is contained, and its containment implies that despite all the propaganda for a future of democratic freedom, the historical national agenda of keeping funk at bay remains. When the wall comes down, it inevitably reveals that East Germans are fearful of learning how to behave like West Germans, and vice versa. Perhaps this is why when the wall comes down, the Schwa believes that building it back up will change something. Before DJ Darky was ever formally introduced to the Schwa, he had unknowingly noticed him as a nameless "eccentric black man who'd periodically come into the Slumberland" and "never spoke, preferring to let the cardboard sign dangling from his neck do the talking . . . HOW CAN WE READ THE WRITING ON THE WALL, IF THERE IS NO WALL" (Beatty 140). The Schwa's sign, like posterizing, assumes that marking something off will keep the truth and change from being revealed, or make it easier to understand. Yet, the experience of the Black German reveals that white West Germans (at least the liberal denizen of Slumberland Bar) and East Germans share some common methods of erasure and disavowal.

As critic Michelle M. Wright has insisted, East Germans are at least recognized as "Others from within," while "Afro-Germans born and raised in Germany are consistently misrecognized as Africans . . . the Afro-German is both an Other-from-Within (a member of that country) and an Other-from-Without (misrecognized as African)" (297). DJ Darky witnesses this experience of alienation when two black women, the Von

Robinson sisters, Klaudia and Fatima, come into the Slumberland Bar, and DJ Darky names them the "Rosa Parks of Slumberland integration" (Beatty 164). The eruption of funk that Slumberland represents for white Germans will not be enough for Black Germans.

Black Germans have a different experience, and so the use of interracial sex as an eruption of funk is not necessarily helpful in solving the problem of misrecognition for Black Germans. If Morrison, as stipulated by Susan Willis, writes so that "sexuality converges with history and functions as a register of change, i.e. historical transition" (263), then Beatty's description and characterization of Slumberland has a similar function. Beatty's representation of the indeterminate nature of blackness occurs with sexuality. Even as Black German experience has been one of misrecognition as Wright discussed earlier, it has also been shaped by other more insidious discourses that have everything to do with sex. Tina Campt has shown that the Afro-German experience and existence has been shaped by the need to maintain racial purity: "In the early 20th century, the status of Germany's mixed-race black citizens was contested and constructed in public and political discourse as a threat to the survival of the German nation . . . the threat of miscegenation was articulated through a discourse of racial endangerment in the German colonies in the debates on the status of racially mixed marriages and the Afro-German progeny of these relationships" ("Converging Spectres" 323). Campt links this fear with the use of French African troops in the occupation of Rhineland, which then produces the "Rhineland Bastard" figure that symbolically comes to represent the offspring of children of the soldiers and German women ("Converging Spectres" 324). Knowing this history, Beatty imagines Slumberland as recognition and acceptance of the specter of interracial desire and German national fears. Slumberland Bar exists as the haven for interracial sex, without having to deal with the perceived danger of that sex to the nation. Notably, the presence of Fatiama and Klaudia confronts and makes it impossible to keep the result of slumming separate from slumming itself.

Unlike the white women slumming for sex with black men, Klaudia and Fatima have a different reason for coming into Slumberland—to hear black music organized or produced by DJ Darky. The Von Robinson sisters' interaction with DJ Darky reveals the importance of accepting CP time and indeterminate blackness. Klaudia is light-skinned and Fatima is dark-skinned, but both find it difficult to locate a place of origin for their German heritage and black heritage since neither have knowledge of paternity. Klaudia provides the first fictional account of Wright's assessment of the Afro-German experience when DJ Darky explains the sensitive nature of saying Jew in contemporary Berlin: "Sometimes Klaudia would say it when she felt embittered about the second-class treatment that Afro-Germans received. If she was feeling particularly aggrieved she'd . . . hiss, 'maybe if I was *Jewish*' . . . never finishing the thought" (Beatty 137). Where Klaudia emotes anger and indignation about the lack of concern for the Afro-German experience, Fatima emotes melancholy. According to DJ Darky, Fatima "wore her blackness like the heroine in that Chekhov play, who when asked why she always wears black, replies, 'I'm in mourning for my life'" (Beatty 123). Fatima's melancholy is the beginning of a counter discourse to critique German guilt over Nazism and the wall with no acknowledgement of its current misrecognition and othering of black citizens.

Beatty explores the difference between white German identity and black German identity with a unique focus on sound. The chicken video becomes sonic sex that elicits different reactions from Germans. For white German women, the music, not the image of chicken intercourse, serves as an aphrodisiac. Since DJ Darky uses the tape to coax white German women into sex, he merely plays a few seconds of the tape and they respond immediately. Such absurdity in the text showcases this need to experience and consume funk without incorporating it into the self. The music on the tape can be used to experience individual pleasure, like that at Slumberland Bar, but it isn't needed to produce a collective identity because the wall has already done that. In the case of Klaudia and Fatima, the chicken tape does not act as an aphrodisiac. Instead, it does produce a longing for mechanisms that can be used to create a collective identity. Klaudia and DJ Darky do eventually begin having an affair, while Fatima becomes invested in the music on the tape to create her identity. Akin to DJ Darky's search for the Schwa, Fatima's and Klaudia's experiences of alienation propel them to search for indeterminate blackness so that they might also sample a beat different than that of white Germans. Together, DJ Darky, Fatima, and Klaudia will learn how sampling the sonics of sex (funk) shapes black identity and culture.

MAKE MY FUNK P-FUNK

DJ Darky tells us that "Funk not only moves, it can remove . . . it'll clear your chakras, I'll give it that. But it isn't enlightenment. None of it is. Jazz, classical, blues, dancehall, bhangra—it's all scattered chapters of the sonic Bhagavad Gita" (Beatty 27). DJ Darky alludes to a song of sacred scripture, and because all of the musical forms have roots in or intersections with black culture, the sacred text is blackness itself. Funk acts as indeterminate blackness' vehicle of expression, and Beatty positions Charles Schwa as a disciple of funk. DJ Darky explains, "Charles Stone, aka the Schwa, is a little-known avant-garde jazz musician we Westside DJs had nicknamed the Schwa because his sound, like the indeterminate vowel, is unstressed, up-side down, and backward . . . (Beatty 36). Although it may seem as if there is little connection between the Schwa's free and avant-garde jazz associated with the free-jazz movement, the connection between the two genres is evident for a number of musicians. In his autobiography, *Hit Me Fred: Recollections of the Sideman*, Fred Wesley articulates the connection between jazz and funk, stating that jazz and funk

> are basically the same thing, with emphasis on different elements and playing with different attitudes. Jazz is cool and slick and subtle, emphasizing the melodic and harmonic side of music. Funk is bold, arrogant, and aggressive, emphasizing the hard downbeats and tricky rhythms of the music, and tends to appeal more to the booty-shaking listener. I submit that there is a very thin line separating the two schools of music appreciation. (207)

Like the be-bop jazz musicians credited with coining the term funk,[8] the Schwa uses funk for something other than booty-shaking. While Wesley comments on funk's effect on the body, funk unequivocally has embedded within it tools useful for non-canonical black identity construction. Moving from the earliest manifestation of funk in the work of James Brown to that of Parliament, heavily influenced by Sun-Ra's philosophies about race, space, and time, the Schwa is more P-Funk, or as Kodwo Eshun might say more brilliant than the sun. P-Funk's heavy emphasis on the body in groove is important here since it stands in opposition to the respectable togetherness, passive non-violent use of the body advocated by Civil Rights leaders, as well as distinguishes itself from the militant cool posing, a la the black power fist, of Black Power leaders. According to P-Funk, the body must groove. Beatty, as if he were Dr. Dre in the early 1990s assembling the magnum opus *The Chronic,* establishes a re-recognition of the importance of funk to black culture and identity by emphasizing its use in the art form of sampling in hip-hop culture. DJ Darky proclaims of the personification of funk: "For us the Schwa is the ultimate break beat" (Beatty 36). Further, even as the Schwa recognizes the other subjective means for funk, he never forgets that funk derives from corporeal labor and exertion. DJ Darky claims of Schwa's tendencies to play with his body in ghastly positions, "Most critics theorized that these corporeal contrivances were designed to illustrate that making music is more than a mental process, that a musician brings his body to a gig, not just his brain" (Beatty 38). The same might be said of constructing identity. A person brings her body to the process, not just society's discursive models. Tony Bolden reminds us that through funk, "dancers become 'three-dimensional visualizations' of music" and "invokes a reevaluation of the very notion of textuality" (18). Through his music, the way he plays, his unique audition process to find a band, and the manner in which he can make anything an instrument, the Schwa has defied society's perceptions of blackness by using funk to facilitate indeterminate blackness.

The Schwa also acts as the ultimate break beat for Fatima and Klaudia, helping them to form a basis for a counter discourse that may halt the misrecognition of Afro-Germans in the novel. Karein K. Goertz's "Showing Her Colors: An Afro-German Writes the Blues in Black and White" explains what misrecognition can do over a period of time: "Unlike African diasporic communities that exist on the 'recognized margin' of countries such as the United States or Britain, Afro-Germans have until recently lacked the support of a viable collective identity to develop the 'protective antibodies' necessary to cope with racial prejudice and insensitivity" (308). DJ Darky's descriptions of Fatima perfectly capture Goertz's antibodies metaphor, since he says of her: "Fatima didn't have hobbies or interests. All she had was pronounced bouts of depression and her sister's broad shoulders to lean on" (Beatty 142). Fatima's malaise remains psychological as DJ Darky documents how Fatima, "who showed up more than once at my place with a medical bracelet tied around a bloodstained wrist bandage," was a woman who consistently attempted suicide (Beatty142). Fatima's suicide attempts are temporarily halted after she hears the Schwa's music. At the moment, "when the song came on Fatima literally shook with happiness. She had found her blackness. After that it no longer mattered that her mother never told them who or what their father was beyond being 'ass-hole colored' white, black, Arab, Mexican, asshole, it didn't matter. They'd been reborn black. Pushkin black. Black belt black. First woman in space black. German black. That was their story" (Beatty 144). These are variations of blackness that funk can provide. The revelation produces momentary happiness, but it is short-lived since Fatima eventually kills herself. Still, the nature of indeterminate blackness and how it moves beyond space and time persists. Break beats turn out to be a cultural artifact of CP time, and as Kodwo Eshun notes in *More Brilliant than the Sun: Adventures in Sonic Fiction*, a mechanism of time travel. Eshun observes:

> The Breakbeat is a motion-capture device, a detachable Rhythmengine, a movable rhythm motor that generates cultural velocity. The break is any short captured sound whatsoever. Indifferent to tradition, this functionalism ignores history, allows hip-hop to datamine unknown veins of funk, to groove-rob, not ancestor worship. (14)

The Schwa is Eshun's breakbeat for Fatima, and he generates cultural velocity that Fatima's self-definition of being Black German requires. Yet, after experiencing several apartheid-like incidents that begin with a new exclusionary policy banning "certain" black men from Slumberland, Fatima realizes "there is no camouflage for being black," and commits suicide by setting herself afire (Beatty 188). However, Fatima was not the only recipient for the Schwa's cultural velocity. When DJ Darky and the Schwa finally do play together, it turns into a jam session about the indeterminate nature of blackness. As DJ Darky mixes and samples with turntables and vinyl records, the Schwa falls into playing a section of the Negro national anthem "Lift Every Voice and Sing." DJ Darky takes the Schwa's selection as a dare for him to be black. He resists the dare so that he can hang on to the mantra he has repeated in some form throughout the novel: "blackness is and forever will be passé" (Beatty 228). As they continue to play, the Schwa in his production of blackness and DJ Darky in his rejection of it, they produce a reflexivity of blackness and create a second sonic wall for Berlin and its black citizens. Ironically, DJ Darky observes of his search for the Schwa and their groove-robbing concert: "Thanks to my misguided effort, blackness is back. The Schwa's musical munificence hadn't rendered blackness irrelevant, only darkened it even further" (Beatty 234). However, as funk suggests, blackness never really went anywhere.

NOTES

1. Because several supporting texts spell *break beat* differently, I have chosen to spell it without a space or hyphen. If it appears differently in cited sources, it is because that it is how the writer of the selected text chose to spell it.

2. Paul Gilroy's *Black Atlantic: Modernity and Double-Consciousness* considers the parameters of modernity for blackness, which marks a place in time dependent on linear conceptions of time. In addition, Canadian cultural critic Rinaldo Walcott's talk "The Poor Cousins of Modernity" expresses that black people's modernity and westerness as being out of sync and in disjointed time to Euro-American modernity and westerness.

3. In the PBS documentary *I'll Make Me A World*, there is footage of Baraka performing a slightly different version of his published poem "Nation Time" in front of students at a campus event. All subsequent references to Baraka's "Nation Time" throughout the essay are from this version.

4. In "Sag Harbor-author Dismisses 'Post-black' label," Colson Whitehead responds to journalist Chris Vognar's query about his work as post-black in the *Dallas Morning News* article.

5. Taylor correctly suggests that use of the phrase itself can lend to vagueness and a non-intentional disavowal of blackness (627), while also insisting upon a refinement of the category, rather than totally doing away with it (636).

6. Afrocentrism also accounts for these African Diasporic concepts of time. In "Time in African Culture," Dorthy L. Pennington wrote, "The mathematical division of time observed by Westerners has very little relevance to Africans" (137). Norman Harris's "A Philosophical Basis for an Afrocentric Orientation" argues that the way a group conceptualizes time determines what role history will play in social change.

7. M.W.I suggests that all alternative histories and futures are possible. According to Peter Byrnes, physicist Hugh Everett is responsible for using the wave function to challenge the parameters of physical reality dealing with the macroscopic and microscopic worlds. From there, theories of time travel and multiverses become possible. See also Everett's "The Theory of the Universal Wave Function" in *The Many-Worlds Interpretation of Quantum Mechanics,* philosopher David Lewis's *On the Plurality of Worlds* and physicist Brian Greene's *The Hidden Reality: Parallel Universes and the Deep Laws of the Cosmos* of to see the various non-linear theories of time.

8. See Tony Bolden's "Theorizing the Funk: An Introduction" in *The Funk Era and Beyond: New Perspectives on Black Popular Culture.*

WORKS CITED

Ashe, Bertram D. "Theorizing the Post-Soul Aesthetic: An Introduction." *African American Review* 41, no. 4 (2007): 609–624.

Beatty, Paul. *Slumberland: A Novel.* New York: Bloomsbury USA, 2008.

Bolden, Tony. *The Funk Era and Beyond: New Perspectives on Black Popular Culture.* New York: Palgrave Macmillan, 2008.

Byrne, Peter. "The Many Worlds of Hugh Everett." *Scientific American* 297, no. 6 (2007): 98–105.

Campt, Tina M. "Afro-German Cultural Identity and the Politics of Positionality: Contests and Contexts in the Formation of a German Ethnic Identity." *New German Critique* 58 (1993): 109–126.

———. "Converging Spectres of an Other within: Race and Gender in Prewar Afro-German History." *Callaloo* 26, no. 2 (2003): 322–341.

Ellis, Trey. "The New Black Aesthetic." *Callaloo* 38 (1989): 233–243.

Eshun, Kodwo. *More Brilliant than the Sun: Adventures in Sonic Fiction.* London: Quartet Books, 1998.

Everett, Hugh. "The Theory of the Universal Wave Function." In *The Many-Worlds Interpretation of Quantum Mechanics.* Edited by Bryce S. De Witt and Neill Graham, 3–140. Princeton, NJ: Princeton University press, 1973.

Forman, Murray. *That's the Joint!: The Hip-hop Studies Reader.* New York: Routledge, 2004.

Gilroy, Paul. *Black Atlantic: Modernity and Double-Consciousness.* Cambridge, MA: Harvard University Press, 1993.

Goertz, Karein K. "Showing Her Colors: An Afro-German Writes the Blues in Black and White." *Callaloo* 26, no. 2 (2003): 306–319.

Golden, Thelma. *Freestyle,* exhibition catalogue. New York: Studio Museum in Harlem, 2001: 14–15

Harris, Norman. "A Philosophical Basis for an Afrocentric Orientation." In *Afrocentric Visions: Studies in Culture and Communication.* Edited by Janice D. Hamlet, 15–26. Thousand Oaks, CA: Sage Publishers, 1998.

Morrison, Toni. *The Bluest Eye.* New York: Plume Book, 1994.

Murray, Rolland. "Black Crisis Shuffle: Fiction, Race, and Simulation." *African American Review.* 42, no. 2 (2008): 215–233.

"Nation Time." Dir. Pollard, Sam, Betty Ciccarelli, Tracy Heather Strain, and Denise A. Greene. 1999. *I'll Make Me a World.* Alexandria, VA: PBS Video (VHS).

Pennington, Dorthy L. "Time in African Culture." In *African Culture: The Rhythm of Unity.* Edited by Molefi Kete Asante and Kariamu Welsh Asante, 123–140. Westport, CT: Greenwood Press, 1985.

Potter, Russell A. *Spectacular Vernaculars: Hip-hop and the Politics of Postmodernism.* Albany: State University of New York Press, 2008.

Taylor, Paul C. "Post-Black, Old Black." *African American Review* 41, no. 4 (2007): 625–640.

Vognar, Chris. "'Sag Harbor' Author Dismisses 'Post-Black' Label," *Dallas Morning News.* Last modified January 20, 2010. http://www.dallasnews.com/sharedcontent /dws/ent/stories/DN-whitehead_0120gd.ARTo.State.Edition1.4c1f53c.html

Walcott, Rinaldo. "The Poor Cousins of Modernity." In *Flying Solo Series. World News Online.* Video. August 13, 2008. http://wn.com/Rinaldo_Walcott

Wesley, Fred. *Hit Me, Fred: Recollections of a Side Man.* Durham, NC: Duke University Press, 2002.

Willis, Susan. "Eruptions of Funk: Historicizing Toni Morrison." In *Black Literature and Literary Theory,* edited by Henry L. Gates Jr., 263–285. New York Routledge, 1990.

Wright, Michelle M. "Others-from-within from Without: Afro-German Subject Formation and the Challenge of a Counter-Discourse." *Callaloo* 26, no. 2 (2003): 296–305.

TEN

POST-INTEGRATION BLUES: BLACK GEEKS AND AFRO-DIASPORIC HUMANISM

ALEXANDER G. WEHELIYE

I

On the one hand, this essay grows out of a general interest in taking stock of some significant shifts in African American identity and cultural production subsequent to the Civil Rights Movement, and, on the other hand, it is a result of teaching a course about the recent history of the African American novel.[1] When initially conceptualizing this course a few years ago, I felt it was necessary to provide a topical focus that moved beyond temporal or generic frameworks, and, as a result I named the course "Post-Integration Blues," since all of the texts on the syllabus grappled with the consequences of integration, especially in educational settings. For my purposes, the phrase "post-integration blues" serves as an apt description of how integration has affected black subjects because it amplifies both the immense gains achieved by the Civil Rights Movement and the cultural, political, and psychological fallout from these benefits. In other words, "post-integration blues" insists on coarticulating the positive and negative dimensions of integration without resolving the tensions between them. The blues, as a structure of feeling rather than a particular musical genre, provides a pathway to understanding the central contradictions of the post-integration era. As Albert Murray has argued:

> The blues as such are synonymous with low spirits. Blues music . . . with all its preoccupation with the most disturbing aspects of life, it is something contrived specifically to be performed as entertainment . . . its express purpose is to make people feel good . . . but in the process of doing so it is actually expected to generate a disposition that is both elegantly playful and heroic in its nonchalance. (Murray 45)

Hence, the "post-integration blues" does not dwell solely on the losses precipitated by integration (loss of black cultural specificity, the continued existence of racism and white supremacy, etc.); instead it accentuates the manifold fissures that are integral elements of this particular culturo-historical formation. The figure of the black geek, as it has emerged in literature and popular culture, represents one of the principal embodiments of the "post-integration blues," allowing black cultural practitioners to underscore how larger societal shifts impact specific black subjects and to create avenues for imagining blackness that refuse to be contained by the mutually exclusive poles of assimilation and separatism.

Huey Riley, one of the main characters featured in Aaron McGruder's popular daily comic strip, *The Boondocks,* declared in the spring of 2000 "I am the anti-cool!! I hereby declare myself . . . A NERD" (McGruder 40).[2] Spread across hundreds of daily newspapers in the United States, this statement seemed like a coming out of sorts, given that until recently black people have rarely been portrayed as geeks or nerds in literature and popular culture. What had been bubbling under the surface since the 1970s and gained some momentum during the two subsequent decades, was now part of the mainstream: the geek as a major category of black culture in the post-integration era (Coates 2007; Crew 2002; Ford 2007; Hannaham 2002; Peterson 2009; Phi 2010, Pressler 2007; Rivero 2007, Tocci 2007). Black subjects were rarely imagined as intelligent and/or articulate beyond the confines of Afro-diasporic literatures, where their intellectual dexterity often led to tragedy. The prominence of Steven Urkel (portrayed by Jaleel White) on the long-running sitcom *Family Matters* (1989–98), who is by far the most well-known black geek in contemporary popular culture, suggests a significant shift in this development, since he was not doomed in the same way as his literary progenitors. Still, his intelligence had to be masked and deflected by the character's buffoonish, almost minstrel-like antics. Another version of the black geek appears in contemporary black literature: besides Huey from *The Boondocks,* black geeks can be found in Paul Beatty's *The White Boy Shuffle* (Gunnar Kaufman), Colson Whitehead's *The Intuitionist* (Lila Mae Watson) and *John Henry Days* (J. Sutter), Trey Ellis's *Platitudes* (Earle Tyner), Zadie Smith's *White Teeth* (Irie Jones), Percival Everett's *Erasure* (Thelonious "Monk" Ellison) and Fran Ross's *Oreo* (Christine Clark).[3] What unites the characters is their circumvention of both the pitfalls of the "Urkel syndrome" and their lack of tragic pathos. Despite being confronted with serious difficulties, these black geeks are generally not very comfortable in either the white or the black world but can, nevertheless, exist in both.

This essay charts the emergence of the black geek as the paradigmatic figure of post-integration literature and a reformulation of Trey Ellis's notion of the "cultural mulatto." I argue that black geeks emphasize the simultaneous alienation from both white and black cultural contexts, while also drawing attention how black geeks navigate between these two worlds through their intelligence and wit. I will begin by examining the concept of "post-soul," since it has become one of the central critical frameworks for conceptualizing black culture in the aftermath of the Civil Rights Movement. Then, the argument turns to the racial contours of geek identity and a brief genealogy of black geeks in literature and popular culture.

2

Trey Ellis, Nelson George, Mark Anthony Neal, and Greg Tate have considered "post-soul" as a useful frame of reference for analyzing major shifts in African American life and art subsequent to the Civil Rights Movement.[4] Combined, these authors argue that black culture has undergone momentous shifts in the last forty years that need to be addressed in order to come to a fuller understanding of our current social, political, economic, and cultural landscape. In other words, these writers ask: what happens after all the major goals of black liberation struggles in the New World have been accomplished, at least nominally? In this sense, the "post" in the "post-soul" compound, as with all other "post-" formations, suspends soul in a perpetual afterlife. While "post-soul" critics agree that black life and culture have undergone some significant changes since the Civil Rights era, it seems far easier to designate what distinguishes "post-soul" from earlier cultural patterns than to pinpoint the precise characteristics of this category. Nelson George, perhaps the most prominent architect of this concept, sums up his notion of "post-soul" as follows:

> Post-soul is my shorthand to describe a time when America attempted to absorb the victories, failures, and ambiguities that resulted from the soul years. The post-soul years have witnessed an unprecedented number of

> black people in the public life of America.... Unfortunately, all that prog-
> ress has not been as beneficial to the black masses as was anticipated in
> the 60s. The achievements of role models have not necessarily had a tan-
> gible impact on the realities of persistent poverty, poor education, and lin-
> gering, deep-seated social discrimination. (George ix)

For George "post-soul" encompasses most aspects of black life subsequent to the Civil Rights Movement and "soul" operates as a signifier for
this movement. In other words, "post-soul" stands (assimilation and increased visibility) and falls (the lingering of poverty and discrimination)
with the epochal events of the 1960s.

Trey Ellis's controversial 1989 treatise, "The New Black Aesthetic,"
remains the most succinct and influential theorization of the cultural
and aesthetic facets of "post-soul."[5] In this essay, Ellis homes in on the
figure of the "cultural mulatto," who "just as a genetic mulatto is a black
person of mixed parents who can often get along fine with his white
grandparents, a cultural mulatto, educated by a multi-racial mix of cultures, can also easily navigate in the white world. And it is by and large
this rapidly growing group of cultural mulattoes that fuels the New Black
Aesthetic" (Ellis 189). Included in this category are artists as diverse as
rock group Fishbone, Spike Lee, and Toni Morrison. In addition, for Ellis, the New Black Aesthetic (NBA) is defined by historically trailing
the Civil Rights and Black Nationalist Movements and by its ironic re-
articulation of some of these earlier movements' central concerns. Mark
Anthony Neal's formulation of the "post-soul" concept, which is indebted
to Ellis's NBA, also uses the Civil Rights Movement as a historical foil.
Yet, Neal's version of "post-soul" productively supplements the matrix
provided by George and Ellis by invoking intramural differences (especially gender and sexuality) and a black variant of postmodernism (Neal
3). Accordingly, "post-soul" functions for Neal not only as a marker of
temporal periodization but also as an aesthetic category: black postmodernism, which, just as postmodernism as a whole, accentuates the end
of grand narratives, differences, pastiche, play, etc. Thus, Neal theorizes
"post-soul" as a sociohistorical phenomenon and a set of aesthetic attributes. Although aesthetics and racial difference feature prominently in
Ellis's NBA, his use of "cultural mulatto" takes away from the force of the
analysis by too easily reinstating the raciocultural taxonomies it seeks to
overcome, thereby limiting the NBA to a simple cultural admixture of

black and white. Conversely, Neal's argument turns on the internal differentiation and fragmentation of black culture, showing that the historical period following the Civil Rights Movement has given rise to a plethora of New Black Cultural Practices, and not only the Aesthetic produced by "cultural mulattoes."

What remains consistent throughout George's, Ellis's, and Neal's accounts, though, is their emphasis on the 1960s as the essential moment in the articulation of "soul" within African American politics and culture. Although "soul" featured prominently in 1960s black liberation discourses, it would be useful to span a slightly broader and different historical net vis-à-vis the role of "soul" in the history of Afro-Diasporic culture, since it played such a decisive role in shaping the very notion of blackness in the West from the late eighteenth century onward. Generally speaking, given that slaves were denied the status of being human, oftentimes their claim, as articulated in poetry (Phillis Wheatley), slave narratives (Olaudah Equiano, Frederick Douglass, and Harriet Jacobs), and in the early history of the African American novel (Harriet Wilson), to western humanity was framed by Christian doctrines of the soul. Thus, Afro-Diasporic subjects were capable of humanity insofar as they could demonstrate that they possessed a Christian soul. W. E. B. Du Bois's *The Souls of Black Folk* marks a watershed moment in the secularization of "soul" in its treatment of "sorrow Songs" as cultural and political artifacts rather than as first and foremost sacred musical texts. This shift, although never quite complete, represents a move to secular humanism. The next instantiation of soul, which found its main expression in the notion of soul as a transcendental (racial) unconscious, appeared during the Harlem Renaissance and in the Negritude movement,[6] only to be later revised and critiqued by the antihumanism of Richard Wright and the critical humanism of Frantz Fanon. In this light, the Civil Rights Movement's and Black Nationalist discourses' definitions of soul represent reformulations of these earlier Afro-Diasporic notions of "soul" rather than novel inventions of this crucial concept. Although none of the authors concerned with describing "post-soul" claims that "soul" enters the annals of black thought only in the 1960s, by focusing almost entirely on this historical epoch, they run the risk of implicitly affirming this interpretation. Taking into account the broader historical trajectory sketched here will enable us to see beyond the last five decades in order to come to a fuller and more layered understanding of the central place (post) soul occupies in black culture's vexed relationship with western modernity.

These dialogues concerning the "souls of black folk" allowed black subjects to alternately demand inclusion in the category of the human, show humanity's limits via its constitutive exclusions, and/or reject the western version of humanity in an outright fashion. Sylvia Wynter's thinking concentrates on shifting contours of the human in the West since the Renaissance in which "soul" often played the role of gatekeeper: only those members of the homo sapiens species deemed to possess souls were seen as possessing the property of the human. Wynter writes:

> The first [form of Man] was from the Renaissance to the eighteenth century; the second from then until today, thereby making possible both the conceptualizabilty of natural causality, and of nature as an autonomously functioning force in its own right governed by its own laws . . . with this, in turn, making possible the cognitively emancipatory rise and gradual development of the physical sciences (in the wake of the invention of Man1), and then of the biological sciences (in the wake of the nineteenth century invention of Man2). These were to be processes made possible only on the basis of the dynamics of a colonizer/colonized relation that the West was to discursively constitute and empirically institutionalize on the islands of the Caribbean and, later, on the mainlands of the Americas. (Wynter 264)[7]

For Wynter these two versions of the human are integrally linked to the fate of western Man's various others, particularly the colonized and "the negro." Thus, rather than being wholly outside of western modernity, black subjects are integral to its discursive and material workings via their putative lack of humanity, which, in turn facilitates western man functioning as Man. Put differently, Wynter's contentions emphasize the integrality of race, especially blackness in the formation "humanity" in western modernity. If we consider that "soul" was such a key player in this drama about the "human," "post-soul" ceases to function as a recent problematic, unfolding instead in broader epistemic and historical contexts. Accordingly, (post-) soul should be viewed as one of *the* central concerns of Afro-Diasporic cultural and political discourses since the end of the eighteenth century.[8] The "soul" era would stretch from this time to the 1960s and represent black culture in the age of religious and secular humanisms, while "post-soul" would designate the current transitionary period to an instantiation of blackness that does not rest on being included in or excluded from hegemonic western humanisms. In many ways, then, post-integration provides a more apt delimitation of the cultural formations I have been discussing, because it does not intimate that the struggle over "the souls of black folk" is a recent and historically delimited phenomenon, or that we have progressed beyond it.[9] Rather it facilitates the conceptualization of a particular cultural, historical, social, and aesthetic constellation (post-integration) within the context of the long-standing struggle over the soul (humanity) of black subjects in the West. The geeks in contemporary black literature and culture are prime examples of the "post-integration blues," and therefore also engaged in (re)defining reigning notions of humanity.

3

Barack Obama's campaign for and historic ascendancy to the presidency of the United States have been accompanied by debates about his geekiness, especially as it stands in putative contrast to his blackness. On the one hand, self-proclaimed geeks of all races claimed Obama as one of their own (Asim 2009; Blum 2008; Chris 2008; Moylan 2009) and, on the other hand, Obama was scrutinized for being "articulate while black" and speaking in the "edubonics" (Moore 2007; see also Coates 2007 and Crawford 2007). Obama's complex racial/national heritage and his ostensible ability to smoothly move between black and white worlds (especially his linguistic code-switching dexterity) were frequently summoned as indices of his "inauthentic blackness."[10] Since oratorical skillfulness has been a hallmark of African American political, cultural, and religious practices (Frederick Douglass and Martin Luther King, Jr., to name the most prominent examples) since the nineteenth century, why were Obama's blackness and his rhetorical aptitude deemed antithetical?

Given its fairly recent appearance and etymological genesis, the definition of "geek," especially in relation to its twin "nerd," is fairly elusive. According to *Wikipedia* a geek is a "person who is fascinated, perhaps obsessively, by technology and imagination. A derogatory term for one with low social skills, often with average intelligence, as opposed to nerds, who are generally viewed as having low social skills but high intelligence."[11] However, I would suggest a slightly different circumscription of this type, using technology and science as the main distinguishers: the nerd relates compulsively to the technological and/or scientific, while the geek obsesses over information/knowledge; both are intelligent and socially discomfited to varying degrees.[12] Finally, a new form of geek has emerged in recent years who traffics in arcane pop cultural knowledge that is presented in a hip, loquacious, self-deprecating, and idiosyncratic verbal style.[13] In this definition, science and technology can be part of "geek" identity but they need not be essential attributes of this figure. More importantly, bracketing techno-science in this context works against the hegemonic racial and gender dynamics of geek identity.[14]

Whether explicitly avowed or not race spectrally suffuses geek identity in several significant ways, especially since it has usually been reserved for white and Asian men (Eglash 2002; Nugent 2008). Ron Eglash describes the racial continuum of geek/nerd identity thus: "There exists a stereotype of Africans as oversexual and Asians as undersexual, with 'whiteness' portrayed as the perfect balance between these two extremes. Given these associations, it is no coincidence that many Americans have a stereotype of Asians as nerds and of African Americans as anti-nerd hipsters" (Eglash 52). Given that black and female subjects are often represented as hyperembodied, it comes as no surprise that they would be excluded from this category, which gains much of its legitimacy from downplaying embodiment and sexuality. Geeks appear as disembodied minds, which leads to both their strength ("superior" intelligence) and weakness (the inability to maneuver social situations). Drawing on the ethnographic work of linguist Mary Bucholtz, Benjamin Nugent writes, "nerdiness . . . is largely a matter of racially tinged behavior. People who are considered nerds tend to act in ways that are . . . 'hyperwhite.' . . . By cultivating an identity perceived as white to the point of excess, nerds deny themselves the aura of normality that is usually one of the perks of being white" (Bucholtz 2001; Nugent 2007). White geeks/nerds adopt exaggerated mannerisms and speech patterns that draw attention not only to their racial embodiment but also to the racial exclusivity of this persona, since using "superstandard" English often goes hand in hand with phenotypical whiteness and being a "hyperwhite" geek signals ownership of the privileges of whiteness.[15] How does this impact whether black subjects have access to and how they utilize geek identity?[16] What happens to "hyperwhiteness" and "superstandard" English when they encounter blackness? Do they remain white? If not, do they become black or transform into something else altogether? Put simply, what are the conditions of possibility for the merging of "black" and "geek" given their seemingly adversarial nature?

On the whole, rather than seizing whiteness as such, black geeks appropriate and recast a specific type of white identity that is both racially marked ("normal" whiteness generally functions by not calling attention to itself) and tied to educational and economic upward mobility.[17] Ellis's term "cultural mulatto" cannot fully express the racial and cultural complexities of black geeks, because it construes the cultural and racial clash embodied in black geeks as mere admixture, falling short of bearing witness to the specific cultural modalities that comprise this compound and their effects on the benefits of "hyperwhiteness." Obama's "superstandard" linguistic demeanor, particularly when contrasted with other African American leaders such as Jesse Jackson, was perceived as "hyperwhite," and, thus, trespassing on a particular (and valuable) property of whiteness (Harris 1993).[18] In other words, Obama and other black geeks are berated for their deployment of "hyperwhiteness" and not for simply "acting white," as it is frequently described in the news media. If only "acting white" were at stake in these debates, why aren't these critiques leveled at black subjects that speak with audibly white working class and/or regional inflections?[19]

Carlton and Hillary Banks from the television series *The Fresh Prince of Bel-Air* (1990–96), for instance, suggest two different modalities of "hyperwhiteness" bodied forth in black characters. Following a predictably gendered path, Carlton falls squarely into the black geek category through his use of "superstandard" English, social ineptitude, and scholastic aptitude, while Hillary, in addition to being spoiled and shallow, speaks with a discernable valley girl accent. Despite the gender split, both sociolects signify whiteness in conjunction with educational ("superstandard" English) and/or economic (valspeak) privilege. In this way, "acting white" and the black geek figure recast the passing narrative found in texts such as Nella Larsen's *Passing*, Charles Chesnutt's *The House Behind the Cedars*, or James Weldon Johnson's *Autobiography of an Ex-Colored Man*. In contrast to passing, however, contemporary forms of cultural trespassing do not rest on biology or phenotype but on the mastery of cultural and linguistic codes associated with racial, class, and gender identities, especially forms of whiteness associated with monetary and cultural capital.

The black geek protagonists in Trey Ellis's *Platitudes* (Earl Tyner) and Fran Ross's *Oreo* (Christine Clark) adroitly negotiate multiple cultural and linguistic environments. Ross and Ellis, however, offer different depictions of the processes involved in such negotiations. Ross's heroine's mother is African American and her father Jewish, and the narrative chronicles Christine's quest—the novel is based on the Greek myth of Thesseus—to find her absent father. Virtually every character in the novel deploys a particular variant of "nonstandard" English, while Yiddish words and phrases appear throughout the text. For instance, Christine's mother thinks in mathematical equations, a minor character constructs English language sentences that are literal translations from French, and her grandmother's mode of expression is described as follows: "From time to time, her dialogue will be rendered in ordinary English, which Louise does not speak. To do full justice to her speech would require a ladder of footnotes and glosses, a tic of apostrophes . . . and a Louise-ese/English dictionary of phonetic spelling" (Ross 12). In contrast, Ellis's *Platitudes* imagines Earle Tyner's linguistic and cultural bridge building primarily between two poles: the largely white world that Earl usually inhabits and the traditionally black world of Harlem that he discovers over the course of the novel. Ellis puts a "post-soul" spin on "double consciousness," since Earle is estranged from black culture and not the white world, as in Du Bois's theorization of this problematic, yet he still imagines Earle as struggling with a duality. Maintaining this duality results in the calcification of both black and white culture so that each appears unitary. Since Ross's *Oreo* features scores of languages, cultures, behaviors, etc., neither the black nor the white world represents a discrete unit but both exist in manifold iterations. The discrepancy between *Oreo* and *Platitudes* on this question is important because it underscores the limitations of the "acting white" debate, which generally neglects the diversity of black and white cultures and construes the relationship between them as a one-way street, reducing the complexity of racial identity, which leads to the erasure of the power dynamics at the heart of "acting white."

In Zadie Smith's *White Teeth*, Irie Jones, born to a white English father and a black British mother of Jamaican descent, desires to transcend her working-class, immigrant surroundings. She does so by embracing her seemingly innate geekiness and by associating with the lily-white, educated, and middle-class Chalfen family. When the Chalfen's son first encounters Irie, he detects a kindred nerd spirit, because she "had a strong nerdy flavor . . . despite that boy she spent her time with. The Indian one . . . Joshua Chalfen strongly suspected her of being *one of his own* . . . She was a nerd-immigrant, who had fled the land of the fat, facially challenged, and disarmingly clever" (Smith 246–47). Chalfen's presumed connection with Irie rests on the erasure of her ethnic and class background. When Irie explains her ethnographic fascination with the Chalfens, she emphasizes class: "she'd never been so *close* to and beautiful thing, the *middle-class*," and nationality: "she wanted their Englishness . . . It didn't occur to her that the Chalfens were, after a fashion, immigrants too . . ." (Smith 267, 272–73). So, in order for the Chalfen family to serve as the quintessence of white Englishness, Irie disavows those aspects of their family history that would most clearly echo her own familial history. Irie's father, even though white and English, cannot personify a Platonic ideal of Englishness because he is working class and surrounds himself with non-white immigrants in his everyday life. Consequently, Irie's embrace of the Chalfen's Englishness is integrally bound to the fact they are also white, middle class. I am raising this point to underscore how the notions of "acting white" or "cultural mulatto" cannot adequately describe the racial trespassing of black geeks (and other black subjects). Both these concepts fail to ask what particular instantiations of black and white identity are being acted out or intermingled in the practices they are describing. If we take into account these questions, then we would perhaps see that some visibly Caucasian subjects also have to "act white" in order to reap the benefits of bourgeois whiteness and that U.S. mainstream culture has been populated by biological and cultural "mulattoes" of many races for quite some time.

The putative violation of racial conventions has often had catastrophic consequences for black subjects, as can be gleaned from the representation of educated black subjects in African American literary and cultural history. In W. E. B. Du Bois's 1903 short story, "The Coming of John," John Jones embodies the archetype of the "overeducated" black subject at odds with his/her environment due to their learnedness; he is exiled from the white world and is unable to exist in the black world. John's violent death at the hands of a mob dramatically underscores the fact that intellectual aspirations and blackness made strange bedfellows in the age of segregation and lynching. During the Harlem Renaissance (Nella Larsen's *Quicksand* and Claude McKay's *Home to Harlem,* for instance) and afterwards (Richard Wright's *Black Boy*) educated black characters were doomed to similar tragic fates. Wright's autobiographical self, how-ever, represents somewhat of a historical outpost, since the tragic dimen-sions of black intellectuals recede from the horizon, replaced, especially during the 1960s, by a twinning of educated blackness with revolutionary fervor represented by personalities such as Angela Davis, Amiri Baraka, and Malcolm X (Eglash 53–54).[20] Although these literary characters and public figures are not black geeks per se, they highlight the long-standing threat black intelligence has posed to existent racial power structures.

In 1980s yet another significant modification of this type appears in popular culture and literature with the emergence of The Native Tongues (De La Soul, The Jungle Brothers, Queen Latifah, etc.) in hip-hop, tele-vision characters like *A Different World's* Dwayne Wayne, and in liter-ary texts such as Trey Ellis's *Platitudes.*[21] The marked difference between these figures and previous representations is that they do not conform to tropes of respectability (Du Bois and Larsen) or revolutionary national-ism (Malcolm X), instead they are socially awkward yet highly intelligent and navigate their diverse environments with humor and wit, which is coupled with an irreverence for racial boundaries and cultural purities.[22]

Paul Beatty's *The White Boy Shuffle* presents the protagonist's family history not as a succession of heroic role models that have overcome the seemingly insurmountable odds placed before them but a "long cowardly queue of coons, Uncle Toms, and faithful boogedy-boogedy retainers" (Beatty 5). Beatty goes on to describe generations of Kaufmans that al-ways stood on the wrong side of history (by painting "whites only" signs and running away into slavery):

> Unlike the typical bluesy earthy folksy denim-overalls noble-in-the-face-of-cracker-racism aw shucks Pulitzer-Prize-winning protagonist mojo magic black man, I am not the seventh son of a seventh son of a seventh son. I wish I were, but fate shorted me by six brothers and three uncles. The chieftains and queens who sit on top of old Mount Kilimanjaro left me out of the will . . . I am the number-one son of a spineless colorstruck son of a bitch who was the third son of an ass-kissing sell-out house Negro who was indeed a seventh son but only by default. (Beatty 5)

The irony in this passage results chiefly from Beatty's deft inversion of black respectability and heroism, which were hallmarks of prior black liberation struggles.[23] Nevertheless, Beatty could not have crafted Kaufman's tops-turvy familial genealogy without acknowledging the importance of and reframing previous black cultural formations. In this way, the geek persona, when inhabited by black subjects, facilitates the exploration of the increased fragmentation in black culture since the 1960s and the recovery of previously neglected aspects of black cultural history. Despite the irreverence exhibited in this passage, Beatty and other contemporary black writers insist on exploring and dismantling the power dynamics that frame the black geek figure. They focus on those moments when the enactment of certain racial codes are perceived as threatening the status quo, which, however, does not mean that these instances are necessarily more radical or transgressive in any general way. More often than not the perceived breach in racial mores (being a black geek, passing, "acting white," for instance) arises when the hegemony of a particular group wields over economic and cultural capital is at stake.

4

It would be easy to read the humor, acerbic wit, and general irreverence of black geeks in literature as straightforward representations of a sociological condition found among a certain part of the African American populace in the aftermath of the gains achieved by the Civil Rights and Black Nationalist movements. Although these movements enabled the de jure and partial de facto desegregation of the U.S. educational system and the rise of a new black middle class, we should be cautious of this interpretation, at least as the exclusive lens through which to view this bourgeoning phenomenon, as it would leave intact the sociologization of black life.[24] Instead, I want to suggest that black geeks in black literature and popular culture conjure "a people to come," to use Gilles Deleuze and Felix Guattari's formulation; "There is extracted from chaos the shadow of the 'people to come' in the form that art, but also philosophy and science, summon forth: mass-people, world-people, brain-people, chaos-people—non-thinking thought that lodges in the three" (Deleuze and Guattari 1994, 218). Rather than insisting on the representation of a preexisting social reality, the concept of "a people to come" accentuates the positive, productive, and provisional aspects of art and literature. Given that racial identities have shifted and multiplied, despite the continued existence of white supremacy and structural racism, the awkward and self-conscious, yet verbally skilled geek persona serves as an ideal vehicle for amplifying the vexed politics and aesthetics of the "post-integration blues." This "people to come" gels with Sylvia Wynter's thoughts on the end of western style humanism, especially as it relates to western modernity's various others: "the struggle of our new millennium will be one between the ongoing imperative of securing the well-being of our present ethnoclass (i.e., Western bourgeois) conception of the human, Man, which overrepresents itself as if it were the human itself, and that of securing the well-being, and therefore the full cognitive and behavioral autonomy of the human species itself/ourselves" (Wynter 260). Consequently, the black geek denotes one passage to a world beyond "Man" by virtue of projecting blackness, a people to come, as disarticulated from the earlier humanist paradigms (spiritual and secular) that have been part and parcel of blackness's thorny liaison with the western idea of humanity.

Contemporary black literature and culture plays a pivotal role in the creation of the black geek as a prototype for "a blackness to come." The version of blackness does not seek inclusion in or lament exclusion from the mainstream, thereby eschewing the two prevailing models for blackness since the end of the eighteenth century: integration and separatism, which are defined principally by their relation to western humanism. Integration allows black subjects to become a part of the center by proving their "full humanity," while separatism insists on the radical alterity of black folk, which renders them incompatible with western humanity. Black geeks highlight the intricacy of (black) life and culture without insisting on either inclusion or separation from the mainstream, instead they minoritize blackness.[25] If geeks draw attention to the general disquiet of existence, then black geeks make possible, visible, and audible the struggles over the continued significance of blackness in the "post-integration" era. The black geek does not epitomize one form of identity among many but a conduit for exploring the shifting vicissitudes of blackness in the contemporary world. Which is to say, black geeks are not representatives of extant forms of identity, not even novel ones, rather, they are harbingers of the potential for singular forms of humanity that may be imagined but cannot (yet) be described.

POST-INTERGRATION BLUES

This course considers post-1960s literary texts, films, etc., that are concerned with the fate of African American identity in the aftermath of the Civil Rights Era. We will begin the quarter with some secondary readings by Trey Ellis and Mark Anthony Neal, all of who try to account for significant shifts in the culture and life of African Americans over the last thirty years. Using concepts such as post-soul and the New Black Aesthetic (NBA), we will discuss questions of social mobility, education, postmodern passing, as well as the variable contours of class, sexuality, and gender as they appear in contemporary African American literature, film, comic strips, television shows, and music. We will also pay close attention to the formal and structural aspects of the cultural artifacts we will be studying.

Requirements:

   *Regular attendance
   Students who miss more than two classes will receive a lower grade.
   *Two essays.
   To be handed in on the specified dates. Late papers receive lower
      grades.
   *Final Exam
   *In-class participation

Required Texts:

   Paul Beatty, *White Boy Shuffle*
   Octavia Butler, *Dawn*
   Ta-Nehisi Coates, *The Beautiful Struggle: A Father, Two Sons, and an
      Unlikely Road to Manhood*
   Junot Díaz, *The Brief Wondrous Life of Oscar Wao*
   Percival Everett, *Erasure*
   Aaron McGruder, *The Boondocks*
   Fran Ross, *Oreo*
   Danzy Senna, *Caucasia*

Schedule

Week 1: Course Introduction
Ellis, "The New Black Aesthetic" (In *Platitudes*) and Neal, *Post-Soul Babies*
Films: *Guess Who's Coming to Dinner* and *Guess Who?*

Week 2: Ellis, *Platitudes*
Ellis, *Platitudes*

Week 3: Ross, *Oreo*
Ross, *Oreo*

Week 4: Everett, *Erasure*
Everett, *Erasure*

Week 5: Díaz, *The Brief Wondrous Life of Oscar Wao*
Díaz, *The Brief Wondrous Life of Oscar Wao*

Week 6: Senna, *Caucasia*
Senna, *Caucasia*

Week 7: Beatty, *White Boy Shuffle*
Beatty, *White Boy Shuffle*

Week 8: Coates, *The Beautiful Struggle*
Coates, *The Beautiful Struggle*

Week 9: Butler, *Dawn*
Butler, *Dawn*

Week 10: Films: *I'm Through With White Girls* and *Medicine For Melancholy*
McGruder, *The Boondocks* and selected episodes from *Chappelle's Show*

NOTES

1. I have taught several different versions of this course since 2002, keeping the basic structure intact while fine-tuning the selection of class materials and their sequencing. See the syllabus appended to this article and my comments included in the roundtable discussion about teaching contemporary African American literature (Ashe 2007). Some of the ideas included here were initially developed in a discussion on the AfroFuturism listserv. I thank the list members for their valuable insights. An archived version of the conversation can be found on the group's webpage: http://groups.yahoo.com/group/afrofuturism/message/13038

2. As I will discuss later, there are many confluences between geek and nerd terminology and personas. While McGruder uses nerd here, Huey, as opposed to Urkel, is more of geek than a nerd, since the intense interest in science and technology that marks nerds as nerds is not one of his defining characteristics.

3. Black geeks also feature prominently in the following texts: Danzy Senna, *Caucasia;* Mat Johnson, *Drop;* Angela Nissel, *Mixed: My Life In Black and White;* Paul Beatty, *Tuff* and *Slumberland;* Alice Randall, *Pushkin and The Queen of Spades;* Colson Whitehead, *Sag Harbor;* Martha Southgate, *The Fall of Rome: A Novel;* Ta-Nehisi Coates, *The Beautiful Struggle;* Octavia Butler, *Parable of the Sower;* Junot Díaz, *The Brief Wondrous Life of Oscar Wao;* Andrea Lee, *Sarah Phillips;* Z. Z. Packer, *Drinking Coffee Elsewhere.*

4. See Ashe 2003, Ellis 2003, George 2001 and 2004, Neal 2002, and Tate 1992. For discussions of "post-soul" in black musical formations, see Eshun 1998, Neal 2002, and Weheliye 2002.

5. Although Ellis does not use the term "post-soul," he prefers the New Black Aesthetic, his ideas concern themselves with the fate of black identity and culture in the aftermath of the Civil Rights Movement in much the same way as those authors who actually wield the former idiom. I will not discuss Ashe's and Tate's important contributions to this debate in detail here but nonetheless want to note that Ashe provides a useful frame for thinking "post-soul" specifically in African American literature and that Tate includes in his analysis of postnationalist black art not only literature, music, and film/television as the other writers do but also the visual arts. See Ashe 2003 and Tate 1992.

6. While the link between soul and a racial unconscious was most influential in the 1920s and 1930s, it appears as early as 1900 in Pauline Hopkins's *Of One Blood,* albeit with strong religious undertones that recede into the background in the later writings.

7. In a different essay Wynter shows the religious conception of selfhood yielding to two modes of secularized humanity, first, the Cartesian "Rational Man" and then beginning "at the end of the eighteenth century . . . Man as a selected being and natural organism . . . as the universal human, 'man as man'" (Wynter 1989, 645). For different versions, besides the two cited here, of Wynter's important argument, see Wynter 1990 and 2006.

8. Paul Gilroy gives a difference valence to these debates by charting the disappearance of freedom from the horizon of Afro-Diasporic political discourses instead of the demise of soul, as occurs in the writings on "post-soul." However, Gilroy's arguments try to come to grips with much of the same problematics as those conjured by the authors cited above (Gilroy 2000, esp. 177–207).

9. As is hopefully clear, my use of "post" in the context of black culture in no way endorses the idea that we have now entered a "post-racial" era.

10. Clearly, Obama's biography lends itself to this narrative, since he is biracial, spent a considerable amount of time outside U.S. borders, and was raised primarily by his white relatives.

11. Here is *Wikipedia's* description of the relationship between geek and nerd: "The relationship of the terms 'nerd' and 'geek' to one another is disputed. Some view the geek as a less technically skilled nerd. Some factions maintain that 'nerds' are both technically skilled and socially competent, whereas 'geeks' are only technically skilled while socially incompetent; others hold an exactly reversed view, with 'geek' being the socially competent counterpart of the socially incompetent 'nerd', and call themselves 'geeks' with pride." See also Katz 1997.

12. This does not mean that geeks cannot have an intense relationship to technology but that is not a distinctive marker of being geeky.

13. Seth Cohen on Fox's now defunct television series *The O.C.* (2003–2007) is the most prominent exemplar of this type of geek and almost all the black geeks in contemporary black literature fall into this category. Cohen's differently pitched geekiness, which does not rely on technoscience, provides a striking contrast to the nerds that populate the CBS sitcom *The Big Bang Theory* (2007–), all of whom are scientists and exhibit technical mastery.

14. Although many critics use geek and nerd interchangeably or focus only on nerds, I will primarily utilize "geek" for the reasons outlined above.

15. I use phenotype here in order to highlight the visual dimension of racialization as it interfaces with geek identity.

16. For Bucholtz the linguistic demeanor of nerds is defined by the use of "superstandard" English, which "contrasts linguistically with Standard English in its greater use of 'supercorrect' linguistic variables: lexical formality, carefully articulated phonological forms, and prescriptively standard grammar . . . But the recognition of such difference is at least as ideologically as linguistically motivated. It is precisely because of the robustness of the ideology of Standard English in the United States that those linguistic varieties generally classified as nonstandard—African American Vernacular English foremost among them—are regularly held up as divergent from the standard despite considerable overlap in grammar, phonology, and the lexicon" (Bucholtz 2001, 88).

17. In the 1984 film, *Revenge of the Nerds,* which was instrumental in the contemporary pop cultural codification of the geek/nerd persona, the (largely white) nerds succeed in their fight against the (exclusively white) jocks only with help of the national chapter of a black fraternity. Rejected by all other organizations because they deviate from the normative instantiation of whiteness, the nerds form a coalition with the African American fraternity based on both groups' shared exclusion from the mainstream.

18. Eglash cautions against viewing black geeks solely in terms of their transgressive and liberatory potential, writing: "Despite their identity violations, these figures . . . often reproduce the very boundaries they attempt to overcome: not surprising since they are focused on attaching the 'wrong' race to the 'right' identity. While the figure of the black nerd contradicts the normative opposition between African American identity and technology, it does so only by affirming the uncool attributes of technological expertise" (Eglash 2002, 59).

19. As the recent debate about Stuart Buck's *Acting White: The Ironic Legacy of Desegregation* makes clear, this is still a fraught topic (Bouie 2010, Peterson 2010, Neal 2010, The Champ, 2010), especially when "acting white"becomes the prime indicator for the achievement gap between black and white students in the U.S. school system. The 'acting white' phenomenon, which, as all of Buck's critics point out is both far more complex and much less prevalent than assumed, operates as a cultural mask for longstanding structural inequalities in the education system.

20. The nameless protagonist in Ellison's *Invisible Man* represents both a critique of the tragic black intellectual and an in-depth exploration of the various pitfalls that accompany this model of black humanity (Ellison 1952).

21. Although this period in hip-hop also saw the proliferation of explicitly Black Nationalist groups such as Public Enemy, Boogie Down Productions, and The X-Clan that carried on the tradition of Malcolm X, The Native Tongues introduced a novel, playful persona without eschewing Black Nationalism or overt political "messages."

22. Clearly this not a complete shift and my genealogy of this figure is intended as an opening bid rather than an exhaustive catalog. Earlier manifestations of the contem-

porary black geek would include jazz musician, Sun Ra and Roger Thomas's character Raj on the 1970s sitcom, *What's Happening!!!* Oliver Wendel Jones, who appeared in the 1980s and 90s comic strips *Boone County* and *Outland* might be Urkel's closest cousin. One of the most prominent prototypical black geeks is Ralph Ellison, who in his non-fictional writings often exhibits an almost fanatical relationship to sound technologies and photographic equipment. See, for instance, Ellison's remarks about his childhood radio building hobby, his utter dedication to building the perfect stereo-system, and his exchanges about photographic camera equipment in his letters to Albert Murray (Ellison 1995, Callahan and Murray 2000). For critical considerations of Ellison and technology, see Weheliye 2005 and Wright 2003. For a useful survey of the appearance and ensuing ideological containment of black nerds in mainstream Hollywood cinema, see Kevorkian 1999.

23. This is especially evident in the reference to one of the most well-known lines from Du Bois's *The Souls of Black Folk:* "[t]he Negro is sort of a seventh son, born with a veil, and gifted with a second sight in this American world . . ." (Du Bois 1996, 5). Although the folkloric belief in the special powers of the "seventh son of the seventh son" predates Du Bois, it was he who ascribed supernatural abilities to all African Americans.

24. On the social-scientification of black life, see Kelley 1997, 15–42, and on the problem of sociological thinking in the institutional histories of black studies, see Judy 2000.

25. Gilles Deleuze and Felix Guattari refer to the principle that structures racial difference as binaristic, or any form of difference for that matter, as molar or majoritarian. Yet, according to this scheme, the majoritarian has no numeric basis, it represents a system of structuration that creates norms from which a variety of factors are then said to deviate, woman from man, black from white, to name the most obvious examples. The molecular or minoritarian, correspondingly, refers not to any actually existing groups but to another style of thinking about, through, and with difference, which facilitates the emergence of hitherto nonexisent becomings that point to novel modalities of life and thought. Where the molar can only express the already preestablished fixed positions of categories and identities, the molecular creates new forms of identity that represent neither the standard norm nor its deviation, in fact, it abolishes the very idea of representation (Deleuze and Guattari 1986 and 1987).

WORKS CITED

Afro-Futurism. 2001. Future Texts 3.0: The New Black Geek Chic (discussion thread). Yahoo Groups: Afro-Futurism. August–September. http://groups.yahoo.com /group/afrofuturism/message/13038.

Ashe, Bertram D. Foreword. In Trey Ellis *Platitudes & "The New Black Aesthetic,"* vii–xxvi. Boston: Northeastern University Press: 2003.

———. "These—Are—the 'Breaks': A Roundtable Discussion on Teaching the Post-Soul Aesthetic." *African American Review* 41, no. 4 (2007): 787–803.

Asim, G'Ra. "Obama Ruined My Game." *Salon,* May 26, 2009. http://www.salon.com /life/feature/2009/05/26/obama_uncool/.

Beatty, Paul. *The White Boy Shuffle.* Boston: Houghton Mifflin, 1996.

———. *Tuff: A Novel.* New York: Knopf, 2000.

———. *Slumberland: A Novel.* New York: Bloomsbury USA, 2009.

Blum, Matt. "5 Signs President-Elect Obama Is a Geek" *Wired*, November 6, 2008. http://blog.wired.com/geekdad/2008/11/5-signs-preside.html.

Bouie, Jamelle. "'Acting White' Just Standard Bullying, Racialized." *Tapped: The group blog of The American Prospect.* July 7, 2010. http://www.prospect.org/csnc/blogs /tapped_archive?month=07&year=2010&base_name=acting_white_is_just _your_stan.

Bucholtz, Mary. "The Whiteness of Nerds: Superstandard English and Racial Marked-ness." *Journal of Linguistic Anthropology* 11, no. 1 (2001): 84–100.

Buck, Stuart. *Acting White: The Ironic Legacy of Desegregation.* New Haven, CT: Yale University Press, 2010.

Butler, Octavia E. *Parable of the Sower.* New York: Four Walls Eight Windows, 1993.

Callahan, John F., and Albert Murray, eds. *Trading Twelves: The Selected Letters of Ralph Ellison and Albert Murray.* New York: Random House, 2000.

Chris. "Master's Degrees." *Stuff Black People Hate,* February 3, 2008. http:// stuffblackpeoplehate.com/2008/03/02/masters-degrees/.

Coates, Ta-Nehisi. "Is Obama Black Enough?" *Time,* February 8, 2007. http://www .time.com/time/nation/article/0,8599,1584736,00.html.

———. "Nerd Culture and Black People—Not an Oxymoron." *Atlantic,* August 9, 2008. http://tanehisicoates.theatlantic.com/archives/2008/08/nerd_culture _and_black_peoplenot_an_oxymoron.php.

———. *The Beautiful Struggle: A Father, Two Sons, and an Unlikely Road to Manhood.* New York: Random House, 2009.

Crawford, Byron. "He Speaks So Well." *ByronCrawford.com.* February 8, 2007. http:// www.byroncrawford.com/2007/02/he_speaks_so_we.html.

Crew, Adrienne. "BAP Like Me." *Salon,* November 29, 2002. http://www.salon.com /mwt/feature/2002/11/26/bap/print.html.

Deleuze, Gilles, and Felix Guattari. *Kafka: Towards a Minor Literature.* Translated by Dana Polan. Minneapolis: University of Minnesota Press, 1986.

———. *A Thousand Plateaus: Capitalism and Schizophrenia.* Translated by Brian Mas-sumi Minneapolis: University of Minnesota Press, 1987.

———. *What Is Philosophy?* Translated by Hugh Tomlinson and Graham Burchell. New York: Columbia University Press, 1994.

Díaz, Junot. *The Brief Wondrous Life of Oscar Wao.* New York: Riverhead Books, 2007.

Du Bois, W. E. B. *The Souls of Black Folk.* Edited by Donald B. Gibson. New York: Pen-guin, 1996.

Eglash, Ron. "Race, Sex, and Nerds." *Social Text* 71 (2002): 49–64.

Ellis, Trey. *Platitudes & "The New Black Aesthetic."* Boston: Northeastern University Press, 2003.

Ellison, Ralph. *Invisible Man.* New York: Random House, Inc., 1952.

———. *Shadow and Act.* New York: Vintage: 1995.

Eshun, Kodwo. *More Brilliant Than the Sun: Adventures in Sonic Fiction.* London: Quar-tet Books, 1998.

Ford, Sam. "The Black Nerd: A Stereotype to Break Stereotypes?" *Futures of Entertain-ment,* November 4, 2007. http://www.convergenceculture.org/weblog/2007/11 /the_black_nerd_a_stereotype_to_1.php.

"Geek." *Wikipedia.* http://en.wikipedia.org/wiki/Geek.

George, Nelson. *Buppies, B-Boys, Baps & Bohos: Notes on Post-Soul Black Culture.* Cam-bridge, MA: Da Capo Press, 2001.

————. *Post-Soul Nation: The Explosive, Contradictory, Triumphant, and Tragic 1980s as Experienced by African Americans (Previously Known as Blacks and Before That Negroes)*. New York: Viking, 2004

Gilroy, Paul. *Against Race: Imagining Political Culture Beyond the Color Line*. Cambridge, MA: Harvard University Press, 2000.

Hannaham, James. "The Rise of the Black Nerd: Separated From Racial Mainstreams, the Outsiders Make Their Mark." *Village Voice,* July 30, 2002. http://www.village-voice.com/2002-07-30/news/the-rise-of-the-black-nerd/.

Harris, Cheryl I. "Whiteness as Property." *Harvard Law Review* 106, no. 8 (1993): 1707–70.

Johnson, Mat. *Drop: A Novel*. New York: Bloomsbury USA, 2002.

Judy, Ronald A. T. "Untimely Intellectuals and the University." *boundary 2* 27, no.1 (2000): 121–33.

Katz, John. "Geek Backtalk: Part II." *Wired,* August 1, 1997. http://www.wired.com /culture/lifestyle/news/1997/08/5632.

Kelley, Robin D. G. *Yo' Mama's Disfunktional: Fighting the Culture Wars in Urban America*. Boston: Beacon Press,1997.

Kevorkian, Martin. "Computers with Color Monitors: Disembodied Black Screen Images 1988–96." *American Quarterly* 51, no. 2 (1999): 283–310.

Lee, Andrea. *Sarah Phillips*. Edited by Valerie Smith. 2nd ed. Boston: Northeastern University Press, 1993.

McGruder, Aaron. *A Right to Be Hostile: The Boondocks Treasury*. New York: Three Rivers Press, 2003.

Moore, Philip Arthur. "Barack Obama Is AWB: Articulate While Black." *Racialicious,* January 25, 2007. http://www.racialicious.com/2007/01/25/barack-obama-is-awb -articulate-while-black/.

Moylan, Brian. "Barack Obama's Geekiest Moments." *Gawker,* September 17, 2009. http://gawker.com/5361977/barack-obamas-geekiest-moments.

Murray, Albert. *Stomping the Blues*. Cambridge, MA: Da Capo Press, 1976.

Neal, Mark Anthony. *Soul Babies: Black Popular Culture and the Post-Soul Aesthetic*. New York: Routledge, 2002.

————. "'Acting White My Ass': Beyond the Myths of Black Student Underperformance." *Loop21,* August 2, 2010. http://newblackman.blogspot.com/2010/08/acting-white -my-ass-beyond-myths-of.html.

Nissel, Angela. *Mixed: My Llife in Black and White*. New York: Random House, 2006.

Nugent, Benjamin. "Who's a Nerd, Anyway?" *New York Times Magazine,* July 29, 2007. http://www.nytimes.com/2007/07/29/magazine/29wwln-idealab-t.html?ex= 1343361600&en=b023e7baf2d1dac5&ei=5090&partner=rssuserland&emc=rss.

————. *American Nerd: The Story of My People*. Simon and Schuster, 2008.

Packer, Z. Z. *Drinking Coffee Elsewhere*. New York: Riverhead Books, 2004.

Peterson, Latoya. "*The Big Bang Theory,* Nerds of Color, and Stereotypes." *Racialicious,* March 10, 2009. http://www.racialicious.com/2009/03/10/the-big-bang-theory -nerds-of-color-and-stereotypes/.

————. 2010. "Some Thoughts on 'Acting White.'" *Racialicious,* July 9, 2010. http://www .racialicious.com/2010/07/09/some-quick-thoughts-on-acting-white/.

Phi, Bao. "NOCs (Nerds of Color)," *Racialicious,* January 25, 2010. http://www.racialicious .com/2010/01/25/nocs-nerds-of-coloressay/.

Pressler, Jessica. "Truly Indie Fans." *New York Times,* January 28, 2007. http://www .nytimes.com/2007/01/28/fashion/28Blipsters.html?_r=1&pagewanted=all.

Randall, Alice. *Pushkin and the Queen of Spades.* New York: Houghton Mifflin Harcourt, 2004.

Rivero, Raafi. "Black Nerds: The Revolution No One Could Have Predicted." *Des Temps,* October 4, 2007. http://desedo.com/blog/black-nerds/.

Ross, Fran. *Oreo.* Boston: Northeastern University Press, 2000.

Senna, Danzy. *Caucasia.* New York: Riverhead Books, 1998.

Smith, Zadie. *White Teeth.* London: Hamish Hamilton, 2000.

Southgate, Martha. *The Fall of Rome: A Novel.* New York: Scribner, 2002.

Tate, Greg. *Flyboy in the Buttermilk: Essays on Contemporary America.* New York: Simon and Schuster, 1992.

Tocci, Jason. "Black Nerds vs. Nerds Who Happen to Be Black." *Geek Studies,* December 18, 2007. http://www.geekstudies.org/2007/12/some-thoughts-on-black-nerds.

"Valspeak." *Wikipedia.* http://en.wikipedia.org/wiki/Valspeak.

Weheliye, Alexander G. *Phonographies: Grooves in Sonic Afro-Modernity.* Durham, NC: Duke University Press, 2005.

———. "Feenin: Posthuman Voices in Black Popular Music" in *Social Text* 71 (2002): 21–47.

Whitehead, Colson. *The Intuitionist.* New York: Anchor Books, 1999.

———. *John Henry Days: A Novel.* New York: Doubleday, 2001.

———. *Sag Harbor: A Novel.* New York: Random House, 2009.

Wright, John. "'Jack-the-Bear' Dreaming: Ellison's Spiritual Technologies." *boundary 2* 30, no. 2 (2003): 175–194.

Wynter, Sylvia. "Beyond the Word of Man: Glissant and the New Discourse of the Antilles." *World Literature Today* 63, no. 4 (1989): 637–647.

———. 1990. "On Disenchanting Discourse: 'Minority' Literary Criticism and Beyond." In *The Nature and Context of Minority Discourse,* edited by Abdul JanMohamed and David Lloyd, 432–469. New York: Oxford University Press, 1990.

———. "Unsettling the Coloniality of Being/Power/Truth/Freedom: Towards the Human, After Man, It's Overrepresentation—An Argument." *CR: The New Centennial Review* 3, no. 3 (2003): 257–337.

———. "On How We Mistook the Map for the Territory and Re-Imprisoned Ourselves in Our Unbearable Wrongness of Being, of Désêtre: Black Studies Toward the Human Project." In *Not Only the Master's Tools: African American Studies in Theory and Practice,* edited by Lewis R. Gordon and Jane Anna Gordon, 107–169. Boulder, CO: Paradigm, 2006.

ELEVEN

THE CRISIS OF AUTHENTICITY IN CONTEMPORARY AFRICAN AMERICAN LITERATURE

RICHARD SCHUR

The conversation about the purpose and nature of African American literature began when African Americans started publishing stories, poetry, and prose during the late eighteenth and early nineteenth centuries. For much of the twentieth century, this discussion continued on in W. E. B. Du Bois's *The Crisis,* the passing novels of the Harlem Renaissance, and in the articulations of the New Negro and Black Arts movements. Since the 1970s, the discussion has focused increasingly on the concept of authenticity, largely because African American literature became canonized at the very moment that postmodernism and multiculturalism questioned the purpose and effect of canonization and other grand narratives. The resulting tension between scholars seeking to canonize African American literature—because it had long been neglected—and postmodernist or poststructuralist scholars emphasizing difference over homogeneity created, what Antonio Gramsci and Stuart Hall have termed, a "crisis." In particular, this crisis has hinged on the question of authenticity and what African American literature ought to represent about African American life. Hall develops Gramsci's concept of the crisis and argues that it signifies "constant movement, polemics, contestations, etc., which represent the attempt by different sides to overcome or resolve the crisis and to do so in terms which favor their long term hegemony" (Hall 422). While it is beyond the scope of this essay to chart this debate in full, it does seek to consider how two recent novels, *Caucasia* and *Sag Harbor,* envision a different kind of authenticity that might defuse this "crisis" and offer a more productive definition of authenticity for scholars.

Authenticity, whether as vernacular language and culture, a reference to black musical styles, or as signifying, has become one significant rhetoric in ongoing canonization efforts. E. Patrick Johnson argues that authenticity "is yet another trope manipulated for cultural capital." He further asserts that "individuals or groups *appropriate* this complex and nuanced racial signifier [authenticity] in order to circumscribe its boundaries or to exclude other individuals or groups. When blackness is appropriated [in this way] to the exclusion of others, identity becomes political" (3). Johnson and others have noted that the very rhetoric of authentic blackness serves to authorize certain voices and dismiss others.[1] In an incredibly insightful essay, W. T. Lhamon identifies a number of traits of what he terms "optic blackness":

> Optic blackness . . . gives instead a convenient, pliable mediation of the
>   real—a fiction that seems sufficiently real for cultural symbolism.
> Optic black is less about "race" than about the positional binary of its own
>   pretense and binary.
> Optic blackness is not contained in any form, genre, or medium, be it
>   high or low; it weaves through them all.
> The contending forces of optic black and optic white center their dispute
>   in American culture and defend their dominion everywhere Atlantic
>   slavery was. (112)

Johnson and Lhamon outline how blackness, when framed in the terms of authenticity, creates a fiction around racial identity and experience and elides how race, in fact, operates. As conceptions about race become increasingly commodified and many view identity as a mere performance, the greater historical and cultural context that shapes these signs and signifiers is displaced and hidden. bell hooks notes that "mass media bring white supremacy into our [African American] lives and remind us of our marginalized status," frequently relying on and manipulating these very markers of supposed authenticity (110). As much as some might wish to argue that the 1950s and 1960s produced revolutionary change to American social institutions, its effect on dominant visual and literary representation was much more evolutionary, frequently incorporating earlier racist strategies. The result is that contemporary African American writers must still engage with racialized symbols and metaphors in their efforts to rewrite them.

While the issue has been central to post–Civil Rights era literary production, this is not the first time that the crisis of authenticity has taken center stage in African American literature. In *Authentic Blackness*

(1999), J. Martin Favor considers how the concept of the "folk" shaped the Harlem Renaissance and the New Negro movement, which in turn shaped the critical vocabulary to analyze and interpret contemporary African American literature (3–6). Favor ultimately concludes that race and racial literary representations are a "tool of aesthetic and politic change" and that "'race' becomes one possible lever in the cultural work of dislodging stubborn and exclusive institutions and practices from their seemingly stable and natural positions" (138). Candace Jenkins argues that the tragic mulatto novels of the 1920s illuminate how middle-class African Americans negotiated their racial identity and interrogated the "imagined boundaries of their community" (136).[2]

More recently, the very popularity of hip-hop music and culture and the popular conception of hip-hop as black have created a similar debate about authenticity within African American culture. Commercialism and middle-class status threaten, at least rhetorically, whether a particular artist is being authentic or merely *fronting*. Although this "crisis" is not really new, it has become constitutive of post–Civil Rights era African American literary and cultural analysis.[3] This crisis, however, should not concern critics too much. The very intensity of these conversations signals the tremendous creative energies being deployed by writers and critics alike. The primary reason that authenticity has become a crucial issue is that there is an abundance of music, literature, and art being created by African Americans, and it is becoming increasingly difficult to find a single narrative or principle to unify or organize it all. This variety illustrates the historical and cultural changes affecting African Americans and the African American community and how the post–Civil Rights era necessitates a revision and rethinking of literary representation and the appropriate narratives for African American literature.

The post–Civil Rights generation (people born roughly between 1965 and 1985) inherited the legislative and legal victories of the Civil Rights and Black Arts movements, and the affirmative action debate. Furthermore, this generation witnessed the demise of Northern industrial cities, the reaction against the Civil Rights movement during the Reagan years, and the birth of hip-hop. They also endured the War on Drugs. These changes affected traditional African American institutions and exacerbated economic and political rifts within the African American community. Moreover, during this time period, critics, pundits, and corporate marketing campaigns have transformed identity from membership in a particular community into more of a consumer transaction or a performance that can be chosen, modified, or discarded. In this context, authenticity of any kind is frequently understood as much as a matter of consumption and performance as it is connecting to a history, institutions, traditions, or shared struggle. Not unsurprisingly, all these changes have contributed to generational conflict as well between the post–Civil Rights generation and their civil rights generation parents. Some, mostly white commentators, have deployed Barack Obama's 2008 election as President and all the changes from the past thirty years as evidence of a colorblind or "post-race" America. For contemporary African American writers, this situation has presented a fertile space to explore, via fiction, the nature of African American identity amid considerable change and the remarkable persistence of racialized thinking in American culture.

This essay engages in a close textual reading of Danzy Senna's *Caucasia* and Colson Whitehead's *Sag Harbor* to consider how contemporary African American novelists are responding to this conversation around race, identity, and authenticity. Senna's and Whitehead's work is particularly useful in understanding the debate as the main characters in these coming-of-age novels struggle against essentialist and reductive notions of African American identity in their quests for self-understanding. This essay argues that Whitehead and Senna both reiterate the importance of race as a social construct in contemporary American culture and challenge narrow definitions of authenticity in African American life. These novels seek to reveal the "mask of authenticity" connected with much contemporary African American cultural production and make room for "authentic" or "real" narratives that do not fit essentialist, Black Arts, hip-hop, or the New Black Aesthetic paradigms.[4] This essay concludes that these two relatively recent novels are engaged in the broader project of re-defining the core of African American literature, thus challenging both reductive canonization efforts and the common notion that contemporary America is post-race. Senna and Whitehead reveal a broader appreciation for the complexity of African American identities and seek to expand the very category of African American literature to include these "new" narratives.[5]

In these novels, Senna and Whitehead reenvision the concept of authenticity through the lenses of a biracial child of the 1970s and an African American kid with a beach house during the 1980s, respectively. By framing their novels in this way, Senna and Whitehead offer characters who deviate from the putative "norms" and canons that have governed contemporary African American literature. The books then chart their coming-of-age quests for identity. Both Birdie Lee (of *Caucasia*) and Benji Cooper (of *Sag Harbor*) realize they fail to meet some definitions of African American identity, but these novels explore how the two teenagers come to understand and accept their social and cultural locations. Ironically, both novels have been understood primarily through the lens of autobiographical fiction, thus conferring a certain authenticity to the narratives because they are understood to be rooted in the actual lives of their respective authors.

Caucasia (1998) is Danzy Senna's first novel. The story is set during the 1970s and 1980s and revolves around an interracial family. The white mother and black father met in Boston during the 1960s and have two biracial children. The mother gets involved in radical politics, while the father immerses himself in his scholarship about the social construction of race. The mother gets herself into trouble with the law and determines she must go on the lam with her light-skinned daughter, Birdie Lee. They wind up hiding out, under assumed names, in rural New Hampshire, stuck in "Caucasia." The father takes the darker-skinned daughter and travels to Brazil as he hopes to escape the racism of the United States. Birdie Lee becomes a teenager while living a lie as a "white Jewish girl" and lacking all knowledge of the whereabouts of her older, darker-skinned sister and her father. As her mother grows increasingly comfortable with their new monocultural life, Birdie grows increasingly uncomfortable and she runs away in search of her black family. Birdie eventually travels to California and finds her father, Deck Lee, who has written a massive response to Henry Louis Gates, Jr.'s *The Signifying Monkey* entitled *The Petrified Monkey* and is obsessed with proving race a fiction. Birdie also finds her sister, Cole Lee, who is studying at Berkeley. The novel ends with Birdie realizing that the gap between her and her black family, as well as her search for identity, will be ongoing and that she is part of a larger group of biracial Americans for whom the older labels and narratives no longer apply. Senna draws on the ethos of postmodernism to reject the received narratives about African American literature even as she seeks to illuminate the need for a "new" canon related to the stories and experiences of the biracial.

Colson Whitehead's *Sag Harbor* describes the exploits of fifteen-year-old Benji Cooper in the African American vacation town of Sag Harbor during the summer of 1985. The novel meanders through a single summer as Benji and his friends stumble toward adulthood as nerdy, upper-class African Americans who attend predominately white private schools in Manhattan. The novel is set against the backdrop of *The Cosby Show* and the new-found visibility of upper-middle class African Americans and the rise of hip-hop as a form of mass culture. Benji realizes that he has the ability to interact with whites in a way that his parents did not, but he also understands that his knowledge of and participation in dominant or white culture also separates him from significant aspects of African American society. While he shares his "integrated" life with his Sag Harbor peers, they are all too aware that their experiences mark them in sometimes strange ways, including the erection of a barrier between them and their parents. The main character approaches his final summer hurrah as an opportunity to re-cast himself into the kind of man he idealizes. Benji, however, does not quite realize his dream and the novel instead details a lot of pretty humorous events (or non-events) that allow Whitehead to discuss in metaphorical ways how race operates in the post–Civil Rights era.

In both novels, the question of authenticity is a major issue for the characters, and authentic black identity is analyzed and examined through a variety of lenses and perspectives. Much of the critical commentary on *Caucasia* centers on its revision of the passing narrative. Kathryn Rummell reads the novel as a rejection of "the racial binary that limited earlier passers in favor of a postethnic affiliation" (12). Rummell further notes that Birdie survives her journey, unlike the "tragic mulattoes" of earlier periods. For Suzanne Jones, *Caucasia* represents how contemporary individuals possess "the ability to assert their own racial identity and the chance to have relationships with both black and white family members" (103). Ibrahim, however, argues that the novel suggests how "the myth of the mulatta [will be] perpetuated into the future" (170). My own reading of the novel draws on Senna's revisiting of the tragic mulatto genre and also examines its relation to the wider scope of contemporary African American writing and the general anxiety around authenticity. By contrasting the novel with Whitehead's *Sag Harbor*, I argue that "mulattoes" are not the only people who struggle with issues of "passing" but they serve as one of several categories, including gender, sexuality, and social class, against which racial identity is crafted and deployed.

A key moment in the novel's interrogation of authenticity occurs about one-third of the way through the novel. Birdie's parents decide not only to divorce but also to split up the children and part company completely. Birdie's father Deck and her sister Cole will head to Brazil—with this pairing determined by their shared dark-skin color. Birdie and Sandy go underground, hiding out from the FBI in the United States. For Birdie, the separation means severing her connection to African American culture as she must leave the Black Power School she is attending (although she is socially accepted only after her sister secures her identity as "black") and adopting a new identity so that her mother can escape detection. The result is that Birdie must suppress her biracial or African American identity in order to protect her white mother. Before Deck and Cole depart, they leave a present of sorts for Birdie:

> The package my father had left me that night of his departure was a shoe box filled with a collection of strange objects. Scrawled in magic marker on the side of the box was the word "Negrobilia." I recognized my father's chicken-scratch handwriting. My mother scoffed when she saw what was inside. He and Cole had clearly thrown the collection together at the last minute. It included a Black Nativity program, a fisted pick, a black Barbie doll head, an informational tourist pamphlet on Brazil, the silver Egyptian necklace inscribed with hieroglyphics that my father had bought me at a museum so many years before, and a James Brown eight-track cassette with a faded sticker in the corner that said "Nubian Notion," the name of the record shop on Washington street. That, along with Cole's Golliwog, was all that was left of them. (127)

The box and its contents serve as Birdie's touchstone to her father and her sister and their shared identity. Senna, however, comments ironically on the nature of African American identity through this strange blend of items. From the music of James Brown and a hair care product for African Americans to the racist imagery of the Golliwog, African American identity is reduced to a set of contradictory objects and ideologies, including Black Power, consumerism, and black collectables. The box functions in a second way as well. It reveals what Deck and Birdie—individuals whose phenotype clearly mark them as Black or African American—believe will help Birdie remember her black family and, in turn, her black identity. By and large, the box of Negrobilia is filled largely with items concerned with the appearance and social performance of racial identity. In effect, Senna is offering a critique of consumerism and the resultant performances that have become central to the construction of racial identity. She reveals that much of what passes as authentic black identity is merely consumption or the production of a particular image—no matter how stereotypical or false.[6]

These items also serve to ground Birdie's claims to biracial and/or African American identity. After an incident in which a police officer accuses Deck of kidnapping Birdie at a park because the officer cannot imagine that he is Birdie's father, Deck implores her to become a spy or racial double agent (58). Within the logic of Deck's request, Birdie's "true" identity can be maintained if she uses her light skin color to witness and testify to how whites behave when they do not think African Americans are around. Birdie's box of Negrobilia and these bizarre artifacts increasingly become the primary way she can identify as African American and resist her mother's efforts to have her pass as white. The box both represents a key element of Birdie's "authentic" self and ultimately encourages her to break from her mother and seek out the suppressed elements of her racial identity.

As her mother gets increasingly comfortable in New Hampshire, Birdie feels how her identity is getting re-shaped and partially "de-formed" as a result of passing in a predominately white community. Birdie's hidden or suppressed racial identity begins to reveal itself when she visits New York City. Senna describes how she responds to hearing early versions of rap music and the breaking that went along with it: "Before long, a group of black and Puerto Rican teenagers, just around our age, came and sat on the bench next to ours. They were smoking and goofing around and had a boom box. It played some kind of talking music, the first I had ever heard of its kind, and I strained to listen, as if it held some secret." In this scene, Senna relies on hip-hop music—something that Birdie has never heard in "white" New Hampshire to show that she retains a link to her "African American" past. Birdie observes "this music wasn't disco, though the underlying tune was somehow familiar, something I had known once, long ago" (260). She then joins a multiracial circle of kids, watching the b-boys perform, much to the horror of her white companion. Birdie's body then "moves to the music" and reveals what passing has tried to conceal (261). In this section, Senna uses hip-hop music to serve as a proxy for racial authenticity and to symbolize Birdie's "real" identity. Unlike her white friend, Birdie intuitively understands hip-hop, thus underlining her difference from her. By using hip-hop to reveal Birdie's "secret" identity, Senna draws on the stereotypical depiction of hip-hop. As Greg Tate notes, hip-hop's global popularity is frequently the result of "its perceived Blackness" and the attendant qualities of being "hip, stylish, youthful, alienated, rebellious, and sensual" (7). This scene is the beginning of the novel's turning point when Birdie breaks from her white mother and seeks out her black family and speaks to Senna's struggle to employ a more nuanced form of racial representation. Despite Senna's effort to explore the limits of such representations and her satirical usage of the Negrobilia, she nonetheless reinforces the very rhetoric of authenticity through her fairly stereotypical reliance on hip-hop as a proxy for racial identity.

Caucasia culminates with Birdie tracking down her father and her sister. This is the second "moment" I wish to examine. Her father has become an isolated and bitter academic. When she finds him, he shares his theory that the "mulatto in America functions as a canary in a coal mine." Deck posits that "mulattos had historically been the gauge of how poisonous American race relations were" and that "you're the first generation of canaries to survive, a little injured, perhaps but alive" (393). He further argues that race is mostly an illusion and that the Civil Rights movement has primarily helped the black middle class (396). Birdie is shocked by both what her father is saying and his general appearance. Even though her father argues that race is illusory and that the post–Civil Rights generation of biracial children are surviving, Birdie's own experience demonstrates that race remains all too real in her life and that of her contemporaries and that growing up bi-racial is not as easy as her father suggests.

Her father then helps her find her sister. They too engage in a discussion about the nature of identity and what it means for contemporary America. Being a part of the hip-hop generation, Birdie and Cole have a slightly different take on their identity and what it means. Cole tells Birdie that "He's right, you know. About it all being constructed. But . . . That doesn't mean it doesn't exist." Birdie retorts: "They say you don't have to choose. But the thing is, you do. Because there are consequences if you don't." And then Cole finishes the thought, "And there are consequences if you do" (408). In this conversation, Cole and Birdie acknowledge that racial identity is a bit of a moving target, especially as social change has created a new set of race markers and categories. However, they both also acknowledge within this new cultural framework that how individuals plot and live out their identity is crucial. The freedom to choose does not mean there is no responsibility to one's family and one's community. Rather, this freedom requires that individuals and communities take responsibility for their choices.

Cole and Birdie's emphasis on choice and responsibility underscores that mere genetic, phenotype or class-based standards for authenticity are not really the issue. Rather, they focus on how a person positions himself or herself within a broader community. On a surface level, this appears quite different from hip-hop's authenticity rhetoric or the debate about street literature. However, Senna's approach is remarkably consistent with it as she focuses on establishing solid relationships and fulfilling one's responsibilities to the community. While Birdie is engaged in a journey of self-discovery, it is not a selfish one. For Birdie, the challenge is to learn how to balance and respect her complex history instead of merely choosing one side or the other. In this framing, authenticity is more about being true to one's history and one's community than about music, language usage, or membership to a specific social class.

The novel ends with Birdie feeling further confused even after finding her lost black father and sister. She takes to the street again, searching for something. She sees a girl that was "black like me, a mixed girl" (413). In this phrase, Senna seeks to broaden the concept of blackness and make room for multiple ways of being and representing African American identity. Birdie thinks she recognizes her but realizes that it would be impossible. Although Birdie wants to acknowledge the girl, she gets on a bus before Birdie can do anything. "Then the bus lurched forward, and the face was gone with it, just a blur of yellow and black in motion" (413). Instead of providing a determinate ending, Senna insists on leaving the reader with an image of racial identity that is in flux and motion.

The very authenticity Birdie initially sought is not found. Rather, both Birdie and the reader are left with choices, potential responsibilities, and the difficulty of building a sustaining identity. In her very funny essay "The Mulatto Millennium" (in the collection *Half and Half*), Senna pillories the limited vocabulary we have for racial identity. She mockingly concludes there that "[t]he categories could go on and on, and perhaps, indeed, they will. Where do I fit? That's the strange thing. I fit into none and all of the above. I have been each of the above, or at least mistaken for them, at different moments in my life. But somehow, none feels right. Maybe that makes me a Postlatto" (27). One might erroneously conclude that Senna is making an argument for colorblindness here. As I hope my (idiosyncratic) close reading of her novel makes clear, just because something is an illusion or constructed does not make it less real. Rather, the authenticity crisis in African American literature is fundamentally about creating a discursive space that allows for the recognition of the complicated and heterogeneous ways race operates, linking one's persona and self-understanding to a shared history and common set of experiences.[7]

* * *

Sag Harbor engages in a similar examination of identity, albeit from a very different location. Benji Cooper, Whitehead's main character, is a private school boy, more akin to one of the Huxtable children from *The Cosby Show* than he is directly linked to Birdie's journey. While Birdie's racial identity is questioned because of her white mother, Benji's racial identity "suffers" from his having lived in a relatively privileged economic setting. Because the novel meanders, this essay engages in a close reading of two chapters, "The Heyday of Dag" and "The Gangsters," to illustrate Whitehead's critique of authenticity. Here is how Whitehead frames the challenge:

> Black boys with beach houses. It could mess with your head sometimes, if you were the susceptible sort. And if it messed with your head, got under your brown skin, there were some typical and well-known remedies. You could embrace the beach part—revel in the luxury, the perception of status, wallow without care in what it meant to be born in America with money. . . . [or] You could embrace the black part—take some idea you had about what real blackness was, and make theater of it, your 24–7 one-man show. Folks of this type could pick Bootstrapping Striver or Proud Pillar, but the most popular brands were Militant or Street. . . . The customary schedule for good middle-class boys and girls called for them to

get Militant and fashionably Afrocentric the first semester of freshman year in college. Underlining key passages in *The Autobiography of Malcolm X* and that passed-around paperback of *Black Skin, White Masks*. Organize a march or two to protest the lack of tenure for that controversial professor in the Department of Black Studies. Organize a march or two to protest the lack of a Department of Black Studies. It passed the time until business school. (58)

The narrator of *Sag Harbor* is all too well aware of the irony or ambiguity of his position in telling the coming-of-age story of a bourgeois African American boy. This quote both gently mocks the poses adopted by some middle-class African Americans and offers an explanation for these stereotypical stages of racial self-awareness. In this paragraph, Whitehead's Benji explains the multi-step process by which middle-class African Americans come to accept their racial identity.

In the chapter "The Heyday of Dag" (from which the quote above was taken), Whitehead examines how Benji and his friends incorporate African American vernacular expressions—mostly through insults and swearing, handshakes, and music to craft an "authentic" identity that merges their middle-class experiences with the popular image and stereotype of young, urban African Americans. Whitehead writes that "the trend that summer, insult-wise toward grammatical acrobatics, the unlikely collage. One smashed a colorful and evocative noun or proper noun into a pejorative, gluing them together with an -in' verb" (41). These insults contained immense power: "The heart of the[se] critique[s] concerned what you were putting out into the world, the vibes you gave off. Which is what made them so devastating when executed well—this ordnance detonated in that area between you and the mirror, between you and what you thought everyone else was seeing" (42). Although not directly stated in the quotations above, language and insults were a key way for these boys to perform a black identity, albeit one that is marked by region, gender, and socio-economic status. This is probably obvious. Whitehead, however, goes further and explains that this rhetorical game is effective because Benji and his friends are struggling to calibrate their internal sense of self with how they are socially perceived. Through the exchange of stylized insults, these boys ironically gain some self-awareness.

The handshake is another public way of expressing one's racial identity. This, too, is an arena of struggle for Benji:

> Yes, the new handshakes were out, shaming me with their permutations
> and slippery routines. Slam, grip, flutter, snap. Or was it slam, flutter, grip,
> snap? I was all thumbs when it came to shakes. Devised in the under-
> ground soul laboratories of Harlem, pounded out in the blacker-than-
> thou sweatshops of the South Bronx, the new handshakes always had me
> faltering in embarrassment. Like this? No, you didn't stick the landing,
> the judges give it 4.6. (43)

In the chapter's conclusion, Benji does gain some self and social awareness after watching "the most botched handshake of the day" between
NP and Randy. He suddenly realizes that "it was unmistakable. Everybody was faking it" (66). Handshakes, like the use of language, are
performative—conferring legitimacy and authenticity on some while revealing the supposed failings of others. Moreover, by linking identity to
the quickly changing patterns of popular handshakes, Whitehead illustrates how concepts of what is hip, cool, or authentic is evanescent. Literary critics need to attend to Whitehead's symbolism here as he illustrates the dangers of tethering any definition of African American (or
any other) literature to current popular styles as such short-lived practices make canonization nearly impossible because the canon would need
to change every time popular styles did. It also runs the risk of reifying cultural practices that are fluid. For the individual, rooting one's racial identity within a particular set of popular or vernacular practices
would also likely create similar problems as one's identity would change
as those styles did.

In the same chapter, Whitehead examines this same issue through
the lens of early 1980s hip-hop. Benji and his crew are discussing Afrika Bambaataa after his "Planet Rock" began blasting out of his friend's
speakers. Benji comments that Bambaataa "bit that [the main sample] off
Kraftwerk." His friend replies that "Afrika Bambaataa didn't steal anything. This is their song." Benji knew he was correct about the sample's
origin. However, Whitehead's purpose in referencing the originality debate around hip-hop and "Planet Rock" is not so much to examine copy-
right issues, but to look at what hip-hop can teach us about the authenticity debate. Reflecting on the conversation, Benji comes to understand
the stakes of this conversation more fully:

> I didn't understand back then why Marcus was hassling me, but I get it
> now. A couple of years later, if someone said "I stole that off an old Lou
> Donaldson record," and the sample kicked it, you got respect for your ex-

pertise and keen ear. Funk, free jazz, disco, cartoons, German synthesizer music—it didn't matter where it came from, the art was in converting it to new use. Manipulating what you had at your disposal for your own purposes, jerry-rigging your new creation. But before sampling became an art form with a philosophy, biting off somebody was a major crime, thuggery on an atrocious scale. Your style, your vibe, was all you had. . . . If someone was stealing your style, they were stealing your soul. (61)

Examining this conversation and Benji's reflection upon it through the lens of authenticity is revealing, as hip-hop here stands in for the process of self-creation. Bambaataa draws on whatever musical resources to which he has access in order to produce something that is his unique sound. At first, Benji views this "borrowing" or "sampling" as theft even if he is trying to appropriate hand-shakes and African American vernacular language for his own purposes of self-reinvention.[8] Benji, however, knows even if he cannot articulate it that "it was okay to like both Afrika Bambaataa and Kraftwerk." His friend cannot abide Benji's critique of Bambaataa even after Benji says "I was just trying to share some information." The friend replies "Yeah, right, I forgot you like that white music, you fuckin' Souxsie and the Banshees-listenin' motherfucker" (62). Benji, as narrator, defends himself to the reader, noting that he was wearing a "Bauhaus t-shirt," not his Souxsie and the Banshees one,[9] suggesting that he has been misrecognized if only slightly.

Through this exchange and its implicit examination of authenticity in music and language, Whitehead helps the reader understand the complex ways that the rhetoric of authenticity shapes African American post-civil rights era youth. Benji feels compelled to meet dominant constructions— apparently shared by both many African Americans and many whites— about black masculinity even if they do not match his own social conditions and personal history This section also helps illuminate the full range of sources, influences, and experiences that shape Whitehead's writing, drawing on music from Kraftwerk to Bambaataa, and incorporating critical reflection on cultural practices, from handshakes to swearing. For Whitehead, authenticity does not mean just street literature, vernacular-based stories, protest novels, and historical fictions, but the full range of American culture during the 1970s and 1980s. Whitehead deploys this variety and Benji's inability to meet stereotypical expectations of African American youth as a sort of anti-authenticity that is somehow more authentic and "real." Benji becomes more human and a fuller character as he agonizes over his perceived failure to realize his image of the authentic African American male.

Whitehead, while amusing his audience with the follies of this identity creation, also realizes that this is not idle navel-gazing. This work of creating authentic identity can have devastating consequences. In the chapter "The Gangster," Whitehead describes his group's embrace of BB-guns as a portent of the dangers facing the hip-hop generation during the late 1980s and early 1990s. Throughout this chapter, there is continual metaphorical slippage between BB-guns and real guns.[10] "Randy grinned and held up the BB rifle to show it off. It looked real, but that was the point. If it looked real, you could pretend it was real, and if you had a real gun you could pretend to be someone else" (123). A few pages later, Whitehead elaborates on how Benji's peers became fixated on guns: "The next gun was Bobby's. This one was a pistol, a replica of a 9mm" (125). Benji, clearly concerned about this turn in the group's play, observes: "Bobby's real-lookin' gun allowed him to indulge his hard-rock fantasies and bury his deep prep-school weakness. Hide his grandfather's soft features in the scowl of a thug, the thug of his inverted Westchester fantasies. A kind of blackface" (126). While Bobby and Randy brag about using their guns and bringing them to school, Benji mocks their tough talk: "Hunting preppies . . . would cut into [their] daily vigils outside the college counselor's office. . . . This BB-gun shit was making people act like dummies" (127). Significantly and subtly, Whitehead shows how the traditional symbol of minstrelsy, blackface, has been inverted in the post–Civil Rights era and by hip-hop. Now, blackface is not a comic image, but an ultraviolent one.

Whitehead then shifts the focus of the narrative and shares Benji's thoughts about fighting. Benji reveals that his father teaches him to fight white kids who insult him, resulting in Benji walking up to a classmate who had wronged him and punching him in the face (136). Whitehead also observes that "you never fought unless there was an audience" (137) and that "generally you punched someone younger and smaller. Common sense" (136). These physical battles were deeply connected with a person's demonstration of "verbal dexterity." For Benji, his memory of fighting reveals that such battles did not prove one's racial authenticity or toughness. Rather, his friends "discovered that we all had glass jaws and went down like a sack of potatoes at the right combo of words" (138). The chapter then veers off into a discussion of hip-hop boasting and Run-DMC (141) and posing for rap album covers (145). Referencing the transition from Run-DMC to Ice Cube, Benji/Whitehead realizes that "Something happened. Something happened that changed the terms and we went from fighting (I'll knock that grin off your face) to annihilation (I'll wipe you from this Earth)" (146).

This then begins the transition back toward the BB-gun war that Benji and his friends planned. "You were hard or else you were soft, in the slang drawn from the territory of manhood, the state of your erected self. Word on the street was that we were soft, with our private school uniforms, in our cozy beach communities, so we learned to walk like hard rocks, like B-boys. . . . We talked one way in school, one way in our homes, and one way to each other. We got guns. We got guns for a few days one summer and then got rid of them. Later some of us got real guns" (146–47). After many false starts, their gang had one BB-gun fight that resulted in a BB getting lodged just above Benji's eye (153). Because Benji, his brother, and the others feared getting found out, Benji did not go to the hospital and he still retains the "scar" from that gun battle (159). This memory causes Benji to reflect:

> For some of us, those were our first guns, a rehearsal. I'd like to say, all these years later, now that one of us is dead and another paralyzed from the waist down from the actual bullets—drug-related, as the papers put it—that the game wasn't so innocent after all. But it's not true. We always fought for real. Only the nature of the fight changed. It always will. As time went on, we learned to arm ourselves in our different ways. Some of us with real guns, some of us with more ephemeral weapons, an idea or improbable plan . . . about how best to move through the world" (158).

In this passage, Whitehead juxtaposes the very "real" battles they fought against the apparent safety of toy guns, "ephemeral weapons," and "improbable plans." Through this contrasting language, Whitehead inverts the very rhetoric of authenticity because what is vague, ambivalent, and evanescent becomes the location for all too real conflict and suffering. In his revisioning, authenticity is not about external objects or visual spectacles but the result of an internal journey and the processes of self-creation and self-understanding.

Caucasia and *Sag Harbor*, I argue, illustrate the qualities and characteristics of what Monica Miller calls the "New New Black Aesthetic" in her in-process manuscript, *Affirmative Actions: How to Define Black Culture in the 21st Century* (I am drawing extensively on her reading of *Sag Harbor* here). It is common to hear the refrain and/or anxiety that the election of Obama ushers in a new "post-racial" age in which race doesn't matter.[11] What is potentially surprising is that writers, such as Senna and Whitehead, are not creating a literature that reflects that kind of post-racial age. In an insightful book entitled *Post Black: How a New Generation is Redefining African American Identity*, Ytasha Womack argues that this new wave of literary and cultural activity suggests not the end of race but a major revision of how race gets represented. Womack argues that "there [has been] a death-grip hold on a cookie cutter image of black life that just didn't apply to every person of African descent living in America" (7). She astutely notes that much of what has appeared—frequently marketed under the rubric of authenticity—doesn't match up with the actual lives of many African Americans, especially as the term today connotes a wider range of ethnic, professional, regional, and social class positions than ever before (12).[12] Senna and Whitehead illustrate Womack's argument as they seek to redefine the terms of racial identity based on how the social changes of the 1960s and 1970s have altered the terrain of American culture. Moreover, these texts reveal that while some of the older stereotypes about African American life have disappeared, newer ones have taken their place, sometimes developed and adopted by the post–Civil Rights generation. These writers and others are representing the contemporary and continuous effort to craft an authentic racial identity against these popular stereotypes and misconceptions.

The stakes of this authenticity crisis in African American literature are about how African Americans ought to be represented, especially given the heightened interest in African American culture generally and hip-hop specifically. As many critics have noted, Jeffery Ogbar argues that many gangsta, thug, and crunk rappers "have parlayed racist assumptions into a degree of financial success that has proved elusive to most black people (or white ones for that matter). They have created images that reify myopic ideas of black authenticity" (32). Both Whitehead (as discussed earlier) and Senna chart their stories (Whitehead more so than Senna) against hip-hop. For Birdie and Benji, hip-hop music and culture is something that connects them to the African American community and their post–Civil Rights generation peers but also reveals the gap between them and other African Americans. For Benji knows

Kraftwerk, whereas Birdie somehow connects to the elements of hip-hop culture even though she has been disconnected from African American culture during the late 1970s and early 1980s. It is not accidental that Whitehead and Senna chart their alternative narratives of racial identity against hip-hop because hip-hop relies heavily on claims or the rhetoric of authenticity. Hip-hop is constantly struggling to free itself from such stereotypical accounts, especially those that are commercially profitable. In order to take African American literature and culture to a new space, Senna and Whitehead must create this "crisis of authenticity" and inter-rogate the boundaries and rubrics that have defined African American identity and representations of blackness in African American literature. Rather than being a sign that all is not well, debates among critics and writers about authenticity reveal the health and vibrancy of the African American novel as a space to explore the contradictions and paradoxes of race in a putatively "post-racial" age.

NOTES

1. See also Dickson-Carr and Weheliye in this volume for further illustrations of this point. Dickson-Carr articulates the putatively preferred literary styles for African American writers and how those limitations may be easing. Weheliye argues that the figure of the "black geek" in post-soul writing is challenging the constraints of African American writing and indicates a new opening for a wider range of representational pos-sibilities.

2. Jenkins's analysis about how the tragic mulatto novels illustrated the conflict between middle and working class African American readers during an earlier period offers a very apt analog to the contemporary conflict between "literary" novels and "street lit." Danyel Smith argues that this conflict, however, is not really necessary or all that productive and we need to explode this binary ultimately (195).

3. A good illustration of these debates about the canonization of African Ameri-can literature can be found in Winston Napier's edited collection, *African American Lit-erary Theory: A Reader.* Also, the very essays included in this collection are frequently concerned with authenticity questions and the explosion of novels that question pre-vious formulations of authentically black literature. See Dickson-Carr (chap. 2), Wehe-liye (chap. 10), Stallings (chap. 9), and Southgate (chap. 12) in particular.

4. For a discussion of how authenticity plays out in hip-hop culture in everything from the music and the videos to hip-hop fashion and design, see Dyson, 5–8. For an overview of the "New Black Aesthetic," see Ellis generally.

5. These two works illustrate Southgate's argument that many contemporary writers are working to create "post-oppression" novels, in which "[t]heir characters might still be oppressed—but it's not in the same old ways," (3).

6. Birdie's box of Negrobilia is related to but distinct from the contents of the narrator's briefcase in Ellison's *Invisible Man* (568). Both Birdie's box and the invisible

man's brief case constitute a set of objects that create a false sense of identity. The collections symbolize the owner's false consciousness or alienation. There are, however, some significant differences too. Birdie received the items as a going-away present, whereas Ellison's narrator collects a similar bunch of objects during his journey. Birdie holds her objects dear because her family gave them to her even if she does not quite understand their meaning. The invisible man, however, misunderstands the objects in his collection because he initially fails to see how he is a pawn in a racist world. Deck and Cole are not trying to dominate. Rather, the objects symbolize how Cole and Deck are just as trapped by these images and stereotypes as is Birdie. By offering a revision of Ellison's symbolism, Senna is writing herself into that tradition and re-shaping it to speak to current challenges. The author would like to thank Lovalerie King for pointing him in this direction.

7. Stallings's reading of *Slumberland* offers a similar argument. Her analysis of the rhetoric of time in African American criticism and the desire to "posterize" create the space for, what she terms, "indeterminate blackness." For Senna, claims to black identity are clearly rooted in discrete narratives with beginnings, middles, and ends. Racial identity has a key temporal component, which in turn leaves open or indeterminate the very nature of contemporary racial identity.

8. Benji's growth here provides an ironic commentary on law's initial and continued immaturity and its resulting misunderstanding of how sampling operates in hip-hop. The law all too often remains stuck in Benji's young and immature perspective about hip-hop's usage of sampling. See Schur 38–41 and Schumacher 444–447.

9. These were alternative bands from the late 1980s, which were generally identified as "white."

10. I should note the homophonic similarity between BB guns and b-boy.

11. Grassian also hints at the role authenticity is playing in contemporary African American writing throughout his book, but because his study is organized around authors—not themes—this idea is not presented fully.

12. Womack's argument looks more toward popular culture than Dickson-Carr's and hence her conclusion that popular culture—as opposed to African American literature—continues to limit the representations of African Americans.

WORKS CITED

Dyson, Michael Eric. *Know What I Mean? Reflections on Hip Hop*. New York: Basic, 2007.

Ellis, Trey. "The New Black Aesthetic." *Callaloo* 38 (Winter 1989): 233–243.

Ellison, Ralph. *Invisible Man*. 2d Vintage ed. New York: Random House, 1995.

Favor, J. Martin. *Authentic Blackness: The Folk in the New Negro*. Durham, NC: Duke University Press, 1999.

Grassian, Daniel. *Writing the Future of Black America: Literature of the Hip-Hop Generation*. Columbia: University of South Carolina Press, 2009.

Habiba, Ibrahim. "Canary in a Coal Mine: Performing Biracial Difference in *Caucasia*." *Literary Interpretation Theory* 18 (2007): 155–172.

Hall, Stuart. "Gramsci's Relevance for the Study of Race and Ethnicity." In *Stuart Hall: Critical Dialogues in Cultural Studies,* edited by David Morley and Kuan-Hsing Chen. New York: Routledge, 1996. 411–440.

hooks, bell. *Killing Rage: Ending Racism*. New York: Henry Holt, 1995.

Jenkins, Candice. "Decoding Essentialism: Cultural Authenticity and the Black Bourgeoisie in Nella Larsen's *Passing*." *MELUS* 30.3 (Fall 2005): 129–154.

Johnson, E. Patrick. *Appropriating Blackness: Performance and the Politics of Authenticity*. Durham, NC: Duke University Press, 2003.

Jones. Suzanne. "Tragic No More? The Reappearance of the Racially Mixed Character." In *American Fiction of the 1990s: Reflections of History and Culture*, edited by Jay Prosser, 89–103. New York: Routledge, 2008.

Lhamon, W. T., Jr. "Optic Black: Naturalizing the Refusal to Fit." In *Black Cultural Traffic: Crossroads in Global Performance and Popular Culture*, edited by Harry Elam and Kennell Jackson, 111–140. Ann Arbor: University of Michigan Press, 2005.

Miller, Monica. "The New 'New Black Literary Aesthetic': 'Reneging' (on?) Contemporary Black Identity." Washington, DC: American Studies Association (ASA). November 2009.

Napier, Winston, ed. *African American Literary Theory: A Reader*. New York: New York University Press, 2000.

Ogbar, Jeffrey. *Hip-Hop Revolution: The Culture and Politics of Rap*. Lawrence: University of Kansas Press, 2007.

Rummell, Kathryn. "Rewriting the Passing Novel: Danzy Senna's *Caucasia*." *Griot* 26.2 (Fall 2007): 1–13.

Schumaker, Thomas. "'This Is a Sampling Sport': Digital Sampling, Rap Music, and the Law in Cultural Production." In *That's the Joint! The Hip-Hop Studies Reader*, edited by Murray Forman and Mark Anthony Neal, 443–458. New York: Routledge, 2004.

Schur, Richard. *Parodies of Ownership: Hip-Hop Aesthetics and Intellectual Property Law*. Ann Arbor: University of Michigan Press, 2009.

Senna, Danzy. *Caucasia*. New York: Penguin, 1998.

———. "The Mulatto Millennium." In *Writers on Growing Up Biracial*, edited by Claudine O'Hearn, 12–27. New York: Pantheon, 1998.

Smith, Danyel. "Black Talk and Hot Sex: Why 'Street Lit' Is Literature." In *Total Chaos: The Art and Aesthetics of Hip-Hop*, edited by Jeff Chang, 188–197. New York: BasicCivitas, 2006.

Tate, Greg. "Nigs R Us, or How Blackfolk Became Fetish Objects." In *Everything But the Burden: What White People Are Taking from Black Culture*, edited by Greg Tate, 1–14. New York: Harlem Moon, 2003.

Whitehead, Colson. *Sag Harbor*. New York: Doubleday, 2009.

Womack, Ytasha. *Post Black: How a New Generation Is Redefining African American Identity*. Chicago: Lawrence Hill, 2010.

TWELVE

SOMEDAY WE'LL ALL BE FREE: CONSIDERING POST-OPPRESSION FICTION

MARTHA SOUTHGATE

I was asked to contribute to this anthology in late 2009, after attending "Celebrating African American Literature: The Novel since 1988," part of a conference series held biennially at Penn State University. The diverse voices and perspectives of the academics and fiction writers at the conference were fascinating and thrilling to me—I was extremely flattered to be asked to contribute to the collection. But for the life of me, I could not decide what to write about. At the time I received the assignment, the film *Precious* had just been released and the media—both old and new—were on fire with commentary about the film. So, of course, Sapphire's *Push*, the basis for the film, was once again omnipresent. I considered writing a craft essay comparing *Push* and *The Bluest Eye,* which deal with very similar material (sexually and physically abused black girls struggling to come of age and find their way against the vicious strictures of race, class and poverty) very differently. But as I began to tackle that essay, I found my interest in making the case one way or another fizzling out. Okay: Plan B. I started trying to formulate some new thoughts about the linkages between *The Color Purple, The Bluest Eye,* and *Push*. I diligently gathered all three novels from my bookshelf to reread, starting with *The Color Purple.* And that's when I snapped. I remember the moment clearly. I was on the subway doing my literary duty. Celie had just been raped—again—when I slammed the book shut and said (in my mind—I don't think I said it out loud), "I can't take it anymore. I'm sick of reading about us getting beat up and beat down, no matter how well it's written about!" Don't get me wrong: my reaction wasn't about the quality or significance of these books. Toni Morrison has created a number of necessary American masterpieces, *The Bluest Eye* among them. And while I don't admire *The Color Purple* or *Push* (I actually don't admire *Push* much at all, but that's another essay) as much as I do *The Bluest Eye*, I certainly appreciate the significance of both. But in that moment, on that train, I realized that I wanted this essay to consider the work of some black writers who were telling different kinds of stories— stories of now (or at least close to now). Stories in which, maybe tough things happened, maybe they didn't, but the horror was not so relentless, as it isn't in most of our lives. Stories that might better reflect black life at this minute in history.

I would not dream of begrudging or denigrating the work of any African American fiction writer who seriously approaches either historical or contemporary horrors with compassion and skill. What's more, there are many fine writers who toggle beautifully between the past and the present. But the past is not where my passion as a fiction writer lies. My road to Damascus moment on the subway was occasioned by the realization that as we move into the next decade of the twenty-first century, that one of my driving interests as a novelist is to create contemporary narratives of African American life. This feeling was summed up beautifully by novelist Tayari Jones at a reading on October 10, 2010, that was organized and sponsored by Ringshout. In a post-reading Q and A she said, "I am deeply committed to telling contemporary stories. I don't want my granddaughter writing about me because I only wrote about my grandparents. I think at some point we've got to step up into the future, write into the now."

I'd like to term this kind of work by black writers (for argument's sake, written mostly by writers born after 1959) post-oppression fiction. These fictions are not devoid of history. Not outside of it. Not free of the effects of racism and race—but the characters in them experience history—and race—very differently than those who came before us. I (and I think I can speak for a number of black fiction writers of my generation) am well aware that the freedoms we have, both in how we live and how we create, were earned in blood by our parents and their parents before them. We know that race still matters and that oppression still exists—we can see it everywhere; in prisons, in the education system, in the health system, in employment (or lack thereof). On the other hand, consider that while there is plenty of de facto segregation, we are no longer *legally* enjoined from the full rights and privileges of American citizenship. Consider who was duly elected to the White House in 2008. Consider if you ever thought you'd see the day—I sure never thought I would. While some things have remained the same, there's no denying that there have also been some fundamental changes in American life.

A clarification: by post-oppression, I *don't* mean that much and justifiably maligned term "post-racial." Nor do I mean "post-black," a similar term I've seen bandied about. As I will attempt to illustrate, younger contemporary writers are utterly aware of their race and the history around it. They are not past it, ashamed of it or denying it. They operate fully within the context of being "black." That said, the definitions of Blackness, for these writers, are somewhat different and perhaps more capacious than that of writers of an earlier generation. Further, the need to represent or speak for *all* African Americans through their work is felt little or not at all. These authors have access to a very different range of experience than those who came before them and that knowledge and experience is infused into the lives of their characters. Their characters might still be oppressed—but it's not in the same old ways. I'll take a moment here to add that I am well aware that to some extent, the notion of a fundamental post–Civil Rights shift in cultural work, including writing, has been advanced before, perhaps most prominently in Trey Ellis's 1989 *Callaloo* essay, "The New Black Aesthetic." But unlike Ellis, who used the term "cultural mulatto" to describe what he saw as the ways in which these writers borrowed from both white and Black culture, I don't see anything mulatto about the work of the writers I will examine here, nor do I consider my own work to fall into that category. We grew up black in America—and that covers a lot of ground.

First, a few words about my own work in the context of "post-oppression" fiction. I've published three novels: *Another Way to Dance, The Fall of Rome,* and *Third Girl from the Left.* All three have been set for the most part in the time period from the 1990s to the early 2000s, which is when they were written. When I began each of these books, I had no conscious thought that I was going to try to write about "post-oppression." I simply wrote about people that I made up whom I found interesting. But as a black writer born after the gains of the Civil Rights Movement, the people I felt free to imagine were quite different than those that writers of an earlier generation might have felt free to imagine: A self-hating Latin teacher and his students. A fourteen-year-old girl trying to make it in the almost all-white world of ballet. A minor actress of the 1970s, her mother, who lived through the Tulsa race riot, and her filmmaker daughter. I can make no claims for how well or badly I executed these characters. But I can say that while I write *aware* of history (it is a particularly important strand of *Third Girl from the Left*) I don't feel its weight in the same way. I don't feel bound to tell only certain kinds of stories. I don't worry about representing the race or uplifting the race through my fiction. And I don't engage with our long history of oppression in the same way that, say, Toni Morrison does. She (and those before her) lived through a visceral everyday experience of racism that I can only imagine. I've been called names, but I've never feared for my life because of my race (and the name-calling and denigration was not an everyday event). I've never been denied entry to any establishment because of my race. I've never experienced the kind of daily racial violence that was the lot of so many African Americans for so long. That's true of many writers of my generation or younger. Like many of them, I don't feel compelled to engage in narratives of direct and violent struggle with racism and oppression. I believe that's because of both the literal freedom from legal segregation that I have always lived under and because of the creative freedom that Wright, Baldwin, Morrison, and so many other black writers who paved the way have won for me. I find myself more drawn to attempting to make art out of the lives that are left once the most overt battles are over. We are no longer restricted by law—but we are still restricted by internal and external bonds of racism, classism, and sometimes, self-loathing. What stories do you tell once the doors have swung open? A lot of us are working on that question.

For most of the nineteenth and twentieth centuries, much of the best-known, most-lauded fiction by African Americans dealt with how being African American affected the protagonist and his or her status in life, often (and understandably) through the prism of difficulty, oppression, and hardship. *Native Son, Invisible Man, Go Tell It on the Mountain,* and, of more recent vintage, *The Bluest Eye, The Color Purple, Beloved*—in terms of incidents in each of these books, let's face it, things are rough, rough, rough. By this, I don't mean that there is no room for nuance or happiness or laughter in these novels (well, not too many laughs in *Native Son*) but always, there is a weight over the characters, a burden that cannot be laid down. One could discuss the levels of craft and/or the success of each of these novels as art endlessly—and certainly, that's been done. But for the sake of my argument, let's agree that the subject matter of these novels unfolds in large part or in whole in relation to the character(s) oppression, directly or indirectly, by the larger (read: white) world.

Something else to consider: The authors most firmly entrenched in the twentieth-century canon of literature by and about African Americans were born in the early part of the twentieth century, well before the Civil Rights Movement and the changes it wrought. Toni Morrison and Alice Walker are, in mid-2011, 80 and 67 years old, respectively. Wright, Ellison, and Baldwin, as we know, have passed on. While I cannot prove this empirically, it is my sense that the work of these writers tends to be what is most commonly taught to high school students and undergraduates who are not majoring in African American studies. And certainly, that's as it should be—these authors are crucial to understanding American literature and the American experience. But for the contemporary high school or college student, perhaps that's not all it should be.

Suppose you are a black fiction writer born around 1970, shortly after the Civil Rights Movement definitively and permanently changed the laws, if not the attitudes, that made life for your parents and those African Americans before them so difficult. And suppose that while you have a clear and visceral sense of the meaning of race, you don't have the kind of direct experience of physical and emotional hardship that the black writers of earlier generations would have had or at least to which they would have been privy. Slavery, lynchings as common practice, legal segregation—you know about all these things, of course, but you haven't lived them. Your battles are smaller, subtler; your feelings about race and your experience of it are complex and shifting. How would that affect you as a writer? How might it change, subtly or not, the material that you were interested in working with? How would it affect the stories you choose to tell and the way you choose to tell them?

By looking at Colson Whitehead's (b. 1969) *Sag Harbor*, ZZ Packer's (b. 1973) *Drinking Coffee Elsewhere*, and James Hannaham's (b. 1968) *God Says No,* all published since 2000, I hope to begin a discussion about the terrain of some contemporary African American writers and illuminate some of the ways in which they are guiding their (and our) American stories into the future. This essay will also be something of an exhortation to academics: that they find time in their overwhelmed schedules to get acquainted with the twenty-first-century work of African American writers beyond Colson Whitehead (who is no doubt significant and skilled but who has also had many upon many academic essays written about his work) and teach it to their students.[1] (A note of disclosure: I am personally acquainted to varying degrees with all three of the writers whose work I will discuss here.)

Here (slightly abridged) are the opening few paragraphs of ZZ Packer's story "Drinking Coffee Elsewhere":

> Orientation games began the day I arrived at Yale from Baltimore. In our group we played heady, frustrating games for smart people. One game appeared to be charades reinterpreted by existentialists; another involved listening to rocks. Then a freshman counselor made everyone play Trust. The idea was that if you had the faith to fall backward and wait for four scrawny high school geniuses to catch you, just before your head cracked on the slate sidewalk, then you might learn to trust your fellow students. Russian roulette sounded like a better way to go.
>
> "No way" I said. . . . "It's cool, it's all cool," the counselor said. Her hair was a shade of blond I'd seen only on *Playboy* covers, and she raised her hands as though backing away from a growling dog. "Sister," she said, in an I'm-down-with-the-struggle voice, "you don't have to play this game. As a person of color, you shouldn't have to fit into any white, patriarchal system."
>
> I said, "It's a bit too late for that." (117–118)

Dina, the protagonist of this story, is wised-up, fiercely smart . . . and scared to death. She is bristlingly aware of her race, her class (Packer elegantly conveys this in a flashback in which Dina and her mother rummage through the sofa for enough change to buy groceries after a mishap with their food stamps) and the ways in which her privileged position as a scholarship student at Yale are a symbol of the effort to transcend the historical bonds of that race and that class. She attempts (with only moderate success) to use her formidable intelligence to manage the degree to which she feels cut off not only from her working-class black neighborhood (by virtue of her bookishness and the determination that has carried her to Yale) and those at Yale (by virtue of race, class, sexual preference, and just about anything else you could name). The primary emotional arc of this story is the way in which a white lesbian classmate named Heidi nearly breaches Dina's carapace of savage wit and racial isolation. The two young women, both outcasts by both temperament and status, form a bond that is first friendship and then, as it begins to edge over into a gentle sexual attraction and real love, becomes so terrifying to Dina that she lashes out and damages the relationship in a way that is unlikely ever to be repaired. The consequences of this decision send Dina reeling into an uncertain future, away from everything she's fought so hard to achieve.

In this story, the white world is never far from Dina's consciousness—but in fact, no one in it ever attacks her directly. There are no racist remarks or encounters; Heidi is not revealed to have some secret race-based animosity toward Dina. Her affection for Dina is simple and sincere, if a bit naive. One of the things that is most frightening to Dina is the white gaze, the sense of being always on display to a world that has invited you in but whose inhabitants (you fear) could turn on you at any moment. An aside: as a scholarship kid myself (prep school in my native Cleveland and then Smith College) I identified strongly with how Packer shows the reader the tensions, internal and external, of being an affirmative-action baby. She also deftly illustrates how making this leap can leave you betwixt and between—you've left the world of working-class and poor African America but you're not really at home in the lap of white luxury. As afraid as Dina is of the white gaze, she is also afraid of opening her heart up to anyone of any race (as we see when she shuts out Heidi, who she truly loves, as well as through a remembered encounter with a black boy back in Baltimore). She reacts defensively to the environment at Yale out of the knowledge of the long reach of history, an awareness that people often keep to themselves the biased sentiments that they might have shared openly in an earlier time and out of a sense of herself as an interloper in a world that has been closed to people like her for hundreds of years (and only began to welcome them in tentatively within the last 30 years).

In "Drinking Coffee Elsewhere," a crucial way in which Dina's story differs most significantly from narratives of an earlier time is that she has been *invited into* an elite, predominantly white institution. In earlier narratives, a black character might not face the direct attack of a white character or characters over the course of a novel or story (often they do, but not always); they are never able, in any concrete or lasting way, to enter the bastions of white power and begin to navigate them, possibly even to join them. That is one of the most significant changes that the Civil Rights Movement brought about. From Packer and Hannaham (Yale graduates) to Whitehead (Harvard graduate) to President Obama (Columbia graduate, then Harvard law), the admission of large(r) numbers of black students into not only the most elite educational institutions but into many other venues previously reserved only for whites, has sped up and cemented a significant increase in the meaning of class within the African American community, along with the meaning of race; meanings that Packer wrestles with elegantly in this story.

Throughout this story collection, Packer continues to consider questions of isolation, both personal and racial, and the assumptions that people make about one another based on race, among other factors. She also delights in both humor and in subverting certain tropes of African American fiction. And perhaps most telling, her stories are all rather open-ended. There is neither the sense of final ruin of her protagonists that one finds in, say, *The Bluest Eye* or of final redemption as in *The Color Purple*. The characters in Packer's stories are in the middle of a great cultural shift and many of them aren't sure where they are going; Packer is content to let it be so to a degree that might not have felt comfortable for a young black woman writer of an earlier generation. In "The Ant of the Self," a brainy, awkward boy is dragged to the Million Man March by his con man father—but rather than feeling elevated to some sort of coming of age, he feels no kinship, only frustration and alienation, at this event that is supposed to cement his ties to the long line of African American manhood. And in "Speaking in Tongues," the old, old story of a young girl who runs away from home without a dime to her name and is taken in, seduced, and then turned out by a pimp is deliciously subverted when the older hookers pool their money, attack their pimp, and help her get away. In Packer's stories, the unexpected is never far away.

In the promotional video for his novel *Sag Harbor*, Colson Whitehead describes it thusly: "Not a lot happens; it's really a slice of life. . . . So, there's no dead body they find like in *Stand By Me*; there's not a lynching and the KKK is not chasing them through the Hamptons."[2] As this remark makes clear, and as readers of his earlier work know, Whitehead has always been deeply interested in subverting genres and expectations. *Sag Harbor,* while it is much more intimate and autobiographical than his earlier work, continues that tradition (like the novel's protagonist Benji, Whitehead was a teenager in the 1980s and spent summers in the affluent black beach community of Sag Harbor outside of New York City). Whitehead's comment in the video is also representative of the tone of the novel: Like both Packer and Hannaham's books, *Sag Harbor* is often very funny—which I believe is indicative of the degree to which African American writers of this generation feel much freer to just plain old crack jokes (Toni Morrison has her moments but let's face it—there aren't a lot of laughs in most of black literature's greatest hits. See Paul Beatty's *Hokum: An Anthology of African American Humor* for more about that). One of the funniest moments in the book involves an elaborate handwritten chart describing the "grammatical acrobatics" that Benji and his friends use that summer to trade idle teenage boy insults. "You fuckin' Cha-Ka from Land of the Lost-lookin' mother fucker" (52) is a typical construction delineated in the chart.

And still, for all that *Sag Harbor* is simply a meandering journey through one summer in the life of a black teen, even though the humor in it is overshadowed and/or shaped, as in "Drinking Coffee Elsewhere" by the white gaze. The above-mentioned section is funny partly because of the ways it is specifically and entirely "black," rooted in hundreds of years of the way we talk and play the dozens and mess around. All the language and interaction between Benji and his friends carries this same casual play of blackness, the same recognition and, in the same breath, dismissal of the white world. This play continues throughout the novel. There were moments when I was reading that I wondered if anyone who hadn't been a black person in the 1980s would get all the references. And then I thought, "Well, you know what? That's okay. Great, even. Heaven knows we've had to figure out cultural signifiers in 'mainstream' fiction for long enough." In much the same way that Junot Diaz uses untranslated Spanish and Spanglish in his work, Whitehead does not invest energy in translating certain argot and ways of being.

Along with that comfort in black culture though, there is still the white gaze, as in Packer's fiction. As Whitehead notes in his video, there's not a directly oppressive white person (there are hardly any white people at all) to be found in the book, but whites are rarely far from the mind:

> You didn't, for example, walk down Main Street with a watermelon under your arm. Even if you had a pretty good reason. Like, you were going to a potluck and each person had to bring an item and your item just happened to be a watermelon, luck of the draw, and you wrote this on a sign so everyone would understand the context, and as you walked down Main Street you held the sign in one hand and the explained watermelon in the other, all casual, perhaps nodding between the watermelon and the sign for extra emphasis if you made eye contact. This would not happen. We were on display. (107)

That awareness of being on display is referred to over and over throughout the book, as is the relief of being out on Sag Harbor and not having to interact with curious whites all day long. The awareness of his position doesn't cramp Benji's style though. Rather, as is true for many of us who found ourselves pioneers in the integration of the upper middle class, this uncomfortable awareness is simply part of his style, as natural—if not as pleasant—as breathing the salt air of Sag Harbor.

Sag Harbor is also marked as a post-oppression novel by its very aimlessness, much as Packer's is marked by its open-endedness. There are no climactic confessions or discoveries—it is just a bunch of boys hanging around until the end of summer. But think about it—how many late-twentieth-century novels *by* a young black man *about* young black men can you name that are about simply hanging around? Personally, I can't think of one. No growth. No disaster. No attacks from the outside world. No racial reckoning of any kind. Whether you find yourself interested in hanging around with these guys or not, there is no doubt that it is something of a bold move—a new move—to present this tale in this way. What's more, the extent to which Whitehead's characters are free to just hang around with relatively little racial pressure hanging over their heads is the marker of change in and of itself. To some extent, chronicling that change is the signal achievement of this gentle novel.

I'll conclude with a brief look at James Hannaham's *God Says No,* the most recently published of the novels I'll examine. The protagonist of this book is an overweight black fundamentalist Christian named Gary Gray who, much to his distress, has an unquenchable sexual desire for men. He tries his best, as the slang has it, to "pray away the gay." But it doesn't work (does it ever?). He doesn't want to leave his version of Christianity; in fact, he wants desperately to live the heterosexual life he's been taught is the only safe path. But the heart—and the flesh—wants what it wants, which leads Gary to some uncomfortable (and explicit) encounters in men's rooms and local parks. In many ways, this novel is kind of a funhouse mirror of the classic "passing" narrative—Gary is desperately trying to pass as straight but the truth keeps making itself known, no matter how hard he fights. And in the end, his redemption comes only when he admits and accepts his homosexuality.

Hannaham has taken—not directly, but obliquely—that old story of "passing" and turned it to his own purposes in considering the meaning of sexuality. What is most striking about this book in the context of the "post-oppression" novel is that even less than Whitehead or Packer's characters Gary's biggest problem is not his race. He's not concerned about the white gaze; he never muses within the narrative about what white people might think of him. What's more, he is often profoundly attracted to white men, but he neither fetishizes nor especially fears this attraction. He hates being gay—but desiring a white guy doesn't make him hate it any more or any less. The primary way that Gary's race enters the novel is as either an attraction or a turn-off for his white partners on the down-low (after his first bathroom encounter, the white man he's just fellated says, "I love me some chocolate chubbies. . . . It ain't enough around these parts for me" [40]). But as you can see by this remark (and Gary's reaction to it later in the scene), his weight is as big a concern and part of his self-conception as his race. In this book, the gaze isn't about white or black—it's about straight or gay.

By choosing, consciously or not, to subvert the passing narrative and make Gary's race incidental to his story (though not denied or elided), Hannaham has taken a big step toward moving the African American novel to yet another place—a place that is wholly of the twenty-first century. So, in their own ways, have Whitehead and Packer. And so have many post-millennial writers that I haven't named here (and not all of them are under 40). As we move through years to come, there will be many other African American voices telling their stories differently still: What will happen as the children of interracial couplings, more numerous than ever, grow up and begin to incorporate their experience into fiction. What will happen if the class divide in the black community, so large now, only grows? Or if (as seems less likely) it shrinks? The narratives being created now add another layer to our already dense and vital literary history and lay the groundwork for what's next, just as Morrison, Baldwin, Ellison, and so many more laid the groundwork for us. The work goes on and the voices carry on, in dialogue, in counterpoint and in harmony. No one can know exactly where it will go. But it's up to wise readers to follow.

NOTES

1. Internet resources can help with this search. One that I helped create, along with novelists Eisa Ulen and Bridgett Davis, editor Chris Jackson, and the director of Cave Canem, Alison Meyers, is a loose coalition called Ringshout (www.theringshout .com). On our website we have a list of ambitious contemporary fiction by black writers. Another good resource is Carleen Brice's always entertaining and thoughtful blog, "White Readers Meet Black Authors" (http://welcomewhitefolks.blogspot.com/). A further help, of course, is anthologies like this one.

2. The promotional video in which Whitehead makes this statement can be found at http://www.youtube.com/watch?v=aILSfknGqFY.

WORKS CITED

Baldwin, James. *Go Tell It on the Mountain*. New York: Dell Publishing, 2000.
Ellis, Trey. "The New Black Aesthetic," *Callaloo* 38 (Winter 1989): 233–43.
Ellison, Ralph. *Invisible Man*. New York: Vintage, 1995.
Hannaham, James. *God Says No*. San Francisco: McSweeney's Books, 2009.
Morrison, Toni. *The Bluest Eye*. New York: Vintage, 2007.
Packer, ZZ. *Drinking Coffee Elsewhere*. New York: Riverhead Books, 2003.
Sapphire. *Push*. New York: Vintage, 1997.
Southgate, Martha. *Another Way to Dance*. New York: Laurel Leaf, 1998.
———. *The Fall of Rome*. New York: Scribners, 2002.
———. *Third Girl from the Left*. New York: Houghton Mifflin Company, 2005.
Walker, Alice. *The Color Purple*. New York: Pocket Books, 1990.
Whitehead, Colson. *Sag Harbor*. New York: Anchor Books, 2010.
Wright, Richard. *Native Son*. New York: Harper Perennial, 1996.

PART FOUR

PEDAGOGICAL APPROACHES AND IMPLICATIONS

UNTANGLING HISTORY, DISMANTLING FEAR: TEACHING TAYARI JONES'S *LEAVING ATLANTA*

TRUDIER HARRIS

Slavery. Reconstruction. Lynching. Black codes. The Ku Klux Klan. Segregation. Jim Crow laws. The Great Migration. School desegregation. The murders of Emmett Till, Dr. Martin Luther King, Jr., Malcolm X, and a host of others. The Greensboro sit-ins. The Atlanta Child Murders. These significant historical events—and countless others that are less iconic—have repeatedly found their way into the imaginings of African American writers, including Tayari Jones, who, in her debut novel, *Leaving Atlanta* (2002), steps into the fear and lack of information surrounding the Atlanta Child Murders to yield an engaging novel about racial violence and childhood nightmares coexisting with attempts to showcase normalcy during extraordinary times. Jones is thus on the contemporary end of a long, long line of foremothers and forefathers who have found their creative imaginings in historical events.

Indeed, one could just as easily chart a history of peoples of African descent on American soil by reading their imaginative writings as he or she could chart that history through nonliterary sources. From Phillis Wheatley, Jupiter Hammon, and Frederick Douglass through the twentieth century and into the twenty-first century with a novel such as Toni Morrison's *A Mercy* (2008), African American authors have found the circumstances of African American existence upon American soil to be just as inspiring as fodder for their creative imaginations as any fertile ground they could till out of totally virgin fields. Consequently, a scholar could argue that American history, specifically as it relates to persons of African descent on American territory, has provided the majority of creative inspiration for African Americans.

Certainly that inspiration begins in the realm of the autobiographical, with formerly enslaved narrators such as Frederick Douglass and Harriet Jacobs (Linda Brent) penning the tales of their lives during slavery. Whether they documented atrocities during slavery, as Douglass did in his *Narrative of the Life of Frederick Douglass, An American Slave* (1845), or documented some and hinted at others, as Jacobs did in *Incidents in the Life of a Slave Girl* (1861), their primary objective was to bring about an end to slavery. That goal-orientation through literary creation linked Douglass and Jacobs with the majority of writers who followed them in the nineteenth century as well as those in the twentieth and twenty-first centuries. Writers such as Frances Ellen Watkins Harper and Paul Laurence Dunbar in their poetry added their voices in representing slavery and newly freed blacks in the late nineteenth century, while James Weldon Johnson, Claude McKay, Jean Toomer, Langston Hughes, and others treated lynching, migration, segregation, and other historical topics in the first few decades of the twentieth century, especially during the Harlem Renaissance of the 1920s. In *The Autobiography of An Ex-Colored Man* (1912; 1927), Johnson depicts a graphic lynching/burning that leads to his protagonist passing for white; he also includes other depictions of the segregated lives of black people in the southern United States and the general limitations placed on their life possibilities. Both McKay and Toomer join Johnson in depicting lynching, McKay in poems such as "The Lynching" and Toomer in "Blood-Burning Moon," which appears in *Cane* (1923). Hughes, who may properly be called a *blues documentarian* of all things African American, portrays blacks leaving the South ("One-Way Ticket," "Bound No'th Blues"), caught in the strictures of Jim Crow ("Mother to Son," "I, Too," "Lunch in a Jim Crow Car"), suffering after their arrival on the so-called promised land of the North ("Ballad of the Landlord," the Madam poems, "Harlem" ["Here on the edge of hell / Stands Harlem"]), and always finding themselves on the short end of the stick in racial matters (there are dozens of examples in *The Collected Poems of Langston Hughes*).[1]

Richard Wright in *Native Son* (1940) and Ann Petry in *The Street* (1946) both charted the course of migration from the South to the North and the consequences of northern living on black migrants in the 1940s, as did Gwendolyn Brooks in her depictions of blacks on the south side of Chicago in *A Street in Bronzeville* (1945), *The Bean Eaters* (1960), and other collections of poetry. Restrictions on opportunities that African Americans had expected as a result of migration to the North also received treatment from James Baldwin and Ralph Ellison in the 1950s. Baldwin's Gabriel Grimes, the father in *Go Tell It on the Mountain* (1953), is a disgruntled migrant from the South whose troubling brand of fundamentalist religion leads him to make life miserable for his Harlem family; having been so saturated with white racism in the South, he cannot imagine a future in which blacks claim their own destinies, so he reins in his family, especially the intelligent and creative protagonist John, whenever they try to deviate from his racially restrictive path. Ellison's narrator in *Invisible Man* (1952) migrates from Alabama to opportunity in New York, but he becomes as much a problem to himself, with his inability to adjust to northern mores, as do the persons around him who actively seek to place strictures on him. In every instance, the history of race relations in the South has acutely informed the personalities of characters and the shaping of narratives on northern soil.

A furious blossoming of the impact of historical events upon the literature was especially observable from the 1970s into the twenty-first century when many African American writers found slavery to be an irresistible attraction in their creative efforts. Sherley Anne Williams, Octavia E. Butler, Charles Johnson, Toni Morrison, Edward P. Jones, and several others ushered in the heyday of the neo-slave narrative, and that subgenre continues to thrive.[2] Of course, Margaret Walker might properly be credited with the inaugural volume in the subgenre when she published *Jubilee* in 1966; the story begins in slavery and ends well into reconstruction. Neo-slave narratives seek to revise if not fully to rewrite the roles African Americans played in the history of slavery. These narratives give more agency and power to enslaved persons than most historical texts corroborate. When Williams gives a black woman the power to be one of the leaders of an uprising during slavery as depicted in *Dessa Rose* (1986) or when Butler gives her female protagonist the ability to influence the ways in which other enslaved persons are treated on a plantation, the potentially corrective or revisionist possibilities of such narratives become clear. Writers revisit slavery with a mission, and that mission is to restore as much humanity and responsibility for one's own existence as can possibly be imagined from the vantage point of the twentieth and twenty-first centuries.

This constant focus on looking back might be assumed to suggest a dominant reactive mode in African American literary creation. That would be an erroneous assumption. Authors of neo-slave narratives paint on a canvas that allows them to right wrongs, grant agency to persons presumed not to have any, and revise, if not completely transform, the historical landscapes that they find so inspiring. There might be a slight documentary quality to these creations, but the writers move their narratives into realms that posit history as possibility, not history as static or limited. The same argument might be made of topics such as segregation, violence, and murder. Writers use the historical basics to move into other ways of thinking about creativity, as Marilyn Nelson and Daniel Black do when they evoke the murder of Emmett Till in their works. Nelson in *A Wreath for Emmett Till* (2005) creates a "heroic crown of sonnets" for adolescent audiences, a move that instantly changes the dynamic of how an author can represent a racially motivated murder. Black, in *The Sacred Place* (2007), imagines a world in which blacks fight back when the white marauders come in the middle of the night to take an innocent child away to kill him.

In the hands of African American writers, history is a tool, a shape-shifting set of possibilities for scripts that historians—and even persons who lived in those historic times—can only imagine. That is no less true for Tayari Jones, who was born and raised in Atlanta and who was aware of the racial madness that ensued there when she was a child. In 1979, when Jones was in the fifth grade, several children and adults from the southwestern part of Atlanta simply disappeared from their homes and families. Various estimates suggest that between 28 and 31 African Americans disappeared. Some of their bodies were recovered and others were not.[3] The disappearances gripped the nation, and an aura of fear surrounded not only Atlanta, but every city in America where large populations of black people resided. Suspects ranged from the CIA, to the Ku Klux Klan (KKK), to the Centers for Disease Control (CDC—whose headquarters is located in Atlanta), to the FBI, to local law enforcement officers and taxi cab drivers. The pervasiveness of the snatchings and the persistence of the killer or killers turned this historical moment into one of the iconic reference points for African Americans. The actual disappearances and rumors combined with lack of official information (the powers that be were accused of trying to save the city's reputation instead of working to solve the cases) to create one of the most frightening scenarios of threats to African American existence on United States soil.

Jones takes the horror and "domesticates" it, in that she brings it front and center to the children in a fifth-grade class whose home lives are in turmoil even as they endure the snatchings and murders of two of their classmates (one body is recovered, the other is not).[4] Divided into three sections, *Leaving Atlanta* focuses first on LaTasha Baxter, her younger sister, and their parents and narrates from a third-person limited perspective. We learn how desperately Tasha wants to be accepted by her classmates, how her father has moved out, and how both situations change when children start disappearing. Her father returns home, the family buys a television for their kitchen, changes their habits about watching television while eating, and glues themselves to the television for the six PM and eleven o'clock news when newscaster Monica Kaufman provides updates on the disappearances. Although Tasha still has a desperate need to be accepted by the most popular girls in her class, she also assumes the role of "protector" for her younger sister. The second section of the novel, the one that will perhaps prove most challenging for students, focuses on Rodney Green and renders his story from a second-person point of view. Through that slightly disorienting approach, we learn of Rodney's inability to do anything to please Mr. Green, of Rodney's hatred for his father, and his voluntarily getting into a car with a stranger after his father has come to school and paddled him in front of his entire class. A middle-class and gifted child who has no hopes—or desire—of living up to his father's expectations (he even imagines his father at one point as a potential child snatcher), Rodney muddles his way through life in a pattern that mirrors the distancing effect of the second-person narrative in which his plight is presented to us. Rodney's only "friend" is Octavia "Sweet Pea" Fuller, a projects' kid whom the other students reject as much for her extremely dark skin coloring (they call her "Watusi") as for her poverty and deliberate lack of social skills. Octavia must spend evenings alone while her mother works third shift. She keeps abreast of the kidnappings and murders by watching late-night television once her mother leaves for work. More mature and perhaps even more sensitive than Rodney and Tasha, Octavia narrates her own story.

Starting places for historical approaches to the novel need to be two-pronged. First, focus briefly on how African writers throughout their ten-

ure on American soil have used history. That is clearly a huge assignment, so perhaps a couple of cases would suffice—perhaps the deaths of
Emmett Till and Martin Luther King, Jr.—to provide students with sufficient information and readings on these cases to enable them to have
informed opinions in discussing them. Then, perhaps give them a short
assignment to reexamine evidence from their own perspective and see
what new conclusions, if any, they can reach about what happened in
both instances. What have writers done with the history in each case?
Into what genres other than poetry and fiction have these events found
their way?[5] How have writers treated the events? In other words, how has
history shaped the creative imagination or how has the creative imagination shaped history?

More specifically in connection with *Leaving Atlanta,* the obvious
place to start in teaching the narrative is to allow students to become
acquainted with the actual events of the Atlanta Child Murders. You
will find that many students today—sadly—know nothing of this iconic
event. They may begin by simply typing "Atlanta Child Murders" into
Google. That will yield several sites—and a Wikipedia article—that provide information about whom the victims were, their ages when snatched,
photographs of them, and when/if their bodies were recovered. From
this broad base of the pyramid of information, you may direct your students to Patricia A. Turner's "The Atlanta Child Murders: A Case Study
of Folklore in the Black Community."[6] Turner does an excellent job of
exploring what happens in a situation in which official information is
not readily forthcoming. Individuals in such situations begin to modify
whatever they have heard and at times to manufacture information that
they need/desire. Turner's essay therefore provides an opportunity to explore the impact of rumor upon nightmarish conditions, which can lead
to a discussion of rumor in any racial situation.[7] With these two scholarly studies as background, students can then engage the effect of rumor
in *Leaving Atlanta* and begin to articulate comparisons between the folk-
based stories surrounding the cases of murdered and missing children
and events with which they may be familiar of a more contemporary nature. Rumors surrounding 9/11 or the (almost) Times Square bombing
come immediately to mind.

Some questions that might engage students in terms of information,
lack of information, manufactured information, and rumor are, How

does each child in *Leaving Atlanta* learn of the missing children? What sources do they rely on to supplement what they initially learn? At what points do the children begin to become "experts," in that they manufacture their own narratives about what is happening around them? In what ways can the communities of children in *Leaving Atlanta* be viewed as folk communities, that is, as communities that create and pass on their own lore? To what components of the larger narratives that surround them do the children seem to be most drawn? How are these attractions in keeping with or deviations from the official narratives? What is the relationship between narratives the children create and their actions— or lack thereof—about protecting themselves and those around them? Does the novel suggest ways in which the sore of this particular history can be healed?

In connection with this last question, direct your students to Tayari Jones's blog about the Atlanta Child Murders. What is her sense of the healing power—if any—of narrative? In what ways does her assessment of what she hoped to accomplish in *Leaving Atlanta* seem plausible to you and your students? In what ways does it not? How does Jones's sense of fictionalizing a historical event coincide with what you and your students may have discovered about the murders of Emmett Till and Martin Luther King, Jr.—or about some other historical event you discussed? From what you read about the Atlanta Child Murders as a historical event, what conclusions do you draw about how well Jones has succeeded—or not—in bringing this event to imaginative realization?

So far, focus on the novel and the historical events surrounding it has been discussion-centered (except perhaps for the photographs on the Internet). Now, introduce a visual component by having your students watch the movie or the documentary based on the cases. The movie, simply titled *The Atlanta Child Murders*, appeared in 1985 and included such notable actors and actresses as Morgan Freeman, James Earl Jones, Rip Torn, Ruby Dee, Gloria Foster, and Martin Sheen. The documentary was produced for A&E and is entitled *155—The Atlanta Child Murders*. It appeared in A&E's *American Justice* series during the 2000–2001 programming season. After viewing, have your students contemplate what differences seeing the dramatization or listening to and viewing the documentary make in their understandings of the cases and their reactions to and evaluations of Jones's novel. Does Jones capture the fear factor sufficiently, or is film a better medium for capturing fear? Compare the ending of the film and the ending of the novel? Which is more satisfactory? Why? What about the documentary—did it answer questions you may have had adequately? What, overall, would you say is the purpose of the documentary? Of the film? To what audiences do you believe each is directed?

At this point, consider Jones and *Leaving Atlanta* in dialogue with other writers (essayists, poets) who have written about the Atlanta Child Murders. Get a copy of Nikki Giovanni's "Flying Underground (*for the children of Atlanta*)" and have students read it carefully.[8] How effective is the poem in bringing to fictional "life" the incident that it portrays? What strategies does the poet employ in attempting to engage readers with the poem? What prior knowledge does Giovanni assume that readers will bring to the poem? Are her assumptions correct? As an isolated attempt to capture what kidnapped and murdered children may have done and felt, how does the poem offer transcendence of the tragedy? In what ways is that attempted transcendence successful? In what ways is it not? Select one of the poems from Marilyn Nelson's *A Wreath for Emmett Till* and compare how that sonnet attempts to deal with a tragic historical event with what Giovanni does. What does this comparison suggest about how writers deal with painful historical materials? How do these treatments shed light—if they do—on your discussion of *Leaving Atlanta*?[9]

After almost two years of fear and lack of resolution, authorities in Atlanta finally arrested, tried, and imprisoned Wayne Williams, a young black man, for the murders of two of the adults (the other cases remain unresolved, which means that no one has ever been arrested for murdering any of the children who were so brutally dispatched). Essayist, novelist, and activist James Baldwin traveled to Atlanta for segments of the trial and to interview various people about it. He published the result of his forays as *The Evidence of Things Not Seen* (1985), which is essentially an essayistic meditation on Wayne Williams, the circumstances surrounding his arrest and trial, and the racial politics of Atlanta. You might want students to explore the volume in enough detail to discover what it is *not* about. It is not about the blood and guts of young bodies being lost and found—or not. It is not necessarily about justice or resolution. It is not, in any great detail, about any of the families that lost children to kidnapping and death. It is, as stated, a *meditation* on a particular moment in history and what it evokes about other moments in history. The challenge in considering *The Evidence of Things Not Seen* in relation to the Atlanta Child Murders and/or *Leaving Atlanta* is that it seems at best almost peripheral to the central issues. And yet it stands as one of the major publications following the murders. A conversation with students, therefore, might center upon Baldwin's positioning in electing his own historical meditation. Why does a northern, black, then-expatriate writer find the case so viscerally engaging? What did he hope to accomplish? In what ways—or not—is that purpose clear to you? What conclusions can you draw about what, if anything, Baldwin's volume achieves in *The Evidence of Things Not Seen*?

Just as students viewed a film and/or a documentary about the Atlanta Child Murders themselves, they also have the opportunity to view one about Wayne Williams. *"Mugshots"—Wayne Williams and the Atlanta Child Murd*ers was produced in 2000. It seeks to answer questions surrounding Williams's involvement in the cases, his arrest, his trial, his conviction, and his possible innocence or guilt. This documentary, whether it is considered sensationalist, titillating, or accurate, is another way of layering as well as complicating the circumstances surrounding the disappearances and deaths of all those young African Americans between 1979 and 1981. Even after the movie and the two documentaries, however, questions still remain—and I am sure your students will still have questions. For example, if Wayne Williams was convicted in only two of the cases, why has there not been sustained effort to uncover the culprit(s) in the remaining nearly thirty cases? Who made the decisions to close those cases, and why were those decisions made? The cases have been reopened twice since the official closings. Neither reopening yielded enough evidence to go forward with the expectation of producing a different outcome. Students might return to Tayari Jones's blog to see what she has written about reopening the cases.

While Wayne Williams came to symbolize villainy in the historical cases, the idea of perpetrators in the novel is left in the realm of the imagination. Discuss how Jones treats the possibilities of who could be responsible for the kidnapped and murdered children. This discussion could circle back to the idea of rumor and could now be combined with how children make a world of their own when they do not have the consistent stabilizing effects of healthy adult influence. Who do the children posit as possible culprits in the text? Indeed, how many different culprits do they imagine? What are their rationales for thinking the way they do? What do their imaginings about perpetrators contribute to discussions of the class dynamics that are operative in the novel? As the fifth graders imagine them, how do perpetrators stack up along class lines for those doing the imagining? How do such imaginings reduce—or even increase—the fear factor in the novel?

As a historical phenomenon, the Atlanta Child Murders can easily be lifted out of their immediately surrounding context. That is, we can focus on the whys and wherefores of the murders and neglect to consider the overall racial climate in Atlanta at the time of the murders. A useful endeavor, therefore, would be to *reinsert,* so to speak, the murders into the racial and social climate of Atlanta between 1979 and 1981. For the twenty-two months that the murders were being committed, what else was happening in Atlanta? Or, as the city had progressed in its historical development through the twentieth century and the struggle for civil rights, what was the racial climate in Atlanta in the late 1970s? Who was in charge of city government? How was it structured? How prominent were African American politicians and other spokespersons for the black community? Popularly billed as "the city too busy to hate," was that really an accurate description of the city's climate immediately before the disappearances began? If there were sources of unrest, were they primarily racial or economic or class based—or something else? How was the southwest side of Atlanta viewed in relation to other parts of the city? Did the people and neighborhoods in this section of Atlanta have political or social advocates comparable to those in other parts of the city? What made this part of the city particularly easy to get in and out of for the perpetrators of these violent acts? In other words, explore in detail the relationships among politics, geography, race, class, and education as they developed historically in Atlanta and manifested themselves in the late 1970s and early 1980s. From Atlanta's historical development, can you reach any viable conclusions about why this section of the city was targeted for the kidnappings and killings? Again, the idea is to layer discussion of the novel; reaching definitive conclusions is obviously nearly impossible.

Students can also layer their discussions of this part of the historical approach to the Atlanta Child Murders by examining in detail the media outlets that covered the cases. Tasha learns about the first missing children by watching television, but television news in 1979 was a far cry from the every hour on the hour sources of information currently available. What other media outlets were available, and who controlled them? An interesting exercise might be to examine a predominantly white media outlet and a predominantly black media outlet for comparisons of how coverage proceeded. Were there other sources of media coverage, such as church bulletins or neighborhood broadside-type handouts? If you are successful in locating such, try to determine what their particular biases are, no matter the direction in which those biases might lean. In terms of a visual media outlet, such as television, another exercise might be to determine whose reputations as newscasters were made/secured during this period. Explore and discuss the ethical issue of how one profits from tragedy, whether that profit is increased newspaper sales, increased newspaper reporting and thus increased reputations for news reporters, increased working hours for officers of the law and others, or even increases in sales of such items as paper products as relatives of victims copied images of their lost loved ones and circulated or posted them in various neighborhoods.

Teaching the novel in the context of the directly related historical events surrounding the Atlanta Child Murders is undoubtedly fruitful. However, another historical perspective will enable your students to place the actual composition of the novel, its structure, in a long line of African American texts. I refer specifically to the first person narrative that Octavia employs in the third section of the novel. A quick perusal of African American literary creations from the original slave narratives through the neo-slave narratives of the twenty-first century will reveal that first person narration has been a preferred mode of poetic, autobiographical, and fictional composition for African American writers since the documentation of their literacy on American soil. One of the most studied examples, obviously, is Frederick Douglass's *Narrative of the Life of Frederick Douglass.* Contemplate with your students this historical phenomenon and what it meant—and means—for African American writers to tend toward first person narratives. A short sampling from Douglass's narrative or another text might serve to provide comparison. A series of possible questions might guide your exploration. First person narratives inevitably presuppose audiences. To what audience(s) did Douglass direct his narrative? What was his purpose in so directing his narrative? How do we measure whether or not he achieved his purpose? What are the intersections between Douglass's use of this device and other first person narrators who appear between 1845 and the time Jones published *Leaving Atlanta* in 2002?

In specifically turning to the novel, consider Octavia's circumstances and the impetus to her creation. To whom is Octavia crying out, so to speak? What, if anything, does she hope to accomplish? Do her circumstances intersect at all with Douglass's, or is her use of first person a measure of how different, instead of how similar, the two narratives are? Douglass experienced various threats during his life as an enslaved person. Consider the threats to Octavia. How does she deal with those threats? In terms of an atmosphere of fear, personal threats, and inability to control one's fate, in what ways can you argue that Octavia's circumstances mirror, if only in small ways, those of persons enslaved in the United States during Douglass's lifetime?

Now, try to remember as precisely as possible what your responses were as you read Octavia's section of the novel. Was she able to tug at you emotionally? If so, how was she able to achieve that objective? What are the features, the rhetorical strategies, of her narrative that succeed in drawing readers into and empathizing with her circumstances? Try to articulate those as precisely as possible, even if it means making a list of the constructions, images, or smaller narrative features that Octavia uses to draw readers into the text. Consider other contemporary first person narratives with which you are familiar; they can be as short as a poem or essay or as long as a novel. Think about your responses to reading those texts. How do the plights of characters in your comparison examples help you to articulate your responses to Octavia and her narrative?

Octavia's narrative is designed to close the potential gap between narrator and reader. By contrast, Rodney's is designed almost to push readers as far away from him as he feels he is emotionally from his father. Examine the strategies that Jones allows Rodney to use and compare those to the ones she assigns to Octavia. What, specifically, in the language, distances readers from Rodney? What distances Rodney from his father? How does language play a role in Rodney's getting into the car with the stranger? While there is little historical African American precedent for what Jones does in the Rodney section of the novel, it is nonetheless compelling and acutely relevant for the sense of isolation that many children and adults felt during the Atlanta Child Murders. Consider, then, the ways in which this unusual and disconcerting narrative strategy might actually be reflective of the historical events that the novel uses as its inspiration.

The same consideration might be offered for the Tasha section of the novel. The third person limited point of view is a very traditional approach to narrative. Indeed, we might assert that it is a "comforting" narration. Everyone is in place, and the narrator has the ability to show us around corners and into Tasha's head. Tasha is the child whose family becomes nuclear again once the child snatchings are publicized. An approach to her section and style of narration, then, might be to explore how this resumed "normalcy" is also achieved through the kind of narrative style allotted to Tasha. The positive intent of the family's reconstitution is in dramatic contrast to the pathological nuclear family of which Rodney is a part, and Octavia is being raised by a single mother. Rodney's confusion, Octavia's independence, and Tasha's delayed maturity can all be tied, in some ways, to the styles of narration in which their stories are rendered. What details can students provide from each section of the novel to support such an assertion?

As you near the end of your discussion, bring your students to focus more intently on Tayari Jones as author of the novel. When an author places herself—or at least a fictional replica of herself—in a text, as a Tayari Jones appears in the fifth grade class portrayed in *Leaving Atlanta*, what interpretative possibilities does that placement allow? In what ways can an author's vision be clouded—or enhanced—by such a move? Were you disconcerted by this narrative move? Did you find it perhaps a bit too cute? Or is it recognition that the author herself was subjected to as much possible trauma as were the young people who were kidnapped and died during that twenty-two month period? Since such placement is unusual, try to reach some conclusions about how best to respond to this fictional phenomenon.

A final assignment might be this: have your students assume the roles of novelist, poet, or playwright. By using the material from *Leaving Atlanta*, how would you revise, transform, or improve upon what Jones has done? Students might literally attempt the creation of a poem, a short play, or a short chapter. If they do so, have them determine afterwards what the greatest challenges were to their creative endeavors. Some questions might include the following: Given your own readings about the Atlanta Child Murders, what compelling features, if any, seem to be missing from Jones' narrative? What would you add? What would you delete? If you are thoroughly satisfied with the novel as it is, articulate precisely why.

As this extended meditation makes clear, how African American writers use history is never a simple or simplistic matter. Their creative motives are complex and engaging, and their created characters are equally so. Even when they begin with a specific and well-known historical occurrence, they can go in myriad directions in responding to that specificity. History in African American literature, therefore, is never a matter of merely attempting to replicate the already known; it is a matter of allowing the imagination to work on the known, to ponder its many tentacles, and to shape something so new that evocations of the historical event are more a whiff of memory than a sustained, smothering, heavy-scented recollection.

NOTES

1. Arnold Rampersad, ed., *The Collected Poems of Langston Hughes* (New York: Knopf, 1994).

2. Some of these novels are Margaret Walker's *Jubilee* (1966), Gayl Jones's *Corregidora* (1975), Ishmael Reed's *Flight to Canada* (1976), Alex Haley's *Roots* (1976) and *Queen* (1993), Octavia E. Butler's *Kindred* (1979), Barbara Chase-Riboud's *Sally Hemings* (1979), David Bradley's *The Chaneysville Incident* (1981), Charles Johnson's *Oxherding Tale* (1982) and *Middle Passage* (1990), J. California Cooper's *Family* (1991), Sherley Anne Williams' *Dessa Rose* (1986), Toni Morrison's *Beloved* (1987), Louise Meriwether's *Fragments of the Ark* (1994), Caryl Phillips's *Crossing the River* (1994), John Edgar Wideman's *The Cattle Killing* (1996), Phyllis Alesia Perry's *Stigmata* (1998), and Edward P. Jones's *The Known World* (2003).

3. Several Internet sources feature information about the disappearances and murders of the children and adults in Atlanta. A simple Google search for "Atlanta Child Murders" will yield police reports, lists, and photographs of the victims, crime journal analyses, and a plethora of other materials. Tayari Jones's blog also refers to the cases. See also Eric Gary Anderson's "Black Atlanta: An Ecosocial Approach to Narratives of the Atlanta Child Murders," *PMLA* 122:1 (January 2007): 194–209. Though Wayne Bertram Williams was convicted of killing two of the victims, the majority of the remaining cases have not been solved. Folklore scholar Patricia A. Turner treats the cases from the perspective of the impact of rumor upon African American communities. See "The Atlanta Child Murders: A Case Study of Folklore in the Black Community," in *Contemporary Legend: A Reader,* edited by Gillian Bennett and Paul Smith

(New York: Garland Publishing Inc., 1996), 299–310. See also James Baldwin, *The Evidence of Things Not Seen* (New York: Dial Press, 1985). There is also a docudrama about the murders as well as a fictional film version of them.

4. I use the idea of domestication to discuss Jones's effort to contain fear in the novel in a chapter that I include in *The Scary Mason-Dixon Line: African American Writers and the South* (Baton Rouge: Louisiana State University Press, 2009); see pp. 151–173.

5. A particularly powerful poem to consider that depicts reaction to the death of Martin Luther King, Jr., is Nikki Giovanni's "Reflections on April 4, 1968," which appears in *Black Feeling Black Talk Black Judgement* (New York: William Morrow, 1970), 54–55. A novel is Charles Johnson's *Dreamer: A Novel* (New York: Scribner, 1998).

6. See note 3.

7. Turner explores this general phenomenon in her critical study *I Heard It Through the Grapevine: Rumor in African American Culture* (Berkeley: University of California Press, 1993).

8. Nikki Giovanni, *Those Who Ride the Night Winds: Poems* (New York: William Morrow, 1983), 33.

9. Novelist Toni Cade Bambara also wrote about the Atlanta Child Murders. Her novel, *Those Bones Are Not My Child,* was edited by Toni Morrison and published in 1999, a few years after Bambara's death.

WORKS CITED

American Justice: 155—"*The Atlanta Child Murders.*" 1985. Arts and Entertainment Television, 2008. DVD.

Anderson, Eric Gary. "Black Atlanta: An Ecosocial Approach to Narratives of the Atlanta Child Murders." *PMLA* 122:1 (January 2007): 194–209.

Baldwin, James. *The Evidence of Things Not Seen.* 1985. New York: H. Holt, 1995.

———. *Go Tell It on the Mountain.* New York: Delta Trade Paperbacks, 2000.

Bambara, Toni Cade. *Those Bones Are Not My Child.* New York: Pantheon, 1999.

Black, Daniel. *The Sacred Place.* New York: St. Martin's Griffin, 2008.

Brooks, Gwendolyn. *A Street in Bronzeville. Blacks.* Chicago: Third World Press, 1992.

———. *The Bean Eaters. Blacks.* Chicago: Third World Press, 1992.

Douglass, Frederick. *Narrative of the Life of Frederick Douglass, An American Slave.* New York: Barnes and Noble Classics, 2003.

Ellison, Ralph. *Invisible Man.* New York: Random House, 2002.

Giovanni, Nikki. *Those Who Ride the Night Winds: Poems.* New York: William Morrow, 1983.

Harris, Trudier. *The Scary Mason-Dixon Line: African American Writers and the South.* Baton Rouge: Louisiana State University Press, 2009.

Jacobs, Harriet. *Incidents in the Life of a Slave Girl.* Mineola, NY: Dover Publications, 2001.

Johnson, James Weldon. *The Autobiography of An Ex-Colored Man.* London: X Press, 1998.

Jones, Tayari. *Leaving Atlanta.* New York: Warner Books, 2002.

McKay, Claude. *Harlem Shadows.* New York: Harcourt, Brace and Company, 1922.

Morrison, Toni. *A Mercy.* New York: Knopf, 2008.

"*Mugshots*"—*Wayne Williams and the Atlanta Child Murders.* Directed by Mark Mori. Austin, TX: Single Spark Pictures, 2000. DVD.

Nelson, Marilyn. *A Wreath for Emmett Till.* 2005. Boston: Houghton Mifflin, 2005.

Petry, Ann. *The Street*. London: Virago, 1986.

Rampersad, Arnold, ed. *The Collected Poems of Langston Hughes*. New York: Knopf, 1994.

Toomer, Jean. *Cane*. New York: Modern Library, 1994.

Turner, Patricia A. "The Atlanta Child Murders: A Case Study of Folklore in the Black Community." In *Contemporary Legend: A Reader*, edited by Gillian Bennett and Paul Smith, 299–310. New York: Garland, 1996.

———. *I Heard It Through the Grapevine: Rumor in African-American Culture*. Berkeley: University of California Press, 1993.

Walker, Margaret. *Jubilee*. Boston: Houghton Mifflin, 1999.

Williams, Sherley Ann. *Dessa Rose*. New York: W. Morrow, 1986.

Wright, Richard. *Native Son*. New York: HarperPerennial, 1998.

FOURTEEN

READING KYLE BAKER'S NAT TURNER WITH A GROUP OF COLLEGIATE BLACK MEN

HOWARD RAMBSY II

When I set up a blog to discuss African American comic strips, I never thought we would end up concentrating on the revolutionary freedom fighter, Nat Turner. Nevertheless, our extended conversation involving a group of collegiate black men interested in multiple views of African American progress and resistance eventually did just that, leading us to Kyle Baker's *Nat Turner* and the sagas of rebellious slaves. Our reading group, which began in 2007, is coordinated by the Black Studies Program at Southern Illinois University Edwardsville, a state university consisting of roughly 300 African American men among the school's approximately 14,000 students. Our extracurricular reading group of black men, consisting of 20 or so undergraduates, one graduate student, and one literature professor, typically meets for weekly online discussions focusing on Aaron McGruder's *The Boondocks* and editorial cartoons by Keith Knight. Occasionally, however, we take deliberate detours, as we did in 2009 and 2010, by covering Baker's *Nat Turner*, a graphic novel that provided us with new opportunities to expand our views of black history, slavery, insurrection, and cultural literacy and competency.

Often, scholars and commentators concentrate on the troubling economic and academic plights of African American males.[1] There is little research on how black men sharpen and display imaginative and intellectual processes while reading. More attention to the reading practices of black men, however, could provide useful understandings of how we accumulate and produce knowledge as well as how we exercise visual literacy. In addition, examining illustrated narratives showcasing black resistance, cultural ideas, and artistic thought compels us to expand the canon of American and African American literary art to include more action-filled narratives about rebellious heroic figures like those found in graphic novels. Among African American graphic novelists and graphic novelists in general, Kyle Baker stands out as particularly accomplished.

An award-winning artist, Baker has drawn and authored several comic books and graphic novels, including *Why I Hate Saturn* (1990), *King David* (2002), and *Special Forces* (2009), to name just a few. He illustrated the graphic novel *Birth of a Nation* (2004), written by Reginald Hudlin and Aaron Mcgruder, and he drew the images for *Truth: Red, White & Black* (2004), written by Robert Morales. In particular, Baker's *Nat Turner* yields important information about a potential future direction for teaching the black novel tradition and at the same time reveals why African American illustrated narratives might be especially appealing and thought-provoking for collegiate black men. Baker's visually stimulating presentation of Nat Turner's "confession" to Thomas Gray situates one of the most well-known slave rebellions in the discourse of graphic novels, and at the same time, Baker utilizes illustrations to narrate a dramatic and action-filled sequence of events in African American history. Baker, no doubt, emphasizes the *action* of the historical narrative as a way of making Turner's story more engaging, staying in line with the conventions of the comics genre.

Baker's graphic novel extends and departs from the larger tradition of the African American novel by presenting a narrative about black characters primarily through the use of illustrated images rather than words. Baker's book made participants in our reading group more aware of the value of viewing illustrated narratives concerning slavery and rebellion as a fruitful way to expand our knowledge of black history and mixed media approaches to reading. *Nat Turner* also gave us an unusual and important opportunity to better understand an intelligent, rebellious slave through the graphic novels.

A PRIMARILY WORDLESS NARRATIVE ABOUT ENSLAVEMENT AND RESISTANCE

Baker initially produced a four-part series of volumes on Nat Turner, self-publishing volume one in 2005. "I originally chose to publish *Nat Turner* myself, rather than through the comic book publishers I usually work for," wrote Baker. "I liked that one of my first books as an independent publisher would be about a self-freed slave" (7). A short mention in *Entertainment Weekly* describes the first part of Baker's series noting that the book "follows Turner's mother from her idyllic African village to the feces- and corpse-littered slave ship and onto the block. It's a hauntingly beautiful historical spotlight."[2] Wil Moss, a reviewer for the *Nashville City Paper*, cites part one of Baker's series in a list of the top graphic novels and comic strips published in 2005: "This is no dry historical retelling, this is a dramatic story that brings Turner's world to life in one of the most fascinating books of the year."[3] In a brief description in *The Washington Post*, Evan Narcisse notes that readers will appreciate that "Baker's intricately [drawn] expressive faces and trenchant dramatic pacing evoke the diabolic slave trade's real horrors."[4] Thanks to the reviews in *Entertainment Weekly* and *The Washington Post*, explained Baker, his self-published book sold through two printings and was eventually picked up and published by Abrams Publishers in 2008.

The Abrams edition of Baker's *Nat Turner* contains four main sections—Home, Education, Freedom, and Triumph. The book presents the experiences of people who could have been Turner's forbearers as they are enslaved in Africa and forced to endure a horrific journey on slave ships, shows glimpses of Turner's childhood experiences, highlights his leading role in the violent insurrection in 1831, and concludes with scenes from his eventual capture and execution. Baker utilizes charcoal style drawings to present illustrative scenes that coincide with Turner's words as presented in Thomas Gray's pamphlet *The Confessions of Nat Turner*, which contains Gray's version of Turner's testimony about the slave revolt. Relatively few graphic artists focus on African American history and culture, which means illustrated narratives about slave revolts are rare. Thus, in the field of contemporary graphic novels, Baker's *Nat Turner* has little company, particularly when it comes to the subject of slavery. When placed within the realm of the black novel tradition, however, Baker's work relates to several notable books such as Ishmael Reed's *Flight to Canada* (1976), Toni Morrison's *Beloved* (1987), and Charles Johnson's *Middle Passage* (1990). Similar to the authors of those works, Baker presents a narrative about slavery produced during the modern era. Yet, unlike those novels, *Nat Turner* presents a narrative of slavery while utilizing relatively few words.

The primarily wordless vivid images used to communicate an unfolding drama about black people being attacked, enslaved, branded, and
loaded onto slave ships troubled and intrigued members of our reading
group when we began covering *Nat Turner* in the fall of 2009. "Baker
gives you pictures," noted Sean, one of our participants. "And you kind
of take them and put them with the information you already know about
slavery and become the author of the early part of the book." The first two
dozen pages of the narrative read like a silent film; with only two or three
panels of images on many of the pages; the book encouraged us to make
our own mental interpretations of the sequence of events taking place.
At several moments in the opening section Home, Baker presents series
of images that highlight the drama of a slave raid and the intense, sometimes intensely troubling decisions people must make when confronted
with the possibility of enslavement.

During one sequence of panels, a woman runs from her captors until
she reaches the edge of a high cliff. She pauses and considers whether
to submit to her captors or jump to her death. A panel focuses on her
face as she looks terror-stricken at her pursuers; a subsequent smaller
panel presents a headshot of the woman looking forward as she considers suicide; and the next, nearly full-page panel shows the woman with
her arms spread wide apparently moments after jumping from the cliff
(Baker 26–27).

Baker's image presenting the woman hovering high in the air after
leaping off the cliff is a suspenseful moment, the outcome of which can
only be revealed to readers by turning to the next page where a rope is
shown encircling the woman's leg as she descends from the cliff. The subsequent image reveals that her captors prevented her from taking her
own life as the image shows her in a coffle with other enslaved people
(28–29). Over the course of a relatively small number of panels, Baker
presents viewers with just enough visual evidence to draw their own conclusions about several series of actions taking place as well as the woman's internal struggles about whether she should stop running or dive to
her death. No doubt, Baker's image of a black woman jumping off a cliff
as if she is taking flight corresponds to the myth of flying Africans in
black folklore, and the woman's willingness to leap to her death invokes
the long history of slaves who committed suicide rather than become or
remain enslaved.[5]

Baker's recurring images of black people willing to kill themselves to escape the hardships of slavery provide dramatic visual manifestations of the lines from an old spiritual: "before I'd be a slave, I'd be buried in my grave." Similar to Toni Morrison's *Beloved*, which is based on the experiences of Margaret Garner who attempted to kill her children rather than have them returned to slavery, Baker shows an enslaved black couple on the ship who conspire to murder their infant as an alternative to a life in slavery by tossing the child overboard into the waiting mouth of a shark. In the panels leading up to the baby's infanticide, images show the couple's horrified looks as they observe the death and horrors of their fellow captives on the slave ship. At one point below deck, the woman lies next to a dead or dying corpse, and later above deck, the couple looks on as one of the slavers beats a young boy with a whip (42–43, 47). A series of images shows the couple standing together silently as they hold their child and seemingly contemplate his life under the gruesome conditions they are witnessing. When their captors are distracted, the woman runs with her child and attempts to throw the baby overboard to waiting sharks. One of the slavers grabs the child's hand and almost prevents the infant from being thrown overboard, but the baby's presumed father leaps forward and bites the slaver on the arm, causing him to release the baby into the waiting mouth of a shark (50–55).

The aforementioned struggles against enslavement, along with several other instances of revolt throughout the book, allow Baker to highlight the notion of black resistance as central to the circumstances of slavery. For students especially interested in the history of black resistance, it is worth introducing them to work that preceded Baker's work such as *American Negro Slave Revolts* (1943) by Herbert Aptheker and the two-volume set *Encyclopedia of Slave Resistance and Rebellion* (2006) edited by Junius P. Rodriguez reveal that Baker's illustrated narratives of black revolt relate to larger, extensive histories of African American resistance. Notably, even prior to Nat Turner's actual insurrection, Baker presents viewers with scene after scene indicating varying degrees of militancy and insurgency among black captives. Members of our reading group were hardly aware that black people could have been so rebellious and courageous at every stage of enslavement and along the Middle Passage, nor had we adequately imagined just how far some slaves would go in order to resist enslavement. We had read Frederick Douglass's narrative and knew of his fight with Covey, as well as Douglass's eventual escape. We had also heard, like many black folks, about the heroics of Harriet Tubman. Baker, however, gave us rare and dramatic visual accounts of anonymous black people engaged in multiple forms of resistance, and his depictions of Africans resisting enslavement long before they arrived in the Americas reminded us that well known figures like Douglass, Tubman, and Turner were the descendants of a host of unacknowledged freedom fighters.

But Baker, of course, does more than simply provide us with poignant images of resistance. Throughout *Nat Turner,* we viewed unsettling images concerning the brutality committed against black peoples who were forced to endure the physical and psychological agonies of slavery. We found the images that Baker presented of Africans being hunted, killed, captured, degraded, and transformed into human cargo, and then finally being remade as slaves in America appalling and accurately representative. Jonathan, one of our participants, explained that "Early on in life, it seemed as though teachers always tried to present slavery to me in the nice way as opposed to the real way." The depictions in the *Nat Turner* book, on the other hand, offered "a more real view" of slavery that was anything but pleasant.

At one point, Baker illustrates scenes of an elder slave punished for playing an African drum. A panel shows the slave shirtless and strung up to a tree being beaten with a bullwhip by a larger, muscular slave presumably under the orders of a white overseer. A subsequent panel shows the elder slave screaming as salt is rubbed into his wounds by the larger slave; and as further punishment for his transgressions of playing an African drum, the elder slave's hands are cut off with an axe in a scene that resembles the grisly amputation of Kunta Kinte's foot in the novel and television miniseries *Roots.* In his poem "Wise 1," Amiri Baraka presents the idea that when slaveholders banned enslaved people from playing drums or their "oom boom ba boom," they were further alienated from their cultural practices and traditions, which put them in "deep deep / trouble" (7). A final scene in Baker's sequence of images shows the shattered pieces of the slave's drum lying alongside his severed hands (60–68). The gruesome illustrations of enslaved black people being emotionally and physically severed from cultural practices offered members of our group rare and ghastly visual manifestations of narratives we had only read or heard about slavery.[6]

We had seen movies, such as *Roots* (1977), *Amistad* (1997), and *Beloved* (1998), depicting cruelty to slaves, but Baker's visual depictions in a graphic novel demanded that we witness slave experiences in ways that were fairly unfamiliar to us. Novels about slavery—Morrison's *Beloved*, Margaret Walker's *Jubilee*, and Alex Haley's *Roots*, for instance— challenge readers to imagine enslavement and struggles for freedom by paying attention to authors' words. Comics or graphic novels, Douglas Wolk has explained, are "more visual" and "*less* verbal" than conventional literary narratives and allow artists to "get across the image of physical setting or person or object or any other visual phenomenon much more easily than prose" (25). Baker's graphic novel encourages audiences to *read* a visual narrative about slavery, which includes scenes that display varying degrees of enslavement and resistance. Baker's "novel" challenges readers to examine wordless illustrations and then later to interpret the juxtaposition of illustrations with excerpts from Turner's/Gray's confessions. For our group, a close reading of the images throughout *Nat Turner* led us to utilize and enhance our visual literacy skills to follow a historical narrative about enslavement and liberation. Baker's book gave many members opportunities to expand their knowledge about the appalling experiences of slavery and the specifics of a well known yet understudied slave rebellion.

Graphic novels, we discovered more and more as we read and discussed Baker's book, engage the imagination on multiple levels, because we were charged with interpreting the narrative's words and images. During the course of our online discussions, Henderson, one of our members, began to direct our attention to how Baker drew facial expressions: "Did you all notice that a large percentage of the panels feature close-ups of characters' faces? And it's all in the eyes. Baker seems to have mastered the art of imbuing eyes with expression (check the eyebrows too)." We concurred and began to read or reread the illustrations in Baker's book with careful consideration to his characters' eyes. Shortly after Henderson's comment, Sean noted that "[t]he eyes and faces tell the story. You take their facial expressions and what you know about slavery and run with it from there." Next, Terrell, another participant, observed that closely studying the black characters' faces allowed him to empathize more with their "pain, [and] sorrow." And our participant Dometi observed that he was particularly moved by the looks of surprise and dread on the characters' faces: "The senses of bewilderment, anger, and fear in the eyes of the characters said a lot. The look of bewilderment stood out the most to me because I can only imagine being suddenly attacked by people I'd never seen before." The focus on facial expressions was an unexpected yet crucial experience in our processes of reading a graphic novel about slavery. The looks of horror, contempt, anger, shock, fear, pain, rage, and determination allowed us to empathize with the emotions, if not the experiences, of the enslaved people throughout the book in ways that would have been less possible if we only read words about their feelings and conditions on the page. Most of our members did not need to be convinced about the value of reading graphic novels, for many had grown up playing videos games and were all attuned to the visual displays of YouTube and various other sites on the Internet. Yet, reading Turner's book was providing new lessons about how reading this particular narrative could broaden our understanding about the intensity of Turner's feelings and other enslaved people. We had of course all heard of Nat Turner before reading Baker's book. However, how many of us actually considered the look of determined rage on Turner's face as he raised his axe to strike his master?

Comics writers often concentrate on the minute details of their characters' facial expressions, so Baker's artwork in that regard was hardly unique. However, when placed in the context of African American literature and black studies, illustrated novels such as *Nat Turner* create new possibilities.[7] Relatively few novels utilize illustrations to the extents that Baker does in order to communicate a narrative about slavery. The wordless images throughout the book required us to pay close attention in order to comprehend what we were viewing and reading. The kinds of new insights gained by studying Baker's work suggests that more efforts should be made in literature and history courses to incorporate illustrations that display the horrors of enslavement, the drama of liberation, and the details and complexity of black people's facial expressions. The many sequences of images highlighting resistance to enslavement throughout *Nat Turner* prompted us to visualize a host of unknown black heroic figures and to consider how written and spoken accounts had prevented us from seeing their acts of rebellion. Baker's graphic novel and our discussions made the group more aware of the significance of a tradition of black resistance and empowered us to expand our approaches to reading visual components of slavery and slave revolts.

THE ACTION-FILLED SAGA OF AN INTELLIGENT, REBELLIOUS SLAVE

Malcolm X describes the differences between the "house Negro" and the "field Negro" in his 1963 speech "Message to the Grassroots," noting that the house Negro "loved his master" while the field Negro, on the other hand, carried extreme disdain for his master to the point of praying for his master's death. According to Malcolm X, the field Negro "hated his master. I say he hated his master. He was intelligent" (11). Malcolm X, along with his vocal and approving audience, celebrated the intellect of slaves who would plot against their captors and seek freedom by any means necessary. Over the years, black artists have shared Malcolm X's conviction, and more importantly, the subject of house slaves and field slaves gave Malcolm an opportunity to weave an informative and entertaining narrative, literary artists have taken opportunities to produce historically informed tales and episodes about enslavement and liberation, which stand as useful resources for readers. Black poets, for instance, have regularly depicted the inner thoughts of slaves and presented their subjects as highly intelligent, contemplative figures.

In her poem "Peeling off the Skin," Adisa writes from the first-person perspective of Nat Turner and projects him as a thoughtful, brooding ghost who reflects with no regrets on his rebellious acts and asserts that he would do it again if presented with the opportunity. In "slaveship," Lucille Clifton adopts the personas of a group of enslaved people who perceptively recognize the troubling irony of men who chain and load humans on ships named "Jesus," "Angel," and "Grace of God." Frank X. Walker's two book-length volumes of poetry, *Buffalo Dance: The Journey of York* (2004) and *When Winter Come: the Ascension of York* (2008), concentrate on the ruminations of York, a slave who traveled on the famous Lewis and Clark Expedition. Thylias Moss' book-length volume *Slave Moth* (2004) presents an intelligent slave girl who chronicles her thoughts and experiences on cloth and through quilting. Adisa, Clifton, Walker, Moss, and several other black poets show a tendency to project the intellectual musings and talents of enslaved people, all of which complement Baker's graphic novel and also provide readers with useful resources for further considerations of studying how modern writers render the thoughts and experiences of black historical figures.[8]

Novelists, like poets, reveal an interest in showcasing slaves who possess elevated thinking abilities. Ishmael Reed's *Flight to Canada* and Charles Johnson's *Middle Passage,* for example, present ex-slaves as scholarly minded protagonists who are also talented writers. Similar to these poets and novelists, Baker highlights the intellectual gifts of his lead character, utilizing illustrations to represent Nat Turner as a thoughtful, heroic figure whose rebellious actions are strongly motivated by his vivid and expansive memory of the pains that black people endured in slavery. Baker's artistic efforts add dimension to Turner's character that go well beyond the static oppressed victim of slavery by depicting a figure with a range of emotional responses. In the eyes of Baker's Nat Turner alone, we view outrage, bewilderment, terror, frustration, and resolve. The depictions of slaves and ex-slaves as intellectual stand as empowering counterarguments to the widespread presentations of slaves as unintelligent and docile.

The illustrations used to complement excerpts from Turner's confessions ultimately project the rebellious slave in more complex ways than the words could alone, encouraging our reading group to observe Turner from multiple viewpoints. Since Thomas Gray recorded and inevitably presented Turner's testimony to fulfill his own interests, the reliability of Turner's "confession" has always been the subject of debate. Thus, Baker's illustrated rendering of Turner's life and the insurrection contributes to our understanding of historical events that have not been fully accessible to us. Baker's graphic novel simultaneously exposed members of our group to multiple presentations of Nat Turner—the first-person perspective of Turner, a perspective that was definitely mediated by Thomas Gray and the view of Turner presented in Baker's drawings. On the one hand, Baker's images offer a kind of visual translation of the words presented by the double-voiced collaboration between Turner and Gray; at the same time however, Baker continually utilizes creative license to project what results in more dramatic scenes from Turner's life than what his actual confessions suggest. Of course, Baker had likely read or viewed various works on slave rebellions; he cites Stephen Oates's *The Fires of Jubilee: Nat Turner's Fierce Rebellion* (1975) and Velma Thomas's *Lest We Forget: The Passage from Africa to Slavery to Emancipation* (1997) among others in his book's bibliography. For instance, Turner mentions that when he was three or four years old and was playing with other children his mother overheard him talking and said that he had spoken of events that "had happened before I was born," prompting people to predict that Turner "surely would be a prophet, as the Lord had shown me things that had happened before my birth" (Baker 57). Turner does not reveal the exact event that he had spoken of that took place before his birth; however, Baker presents an illustration next to Turner's words that shows Turner as a youngster surrounded by children and astonished looking adults as he references the moment when the couple aboard the slave ship had thrown their baby overboard to a shark rather than have him live in slavery (57). Baker's illustration suggests that Turner has a mysterious skill or gift to recall the past and particularly horrific moments along the Middle Passage that occurred before he was born.

The notion that Nat Turner, even as a young boy, had special gifts or powers fits well within the realm of comics, a form full of characters known for their extraordinary talents and supernatural abilities and thus provided the young black men in our group with a new or additional black heroic historical figure. The young Turner is also presented as an outsider, another well known feature of comic book protagonists. In one image, Baker presents the young Turner as distant from other adolescent slaves, and on an adjoining page, Baker illustrates a scene showing the young Turner being prevented from receiving formal education along with white peers (70–71). According to novelist and comic book enthusiast Jonathan Lethem, books in the "geek genre," such as graphic narratives and science fiction, often showcase "an incredibly sensitive, beautiful main character [who] is misunderstood by everyone around them." Lethem says that "the energy" of such books derives from a recognition among readers that those alienated protagonists are "smarter and more sensitive than the people around them who are treating them so badly" (Schiff 124). The depiction of Nat Turner as an exceptional young black boy struggling under the harsh circumstances of slavery made him an even more endearing figure to members of our group.

A long tradition of African American writers has presented exceptionally talented black males boys who survive in the face of incredible odds. The early sections of Frederick Douglass's *Narrative of the Life of Frederick Douglass* (1845) and James Weldon Johnson's *Autobiography of an Ex-Colored Man* (1912) depict the experiences of resourceful young black males who must negotiate unbelievably difficult social and emotional terrains. The precocious young Richard in Richard Wright's autobiography *Black Boy* (1945) and the unnamed protagonist of Ralph Ellison's *Invisible Man* (1952) struggle under the weight of Jim Crow. The young Gunnar Kaufman, the lead character in Paul Beatty's *The White Boy Shuffle* (1996), and Huey Freeman, the ten-year-old militant in Aaron McGruder's comic strip *The Boondocks* (1996–2006), are gifted intellectuals who reside in hostile environments. So while Baker's depiction of the young Nat Turner certainly corresponds to the "geek genre" tendency to present special yet misunderstood persecuted protagonists, Baker's book also resides firmly within the African American narrative tradition of highlighting the experiences of extraordinary black boys struggling to overcome tremendous obstacles.

We had all previously heard and read stories about the famous rebellious slave, but Baker's illustrations gave us a rare view, among other things, of Turner as a thoughtful and inquisitive child deeply disturbed by his life as a slave. Perhaps the primarily collegiate black male composition of our group explains why so many of our participants frequently identified with Turner. They likely saw something of their own adolescent experience reflected in Baker's depictions of Turner's experiences of alienation as a child. On the other hand, by the time we encountered Baker's images of an apparently talented juvenile black male, we had all been previously and thoroughly immersed in the sagas of a Huey Freeman. McGruder's depictions of the brainy and militant Huey prepared us for Baker's portrayal of Turner. Like Huey, the young Turner was apparently a brilliant and introspective outsider in a troubled world. In other words, he had the ingredients of a typical young hero.

Baker's inclusion of scenes showing black people in Africa, the horrors of the Middle Passage, and aspects of Turner's childhood helped shape our understanding of the broader context of enslavement and resistance. Baker's creation of scenes in Africa and enslavement in South in the opening Home and Education sections of *Nat Turner* changed how we viewed the lead-up to the insurrection, and it was Baker's dramatic use of illustrations during the Freedom section of the book that transforms the so-called "confessions" into an action-filled saga of rebellion. The scenes throughout the Freedom section show a variety of close-ups of enslaved persons with impassioned looks on their faces, highlighting the intensity of emotions among the black people during the insurrection. One image shows Turner looking upward and surprised with a bible in his hand as he recognizes "signs in the heavens"; another series of images shows an intense and concentrated looking Turner with an axe above his head preparing to strike a blow on his master; and another image shows an authoritative Turner appearing to shout orders at his fellow slaves (110, 114, 143). The dramatic facial expressions of the rebelling slaves presented in the illustrations are as much a part of Baker's narrative as the "confession" that Turner tells. Baker's detailed attention to facial expressions gives him the opportunity to project the interior and highly intense feelings of terror experienced by enslaved people through vivid illustrations.

Baker further dramatizes events by showcasing the acts of extreme violence and slaughter that took place at the time of the insurrection. During the "Freedom" section, Baker depicts nearly a dozen brutal scenes of murder enacted by the slaves upon their former masters and their masters' families. The scenes are gruesome, showing men, women, children, and infants being killed with axes, guns, and planks of wood. The death of the black infant by shark earlier in the narrative may have been a way of preparing readers/viewers to accept the death of white infants later in the story. The participants in our group admitted that although they had previously heard stories about Turner's insurrection, it was only after viewing Baker's horrific illustrations that they more fully considered what the scenes of a violent insurrection might look like. The experience of reading Baker's book may have accomplished one of our major goals of developing a better, more complex understanding of Nat Turner and the general experiences of enslaved people who sought to liberate themselves. At the same time, the enjoyment of reading a graphic novel may have done little to increase our participants' interest in reading canonical novels about slavery. In fact, just as the wordless first chapter of Baker's book piqued the interest of our members, it is reasonable, though perhaps unfortunate for many literary scholars, to assume that illustration-less novels by Charles Johnson, Toni Morrison, Margaret Walker, and others might fail to adequately grab the attention of the kind of young black men who participated in our group.

For Baker, action, not just words on the page, are vital in the narration of an effective graphic novel. In an interview, while discussing his collaborative work with Aaron McGruder and Reginald Hudlin on the graphic novel *Birth of a Nation,* Baker noted that McGruder's *The Boondocks* comic strip is "very talky, and his characters don't move." In his own work, Baker makes his characters less talkative and instead determines that their many movements—through their facial expressions, physical efforts, and involvement in dramatic actions—will be utilized to convey ideas. "The thing is," explained Baker, "my stuff is usually very visual, because I know I'm in a comic book."[9] Baker knew he was dramatizing Turner's story in a comic book, and the results reveal a focus on making the narrative very visual, action and picture-oriented. In one remarkable scene, Baker presents an image of Turner charging forward with a sword in his hand as he leads a large group of men on horseback that covers a page-and-a-half (146–147). The image confirms Baker's interest in utilizing sparse wording and signaling dramatic movements in order to effectively communicate ideas in a comic book. The privileged place of action sequences in Baker's *Nat Turner* made the narrative of the insurrection enthralling for our reading group and relatable to the drama of action movies, television programs, and video games so familiar to our participants.

SOME CONCLUDING IMPLICATIONS AND QUESTIONS

How does the enjoyment that collegiate black men have in reading a comic book about a historical moment diminish or enhance their learning experiences? What does the group's heightened interest in graphic novels over conventional novels indicate about the need to expand discussions about literacy to include topics related to artistic illustrations? While we continue to explore answers to these kinds of questions, observations based on one black men's reading group suggests that Baker's book created special opportunities to develop a better understanding of topics like black history, slavery, and resistance, and encouraged a rethinking of the experience of "reading" and conversing about artistic compositions through the use of a blog or, more broadly, through the development of an online learning community. Baker's illustrations gave many of us our first extended views of what a slave insurrection might have looked like and just how far rebellious enslaved black people would have been willing to go in order to free themselves.

Our focus on the details of Baker's drawings such as skilled illustrations of facial expressions to convey ideas and Baker's transformation of Turner's insurrection into an action-packed narrative were two of our most important discoveries. We came to recognize those discoveries through online and face-to-face discussions as we worked our way through Baker's book. The results of our discoveries and, more importantly, our overall learning experiences confirmed our sense that utilizing multiple modes of technological and analog communication, and reading, writing, and talking about what we were observing could be intellectually enriching. Utilizing a blog format, of course, had various benefits for the participants. "The best thing about a blog is that it's what we're used to," wrote Dometi. "Most of us are on Facebook and follow other blogs, so it's definitely beneficial to have a place to discuss literature in a format we're used to." Curtis, another participant, added that blogging "is more beneficial and feasible for people who want to discuss and interact at times that are more convenient for them. This is definitely great for people who have classes at all times of the day." For these and other members of our group, the familiarity of online interactions and the convenience of using a blog for those with hectic schedules were important benefits of the program.

Over the years, many of us have followed discussions and coverage concerning troubled black men. The National Urban League's 2007 annual State of Black America special report, "Portrait of the Black Male," contains statistical documentation and essays designed to address the distressing conditions of African American men. The quantitative data regarding high levels of poverty, low literacy rates, and other challenges facing black males highlight a troubling "crisis," and so the kind of online reading group that we established might serve as one useful alternative for more actively engaging young black men in beneficial educational processes. The representation of black men in these ways are useful but provide hardly any information regarding the diverse and dynamic processes associated with how black men build knowledge and present ideas in particular settings. According to comics scholar Douglas Wolk, "leaps of imagination are an enormous pleasure," and comics serve as useful guides for "imagining the visual aspect of a story as it is transformed through the cartoonist's perception" (133). Observing Baker's leaps of imagination in the process of representing Turner's insurrection and the discussions of collegiate black men following Baker's lead was a rewarding educational experience. The graphic novel should not be seen as a replacement for reading canonical novels about slavery by authors such as Toni Morrison, Charles Johnson, and Ishmael Reed. Instead, African American graphic novels, such as Baker's *Nat Turner,* serve as viable additions to the canon for stimulating new and extended conversations about history, artistic composition, and multiple modes of literacy.

NOTES

1. See William Julius Wilson, "The Economic Plight of Inner-City Black Males." *More Than Just Race: Being Black and Poor in the Inner City.* New York: W. W. Norton and Company, 2009. 62–94; Elijah Anderson, ed., *Against the Wall: Poor, Young, Black, and Male.* Philadelphia: University of Pennsylvania Press, 2008.

2. Before Abrams published the four-part series of Baker's *Nat Turner* as a single book in 2008, Image Comics published issues #1 and #2 as a single volume *Nat Turner* (Encore Edition Vol. 1 of 2) in 2006 and issues #3 and #4 as a single volume (*Nat Turner Volume Two: Revolution*) in 2007. Therefore, it is likely that in addition to the *Entertainment Weekly* and *Washington Post* bringing attention to the book, the Image Comics volumes also assisted in bringing Turner's book to a wider audience. Abby West, "Nat Turner," *Entertainment Weekly,* September 16, 2005, http://www.ew.com/ew/article /0,,1105405,00.html.

3. Wil Moss, "Graphic Content," *Nashville City Paper,* December 16, 2005, http:// nashvillecitypaper.com/content/lifestyles/font-colorgreenweb-only-columnfont -graphic-content-4.

4. Evan Narcisse, "Nat Turner. No. 1," *Washington Post,* July 3, 2005: M8.

5. See Lovalerie King, "Myth of Flying Africans," in *The Toni Morrison Encyclopedia,* ed. Elizabeth Ann Beaulieu (Westport, CT: Greenwood Press, 2003): 122–124; Julius Lester, "People Who Could Fly," in *Black Folktales* (New York: Richard W. Baron, 1969): 147–152.

6. Members of our group had read Frederick Douglass and expressed being disturbed by the violence against slaves presented in the book.

7. Children's books, even those about slavery, such as Ellen Levine and Kadir Nelson's *Henry's Freedom Box,* based on the life of Henry Box Brown, and Carole B. Weatherford and Kadir Nelson's *Moses: When Harriet Tubman Led Her People to Freedom,* have frequently relied on sparse words and visual images to convey narratives. But unlike Kyle Baker's book, children's books about slavery are necessarily inclined to downplay the horrid and violent nature of slavery and resistance.

8. Modern and contemporary black poets regularly utilize persona poems to present the first-person perspectives of thoughtful and clever slaves and ex-slaves. See,

for instance, Opal Palmer Adisa, "Peeling Off the Skin," in *Gathering Ground: A Reader Celebrating Cave Canem's First Decade,* eds. Toi Derricotte and Cornelius Eady (Ann Arbor: University of Michigan Press, 2006), 14–16; Lucille Clifton "slaveship," in *The Vintage Book of African American Poetry,* eds. Michael Harper and Anthony Walton (New York: Vintage Books, 2000), 250; Frank X. Walker, *Buffalo Dance: The Journey of York* (Lexington: University Press of Kentucky, 2004); and Thylias Moss, *Slave Moth: A Narrative in Verse* (New York: Persea Books, 2004).

9. Andrew Farago, "Special: An Interview With Kyle Baker," *Comics Reporter,* May 1, 2005, http://www.comicsreporter.com/index.php/resources/interviews/2251/.

WORKS CITED

Adisa, Opal Palmer. "Peeling Off the Skin." In *Gathering Ground: A Reader Celebrating Cave Canem's First Decade,* edited by Toi Derricotte and Cornelius Eady, 14–16. Ann Arbor: University of Michigan Press, 2006.

Baker, Kyle. *Nat Turner.* New York: Abrams, 2005.

Baraka, Amiri. *WISE, WHY's Y's.* Chicago: Third World Press, 1995.

Clifton, Lucille. "slaveships." In *Blessing the Boats: New and Selected Poems 1988–2000.* Rochester, NY: BOA Editions, 2000.

Farago, Andrew. "Special: An Interview With Kyle Baker." *Comics Reporter.* Last modified May 1, 2005. http://www.comicsreporter.com/index.php/resources/interviews /2251/.

Jones, Stephanie J., ed. *The State of Black America 2007: Portrait of the Black Male.* New York: National Urban League, 2007.

Malcolm X. "Message to the Grassroots." *Malcolm X Speaks: Selected Speeches and Statements.* Edited by George Breitman. New York: Grove Press, 1994.

McGruder, Aaron. *The Boondocks: Because I Know You Don't Read the Newspaper.* Kansas City: Andrews McMeel, 2000.

———. *The Boondocks Complete First Season.* New York: Sony Pictures, 2006.

Moss, Thylias. *Slave Moth: A Narrative in Verse.* New York: Persea Books, 2004.

Moss, Wil. "Graphic Content." *Nashville City Paper.* Last modified December 16, 2005. http://nashvillecitypaper.com/content/lifestyles/font-colorgreenweb-only-columnfont-graphic-content-4.

Narcisse, Evan. "Nat Turner. No. 1." *Washington Post.* July 3, 2005: M8.

Schiff, James. "A Conversation with Jonathan Lethem." *Missouri Review* 29.1 (2006): 116–34.

Walker, Frank X. *Buffalo Dance: The Journey of York.* Lexington: University Press of Kentucky, 2004.

———. *When Winter Come: the Ascension of York.* Lexington: University Press of Kentucky, 2008

West, Abby. "Nat Turner." *Entertainment Weekly.* Last modified September 16, 2005. http://www.ew.com/ew/article/0,,1105405,00.html.

Wolk, Douglas. *Reading Comics: How Graphic Novels Work and What They Mean.* New York: Da Capo Press, 2007.

FIFTEEN

TOWARD THE THEORETICAL PRACTICE OF CONCEPTUAL LIBERATION: USING AN AFRICANA STUDIES APPROACH TO READING AFRICAN AMERICAN LITERARY TEXTS

GREG CARR AND DANA A. WILLIAMS

Africana Studies is an academic extension of what Cedric Robinson has called "The Black Radical Tradition." This tradition is notable for emerging out of a pre-existing constellation of African intellectual work, shaped by millennia of subsequent migration, adaptation, and improvisation. Through the central acts of translation and recovery,[1] Africana Studies seeks to theorize out of long-view genealogies of African intellectual work. This process has been captured with striking impact by the writer and translator Ayi Kwei Armah, both in his fictional texts *Two Thousand Seasons* (1972), *KMT: In the House of Life* (2002), *Osiris Rising* (1995), and in his memoir/historiography *The Eloquence of the Scribes* (2006). Armah and other key theoreticians have set themselves the task of intentionally linking that series of migrations, adaptations, and improvisations from the origins of humanity to the present, integrating wave after wave of challenges and solutions to the problems of African human existence as a series of interlinked episodes, of which the period of enslavement and colonialism is a very recent and very temporary set of moments.

The key factor in assuming both this task and the intellectual posture that grounds it is the deliberate embrace of "long-view" memory: the same type of broad envisioning of the human experience that has long informed the intellectual posture of other societies (including the West) as an ideational construct. In fact, the truncation of the time/space coordinates of memory—the amputation of memory as a consequence of the failure of educational institutions designed in part to reinscribe those memories as a critical element of equipping Africans to negotiate their futures on their terms—presents a theoretical crisis that the academic field and discipline of Africana Studies has set out purposely to engage and correct. The term "Africana," then, should be used in the academic context of "Africana Studies" as a term that describes the creation of methods that fully integrate the study of people (Africans and African-descended communities), geography (Africa as well as any physical place populated by Africans), and culture (concepts, practices, and materials that Africans have created to live and to interact with themselves, others, and their environments).[2]

Any study of African people that does not begin with the recognition of and systematic reconnections to both the concept of African cultural identities and the specific, lived demonstration of them will only continue to erase Africans as full human beings and actors in world history. Indeed, among the most important questions to consider in any study of the human experience are the following:

- Who are the people being studied? Where did they come from, and how did they come to the experience being studied?
- How do people view themselves, their origins, and their world in any given time and place?
- How do people organize and govern themselves around common goals? How do they make decisions, resolve disputes, recognize authority, interact with others, and establish common tastes and styles, etc.?
- How do people use the materials and tools available to them to shape their physical environment?
- How do people remember what they have done, and how do they pass those memories to future generations?
- What have people created to express their thoughts and emotions to themselves and others?

Arguably, these questions are, or should be, present regardless of the people being studied. Scholars of the African experience in the United States and elsewhere must ask these questions as a continuing process of tracing and re-tracing the African experience from its origins in Africa to the present. It also allows us to see African American contributions to the formation of "American identity" and other geographically local identity formations without reducing the person, people, texts, practices, and/or narratives to only the sum of those contributions. Approaching the African experience in the creation, evolution, and continuing reconfiguration of the United States requires seeing African American life as both an extension of African experiences and as contributions to the multinational society and culture that is the United States. Such an approach exposes the reader to the rich connections, differences, and shades of distinction among Africans across time and space.

The time between the beginning of documented settled human societies in Africa to the present is roughly approximate to twenty four times the period between Columbus's Atlantic voyages and the present. The study of African people, however, is usually restricted to their experiences in European colonies, a time frame covering less than one thirtieth of the period of human history for which some type of record exists. Even though some mention is usually made of "preslavery" or "precolonial" Africa, the emphasized experience is the "modern" period, so named because of a framework that connects its institutions and cultures to "classical" and "medieval" Europe.

Most scholarship on the African American experience follows this narrative framework, outlining a "black" experience that shadows the themes that mirror the goals, objectives, systems, and narratives of European/ United States history. This framework sees the African American experience only as it contributes to a United States narrative that begins with the establishment of "New World" European colonies and then connects the establishment of an independent United States to Manifest Destiny, the Civil War/Reconstruction, and finally to the emergence of the United States as a hemispheric and world power.

The African American experience is much more complex than the experience contained in this narrative frame. In fact, the continuing attitudes of many if not most African Americans toward United States domestic and foreign policy cannot be understood without recognizing the distinct experiences, worldviews, and perspectives of United States citizenry of African descent. The conceptual categories outlined throughout the rest of this chapter allow scholars to organize African experiences in the United States in ways that take them out of any particular narrative structure, thereby prompting them to raise the underlying questions of how Africans looked at and experienced their worlds through time and space. Reading texts and experiences using these categories encourages students to ask differently prioritized questions about the subjects covered in coursework. These types of questions prompted by utilizing the Africana Studies Conceptual Category approach will make visible the choices made by the preparers of the course lessons, textbooks, anthologies, and teaching materials around what elements of Africana life to emphasize. The answers to most of the questions raised under each category will not be found in the text of the lesson or the textbook: they will require speculation and further research on the part of both student and teacher, the "extended learning" and "higher order" goal of classroom work.

CATEGORIES OF HUMAN INSTITUTIONS

While we can imagine an endless variety of approaches to organizing human culture and experiences, using the conceptual categories discussed below satisfies a threshold requirement of translating and recovering African experiences as part of a discipline-oriented Africana Studies approach to producing new knowledge about these experiences. A graphic depiction of the Conceptual Categories in a form that could be replicated for the classroom in an effort to have students consider the categories as a contrastive ensemble is included below:

Social Structure	Governance Structure	Ways of Knowing	Science and Technology	Movement and Memory	Cultural Meaning Making
What is/are the social structure(s) in place for the people discussed?	How did the Africans organize themselves during this period?	What kinds of systems did African peoples develop to explain their existence and how did they use those systems to address fundamental issues of living?	What types of devices were developed to shape nature and human relationships with animals and each other during this period and how did it affect Africans and others?	How did/do Africans remember this experience?	What specific music, art, dance, and/or literature/ oratory did Africans create during this period?

SOCIAL STRUCTURES

"What was the social, economic, political, and/or cultural environment that Africans found themselves living under during the period under study?" Scholars and students asking this question are required to develop their ability to recognize the various types of social relations that African people found themselves in with regard to other Africans as well as with non-Africans. For example: any topic involving African people in the United States involves the emergence of an economic system that stressed capitalism, democracy, and Western-style Christianity. The various regional and local approaches to this system form the social structures under which African people lived as distinct from any ideas they had and/or developed about either the system or their engagement with it.

From the beginning of the United States national project, African people were positioned in a social structure that interacted with them as either chattel property or quasi-property—what most historians would call "free blacks." At no time prior to the end of the United States Civil War did any Africans attain the federal status of United States citizen. After the United States Civil War, the reinscription of unequal race relations created a situation that remains unresolved: the economic, cultural, and political dimensions of full citizenship status of African people is still a subject of open debate, both within and without African American communities.

Africana Studies approaches to examining contemporary texts and practices begin with the varied physical environment of Africa, emptying into an enumeration of the range of social structures that Africans designed in these various regional contexts from prehistory through the modern era. Enumerating these African-derived structures as the exclusive structures that gave contour to their governance structures prior to their encounters with non-Africans allows the scholar to distinguish between these structures and the social structures that developed in the wake of African interaction with others that arose as a consequence of what became known as both the Arab and European (read: Atlantic) trade in material and human commodities.[3] Scholars and students can now consider the texts and practices of African people in the specific context of emerging social structures under which Africans in West Atlantic societies lived and continue to live in increasing complex ways, as well as their varying status within them.

GOVERNANCE

"What sets of common rules and/or understandings did Africans create to internally regulate their lives in the situation under study?" The historian Jan Vansina has written that all common societies create forms of governance to unite different communities into a larger whole. He goes on to say that such a whole will presuppose common goals, legitimacy based on a common worldview, a framework for resolving individual and social ills, and common leadership as well as common cultural tastes.[4] Teachers utilizing an Africana Studies approach to investigating narratives must encourage students to search texts and learning materials for the varying sets of rules created, adapted, and encoded by African people to guide relations among themselves. What were the social units and customs created by Africans to manage their daily affairs and life activities, as well as those that emerged to govern how they interacted with non-Africans?

Arguably, most narratives on African Americans (fictional and nonfictional) have focused largely on the last category. As a result, students of African American history have become adept at equating how African people interacted with Whites with how they governed themselves, rather than distinguishing between the first conceptual category (Social Structures) and the second (Governance). Unlike questions raised under the category of Social Structures, questions under the Governance category will never move to focus on the external forces that govern African American life at any moment. As a result, the first and, by far, the longest period of African existence will see a convergence of these first two categories as long as African life is studied within a wholly African geographical, political, economic, and cultural context. The differences between Social Structure and Governance will focus on different types of African systems as they come into contact with each other. For example: how did the expansion of the "empire-style" governance systems represented by Ghana, Mali, Songhai, etc., differ from and or impact the lives and governance systems of those not previously subject to them?

How, for example, in the formation of Vodun in Haiti, did the type of governance structures incorporated by various Yoruba people help organize the conceptual contributions of Fon, Dahomey, and Akan Africans in a more systematic way reflective of the first group's orientation toward large-group, urban, and larger territorial arcs?

The historical period of most relevance regarding questions that focus on African encounters with Arabs and Europeans prior to and during the enslavement periods witnesses the occasion of the first major splits between "African" and "non-African" "races," cultures, social structures, etc. Africana Studies–anchored questions of texts, practices and narratives that emerge from this period forward require students to continue to look for evidence of internal governance among Africans, whereas most disciplinary studies of Africans do not stress—and many do not explicitly identify—unbroken genealogies of internal mechanisms for regulating "Black communities" as governance systems, however small, discrete, "subaltern," and/or peripheral to the seemingly dominant social structure in which they are retained, adapted, and utilized to order the private spaces of African life.

WAYS OF KNOWING/SYSTEMS OF THOUGHT

"What kinds of systems did African peoples develop to explain their existence, and how did they use those systems to address fundamental issues of living?" Making students aware that Africans developed their own systems of thinking about reality enables students to ask how Africans in the United States have retained elements of their African identities while adapting new experiences and cultures to the challenge of living. It also enables scholars and teachers to reorient their intellectual work in this regard to a methodology and method freed from the first-order question of whether or not these ways of knowing/epistemologies exist and, if so, whether or not they retain some explanatory force distinct from other cultural geographies or modalities.

Typical contemporary discussions of African American thought usually include discussions of African ways of knowing or systems of thought in specific references to "religion," "philosophy," "worldview," and/or related categories. Scholars and students oriented toward this Africana Studies approach should be encouraged, however, to question how Africans' ideas about themselves, the world, and the universe influenced every aspect of their lives and experiences, whether or not this question is addressed in a specific subject. Examples of African ways of knowing include but are not limited to: sacred written, oral, or material texts; systems of divination; creation stories; ideas about what is beautiful and/or good; ideas about life and death; and ways of understanding human beings relationships to each other and to nature, among other subjects. Importantly, students must be encouraged to search textbooks and learning materials to see how Africans continued to use their extended, adapted, and improvised worldviews to make sense of their struggles for self-determination. For example: A question might be conceived that leverages adapted African ideas about mass participation growing out of the Afro-Christian orientation of Mississippians, Alabamians, Georgians, Louisianans, etc., that envisions the so-called "Civil Rights movement" as the Africanization of contemporary American ideas about citizenship and participation.

SCIENCE AND TECHNOLOGY

"What types of ideas about how nature works (science) did people develop, and/or what devices (technology) did people create to shape their natural, animal, and human environments?" Answers to this question will differ depending on the people being studied and the material circumstances that require the application of creative intelligences emerging from attitudes about nature and the human being; scholars should think about and students must be encouraged to identify how Africans expressed ideas about relationships between culture, science, and technology.

At the onset of human life on Earth, initially African uses of science and technology preceded and set templates for subsequent human innovations, including the creation of tools for hunting and gathering, animal domestication and husbandry, and the creation of sedentary societies organized around agriculture. Investigation of texts and practices that involve ongoing African technological adaptations should explore the appearance of this subject, from classical African hydraulic science and technology to subsequent innovations in transportation, food storage, and preservation, mineral extraction, and architecture, among other subjects. Any narrative involving African people will likely feature some dimension of science and technology that could be investigated as a part of the integration of this category into the overall arc of inquiry. Such a process would introduce technological creations from multiple cultural sources, from the intervention of maritime technology from outside of Africa as well as the merging of African and non-African technologies in fields such as agriculture and warfare.

MOVEMENT AND MEMORY

This conceptual category asks the question, "how did Africans during the moment being studied preserve memories of where they had been and what they had experienced, and how did they pass these memories to future generations?" This subject is often reduced in scholarship to studies of written documents such as "slave narratives," "folk tales," or other categories similarly associated with history.

Scholars, teachers, and students utilizing an Africana Studies approach must be encouraged, however, to expand their ideas about memory to include any and all ways of communicating ideas about the past to future generations. Germaine subjects include searching for narrative traces of how Africans created architecture, writing systems, music, art, and oral narratives to preserve individual and group memory across Africa. Subsequent lessons give examples of how Africans began to see themselves as members of cultural—and, with the onset of enslavement, racial and subsequently class (and even gender)—groups, and how their memories of their experiences differed from the memories constructed by other groups about who Africans were. Narratives dealing with the experience of enslavement, for example, contain language describing how African people remember the stages of their capture and deportation from Africa as well as their slow process of building life and memory in the various countries of the West Atlantic.

CULTURAL MEANING MAKING

Closely related to the category on Movement and Memory, this conceptual category asks the question, "What specific types of music, art, dance, and/or narratives did Africans create during the period under study?" Unlike their search for answers under the previous category, scholars and students should be encouraged to do two things: search for examples of African cultural production for the periods and subjects under consideration and provide contemporary examples of Africana cultural texts and practices that demonstrate elements of African meaning-making.

The work of scholars such as Yvonne Daniel and Robert Farris Thompson outlines and explains cultural elements that are found in some form in most if not all African cultural systems as they diverge and develop across time and space.[5] Searching texts, practices, and narratives for historical and contemporary evidence of these elements will allow students to recognize the ongoing Africana in their contemporary lives as well as in the lives of the many countries in and outside of Africa where Africans currently reside. This exercise will reinforce the relevance of historical memory related to specific figures, events, and ideas in the African American experience by connecting them to the cultural production of the majority of Africans in the place and during the period under study. It also places the ideas and contribution of social, economic, political, and/or cultural elites—usually the most visible to communication networks beyond the African American community—in a more appropriate and less outsized representative context. This last objective lies at the center of the field and discipline of Africana Studies, the first and only academic field born directly out of mass protest, community organizing, and the leveraging of political and cultural capital for structural and institutionalized academic space in the Western academy.

In order to achieve the methodological objectives of Africana Studies contained in the questions that undergird the Conceptual Categories approach, scholars, teachers, and students must leverage the social, political, and cultural capital that attend the production of African narratives, texts, and practices to discern intellectual connections and engagements necessary to widen the tributaries flowing from African contributions to human knowledge and advancement.

From its inception, African American literature has been concerned foremost with ideas of liberation. Much of the early literature that made its way to print, in fact, was published for the express purpose of supporting the abolitionist cause. Even after slavery was abolished, African American writers were interested in a psychological and social liberation; and in more contemporary times through the present moment, a considerable class of African American writers actively engages the idea of historical liberation—in other words, the liberation of diasporic African experiences from history's falsities. More often than not, the central conflict in this contemporary African American historical fiction turns on the tension between a member of the African American community, who serves as a representative narrating central consciousness, and the white community, which serves as the implied antagonist. This subgenre of African American literature poses a basic question: *what happens when an outsider tells the story?* A crucial question that emerges from the above outlined conceptual categories and extends that basic question is: *what happens when an outsider also influences our ways of reading, knowing, and being?*

The attempt to use these conceptual categories to read a contemporary African American text is not without its challenges—the impetus to offer an Africana Studies reading (using the conceptual categories as the incubator for such a pursuit) of African American literary texts without consideration of and engagement with the full range of Africana Studies methodologies is a seductive (and potentially reductive) one. Yet, the dormant possibilities potentially made manifest by situating the two distinct disciplines (literary study as the discipline in the case of African American literature) beside each other are perhaps among African American literature's few sources of meaningful liberation.

That African American literature and its correlative critical gaze stand in need of liberation (particularly as it relates to its tenuous relationship with mainstream Western theory) is at least part of the point Sandra Adell makes in "The Crisis in Black American Literary Criticism and Postmodern Cures of Houston A. Baker, Jr. and Henry Louis Gates, Jr."[6] While Adell focuses her critique on Baker and Gates specifically, the point she makes—that "the current crisis in the critical reading of twentieth-century Afro-American writing has been deepened by certain philosophical and epistemological paradoxes arising from the incompleteness and inconsistencies of formal networks of principles such as the ones posited by . . . Baker . . . and . . . Gates" (523–24)—applies more broadly to the limitations of contemporary African American literary criticism that continue to plague the field even today. She argues convincingly that while Baker's *Blues, Ideology, and Afro-American Literature: A Vernacular Tradition* and Gates's *The Signifying Monkey: A Theory of Afro-American Literary Criticism* both seek to generate theories of reading that emerge from and draw upon African American expressive culture and its traditions and that, correspondingly, differ meaningfully from traditional American (and perhaps Western) theoretical concepts, "both appropriate and marshal formidable epistemologies from structuralism, post-structuralism, and deconstruction in order to make certain truth claims on behalf of the [African American] tradition" (525). As she makes clear, their appropriations are not problematic; in the sense that the obsession with contemporary literary criticism has undeniable roots in efforts to quell rising interest in ethnic literatures in general and African American literature in particular, their mastery of theory was quite the unexpected coup. Their appropriations do, however, reveal in full view the paradox, if not impossibility, of generating frameworks that emerge from within the culture but that assume the posture and structural (re)semblance of traditional epistemologies. In short, Baker's invocation of Michel Foucault, Fredric Jameson, and Hayden White and their epistemological assumptions about archeology and ideology and Gates's Hegelian conceptualization of chiasmus to bring together hermeneutics as the Yoruban Esu and rhetoric as the diasporic trickster, she argues, set into motion the collapse of their version of blackness into itself, even as the noble goal is to recover and reveal African American expressive culture.[7] Finally, in the essay's penultimate paragraph, she observes that while both texts

> fall short of their emancipatory goal of freeing Afro-American literature from the hegemony of Eurocentric discourses, both studies bring into sharp relief what can best be described as a nostalgia for tradition. For to summon tradition . . . by reconstructing it, is to search for an authority, that of the tradition itself. Such an enterprise . . . is inherently conservative. Something is always conserved; something always remains the Same. This is what makes the role of the black critic or anyone else concerned with advancing certain emancipatory ideas particularly burdensome (538).

Adell's observation, I contend, is a sort of rhetorical/epistemological paradox itself since its recognition of the desire or nostalgia for tradition is wholly accurate, while its assumptions about the emancipatory potential of the summoning and reconstruction of tradition are marred by its epistemological conception of the very notion of tradition, which must be (and is not for her) informed by the long-view genealogies of African peoples outlined above. Similarly, the recognition that advancing emancipatory ideas is burdensome is indisputably adept; but the burden is not tradition's assertion of an authority or its tendency to conserve an idea. Instead, the burden is to recover tradition (and by extension its authority) at its point of genesis and then to sustain (or conserve) that tradition's ways of being and knowing in any and all attempts to generate sound theory about the tradition's progeny in all its cultural manifestations.

Again, the temptation to impress a superficial "Africana Studies reading" upon African American literary texts (logical though it seems to those less aware of the former's underlying disciplinary assumptions, methodologies, and objectives—assumptions, methodologies, and objectives that are in direct and purposeful opposition to those in literary studies) is one that must be suppressed. What reading African American literary texts (those that lend themselves to such readings) through the lens of these conceptual categories can achieve here, however, and with much greater success in the future if done deliberately and with great care is the emancipatory goal to which African American literature has perpetually committed itself as a tradition.

EARLY AFRICAN AMERICAN LITERATURE AND THE NORMATIVE CONCEPTUAL CATEGORIES

In many regards, the application of the Africana Studies normative conceptual categories is most revealing when applied to early texts written by continental Africans in America. One such author might be Phillis Wheatley, whose *Poems on Various Subjects, Religious and Moral* (1773) identifies the author as "Phillis Wheatley, Negro Servant of Mr. John Wheatley of Boston, in New England." Literary scholars consistently celebrate Wheatley's achievements on the basis of her identity as an enslaved person. If she were indeed simply a "slave girl," if such a person can exist (Linda Brent notwithstanding), her abilities might be rightly viewed as exceptional, difficult to believe. The eighteen so-called "noble citizens" who encircled her to affirm her abilities would be justifiable. But

Wheatley was not simply a "slave girl." When we consider her identity on Africana terms, she becomes a young Senegambian, who likely had no less than three tongues, her native Wolof, Arabic, and Fulani.[8] And if she was taken from a part of the country where trade was common, she would have known even more dialects. If she had friends with parents from neighboring communities who spoke other dialects, she would have known those too.

Perhaps because of the limitations related to African American literature's alliance with a mainstream discipline, little scholarship on Wheatley considers her African heritage in any meaningful way.[9] Repeatedly, she is the "shining example of Negro genius" (Brawley in Flanzbaum 72), not Fatu, named after the Prophet's daughter, not her siblings' sister, not her peer's playmates, not the average Senegambian child fluent in multiple tongues and, by her culture's standards, far from illiterate. If we consider Wheatley in the context of continental Africa, she is the daughter of the first peoples to produce and preserve meaning through inscription; she is not an anomaly.

A cursory reading of "On Being Brought from Africa to America" using merely the first three categories makes the point here. When we consider the first category, social structures, we ask: *what social structures inform the text*—slavery and religion as intertwined institutions are readily apparent. The second category concerns self-governance, so we ask: *what rules govern the way Wheatley relates to others*; and *how does she orchestrate her social movement in light of her social structures*—slavery and its religious justification? With this question, we must be careful to consider the rules as Wheatley establishes them for herself, not as her enslavers establish them because the responses are very different based on whose rules we consider. Her rules of self-governance, as her letters to fellow Africans and her marriage to a man whom many saw as beneath her reveal, make clear that she does indeed create a social network independent of the one established for her by the Wheatleys. One rule that governs her movement is her memory of and fidelity to Africa, a fidelity that not only her letters but also much of her poetry supports. One can see how this complicates traditional readings of the poem, which suggests that she is grateful for the so-called "mercy" that brought her to America. Queries about her rules of self-governance, then, lead us to investigations of the black community of which she was a part and, minimally, of their religious beliefs and ideological positions on slavery as a capitalist (rather than religious or moral) institution.

The third category, ways of knowing, requires us to ask: *what ideas about the nature, purpose, function, and process of existence and being could Wheatley have accessed to develop explanations of the world into which she was thrust?* How might she have used this newly developed but no less informed way of knowing to address issues related to her living in this period? When we consider the region from which she was likely taken, we must consider the probability that she and her family were Muslims. If this is true, we can assume that even as a seven year old, her consciousness was very much informed by a distinctly continental-African religious background. How then would a young woman who has been converted to Christianity but wrought with the memory of Muslim sensibilities have interpreted the word *pagan?* How would the fact that this same young girl knew Latin influence that interpretation further? Finally, how might she interpret Christianity as an alternate way of thinking about the nature, purpose, function, and process of existence and being to develop an explanation of her new world? The categories encourage if not implore us to consider as a possibility that Wheatley saw Christianity as an accretive religion that drew from traditions much older than itself. Under these terms, her seeming religious devotion is not to Christianity exclusively but rather to a broadly informed system of divination. Under these terms, too, her reference to Africa in "On Being Brought from Africa to America" as a "pagan land" refers not to its godlessness but rather to an awareness and acceptance of a much longer arc of religious traditions. *Pagan,* as Wheatley likely knows, does not have one accepted, static meaning. So she likely chooses the word purposefully and ironically (as indicated by her use of italics for the word in the poem) to refer to the religion from which early Christianity drew its rituals and to its use during the Roman Empire to mean *civilian,* or a nonmilitary person, in which case her land is one of peace and civility. Such a reading heightens the irony that the end of the poem presents—a reminder that Negroes can be angels too.

In short, the normative conceptual categories, as pedagogical imperative, demand new ways of reading and new sets of questions. No longer can we ask simply if and why Phillis Wheatley's poetry forced America, as represented by her panel of judges, to read anew, in the sense that her poetry demanded reconsiderations of the African's intellectual capacity. We can no longer simply consider her use of Latin to complicate and code her double-voiced poetry. Rather, we must read the text through language and cultural systems grounded in a politics of memory and translation germane to both Africana Studies and African American literary studies.

READING LALITA TADEMY'S *RED RIVER:* THE NORMATIVE CONCEPTUAL CATEGORIES AND CONTEMPORARY HISTORICAL FICTION

Many of the earliest authors of "African American" literature remember Africa and invoke distinctly African cultural and historical experiences in their writing, assuring a useful reserve of material to facilitate textual readings using the conceptual categories. Yet, it is historical fiction in contemporary African American literature that likely benefits most from the application of the conceptual categories since contemporary texts require students to recreate from whole cloth the cultural and historical experiences the texts engage. Lalita Tademy's *Red River* (2007), set alternately before 1873 and after 1873 (through 1937), fictionalizes the massacre of 150 African Americans in Colfax, Louisiana. The novel seeks to correct the story and its misrepresentation by a marker that reads "*On this site occurred the Colfax Riot in which three white and 150 negroes were slain. This event on April 13, 1873 marked the end of carpetbag misrule in the South*" and by a "massive marble obelisk memorial almost twelve feet high dedicated to the three white men who died on that day" (416–17). The memorial is "*Erected to the Memory of the Heroes of Stephen Decatur Parish, James West Hadnot, and Sidney Harris Who Fell in the Colfax Riot Fighting for White Supremacy, April 13, 1873*" (417).[10] From its opening lines to its final ones, the novel complicates ideas of history and tradition. It is the tradition and history of white supremacy that informs the markers, and it is the tradition and history of self and race pride that fuels the black community's resistance to this ill-begotten supremacy. A reading of *Red River* through the conceptual framework offers a culturally based pedagogy that begins to address the limitations of history and tradition and emancipates the narrative from its oppressive discourses.

The novel's prologue warns the reader that "This is not a story to go down easy.... don't nobody want to talk about the scary time. Don't nobody want to remember even now, decades removed.... I don't hold with that point of view.... All I do now is remember and pray the story don't get lost forever...." (Tademy 1). In this regard, the novel is concerned with the use of memory to negotiate, challenge, and generate varied levels of discourse and explanation, despite (or perhaps because of) the silence around the experience and legacy it narrates.

The first category calls for consideration of the social structure that undergirds the text. Students should readily recognize that *Red River's* narrative is mulitlayered, moving back and forth between the past and the present. So, they should be encouraged to consider how the social structure is similarly multifaceted. On one level, the experiences of the novel's characters are informed by the failure of Reconstruction; and on another, they are informed by the legacy of the black townspeople's attempt to "keep the courthouse" until Federal troops come (which never do) to ensure that the newly elected Republicans are allowed to govern in the majority black parish. On yet another level, the novel's social structure is informed by the period of enslavement; and that period too, has layers, recalling slavery before, during, and after the Civil War. Accordingly, students should be encouraged to consider each of these layers before they attempt to answer the questions *who are the people in the novel, where did they come from and when,* and *how did they come to the experience the novel explores?*

Considerations should minimally include the social, economic, political, and cultural environment that informs each of the layers. What is the circumstance of Reconstruction? How do Republicanism and carpetbaggers influence the novel's milieu? Why is segregation the rule of the day? Why do some whites side with the black townspeople? How do American ideas about land ownership influence the characters' choices and why? Why do the black townspeople risk their lives to vote? Why do they equate Reconstruction with citizenship and manhood? How do regional (north and central Louisiana) and local (Franklin and neighboring parishes) realities inform the social structure? How is the local social structure different from the other social structures invoked in the narrative? An in-depth engagement with this category also requires students to research or to be made aware of the social structure of the African communities from which the black townspeople might have conscious or unconscious memory. Students are then able to identify how these social structures have been maintained and adapted (and in some instances integrated into American society), and this awareness makes clear the distinction between an externally imposed social structure and an internally generated system of governance.

Questions related to the second category, governance, consider the common rules Africans created to structure and guide their communities internally. Students should identify rules that guide the way the black townspeople interact with each other. They should consider internal governance among families that know each other well and then among families who have only a passing familiarity with one another (taking some note of how negligible the distinction is in terms of behaviors, especially in moments of crisis). Students should be prompted to ponder things like why Hansom Brisco, upon his first encounter with Israel and Lucy Smith, convinces them to allow Hansom and his wife to take the infant Noby Smith (whom Israel and Lucy have resolved will die before the day's end) to see if Noby's life can be saved; and why Israel and Lucy agree to it. What undergirds Hanson's statement to Israel after the Briscoes have nursed Noby back to full health: "'He's your son, always be yours, but they belong to all of us. . . . We can't spare a single one. I be watching this boy, not only for health for what use he put it to" (23). Why are the townspeople who are unwilling to participate in the efforts to "keep the courthouse" willing to risk their safety by providing shelter to those in danger once the massacre begins? Why do the men of the town insist on starting their own black freemason lodge? What are the implications of and what is the context for this institutionalization of community?

Notably, one of the novel's most crucial metanarratives—the practice of "shouting out" one's name—makes clear the ways self-governance can influence adaptability to or rejection of the social structure. Sam Tademy, one of the town's revered defenders, remembers the one time he saw his father before emancipation. The night before Sam's father runs away (he is to be sold the next day), he tries to persuade his family to run

with him. When Sam's mother refuses to go or to allow his father to take
Sam and his brother, his father tells his sons the story his father told him.
As the narration makes clear, his memory of and commitment to self-
governance inform his rejection of the oppressive social structure. He
passes this memory, which invokes Africa, on to his children, thereby in-
fluencing their ways of knowing, our third category. Imploring his sons
to stretch out their hands, he tells them,

> "Spread your fingers apart far as they go. . . . It's like your arm the river,
> and your fingers the smaller rivers running to the sea. The big one the
> river Nile. Bigger than any river you ever see. We come from the part with
> the little rivers, call the Nile Delta. Alexandria in Egypt, and Egypt in
> Africa. That where you from. Not this place. . . ."
> "We got a name, a family name. My father tell me, and now I tell you."
> "Our real name Ta-ta-mee." (105–106)

Careful attention to the enslaved community's interaction one with another and in contrast to its interaction with whites, in short, reveals the
ways the enslaved adapted to their social structure by recalling their pre-
enslavement existence to create for themselves rules of self-governance
that allowed them to retain their ways of knowing even in the most difficult of circumstances.

The third category—ways of knowing/systems of thought—connects
with the governance category in prompting students to consider how
the characters' ideas about themselves and their world impact their daily
lives and experiences. In addition to the previously discussed transmission of naming and memory, important to the ways of knowing, governance, cultural meaning-making, and movement and memory categories, the question of the significance of education is raised by the
ways of knowing category. Why is formal education—having a school
and reading in particular—so important to the black community in *Red
River,* and how does the community imagine that education will impact
their lives? How does informal education, passed down from elders to
apprentices in this community, reveal an understanding of humans' relation to the world that is distinct from the beliefs of the white community
and that dictates the community's actions with its members and those
outside of it? What worldview undergirds their quests for and achievement of self-determination? If their insistence that it be the black men

of Colfax (not the whites or the carpetbaggers) who defend the town is driven by an improvised world view that reaches back farther than slavery, what are the sources of this worldview? How or at what points does the novel begin to unravel Polly's claim in the prologue that "There [sic] a special way of seeing come with age and distance, a kind of knowing how things happen even without knowing why. Seeing what show up one or two generations removed, from a father to a son or grandson, like repeating threads weaving through the same bolt of cloth" (4)?

Interestingly, this "special way of seeing" and "kind of knowing how things happen" in the novel extends to the fourth category where students seek to uncover what ideas the narrative reveals about characters' awareness of how nature works. When Noby asks Israel "How long to Easter, Papa," for instance, students should note that Israel does not provide Noby with calendar dates. Rather, Israel responds: "Go look at that pecan tree, tell me what you see" (14). When Noby assesses the size of the leaves as the size of his thumbnail, Israel informs Noby that "Spring don't come to Louisiana till the pecan trees leaf out, leaves at least big as the quarter dollar we got buried in the backyard. . . . Easter come about the same time. We got almost three weeks till it safe to plant new in the garden, otherwise late frost likely come and steal up all our labor" (14). Students will likely recognize Noby's awareness of nature and his surroundings as both learned and intuited and equally of practical and cultural/political import. When Noby hears his father say that the white men are gathering at Summerfield Springs and that no one knows what they are planning, Noby, determined "to be a part of what the colored Colfax men are doing" (59), knows that "a nine-year-old colored boy by himself can slip in and out of places none of the men in the courthouse can" (59). The narrator reveals:

> Noby has always been good at course-plotting, as his father taught him, interpreting the clues offered by the sun, stars, or moon, observing wildlife and vegetation, monitoring where moss grows on trees or how the mistletoe drapes. His sense of direction is keen and specific, and once he travels a path, the most obscure landmark is implanted in his head from that day forward (59).

He reaches Summerfield Springs undetected, hears the white men's plan, and returns to the courthouse to warn the black men of the ensuing attack. Here, students should contemplate what the novel reveals about the relation of nature to the cultural and political. Students might also consider the novel's commentary on hunting, noting that Jackson Tademy prefers to trap rather than to shoot his prey, while his brother Green, who accidently shoots and kills himself while hunting, consistently shoots his prey at first sight. Some attention should also be given to the technologies used for warfare in the novel, so students should consider minimally how technology influences the outcome of the massacre and how the black community relies on nature to survive in the years following the massacre. Does the novel suggest that there is any point in distinguishing between nature and technology?

The fifth category, movement and memory, implores students to search for textual markers such as architecture and/or written and oral inscriptions that reveal the preservation of memory. Students will likely note that the most notable architecture in the novel is the obelisk that memorializes the three white men who were killed. What they must take even greater care to note, however, is the fact that the obelisk has origins in Egypt, which is where the Tademys, through memory handed down orally, trace their African origins. Students' awareness of the African origins of the obelisk, coupled with their consideration of the novel's references to black and white freemasons, will prompt them to note the relation of architecture and inscriptions of memory. The obelisk, they will discover, is one of many architectural achievements of Egyptian influence that inspires cemetery memorials in the nineteenth century. This awareness will also, no doubt, complicate the novel's commentary on movement and memory, causing students to query why the whites publically perform movement and memory, while the black community does so privately and ambiguously? When their manhood is threatened, the Tademy men shout out their African family name in a private ritual inspired by Sam's father's concession that while he can only whisper the family name on the night he runs away, "one day [Sam and his brother] gonna shout it out so everybody hear, and your children gonna shout it so they remember who they is. . . . You got strong, free, fighter's blood in you . . . and when you make your own sons, teach them to shout out they name like they know who they is" (107). The basis of the ritual is their Egyptian ancestry (their lineage as descendants of peoples phonetically called "Ta-ta-mee" from the Nile delta), yet the one public inscription of Egyptian memory (the obelisk) is confined to white freemasons who are undoubtedly unaware of its African origins. This irony alone will encourage students to recover African culture and to see how its integration into Western societies requires higher order thinking to access revelations about movement and memory.

The final category, cultural meaning making, requires students to search the text for examples of African cultural production (music, art, dance, narrative, etc.) that demonstrate how characters make meaning that is distinctly African in a particular temporal/spatial experience. What ongoing extensions of African cultural life are present? How does the shouting out of the Tademy name mirror or extend the African ring-shout? How have the religious practices narrated in the novel been modified to reflect African culture? This category might inspire students to consider McCully's oratory about his "voting hat," a brown fedora with a "phoenix" feather in the brim. When Sam teases McCully that the feather "come from one of the birds common as dirt around here," (32), McCully chides: "You showing a terrible failure of imagination. This here a rare feather from the phoenix bird what lived in the desert for five hundred years, go up in flames, and raise itself up brand-new from the ashes" (32). McCully makes his own meaning for the hat: "I wear it the day we vote them men in, and I keep on wearing it till they take up the office for good. Just like this here phoenix feather, we gonna get stronger and stronger and rise from the ashes where we been" (32). Sam accepts McCully's lore about the hat, and he accepts the hat and its meaning from McCully just before he dies protecting the courthouse. Sam then passes the hat to his son Jackson, who accepts it along with the challenge of uplifting the race; Jackson passes it on to his grandson Ted, who knows it only as his GrandJack's "funeral hat" until Jackson tells him about McCully (who is also Ted's great-grandfather), the phoenix (Ted rightly calls it a heron feather), and the responsibility that comes along with possession of the hat. Bequeathing the hat to Ted, Jackson, just before he "consume[s] himself with the selfishness of dying," tells Ted:

> "This not a gift. . . . This hat a responsibility. Names of men you never gonna know lay buried in the ground for you. Can't change the past, but don't mean you not in somebody's debt. This hat mean no matter how much time pass, no matter how dark it seem, you not allowed to turn your face to the wall, throw up your hands, forget. . . ."

> "Your day coming, and when it does, it be clear to you.... A man
> sometime don't know who he is until somebody expect something from
> him. We all expecting in abundance. Don't disappoint." (408)

Ultimately, the text itself becomes an African cultural production, imploring memory to give voice to meaning-making systems the black people in Colfax create before and after the massacre that is memorialized by the whites as a "riot." As Sam and Polly note: "Words matter in how people see, how they gonna remember. Easter Sunday 1873 be the Colfax Massacre, not the Colfax Riot, and the only shame be we didn't get the parish power to the hands of the Republicans" (209).

Polly warns us from the beginning that the story "won't go down easy." Using the categories to enhance traditional readings of the novel inevitably encourages and requires students to move beyond first order thinking as it relates to the novel to complicate our ways of thinking, reading, and being and, ultimately, to liberate the text from the limitations of the noteworthy and historical but decidedly hegemonic discourses such as lynching, masculinity, white supremacy, and citizenship that it engages. Notably, the novel does not provide the answers to the questions raised when reading it through the lens of the categories. Nor should it; rather, the novel, like all good literature, should provoke inquiry, incite curiosity, inspire new thinking. It is our task as readers—as teachers and learners—to bring to the text an approach to reading African American literature that is committed to avoiding the philosophical and epistemological paradoxes that plague traditional African American literary criticism. Such an approach must begin and end with underlying assumptions that emerge from and privilege the ways of being and knowing that characterize and reflect the people and experience being studied as revealed by the long arc of their history. As *Red River* and so many African American texts unveil, reading our literary cultural heritage in light of memory and of the genealogical heritage of historical and cultural experiences matters. Such readings will undoubtedly render fully visible, for the keen eye and introspective student, principles, practices, and rules that lend themselves wholly not only to fertile advances in African American literary criticism and pedagogy but also to rewarding revelations about the African American text's interminable ability to negotiate, control, and generate multiple levels of discourse that are both regenerative and liberating.

NOTES

1. See Ngugi wa Thiongo, *Something Torn and New: An African Renaissance,* (New York: Basic, 2008).

2. This critical point identifies the line of demarcation between Africana Studies as an academic discipline and the other academic fields and disciplines. Much of the work currently categorized under the title "Africana, Black, and/or African American Studies" is in fact a potpourri of scholarship that has only the subject matter—African people, experiences, texts, and/or practices—in common. For two generations, scholars trained and training graduate students in the field and discipline of Africana Studies have struggled to establish and maintain autonomous disciplinary spaces for this work. This essay serves in part to suggest one possible approach to both establishing a disciplinary approach to the field and engaging in interdisciplinary work with other fields. On the subject of Africana Studies, disciplinarity and the distinction between what is and is not representative of the field and discipline, see Carr, "What Black Studies is Not: Moving From Crisis to Liberation in Africana Intellectual Work" (Donald Smith Distinguished Lecture at Baruch College, New York, December 6, 2010).

3. David Levering Lewis notes that in a 1906 research proposal to the Carnegie Institution of Washington, DC, W. E. B. Du Bois outlines a substantially similar project of separating African life and experience from a reduction to the social structures that Africans encountered during enslavement. Lewis writes that Du Bois proposed that Carnegie fund a mulityear research project that would begin with historical studies of Africa before adding an analysis of the period of United States enslavement and the systems of postbellum education, economics, and politics before adding a comparative study of enslavement throughout the Western Hemisphere and in Africa. This enumeration of social structures would have been accompanied by a simultaneous consideration of racial types, intermixtures, and, critically, "ethnic and cultural variations on the African continent" and would culminate with "sociological studies intended to consolidate, classify, and derive 'scientific' generalizations" (242–243).

4. See Vansina's *How Societies are Born: Governance in West Central Africa before 1600* (Charlottesville: University of Virginia Press, 2005).

5. See Daniel's *Dancing Wisdom: Embodied Knowledge in Haitian Vodou, Cuban Yoruba, and Bahian Candomble* (Urbana: University of Illinois Press, 2005) and Thompson's *Flash of the Spirit: African and Afro-American Art and Philosophy* (New York: Vintage, 1984).

6. Adell's comments should be considered amid the myriad of responses to the post "Reconstruction of Instruction" moment in African American literary criticism. Key among these conversations are the dialogic exchange between Henry Louis Gates, Jr., Houston A. Baker, Jr., and Joyce Ann Joyce in *New Literary History* (the Winter 1987 issue), among others; Barbara Christian's "The Race for Theory" and Michael Awkward's response to Christian in "Appropriative Gestures: Theory and Afro American Literary Criticism"; and most recently Reggie Scott Young's "Theoretical Influences and Experimental Influences: Ernest J. Gaines and Recent Critical Approaches to the Study of African American Fiction."

7. Adell argues of Gates especially: "the more the black theorist writes in the interest of blackness, the greater his Euro-centrism reveals itself to be. . . . [Esu and the Signifying Monkey] are de-Africanized, as it were, and in Gates' version, they 'speak'

like transmogrifications of all the hermeneutial (Esu) and rhetorical (Signifying Monkey) paradigms post-structuralism has made ready-at-hand for him" (534).

8. See Carole A. Parks's "Report on a Poetry Festival," *Black World* 23.4 (February 1974): 92–97.

9. Recent criticism that seeks to defend what seems to be a reluctance on Wheatley's part to be critical of slavery fails in this regard as well. Walt Nott, for instance, argues in "From 'Uncultivated Barbarian' to 'Poetical Genius': The Public Presence of Phillis Wheatley" that Wheatley's "symbolic transformation in the eyes of contemporary white Anglo-American culture from 'Barbarian' to 'Genius' suggests her successful crafting of a public persona" (22). While he celebrates her ability to craft a public self, he fails completely to consider her existence beyond the immediate context of the eighteenth century and its public discourse. Again, in Wheatley's defense, R. Lynn Matson, in "Phillis Wheatley—Soul Sister?," an article published at the height of "corrective," pro-Wheatley scholarship, seeks to deconstruct longstanding and prevailing arguments that Wheatley can be condemned for "failing to espouse in any way the plight of her race" (222). But Matson does not attempt to construct Wheatley as a "Soul Sister" by reconstructing her as a continental African first and foremost. Instead, Matson argues for Wheatley's affinity to blackness on the basis of her written correspondence, or, her letters. Indeed, some of the letters are revealing in this regard. And while the points Matson makes are valid, she depends on the letters, not Wheatley's poetry, as the source from which we are to make the case for the racial readings of the poet. A reading of her poetry using the conceptual categories allows her poetry to accomplish this as, if not more, effectively.

10. Both markers still stand in Colfax, Louisiana, the first at the courthouse and the second at the cemetery. As Tademy writes in the Author's Note, her visit to the courthouse was initially to research her father's family history. Only after seeing the marker and then the memorial and hearing her aunt's curt confirmation ("Our people were there. . . . Some got out, and some didn't") does the incident that ultimately shapes the narrative inspire parallel research and provide the lens through which to narrate her father's family history.

WORKS CITED

Adell, Sandra. "The Crisis in Black American Literary Criticism and the Postmodern Cures of Houston A. Baker, Jr., and Henry Louis Gates, Jr." In *African American Literary Theory: A Reader,* edited by Winston Napier, 523–39. New York: New York University Press, 2000.

Baker, Houston A., Jr. "In Dubious Battle." *New Literary History* 18 (Winter 1987): 363–69.

Carr, Greg E., ed. *Lessons in Africana Studies.* Philadelphia: Songhai Press and the School District of Philadelphia, 2005.

———. "What Black Studies is Not: Moving from Crisis to Liberation in Africana Intellectual Work." Donald Smith Distinguished Lecture at Baruch College, New York, December 6, 2010.

Daniel, Yvonne. *Dancing Wisdom: Embodied Knowledge in Haitian Vodou, Cuban Yoruba, and Bahian Candomble.* Urbana: University of Illinois Press, 2005.

Flanzbaum, Hilene. "Unprecedented Liberties: Re-reading Phillis Wheatley." *MELUS* 18, no. 3 (Fall 1993): 71–81.

Gates, Henry L., Jr. "'What's Love Got to Do with It?' Critical Theory, Integrity, and the Black Idiom." *New Literary History* 18 (Winter 1987): 345–62.

Joyce, Joyce A. "The Black Canon: Reconstructing Black American Literary Criticism." *New Literary History* 18 (Winter 1987): 335–44.

———. "Who the Cap Fit: Unconscionableness in the Criticism of Houston Baker and Henry Louis Gates, Jr." *New Literary History* 18 (Winter 1987): 371–84.

Lewis, David L. *W. E. B. Du Bois: A Biography.* New York: Henry Holt, 2009.

Matson, R. Lynn. "Phillis Wheatley—Soul Sister." *Phylon* 33, no. 3 (1972): 222–230.

Nott, Walt. "From 'Uncultivated Barbarian' to 'Poetical Genius': The Public Presence of Phillis Wheatley." *MELUS* 18, no. 3 (Fall 1993): 21–32.

Parks, Carol. "Report on a Poetry Festival." *Black World* 23, no. 4 (February 1974): 92–97.

Tademy, Lalita. *Red River.* New York: Warner, 2007.

Thompson, Robert Farris. *Flash of the Spirit: African and Afro-American Art and Philosophy.* New York: Vintage Books, 1984.

Vansina, Jan. *How Societies Are Born: Governance in West Central Africa before 1600.* Charlottesville: University of Virginia Press, 2005.

Young, Reggie Scott. "Theoretical Influences and Experimental Influences: Ernest J. Gaines and Recent Critical Approaches to the Study of African American Fiction." *Contemporary African American Fiction: New Critical Essays,* edited by Dana A. Williams, 11–36. Columbus: Ohio State University Press, 2009.

wa Thiongo, Ngugi. *Something Torn and New: An African Renaissance.* New York: Basic Books, 2008.

AFTERWORD

ALICE RANDALL

On behalf of the novelists, I applaud the scholars. And I thank the scholars for including fiction writers in the important conversation about the evolving shape of the African American novel that took place at the Nittany Lion Inn October 23rd and 24th of 2009. That conversation is powerfully continued in this volume. Again the writers are invited.

Mat Johnson opened this volume. I close it. During the conference I had the pleasure of hearing Mat read from his surreal masterpiece, then in progress now published, *Pym*. Another pleasure was meeting Martha Southgate and hearing her voice raised in air after admiring her voice on paper throughout *Third Girl from the Left*. A personal highlight was the book launch hosted for my third novel (the novel that followed *The Wind Done Gone* and *Pushkin and the Queen of Spades*) by the Africana Research Center and the Master in Fine Arts program. In thanks for that, I will close with a flash of fiction, the shortest chapter of my longish novel, *Rebel Yell*.

Before I come to that close I want to salute two novelists who provide perplexing signs of our times, Sister Souljah and Sapphire. And I will bow to the two living novelists who most inspired me to become a novelist, Ernest Gaines and Toni Morrison. This seems particularly fitting as the conference was opened with a brilliant analytical keynote presented by Houston Baker on Morrison and drew toward a close with a dinner talk of mine, a talk which touched on Souljah and Sapphire and celebrated Gaines and Morrison.

My talk, associative and autobiographical, engaged Morrison by providing a patchwork of language: readings from my three novels; memories of the poet Alberta Bontemps, Langston Hughes's dear friend and Arna Bontemps's wife; and readings of three striking letters written to me by my readers, including a letter from Harper Lee. It was the talk of a fiction writer.

"My plot, over and over," I said that night, "is what I call 'the baby plot.' The 'baby plot' is about being grown and negotiating responsibilities to others and the future without neglecting the self."

As dessert was being served I mused on birthing, Bontemps, *Beloved*, and "the baby plot." At the center of it all were a few simple recognitions.

"Our families," I said, "are not all attack-the-children crazy. Our fathers are not all rapists. Though all three of my heroines have been raped, not one has been raped by a black man or by her father."

"The stock character at the center of *Push*, the raping black man, is one I'm ready to be done with. I want some portraits of our good fathers. We have them. And I want more complex portraits of all our fathers. And I believe that more artistic portraits of them in literature and film will do much to create more in life."

"My deep appreciation of *The Coldest Winter Ever* lies in its particular exploration of 'the baby plot.' Sister Souljah doesn't fade away from the possibility that Winter's father prepares her in significant ways, even as he imperils her. I like the way Souljah works 'the baby plot,' the way she is able to capture, the whip-lash preciousness of ghetto children, what it is to 'feel dipped' as in 'dipped in gold' highly prized by a one when you are low-valued by the many."

"Winter is valued by her father Santiago and to a lesser degree by her mother. Sister Souljah constructs this reality with an elegant economy. I suspect some resistance to the novel *The Coldest Winter Ever*, some of the low rating, has as its source an inability to read as authentic, a sly and complex portrayal of thug as loving daddy—in the nonerotic sense—as real."

That inability, I concluded, "has less to do with failures of writing and far more to do with failures of reading."

For me, black fiction changed around 1987. Around the time of the publication of Morrison's *Beloved*, I spent months sleeping in Arna Bontemps's library, waiting for my only child to be born, sheltered through bed rest by her great-grandmother, Alberta Johnson Bontemps. After *Beloved* was the first book I read after the birth of my daughter in August of 1987, I became a writer.

I remembered turning the pages and knowing, "A task had been achieved. Evil had been transformed into beauty by layers of loving perception, intelligence and imagination, the past was nailed back into the past, stripped reader by reader of shame. Coming quick on the heels of another masterpiece of twentieth century African American fiction, Ernest Gaines's *A Gathering of Old Men*, the masterpiece *Beloved* is for me the end of a literary era, leaving much significant about our lives beyond plantation desperation for a next era to claim."

At the center of my life and at the center of my fiction is a single understanding: "Doing what is best for the children and not just our own children, all the children, finding a vivid way to do the hard right thing, focused on the future not the past, on our wishes and dreams not our bruises, is to move past survival to thriving no matter what the circumstance."

"African American novels in the present period struggle with engaging the future informed by, but not hobbled by, the past. In doing so some of us have relocated the central historical moment of our collective experience . . . in the civil rights struggles of the [1960s] and the multiple branches of identity and culture that rose from it. I am one of those."

"And others of us have recentered, or centered, our identities in the post-soul street . . . One way or the other, a new road is being walked a new way. The significant aesthetic has shifted from the authentic portrayal of unspeakable tragedy, to the authentic portrayal of nuanced triumph."

For me, nuanced triumph often has much to do with portrayals of provisioning for children. That is the dominant lens through which I have read African American novels since 1987.

This volume provides many alternative lenses and many different frames to read and to teach contemporary African American novels including the lenses provided by working novelists.

Writers need readers. Scholars are a special kind of reader. Writers are another special kind of reader. All readers are significant.

But quiet as it's kept, great readers—powerful, informed, nuanced readers—inspire and sustain writers in particular ways, some of which make the ground for writing more fertile. Great writers need great scholars.

And good writers need them even more. Great scholars get it. They get the spaces. The space between what was tried for and what was achieved; between what the audience understands itself to want and what the audience understands itself to need; between the difficulties of the text and the abilities of the student; between the language and novels of today and the language and novels of yesterday. They see new spaces and create new bridges of insight. They get the spaces and so much more.

I thank them for all of it. And I thank the scholars present at Penn State for all of it and for keeping the conference close to the page.

This book is evidence the Penn State African American novel conference braided creators and critics in a way that informed the elemental alliance of readers and writers; in a way that illumined the elemental tensions between readers and writers; in a way that underlined many profound connections between fiction and life; and in a way that explored the gap between knowing and teaching.

Contemporary African American literature moves many conversations forward and enlarges the spaces for both creation and analysis.

May the pages before these frame and reframe my pages that follow, and all my pages to come.

The news traveled faster than any other news ever. Dr. King had been shot dead. The date was April 4, 1968. Abel's house quickly became a gathering place. Friends and even some people they didn't know arrived at the house on Fifteenth Street without invitation until there were fifty or sixty grown people in the house, crying and getting drunk.

It was a fifth and final blow. Medgar Evers, June 12, 1963, shot walking into his ranch house, leaving two boys and a girl. The four little girls bombed in church on September 15, 1963. November 22, 1963, John F. Kennedy killed in Dallas. February 21, 1965, Malcolm X. Now the daddy of Yolanda, Little Martin, Bernice, and Dexter was dead.

In Big Abel's house it was the end of an era that in Nashville had begun with the bombing at the home of Z. Alexander Looby in April 1960. Abel didn't remember a time when politically active black men weren't dying.

He was over black men. King's death did it. He heard all the sadness. He heard other things too. That King was up in that hotel with a white woman. In his little boy's mind and in his grown man's mind, Abel always blamed Coretta for the death. It would take Hope to almost undo that. No one could undo his sadness that he hadn't saved the wrapper off the candy bar Dr. King had given him.

That very night eight-year-old Abel started saying no when people asked if he wanted to run for his father's seat on the city council when he grew up.

He was over black people. Ever since he could remember he had heard the phrase that all he had to do was be black and die. And now the only two things he for sure didn't want to do were be black and die.

Reprinted by Permission of Bloomsbury

ANNOTATED BIBLIOGRAPHY

PIA DEAS AND DAVID F. GREEN, JR.

Beatty, Paul. *Slumberland*. New York: Bloomsbury, 2009. Author of the satirical coming-of-age story *White Boy Shuffle*, Beatty continues in the satirical vein with *Slumberland*. In this hilariously off-beat novel, Ferguson W. Sowell, a.k.a. DJ Darky, is a man who believes that blackness as a racial category has ended. When, much to his delight, he succeeds in creating the world's perfect beat, he chooses to seek out someone who he believes could truly appreciate his genius, the legendary free-jazz artist, Charles Stone, a.k.a. "the Schwa." The description of the beat captures Beatty's rich, sardonic approach: "a two-minute-and-forty-seven-second amalgamation of samples, street recordings, and original phrases . . . many layers, obscure riffs from pop bands that never popped, folk music from countries without folksiness, sea chanteys from land locked nations, all overlapped with my favorite idiosyncratic sounds and pressed into a musical ore as unidentifiable as a fragment of flying saucer metal in a 1950s sci-fi film" (31–32). At first, he has no idea how to locate the elusive Schwa, but when he receives a mysterious package indicating that the Schwa may be in Berlin, he heads to Germany. Once there, he hangs out at the Slumberland bar where he makes his living as the first-ever jukebox sommelier and pursues his quest to find Stone. This bawdy, fun novel offers an earnest meditation on race in a purportedly "post-racial" world.

Black, Daniel. *They Tell Me of Home*. New York: St. Martins Griffin, 2006. In this engaging first-person narrative, Tommy Lee Tyson tells the story of his decision to return to Swamp Creek, Arkansas. As a young man, he had left after high school graduation in order to pursue his educational dreams. While he originally vowed never to return, he comes back to Swamp Creek with a newly minted PhD in Black Studies. As he disembarks from the Greyhound bus and crosses the field to his parents' home, he is flooded with the bittersweet memories of his boyhood. He fondly recalls his adventures with his cousin and running buddy, Darryl, but he also remembers the backbreaking manual and farm labor in which his father insisted he participate. Now that he has returned, Tyson is forced to confront several mysteries, including how and why his younger sister died, as well as a secret about himself. As he comes to terms with his self-imposed exile from his hometown and the significant rifts between himself and his family, he gains a more positive understanding of himself and his culture.

Butler, Octavia. *Fledgling*. New York: Seven Stories Press, 2005. Continuing to explore themes treated in her 1993 novel, *Parable of the Sower, Fledging* not only provides a critique of social and ideological limitations, but imagines alternative foundations on which to build new a new society. Fledgling is a story about Shori Matthews, a 53-year-old amnesiac vampire who looks like a 10-year-old African American girl. Shori awakes alone in a cave, not remembering anything about her past, and she must divine everything about herself from the clues provided by her body. She soon discovers that she is a vampire, or an Ina—a race of beings that predate humans and share a symbiotic relationship with them. Inas use humans for survival and in return provide them pleasure and extended life by biting them and drinking their blood. After discovering a burned village that feels familiar, but of which she has no memory, Shori is picked up by a construction worker named Wright, and they soon begin a symbiotic relationship. The novel follows these two as they struggle to discover who Shori is, avenge the death of her family, and avoid the vampire that killed her family. Through their journey Shori learns that she is different from other Inas, as she has been genetically manipulated and has human DNA. For instance, she has melanin in her skin and can walk about freely in the sun. Her difference is the reason her family was murdered and also why she is being hunted by *pure* vampires. Butler uses this interesting take on vampire mythology to explore the themes of difference and hate. Shori's experiences help readers to think about what it means to move beyond narrow and repetitive ideological struggles in order to build a new society where reciprocity is a fundamental aspect of its value system.

Danticat, Edwidge. *The Dew Breakers.* New York: Knopf, 2004. In this poignant exploration into the lives of three members of a Haitian family living in New York, Danticat considers the inescapability of the past, while exploring the possibilities of redemption and change. The novel opens with a young woman paying homage to her father in a sculpture she has created and through which she is about to earn her first major commission. The evening before the sale is to take place, the father destroys the sculpture, explaining to his daughter that he is not the man who she has honored in her work. While she has grown up believing her father was a prisoner of Francois Duvalier's loathed Haitian security force, known as "Tontons Macoutes," he explains to her that he was actually one of the prison guards, or "Dew Breaker," so-called because they arrived to apprehend their victims from their homes just before dawn "as the dew was settling on the leaves." The novel develops through varying perspectives of the characters whose lives are haunted by the impact of Duvalier's corrupt and repressive regime, and we come to know the "Dew Breaker" through the stories of his former victims, his pious wife, and his disillusioned daughter. In this gripping and evocative novel Danticat intertwines the personal and the political, the past and the present, interrogating the impact of this legacy of violence on Haiti and its people.

Diaz, Junot. *The Brief and Wondrous Life of Oscar Wao.* New York: Riverhead Books, 2007. *The Brief and Wondrous Life of Oscar Wao* is a witty and wryly humorous novel about an awkward, self proclaimed "ghetto nerd" struggling to gain voice and confidence through the imaginative reading and writing of comic books. The protagonist, Oscar, is a second generation Dominican American, who uses comic books and superheroes to escape his overbearing mother, Beli. By writing his own narrative, Oscar finds a kind of love, acceptance, and confidence that he has always longed for and is thus able to engage his troubled family history. Beli, troubled by her past, attempts to instill in Oscar and his sister Lola values and traditions that are incompatible with their American upbringing. The novel can be read as an allegory about the struggles of postcolonial and African American immigrants who seek to escape the deep structures of domination. Beli's own oppression— the brutal execution of her father at the hands of Rafael Trujillo, the Dominican dictator and antagonist of the novel, and the spousal abuse by her husband—is absorbed and passed on to her children. However, literacy, specifically the ability to rewrite and re-imagine one's life, provides Oscar access to an escape from the repetitive cycle of violence. The novel is entertaining and stinging in its criticisms and analyses of identity, imagination, and hegemony.

Due, Tananarive. *My Soul to Keep*. New York: Eos, 1997. *My Soul to Keep* is the first novel in the African Immortals Series; it is followed by *The Living Blood* and the third book in the series, *Blood Colony*. The novel is a dark fantasy about a young black couple, Jessica and David Wolde. The two represent an ideal black middle class family; David is a professor and Jessica is a journalist. They live in a beautiful house and have a 5-year-old daughter. However, David is secretly an immortal who has lived several hundred years before ever meeting Jessica. He is one among thirty other immortals that roam the earth with unnatural healing properties gained from the blood of Christ; the blood keeps them living by rapidly healing any disease, trauma, or cellular anomaly. However, because the immortals live under a code to never share their blood and never tell anyone of their immortality, a conflict emerges when Jessica begins to investigate a story that could expose her husband's secret. Jessica must come to grips with the fact that the deaths of her family and friends may not be a coincidence, but rather the result of a secret David is keeping with his friends from Ethiopia. The novel offers an original take on immortality myths, tracing the genealogy of the immortals back to Africa and even Christ himself. Due pushes African American science fiction forward with this dark fantasy about morality and the depths to which some will go to protect and preserve knowledge, even at the expense of love and family.

Durham, David. *A Walk Through Darkness*. New York: Doubleday, 2002. Following on the heels of his 2001, novel *Gabriel's Story*, a coming-of-age story set in the reconstruction-era, Durham's *A Walk Through Darkness* is a powerful contribution to the neo-slave narrative genre. In harrowing detail, *A Walk Through Darkness* brings to life one slave's escape and interweaves two stories, the gripping tale of a young fugitive slave, William, and of the slave tracker, Morrison, hired to return him to his owner. William, who had initially been extremely reluctant to seek out freedom, decides to escape from the plantation after his girlfriend, Dover, who is pregnant with his child, is forced to relocate to Philadelphia, a free state, with her mistress. In William's journey, Durham provides a careful, nuanced portrait of the confusion, terror, and obstacles that fugitive slaves faced. Once he arrives in Philadelphia, securing his freedom is a more complex enterprise than he originally imagined, and because of the fugitive slave laws, he and his girlfriend must consider escaping further north, to Canada. This fast-paced tale captures the psychic, geographic, and social disorientation of William as he travels north and must navigate an unfamiliar landscape, ask for assistance from unusual sources, and resolve his own ambivalence about seeking freedom. The view into the slave tracker's mentality provides an additional dimension to the story, and the vivid descriptions of prejudices highlights the inhumanity of the entire slave system.

Ellis, Trey. *Platitudes*. Boston: Northeastern University Press, 2003. Ellis, author of "The New Black Aesthetic," a manifesto outlining what Ellis sees as his generation's commitments and challenges to previous articulations of a black aesthetic, creates his first novel, *Platitudes*, as a meta-fictional meditation on whether or not experimentalist sensibilities and racial aesthetics are necessarily opposing forces. In order to illustrate his point, his main character, DeWayne Wellington, an experimental novelist, strikes up a literary friendship with popular author, Isshe Ayam. As they trade drafts of their work, Wellington's appreciation for including racial experiences in his own work grows, and he begins to rewrite his work and shift his approach to his fiction. The result is a dynamic conversation regarding both the traditional origins of, and the potential new directions in, African American fiction. Although the narrative ultimately sputters to an unsatisfying conclusion when the friendship between DeWayne Wellington and Isshe Ayam turns into romance, the narrative's exploration and demonstration of the process of artistic invention make it worth the read.

Everett, Percival. *Erasure.* Hanover, NH: University Press of New England, 2001. Everett has established himself as a significant contemporary author with nearly twenty novels, one children's book, several short story collections, and even a series of abstract paintings. He is known for his eclectic writing style and his concentrated efforts to expand the thematic and stylistic scope of African American fiction. In *Erasure,* a scathing critique of the publishing industry and imaginative exploration of identity, creativity, and public culture, Everett composes a complex allegory about the struggle between authenticity and success within a contemporary culture that values ostentation and debased representations of African American life. The novel follows Thelonious "Monk" Ellison, an avant-garde writer and English Professor who writes highly esoteric novels that sell very little and affront his African American peers who expect him to write more identifiably black novels. Dismayed by the national success of Juanita Mae Jenkins, an amateur black middle class writer, whose exploitative first novel *We's Lives in Da Ghetto* is hailed as a work of a real creative genius, Monk creates the pen name Stagg R. Leigh and writes *My Pafology. My Pafology* is a painfully wicked story written in first person, untrained prose about the deviant, exploitative, and violent acts of a young Black boy in the ghetto. In an ironic twist the novel gains national recognition and makes the reading list for a coveted and prestigious Book Award. The judges for the book award consider the book an informative and authentic account of black life in America and, against Monk's disapproval, select it as a finalist for the award. The story-within-a-story structure is a clever, hilarious, and imaginative illustration of the postmodern aesthetics and experimental writing style that have become hallmarks of the New Black Aesthetic. Everett manages in one fell swoop to provide stinging criticism of black popular culture, the publishing industry, and academia.

Flowers, Arthur. *Another Good Loving Blues.* New York: Ballantine Books, 1994. This delightful and refreshing turn of the century love story focuses on the relationship between traveling blues pianist, Lucas Bodeen, and conjure woman Melvira. In an engaging subplot, Melvira, who was abandoned by her mother, Effie Dupree, and raised by Hoodoo Maggie, is called by her mother's spirit to make peace with her. In order to do so, Melvira and Lucas travel to the Mississippi Delta and en route stop on Beale Street. The struggle for power and dominance in their relationship naturally creates conflict and estrangement between Bodeen and Melvira, but ultimately, they are reunited when Bodeen swallows his pride and woos Melvira back to him. This story is told in a casual, comfortable Southern cadence and is knowingly indebted to Zora Neale Hurston's *Their Eyes Were Watching God,* with Hurston making a cameo appearance in the narrative.

Gaines, Ernest. *A Lesson Before Dying.* New York: Vintage Books, 1994. Set in the 1940s, *A Lesson Before Dying* examines the struggle for manhood by two Black men in a rural, racist, and segregated Louisiana parish. Grant Wiggins, a local schoolteacher, is asked to help Jefferson, a young man who is sentenced to death after being convicted of a murder he didn't commit. The novel uses the theme of personal growth to frame Grant and Jefferson's relationship. Jefferson, against his better judgment, receives a ride home from some friends who decide to rob the local store. The robbery ends with the death of Jefferson's friends and the store-owner. In a panic, Jefferson steals the money from the store and is quickly caught. At his trial his attorney argues against the death penalty by referring to Jefferson as a hog, as someone with no sense and no way of understanding what he has done. The day he is sentenced, Jefferson's godmother, Miss Emma, asks Grant to visit Jefferson in jail before his execution and to educate him. Unsure of what he can do for Jefferson in the few weeks he has left, Grant is hesitant to help. Grant initially believes Jefferson to be guilty, if not of the crime, then of stupidity; however, through their conversations, Grant comes to respect Jefferson, helping him learn to write, to gain a sense of pride, and to grasp fully the error of his decisions. Through his personal progress, Jefferson comes to understand what it means to be a man and Grant learns to be more aware of his social and cultural responsibilities. Gaines paints a vivid picture of the tensions, humiliations, and injustices that shaped race relations in the pre–Civil Rights South. However, it is the struggle to maintain integrity and community in an unjust society that makes *A Lesson Before Dying* such an inspiring tale of personal and social growth.

Glave, Thomas. *Whose Song? And Other Stories*. San Francisco: City Lights Publishers, 2001. In his first collection of short stories, *Whose Song?*, Glave brings us nine visually striking, innovative, and compelling stories about black gay desire, love, longing, and loss. Glave's narrative gaze is unflinching. In "Accident," a couple fights their way to the front of a crowd to observe a car accident and are riveted by the horror of the crash. This initial incident becomes an extended meditation for the main character on his own unresolved traumatic memories. Then, in "Commitment," Glave examines the personal cost of forsaking gay desire for more traditionally accepted relationships. Lou Jay and Ricky are a young Southern couple who must hide their relationship from their families, including Ricky's patriarchal, homophobic father. When Ricky sleeps with and impregnates his and Lou's mutual friend, Renee, Ricky's father, who suspects that Ricky is gay, seizes upon this opportunity to insist that his son marry. Meanwhile, Ricky tries to convince Lou Jay to run away with him and when he is unable to, he turns his pent-up rage on his fiancée in an explosive, violent ending. These stories with their aggressive and even violent undertones, offer a powerful, poignant exploration of contemporary gay identity.

Gomez, Jewelle. *The Gilda Stories*. Boston: Firebrand Books, 1991. When Gilda, a fugitive slave, needs refuge, two women take her in. Then, the story takes a supernatural turn, as we discover these women are vampires who eventually induct Gilda into their society and thereby extend her mortality. This rich story unfolds over 200 years as Gilda travels from Louisiana, to California, to Massachusetts, and then New York. She experiences slavery, living in a mining town during a gold rush, and participates in the vibrant nightlife of New York City as a singer and performer. As the novel progresses from 1850 to 2050, a horrific, nightmare and apocalyptic vision unfolds. The terrifying future is primarily the result of extensive and severe global environmental devastation, and this crisis is further fueled by rampant drug addiction. Part romance, part fantasy, part morality tale, this is a story of one woman's quest to build kinship, family, and community.

Grooms, Anthony. *Bombingham*. New York: Ballantine Books, 2001. *Bombingham* is a story about Walter Burke's experiences both in the war torn rice paddies of Vietnam and in the tumultuous streets of Civil Rights era Birmingham. Through the eyes of a young Walter struggling to cope with his mother's deadly disease, readers witness the growth of a fledgling Civil Rights Movement, the ever-present tension of segregation, and the social responsibility that compelled so many to act. The novel oscillates between the experiences of a younger Walter as he reflects on his family life and participation in the movement and an older Walter whose growing cynicism makes it difficult for him to understand and cope with the death and violence of the Vietnam War. Ultimately, Walter must find the strength to write a letter to the family of the dead members of his military unit, a letter that leads him to question whether the successes of the movement were little more than hallow victories as he finds himself in a repetitive cycle of fighting for freedom with heavy losses to both sides. Through a powerful and dramatic understanding of voice, tone, and growth, Grooms oscillates between two very different perspectives from the same character, while at the same time merging two pivotal periods in American history into a unique, enthralling, and painful reflection on the American and African American experiences between 1954 and 1975.

Hopkinson, Nalo. *The Brown Girl in the Ring*. New York: Grandcentral Publishing, 1998. *The Brown Girl in the Ring* is a science fiction story set in Toronto, Canada several years in the future. Economic and social downfalls have driven most civil services and wealthy citizens into the suburbs leaving only the destitute to struggle for survival within the heart of the city. The suburbs have become the backbone of society and the city has been transformed into a literal and figurative hole of decay, and together the suburbs and city represent a ring that citizens must navigate stealthily. The story follows Ti-Jeanne, a young mother and Caribbean mystic woman in training, as she tries to control her gift and wrest control of inner city Toronto from Rudy, an obeah sorcerer and leader of the organized crime syndicate known as the posse. Ti-Jeanne's grandmother, a practicing healer and voodoo mystic, tries to help Ti-Jeanne come to grips with her heritage and the visions she has been having as of late. However, Ti-Jeanne's main concern is for her infant son, and the child's father, a former nurse and drug addict who, until recently, has been selling drugs for the posse. Driving the story is a search for a healthy human heart to be donated to the dying mayor of the city, for a price. Hopkinson is able to weave deftly Caribbean mysticism and the politics of social decline into a coming-of-age narrative about a young girl struggling to come to terms with her heritage.

James, Darius. *Negrophobia: An Urban Parable*. New York: Citadel Press, 1992. Presented as a screenplay and interspersed with invented newspaper articles, epigraphs, and miscellaneous material, *Negrophobia* is a raunchy, raucous examination of stereotypes as seen through the contemporary eyes of the white protagonist, Bubbles. As it turns out, Bubbles is in for one wild ride. As the mammy tells Bubbles, "Lookie here, *Miss Whyte 'n' Mighty!! In dis kitchen white is right if it kin kick three hundred 'n' sixty pounds of sweatin' black ass'*" (12). Once she has been confronted and thoroughly beaten up by Aunt Jemima's Flapjack Ninja Killers from Hell, a girl gang at her local high school, she returns home and the maid involves her in an elaborate voodoo ceremony during which Bubbles confronts the stereotypes of her own mind. In her voodoo induced visions Bubbles is transported to the Paint Factory, the Pit, the Cave of Flaming Tar Babies, and encounters Uncle H. Rap Remus, Burrheads, the corpse of Malcolm X, the Zombie Master, Elvis Zombie, and the Talking Dreads. Bubbles observes of her visits, "As those black, hypnotic disks spun larger and darker in the abyss, the farther and farther I fell, confronting the contents of my own mind in full, vivid, and animated relief, not knowing what waited in the wellsprings of my psyche, not knowing how I might transmogrify" (168). This often hilarious, over the top satiric exploration of how stereotypes persist in the postmodern imagination is punctuated by grotesque, graphic, and sexual imagery.

Johnson, Charles. *Dreamer*. New York: Scribner Paperback, 1998. Winner of the 1990 National Book Award for his fictional account of the former enslaved person, Rutherford Calhoun, protagonist of *Middle Passage, Dreamer* tackles another historical epoch. Set in the last two years of Martin Luther King, Jr.'s, life, the novel utilizes King to explore the complexity of identity through themes such as duality, selflessness, and goodness. Johnson does an excellent job of reimagining and conveying the conflicted feelings that King struggled with during certain events of his life and career, and then further exploring these conflicts in other contexts by including a doppelganger of King, Chaym Smith, who, although untrustworthy and mysterious, offers to stand in as King's double. Smith is watched over by a loyal civil rights worker named Matthew Bishop. However, the book mainly serves as an allegory for the universal struggles that all men and women bear as they grapple with conflicting feelings and desires. One scene illustrates this point as King struggles head on with his own internal conflict between lust and spirituality. A young King watches a classmate, on whom he had a crush, become seized by the Holy Spirit one day in church. The sight of the girl writhing on the floor is troubling and arousing to King at once. Thus, Johnson troubles the apparent duality set up between King and Smith as various scenes in the novel become a lesson on the internal struggles between sin and good that are a constant tension in one's life, a tension that molds the character of every person. The story is both moving and revelatory through its study of each character. Johnson strategically shifts narrative voices throughout the novel for dramatic effect, including several chapters where he seemingly narrates King's own thinking in third person. Such practices complicate our reading of each character as the reader is implicated in the very struggles that make up the core of the novel.

Johnson, Mat. *Dark Rain*. New York: Vertigo, 2010. Author of the 2008 graphic novel, *Incognegro*, which told the story of a light-skinned African American journalist who goes undercover during the early 1930s to expose the lynching of black men, Johnson, in *Dark Rain*, takes on a more recent historical moment, turning his literary attention to events that unfold against the backdrop of Hurricane Katrina. This graphic novel, written by Mat Johnson and illustrated by Simone Gane, tells the story of two men, Dabny and Emmit, who use the chaos created by Hurricane Katrina as an opportunity to rob the safe deposit boxes holding the dirty money of mostly criminals, former slave holders and other profiteers. The story develops into a series of moral conundrums, as we learn about the dire circumstances that have driven Emmit and Dabny to their desperate act. As they head into New Orleans while the rest of the city tries to evacuate, they are confronted by the villainous Colonel Driggs who heads the private security firm, Dark Rain, and is ostensibly hired to aid in the protection and rescue of the New Orleanians, but who really uses his power to further terrorize and exploit the ravished city and its people. As the crime plot of *Dark Rain* develops in the days before, during and after Hurricane Katrina, it becomes clear that the storm brought only the first layer of destruction; the indifference of the government and their hired security forces to the plight of the mostly poor and dark-skinned survivors of the storm exposes another, deeper level of devastation.

Johnson, Mat. *Hunting in Harlem*. New York: Bloomsbury, 2003. After his debut novel, *Drop*, in 2000, Johnson creates a deeply disturbing urban noire focusing on a group of ex-cons who have been recruited to be part of the "Second Chance Program," a moving company with an uplift message. Yet, as the plot thickens and unravels, what becomes clear is that underneath the rhetoric, is a dire reality. The moving company is creating its own work supply by murdering the miscreant residents of the Harlem community in order to make room for the wealthier and more respectable middle class. Through staged accidents, a fall in a bathtub for instance, Harlem's violent thugs, abusers, and other bad seeds are extinguished. A diabolical examination of how middle-class progress is at least partially dependent on an urban underclass, the plot pivots on a newspaper reporter's investigation of the crimes and attempts to expose the moving company's real motives. This engaging narrative is a modern day morality tale about the consequences of gentrification.

Johnson, Mat. *Pym*. New York: Spiegel and Grau, 2011. In this witty and satiric rift on Edgar Allen Poe's lone novel, *The Narrative of Arthur Gordon Pym*, Johnson evokes Poe's journey into the heart of darkness as a way to explore what Johnson's protagonist Chris Jaynes refers to as "the pathology of Whiteness." When Jaynes, an untenured professor of African American literature, gets fired from his post at a "good but not great" college, he sets off on a journey spurred by his discovery of a manuscript that suggests an alternative ending to Poe's narrative—an ending that indicates Poe's character Pym and the black shipmate Dirk Peters, as well as Tsalal, the all-black island they visit in Poe's novel, may all be real. In his quest to get to Tsalal, Jayne's joins company with his cousin, Booker, a civil rights activist turned deep sea diver and captain of an all-black crew assembled to go to Antarctica on a water bottling venture, Garth Frierson, his childhood friend who is addicted to Little Debbie snack cakes and obsessed with the popular landscape artist Thomas Karvel, Jayne's ex-girlfriend Angela and her new husband Nathaniel, and the water treatment engineers and adventure duo, Jeffree and Carlton Damon Carter. When the crew reaches the vast white lands of "the last continent," they discover not only the preserved 200-year-old Pym, but also the Tekelians, enormous white Neanderthal-like creatures who end up enslaving the crew and who can only be appeased by the snack cakes Garth has brought along. Johnson's *Pym* entertains and unsettles readers as the all-black crew attempts to navigate the vast white lands and colossal white creatures, and his protagonist seeks to wrest control over the legacy of Dirk Peters out of the clutches of Pym's dying hands.

Jones, Edward P. *The Known World*. New York: Amistad, 2003. Set in antebellum Virginia, and spanning several decades, *The Known World* is an ironic, entertaining, and stunning revision of Harriet Beecher Stowe's *Uncle Tom's Cabin* in which the Uncle Tom character is reimagined as a manumitted slave given his own plantation to run. The story begins with the death of Henry Townsend, a free black man who owns a plantation and African American slaves. The story is a complex patchwork of intersecting experiences involving and revolving around the tense relationships among slaves, free blacks, working class whites, and plantation owners living in Manchester County, Virginia. After Henry's death, his wife Caldonia attempts to run the plantation, but many of the slaves' sense an opportunity to escape. Henry's first slave Moses, who had assumed the role of overseer while Henry was living, begins an affair with Caldonia viewing this as a chance to succeed Henry as Caldonia's husband. However, despite their affair Caldonia rejects him as a potential husband because of his status as a slave, further contributing to the instability of the plantation. Ripe with ironic twists, contradictions, and tensions, Jones's novel explores the complexities and contradictions of human behavior including moral failures and successes. In addition to exploring the politics of black-on-black slavery, Jones examines with nuance and wit, the class and social hierarchies that shape the small town. Reminiscent of William Faulkner's construction of Yoknapatawpha County, including his shrewd depiction of the moral dilemmas, racial conundrums, and social tensions that shaped the setting for a number of his novels, Jones's Manchester County serves as the site for a compelling tale of conviction, class, and the toll slavery exacts from everyone's humanity.

Jones, Tayari. 2002. *Leaving Atlanta*. New York: Warner Books. *Leaving Atlanta* is Tayari Jones's debut novel. Set during the period of the Atlanta child murders that took place between 1979 and 1981, Jones's novel is written from the perspective of three African American children—Latasha Baxter, Rodney Green, and Octavia Harrison—who are coping with the loss of a classmate, the fears and frustrations of their parents, and the cruelty of elementary school caste systems. Split into three sections, the novel begins with Tasha's narrative, then moves to Rodney's story, and ends with Octavia's departure from Atlanta at the height of the murder spree. Throughout the novel, readers are made vividly aware of the struggles of childhood as each child must face the fearful, protective, and sometimes misguided behavior of well-meaning parents, and the unpredictable nature of childhood friendships. Through her language and wit, Jones captures the voice of each child, rendering a painfully beautiful story about the choices children make, the decisions of fearful parents, and the harsh realities that change forever the lives of all black children living in Atlanta during the murders. Each interlocking narrative exposes both the frailty and resiliency of children, and the pain of tragedy that has become a central element of the African American experience.

Lavalle, Victor. *The Big Machine*. New York: Random House, 2009. In *The Big Machine*, Lavalle examines religious extremism, folklore, and the American underclass through a fantastical story about Ricky Rice and a cohort of other reformed social deviants. The novel begins at a bus station in Utica, New York, and follows Ricky as he receives a cryptic invitation to visit a secret compound in Vermont. Ricky, an orphan, janitor, and junkie struggling to find peace in his life, decides to accept the invitation to the compound only to meet a cadre of other junkies and social deviants who have received similar cryptic notes. Together the group is introduced to the Washburn Library where they meet the Dean—the enigmatic

supervisor of the library—and in exchange for housing and clothing agree to become unlikely scholars, a cohort of downtrodden individuals selected to uncover
paranormal mysteries embedded in American news journals. The novel picks up
momentum as Ricky excels at his job as an unlikely scholar and is teamed up with
Adele Henry, a silver haired former prostitute and veteran unlikely scholar. The
two are ordered to San Francisco to stop a former scholar, Solomon Clay, turned
religious extremist bent on making America aware of the underclass it has been ignoring. Ricky becomes a true unlikely hero as he and Adele discover a secret coven
they must protect from the extremist beliefs of Solomon Clay. At the heart of the
novel, Lavalle provides a sophisticated critique of contemporary views on religion,
faith, folklore, and American elitism. As Lavalle notes, "Doubt is the big machine.
It grinds up the delusions of women and men." In the novel, he eschews the traditional notions of genre by incorporating science fiction, detective fiction, folklore,
and urban fiction among others into his tale about doubt, guilt, and atonement.
Although unorthodox and at times violent, Lavalle's novel captures the absurdity,
allure, and ubiquitous presence of dogmatism in all of its various forms, connecting it to a tale with unlikely heroes and supernatural undertones.

McFadden, Bernice. *Sugar*. New York: Plume, 2000. Set in the 1950s in Bigelow, Arkansas, the story revolves around the central character Sugar Lacey, a 30-year-old
prostitute who has just moved to town, and her unlikely friendship with Pearl
Taylor, a respected member of the community who struggles to cope with the
death of her 11-year-old daughter 15 years ago. Afraid for their men and their
morals, the women of Bigelow want Sugar to leave town as soon as she arrives.
However, to their surprise and to Sugar's surprise as well, Pearl, a bible-toting
Christian, is immediately drawn to Sugar who reminds her of her dead daughter. From its tenuous beginnings, Pearl and Sugar's friendship allows each woman
to confront their own inner turmoil. The relationship eventually helps lift Pearl
out of her depression and the two grow closer to one another, despite Pearl's open
disapproval of Sugar's occupation. Pearl begins to "live" again and delights in
the pleasures of makeup, juke joints, drinking, and dancing, and Sugar begins
to attend church with Pearl, eventually curbing her nightly escapades and demonstrating a new modesty in clothing and appearance. The novel's turning point
occurs when Sugar is brutally beaten by a "john" who is also the murderer of
Pearl's daughter. In language that is both rhythmic and stark, McFadden engages
in a powerful exploration of misogyny, grief, despair, hope, and friendships.

McKinney-Whetstone, Diane. *Tumbling*. New York: Scribner, 1996. In the first of her
three Philadelphia-set novels, McKinney-Whetstone focuses on the married life
of Noon and her husband Herbie. Despite their love for each other, their marriage
is troubled. Noon is dealing with a profound personal trauma and when she is not
able to meet Herbie's sexual desires, he begins a relationship with the nightclub
singer, Ethel. The couple adopts two daughters, first a baby, Fannie, who is left on
their doorstep and later Ethel's niece, Liz. Fannie is a spitfire and free spirit, and
Liz is shy, anxious and extremely fashion conscious. Despite their respective differences, the two girls share a close, inextricable bond. Herbie adores Fannie and
dotes on her, but must be urged to extend the same fatherly affections toward Liz.
Against the backdrop of this family's trials and tribulations, the community debates whether or not to sign away their homes to the city developers. The residents

of this South Philadelphia neighborhood become embroiled in a political fight against the city while at the same time discovering they are not all on the same side. The story's focus on how urban development and gentrification change close-knit communities will resonate with contemporary readers.

Morrison, Toni. *Paradise*. New York: Plume Books, 1998. Nobel Prize winner and author of numerous novels, including most recently, *Love* (2003) and *A Mercy* (2008), in *Paradise* Morrison tells the story of two communities—the town of Ruby, a small African American settlement in Oklahoma and the Convent, a small group of women who live in an abandoned convent located on the outskirts of Ruby. Although Ruby itself was formed through the displacement of four black families, when the town's way of life is perceived as being threatened, the men become desperate and use the women in the Convent as scapegoats for their anger. Thus, the novel begins with an attack on the women in the Convent by the men of Ruby, an attack that is quickly suspended as the readers are given multiple perspectives and different backgrounds on each character, providing insight into the events, emotions, and human flaws that lead up to the attack. Although the people of Ruby once trusted, needed, and relied upon each other, change has begun to undermine their unity and a younger generation has begun to challenge their conservative beliefs about life, religion, and family. At the heart of the novel are the convent women and the Morgan twins, Deacon and Steward, brothers who epitomize unified authority; they appear to share one memory, one purpose, and one belief until the attack on the convent ultimately divides them. Throughout the novel Morrison uses Ruby and the Convent to illustrate the dangers of narrow mindedness, conservatism, and fixity. Whereas the Convent serves as an "open house," a celebration of difference, where women of various races, regions, and faiths convene to heal and transform each other, Ruby struggles to maintain a way of life that has long since become archaic. After the smoke of violence clears, *Paradise* leaves the reader trying to understand the relationship between Ruby and the Convent as the human struggle for redemption, healing, and a deeper understanding of community.

Mosely, Walter. *Always Out Numbered, Always Outgunned*. New York: Washington Square Press, 1998. *Always Out Numbered, Always Outgunned* follows Socrates Fortlow, an ex-convict who served twenty-seven years in an Indiana jail for a double homicide and rape. After his discharge from prison, he finds himself in Los Angeles where he struggles to carve out a life worth living in a cramped two-room apartment in Watts. Living up to his namesake, Socrates examines life as it happens, developing a kind of common sense philosophy that he uses to teach and learn through experience. The book reads like a collection of short stories but maintains its cohesiveness through the recurring characters that help to redeem and shape Socrates. In particular, Socrates becomes a mentor to a young boy named Darryl, teaching him to avoid the same mistakes that Socrates made growing up. He teaches Darryl about respect, friendship, and responsibility. Much of the novel follows a problem-solving pattern that often involves Socrates working to resolve each problem through dialogue and deep thought. Throughout the course of the novel, Socrates broods on his past violence, racism, social corruption and the way that each of these has taken a toll on him and people in general. In total the stories create an engaging dialogue between the characters and the reader about a variety of manhood, violence, friendship, freedom, social and familial responsibilities, and morality. The last story in the collection best illustrates this as it provides an interesting dialogue between Socrates and a dying friend. The two men discuss ideas about personal ethics, the right to die, and the definition of a good death. The exchange provides an unresolved but complex exploration of death and euthanasia. As with each story in the novel, Mosley does an excellent job of weaving philosophy and experience to show that the examined life is the only life worth living.

Packer, ZZ. *Drinking Coffee Elsewhere*. New York: Riverhead Books, 2003. In her first collection of short stories, which received widespread praise, Packer focuses on African American urban characters dealing with race and identity in a predominantly white world in surprising, affective ways. In the opening story, "Brownies," a group of African American girls attends a summer camp where the ringleaders of the group decide that a member of another group has called them the n-word. In a surprising twist, the girls accused of using the racial slur turn out to be developmentally challenged, leaving the girls in the African American troupe questioning their initial decision to retaliate. In "The Ant of the Self," a young man confronts his conflicted feelings about his father after posting his bail and then driving him across country to the Million Man March where his father hopes to make a fortune selling exotic birds. In the title story, the main character, Dina announces at her Yale freshman orientation that if she had to be an inanimate object, she would be a revolver. This declaration earns her weekly meetings with the dean, counseling, and her own dorm room (because she is a suicide threat). Despite all of her antisocial provocations, a young white woman, Heidi, befriends her and Dina has to ultimately confront whether or not she might be a lesbian. These stories, along with the others in the collection, constitute deeply nuanced examinations of the complexities of identity in the contemporary world.

Parks, Suzan-Lori. *Getting Mother's Body*. New York: Random House, 2003. The novel follows Billy Beede, the daughter of a late blues singer and con artist Willa Mae Beede, and Billy's Uncle Roosevelt (Willa Mae's brother) and Aunt June. All of them work at a gas station, where Roosevelt and June raised Billy following the tragic death of her mother. Billy becomes pregnant by a married man from a neighboring town and upon discovering that the father of her unborn child is happily married but was too much of a coward to tell her, she decides to raise the money for an abortion by digging up her dead mother's body and pawning her jewelry. However, Willa Mae is buried hundreds of miles away in Arizona. When Billy informs her Uncle and Aunt of her plan, they too decide to join Billy and claim a portion of the treasure. Billy "borrows" a truck from one of Willa Mae's last boyfriends, the transgendered Dill Smiles, who has claimed Willa Mae's diamond ring and pearls for him/herself. Set during the Civil Rights Movement, in a small town in Texas, the story carries a charm of its own. Through a musical display of black vernacular and Southern wit, Parks produces an engaging cast of characters that together spin a tale about anger, deceit, resentment, and forgiveness that is both moving and rich.

Perry, Phyllis Alesia. *Stigmata*. New York: Anchor Press, 1999. Perry, a Pulitzer Prize–winning journalist, makes a powerful contribution to the neo-slave narrative genre. In this deeply affecting and emotionally charged psychological mystery, a young woman struggles to assess accurately what is happening to her. Is she experiencing intense flashbacks, dreams, time travel, a mystical experience, or a profound psychological disturbance? As the story opens, the protagonist, 34-year-old Lizzie, is securing her release from a psychiatric ward by carefully persuading the lead psychologist that she is cured. She convinces him that she agrees with his assessment by dutifully giving the answers that she knows he wants to hear. However, it quickly becomes clear that her own, true understanding of her experience is that she is inhabited by her two female ancestors, including her grandmother, Ayo. Upon her release, she return to her childhood home, where she lives with her parents as she tries to readjust to her life outside of the mental hospital. During her stay with her parents, she realizes that she is her mother's mother who abandoned her daughter an early age. In order to heal her mother's sense of loss and grief, she must, very gradually over many months, convince her conventional, anxious mother that she has come back for her. She does so by working closely with her mother on a new story quilt that details Ruth's mysterious disappearance. This is a beautiful and searing story of how psychic wounds can offer possibilities for transformation.

Raboteau, Emily. *The Professor's Daughter.* New York: Picador, 2005. *The Professor's Daughter* examines race, culture, and class through the life of Emma Boudreaux, a biracial Yale college student. When Emma's older brother Bernie urinates on a train rail and electrocutes himself, ending up in a coma, Emma must negotiate the social and class politics of her biracial heritage alone. Born to a black Princeton professor and a white housewife, Emma and her brother had navigated the politics of their mixed-race parentage together, having received almost no guidance from their parents. The novel itself is a patchwork of narrators, writings—one chapter is a paper Emma wrote for a class on the postcolonial African novel—and perspectives of other characters that together draw the reader into an intricate exploration of race and culture in America. One chapter travels deep into the mind of a recent African immigrant living in Princeton with her academic husband, another chapter journeys back into the boyhood and background of Emma's father and the Boudreaux lineage in general, and yet another chapter follows the mind of the comatose Bernie. The novel's constant shifting of narrative perspective, geographical location, and time periods parallels the apprehensive and bumpy search for identity that Emma embarks on as she struggles to understand herself and escape her family's past.

Randall, Alice. *The Wind Done Gone.* Boston: Houghton Mifflin, 2001. So much more than a wonderful parody of *Gone with the Wind,* Randall's debut novel tracks a journey of self-discovery for Cynara, the mulatta offspring of a plantation master and his house servant Pallas. Through personal journal entries, the reader witnesses Cynara's growing desire as it builds from an infancy of sharing her mother's milk with the master's white offspring (a parody of Scarlet O'Hara called Other) and continues through her shadow life as the disinherited daughter of slavery. Sold to family friends for $1 at puberty, Cynara ends up working as the chamber maid (and the only virgin) in a brothel that is frequented by her future lover and husband R.B. (a parody of Rhett Butler). Randall combines Cynara's journey with an African American perspective on nineteenth century American history as she makes visible America's interracial past through the recovery of Cynara's property and her story, which is presented via her personal journal.

Randall, Alice. *Rebel Yell.* New York: Bloomsbury USA, 2010. Randall's third novel presents a story of the relationship between Abel and Hope, that brings us from the
Civil Rights era to the eve of the 2008 U.S. Presidential election, and takes us from
Nashville and Birmingham to venues across the globe. Reminiscent of Ralph Ellison's *Juneteenth,* the novel offers a discourse on America's racialized past, with
Randall focusing on the implications of the Civil Rights era. She provides an intimate look at the black affluent class that gave birth to today's black conservatives
via the story of Abel, born "colored-baby royalty," whose early run in with the
KKK shapes the course of his life, making him angry and unsettled. When he and
the very light-skinned, mixed-raced Hope meet in college, they form a mutual attraction based on her desire for a stronger identification with blackness and his
desire to be less identified with blackness. Hope unravels his history after his second wife, a white woman of less lofty birth assists his untimely end at a campy
dinner theater restaurant during the annual Rebel Yell celebration. With appearances from Condoleezza Rice and Barack Obama, Randall's story sets bare the
underpinnings of the oft-stated sentiment that African Americans are not a political or social monolith—leaving us with much to contemplate about racial
solidarity in the new millennium.

Rhodes, Jewel Parker. *Douglass's Women.* New York: Atria Books, 2002. *Douglass's
Women* is an imaginative retelling of Fredrick Douglass's relationship with Anna
Murray, a free woman of color, whom he marries after obtaining his freedom
and his affair with Ottilie Assing, a German woman who captures his interest
through her intellectual prowess. The story revolves primarily around the conflict of sharing Douglass with another woman and with the public, as well. Anna
must negotiate her feelings of betrayal with her duties as a mother and wife. Ottilie
must negotiate her desire to move from behind Douglass's shadow as a public intellectual figure and become more than a mistress with her love for Douglass. The
narrative moves along gracefully as Rhodes introduces various romantic angles
and conflicts that provide nuance to the characters. The women are granted a kind
of agency as Rhodes reveals that their positions behind Douglass are ultimately
as much a matter of choice as they are a result of misogyny and social conditions.
Anna's reluctance to become literate or share Fredrick Douglass's passion for
rhetoric and reading contribute to both his infidelity and her dependence on him;
however, this is something that Anna seems keenly aware of and chooses as a matter of preference rather than helplessness. Douglass remains a shadowy figure
throughout much of the novel, constructed largely through his personal relationships with Anna and Ottilie. Rhodes's language is vivid and detailed, navigating
readers through the thoughts and internal conflicts of both Anna and Ottilie in an
attempt to recover two lost voices from an important moment in American history.

Souljah, Sister. *Midnight: A Gangster Love Story.* New York: Washington Square Press,
2008. *Midnight: A Gangster Love Story* is a sequel to Sister Souljah's debut novel,
The Coldest Winter Ever. In this novel, Souljah provides a backstory for the mysterious and strong-willed Midnight from her previous novel, tracing Midnight's
unexplained demons from the first novel to a past that is harsh and painful. Set
in Sudan and Brooklyn, New York, the novel begins with Midnight narrating
his father's teachings and his life in Africa. His father, a powerful and quiet man,
speaks several languages and teaches Midnight the importance of observation and

careful planning. He also teaches him to defend his family at all costs, a lesson that becomes a theme throughout the novel. In Northern Sudan, Midnight lives a life of relative opulence on seventy-five acres of land owned by his father, a doctor of science and an adviser to men in power. Following political turmoil involving his father, Midnight, at age seven, is forced to flee with his mother and sister to the United States. Poor and in exile, his family must live in the projects of Brooklyn, where Midnight uses the teachings of his father to navigate the foreign and dangerous sites of urban American. Thrust into a world different from his homeland, he quickly learns the skills and cunning necessary to protect his mother and little sister from the hostile environment in which they are submerged. Souljah uses a plain but graphic style of first-person narration to explore themes such as racism, drug abuse, violence, poverty, as well as immigration, faith, discipline, and struggle. These themes shape the complex, yet mysterious Midnight we come to know, and along with Winter Santiago, admire for his ability to adapt to a vicious urban environment.

Southgate, Martha. *Third Girl from the Left*. New York: Houghton Mifflin, 2005. *Third Girl from the Left* focuses on three generations of women represented by Mildred, Angela, and Tamara, all of whom dream of escaping the environments in which they grew up. The novel is broken into three parts, each telling the story of these women, starting with Angela whose experiences as an actress in the blaxploitation films of 1970s serves a frame for the bulk of the novel. Angela flees her life in Tulsa, looking for fame in the movies but instead becomes a Playboy bunny that both uses and explores her sexuality in efforts to obtain bit parts in movies and to express her own personal freedom. Her proudest moment in the business occurs when she plays the third girl from the left in a fight scene with Pam Grier in *Coffy*. Angela's promiscuity and lifestyle creates a divide between her and her family, one that could be bridged through conversations with both her mother and daughter. The novel spends a great deal of time exploring the hidden desires, fears, and struggles of these women, as well as the hidden trauma each one passes on to her own daughter. In some way, movies serve as a form of liberation for each woman, a liberation that culminates in Tamara's documentary, which exposes the tragic secrets that have kept all three women bound to a legacy of pain. Through swift and vivid imagery Southgate interlaces a cacophony of memories and experiences that allow readers to be flies on the wall in this tragic and moving story.

Tyree, Omar. *Flyy Girl*. New York: Mass Market Paperback, 1993. This urban novel and coming-of-age story begins in 1977 with 6-year-old Tracy Ellison at her birthday party, but most of the story unfolds in 1988 at the launch of hip-hop's materialistic influence. Growing up in the middle class Philadelphia suburb of Germantown, Tracy is a pretty, curvy, conceited, intelligent, and hazel-eyed young woman armed with a sassy mouth and a belief that the world is hers for the taking. The daughter of a pharmacist and a dictitian she, like most of her friends, is boy crazy. Tyree depicts Tracy as a modern day jezebel, whose rebelliousness, recklessness, and physical desire becomes a hypersexual metaphor for the influence of Hip Hop's bling-bling lifestyle on the maturation of young, urban, black youth. Motivated by money and excess, Tracy and her friends will do anything and have anything done to them to receive the material pleasures they believe is their due. The novel follows them as they plunge themselves headlong into a world of violence, gratuitous sex, and heartbreak. However, Tracy witnesses the effects of her lifestyle when she comes upon a former role model who is drug addicted and prostituting herself. Shocked into an epiphany, Tracy begins to examine her life, her goals, and her sexuality, evolving quickly from a brash, narcissistic "flyy girl" into a socially and intellectually mature young woman. The novel represents one of the first forays into the genre of urban literature and an attempt to comment on the anxieties and beliefs about the insidious effects of the cocaine economy and Hip Hop culture on black communities and black youth. Although many of Tyree's observations are trite and simplistic, such a work is laudable in its portrayal of contemporary urban black culture. Though a rocky narrative prose, disrupted by many italics and an imbalance between neutral narration and vernacular dialogue, Tyree manages to bring controversial and often hidden elements of black life into the literary world and provide the first major statement on the now popular concept of the video vixen.

Wideman, John Edgar. *Philadelphia Fire.* New York: Vintage Books, 1991. In this novel, Wideman uses the imaginative reinterpretation of Shakespeare's *The Tempest* and the 1985 bombing of the West Philadelphia row house owned by the "radical" group Move, to explore black masculinity, community, and loss. The story follows Cudjoe, the narrator, who returns after years of self-imposed exile on an island in the Aegean Sea. Cudjoe is in search of a young boy, Simba, seen running from the bombing. Wideman's language and various shifts in point of view complicate the narrative, but also imbue it with a living voice allowing the narrative to function as a collective response to black experience itself. Ultimately, Wideman directs the reader's attention to the struggles of urban culture and tries to provide a nuanced look at the cycle of violence and disinterest that is linked back to the legacy of slavery and colonialism. Throughout the novel Wideman makes unique connections between Caliban from *The Tempest,* the current forms of oppression that shape black urban culture, and Cudjoe's own guilt for removing himself from these occurrences. Using the bombing as a touchstone, the novel explores the textures of experience that should cause everyone to rethink connections between legacies of oppression and the current struggles within urban culture. In over four decades, Wideman has published several novels and several short story collections. His most recent novel is *Fanon* (2008), which fictionalizes the life of African philosopher, psychiatrist, and revolutionary Franz Fanon (1925–1961).

Whitehead, Colson. *John Henry Days.* New York: Anchor Books, 2001. Author of several novels, including *The Intuitionist* and *Sag Harbor,* Whitehead, in *John Henry Days,* follows protagonist J. Sutter, a young black journalist. Sutter is in the middle of a record "junketeering" run (in which freelance journalists zip across the country on a steady diet of assignments, free food, and other receipted expenses for which they can get reimbursed) as he attends the unveiling of a John Henry stamp in the little town of Talcott, West Virginia, where John Henry is thought to have worked and died. Although J. Sutter serves as the main protagonist in the novel, the novel itself reads more as a collection of vignettes from various time periods that use the African American folk hero John Henry as a metaphor for exploring the personal conflicts of different individuals. One sub-story reflects on stage actor and political activist Paul Robeson's performance in the failed 1940's musical about John Henry. Another subplot follows Jake Rose, a Jewish song plugger on Tin Pan Alley who aspires to make his name as a composer at the turn of the twentieth century by writing the "Ballad of John Henry." However, the novel revolves mainly around the parallel between John Henry, whose own story is interspersed in various chapters throughout the novel, and J. Sutter. Each man battles against the machine for the sake of his future. John Henry is killed by the industrial age only to be revived and immortalized through music and modern technology, while J. Sutter is being destroyed by the digital age, which engages him in a cycle of meaningless travel and the empty quest to meet the word count of his next assignments. Whitehead's novel is a postmodern mystery that uses the John Henry folktale as metaphor for contemporary struggles for purpose and selfhood in a digital age.

Williams, Sherley A. *Dessa Rose: A Novel.* New York: William Morrow and Company, 1986. Williams's novel tells the moving story of Dessa, a young slave woman who is imprisoned for her suspected leadership in a slave revolt. As the story opens, Dessa is being interviewed by Adam Nehemiah. In Nehemiah's eyes, Dessa is simply a "darky," and in his reactions to her story, we see a personalized account of racism and condescension. Through flashbacks that provide a striking and compelling contrast to the central narrative, Dessa and her lover Kaine's story emerges. Dessa, young and pregnant, sought revenge for Kaine's, death. When she escapes and eventually finds refuge at a plantation owned by a white widow, an unlikely cross-racial alliance forms, demonstrating how friendship can be a crucial source of personal transformation and a catalyst for resistance against systemic injustices. This is a powerful, deeply affecting narrative that challenges readers to reimagine a different past of cross-racial alliances and the quest for physical, spiritual, and emotional freedom.

Youngblood, Shay. *Soul Kiss.* New York: Riverhead Books, 1997. In her first novel, Youngblood tells the coming-of-age story of Maria Kim Santos, a young girl abandoned by her mother. Maria's mother is unable to recover from her failed affair with a married man and becomes addicted to drugs, leaving Maria to live with her two aging aunts. This story is book-length meditation on the deep physical and emotional conflict the main character experiences as she attempts to negotiate relations between herself, her friends, and her family. The character's initial hostility towards her aunts softens as she learns to see through their tough exteriors. Still, in her longing for her mother and her romanticization of her father, she ultimately connects with her father and decides to live with him. Perhaps most disturbingly, when she leaves her aunts to live with her father temporarily, she develops an emotionally incestuous relationship with him. She allows him to draw her nude and dreams of sexual experiences with him. This story highlights the emotional vulnerability of a young girl as she attempts to come to terms with her sexual identity.

CONTRIBUTORS

VOLUME CO-EDITORS

Lovalerie King is Director of the Africana Research Center, Associate Professor, and Director of Graduate Studies in African American Studies at Pennsylvania State University. A specialist in African American literary and cultural history, she has authored or co-edited six other volumes, including *James Baldwin and Toni Morrison: Comparative Critical and Theoretical Essays; Race, Theft, and Ethics: Property Matters in African American Literature; New Essays on the African American Novel* and *The Cambridge Introduction to Zora Neale Hurston;* and *African American Culture and Legal Discourse.* She is a regular co-planner of a conference series on African American literature and moderator of the Contemporary African American Literature listserv.

Shirley Moody-Turner is Assistant Professor of English at Pennsylvania State University specializing in African American literature, critical race studies, and folklore studies. She has published in *New Essays on the African American Novel, A Companion to African American Literature,* and *African American Review,* and she recently served as guest editor for a special section of *African American Review,* "*Anna Julia Cooper: A Voice Beyond the South.*" She is the author of *Black Folklore and the Politics of Racial Representation* (forthcoming), in which she recovers African American theorizing about the significance of folklore and folklore studies in the late nineteenth and early twentieth centuries. She has served as a co-planner for the last three conferences in Penn State's Celebrating African American Literature series.

VOLUME CONTRIBUTORS

Houston A. Baker, Jr., is Distinguished University Professor and Professor of English at Vanderbilt University. He has published or edited more than twenty books. He is the author of more than eighty articles, essays, and reviews. His most recent books include *Turning South Again: Re-Thinking Modernism, Re-Reading Booker T* and *I Don't Hate the South: Reflections on Faulkner, Family, and the South.* In 2009, his critique of black public intellectuals entitled *Betrayal: How Black Intellectuals Have Abandoned the Ideals of the Civil Rights Era* received an American Book Award from the Before Columbus Foundation. Baker is a published poet whose most recent volume is titled *Passing Over.* He has served in a number of administrative and institutional posts, including the 1992 Presidency of the Modern Language Association of America. His honors include Guggenheim, John Hay Whitney, and Rockefeller Fellowships, as well as a number of honorary degrees from American colleges and universities.

Greg E. Carr is Associate Professor of Africana Studies and Chair of the Department of Afro-American Studies at Howard University. He served as the School District of Philadelphia's first Resident Scholar on Race and Culture. He led a team of academics and educational policymakers in the design of the curriculum framework for the African American History course now required for public high school students in Philadelphia and edited *Lessons in Africana Studies,* the first secondary school materials to approach African American History from an Africana Studies methodological framework. He is also co-founder of the Philadelphia Freedom Schools Movement, a community-based academic initiative that has involved more than 10,000 elementary school students, 2,000 high school students, and 1,000 college students in an intensive, African-centered curriculum. He is co-editor of the Association for the Study of Classical African Civilizations' multi-volume *African World History Project.*

Pia Deas is a Visiting Assistant Professor of English at Lincoln University specializing in African American literature and satire. She has developed courses on contemporary African American literature. She currently leads an undergraduate research initiative on the Black Arts Movement that trains undergraduates in research protocal and prepares them to pursue academic careers in the humanities.

Darryl Dickson-Carr is Associate Professor of English at Southern Methodist University, where he teaches courses in twentieth-century

American literature, African American literature, and satire. He is author of *The Columbia Guide to Contemporary African American Fiction,* which won an American Book Award in 2006, and *African American Satire: The Sacredly Profane Novel.* His current research focuses on satirical texts of the Harlem Renaissance.

Eve Dunbar is Associate Professor of English at Vassar College, specializing in African American literature and cultural expression, black feminism, and theories of black diaspora. She is also an active contributor to Vassar's Africana Studies, Women's Studies, and American Culture programs. Her book *Black Regions of the Imagination: African Americans Between the Nation and the World* explores the aesthetic and political ties that bind literary genre, American nationalism, and black cultural nationalism in the literary works of mid-twentieth century African American writers. She has contributed articles, essays and reviews to *African American Review,* the *African American National Bibliography* (2008), *Callaloo, Post No Ills: A New American Review . . . of Reviews.*

Kristina Graaff is a doctoral fellow at Humboldt University's American Studies Department (Berlin, Germany). She has been a fellow at the Transatlantic Graduate Research Program Berlin-New York (2008–2011) and a visiting scholar at Fordham University's African American Studies Department and the Bronx African American History Project (2008-2009). Her areas of research include African American "popular" fiction, urban literature, prison writing, and the U.S. penal system and the intersection of entrepreneurial and library practices. Among her most recent projects is the forthcoming anthology *Urban Street Vending in the Neoliberal City: A Global Perspective on the Practices and Policies of a Marginalized Economy.*

Maryemma Graham Graham is University Distinguished Professor in the Department of English at the University of Kansas. Founder and Director of the Project on the History of Black Writing (1983–), she has published 10 books, including *The Cambridge History of African American Literature* (with Jerry W. Ward, Jr.), *The Cambridge Companion to the African American Novel, Fields Watered with Blood: Critical Essays on Margaret Walker, Teaching African American Literature: Theory and Practice,* and *The Complete Poems of Frances E.W. Harper,* and more than fifty essays, book chapters, and creative works. Graham has been a John Hope Franklin Fellow at the National Humanities Center, an American Council of Learned Societies Fellow, a Ford and Mellon Fellow and has received more than 15 grants from the National Endowment for the Humanities. In 2010, she was inducted into the International Literary Hall of Fame for Writers of African Descent. Forthcoming are *The House Where My Soul Lives: The Life of Margaret Walker*; a multi-media text, *Margaret Walker's South* (with photographer C. B. Claiborne); and translingual volume, *Toni Morrison: Au delà du visible ordinaire/Beyond the Visible and Ordinary* (co-edited with Andrée-Anne Kekeh and Janis A. Mayes).

David F. Green, Jr., is an Assistant Professor at Hampton University and a former fellow of the Center for Democratic Deliberation, who specializes in African American literature and rhetoric. He has recently edited *African American Contributions to Community Literacy,* a special issue of *Reflections: A Journal of Writing, Service-Learning, and Community Literacy.* He is currently working on *It's Deeper Than Rap: A Study of Hip Hop and Composition,* a monograph that examines the linguistic and rhetorical practices within Hip Hop culture as a way of reanimating theories of literacy and language used to teach college-level writing.

Trudier Harris is Professor of English at the University of Alabama, Tuscaloosa, and J. Carlyle Sitterson Professor of English Emerita, University of North Carolina at Chapel Hill. Her more than twenty published books include three award-winning volumes: *Black Women in the Fiction of James Baldwin* (College Language Association Creative Scholarship Award, 1987), *Fiction and Folklore: The Novels of Toni Morrison* (Toni Morrison Society Author Award, 1998), and *The Scary Mason-Dixon Line: African American Writers and the South* (College Language Association Creative Scholarship Award, 2010). She edited or co-edited six volumes of the *Dictionary of Literary Biography* and co-edited *The Literature of the American South: A Norton Anthology.* In 2010, she was inducted into the International Literary Hall of Fame for Writers of African Descent. Her latest book, *Martin Luther King Jr., Heroism, and African American literature* is forthcoming.

Mat Johnson is the author of the novels *Drop, Hunting in Harlem,* and *Pym;* the nonfiction novella *The Great Negro Plot;* and the graphic novels

Incognegro and *Dark Rain*. He was awarded a United States Artist James Baldwin Fellowship, The Hurston/Wright Legacy Award, a Barnes and Noble Discover Great New Writers Selection, and the Thomas J. Watson Fellowship. He is a faculty member in the University of Houston's Creative Writing Program.

James Braxton Peterson is the Director of Africana Studies and Associate Professor of English at Lehigh University. He is the founder of Hip Hop Scholars, LLC, an association of Hip Hop generational scholars dedicated to researching and developing the cultural and educational potential of Hip Hop, urban, and youth cultures. He has written numerous scholarly articles on Hip Hop culture; multiculturalism; African American literature, culture, and linguistics; as well as urban studies. He has published in *Callaloo, Criticism,* the *Journal of Africana Studies* and *African American Review*. Essays and other writing have appeared on the Root.com, *Huffington Post,* the Gno.com, Bet.com and the *Daily Beast*. He is currently working on a book, *Hip Hop Figures: Critical Essays on Rap Music*.

Carmen Phelps is Associate Professor of Literature and Director of Graduate Studies in English at the University of Toledo. Her current research interests include sexual identities and gender performance in the African Diaspora, black queer theory, and race studies. Her forthcoming book examining the Black Arts Movement and Chicago Women Writers is entitled *Paradox, Performance, and Collaboration: Revisiting the Black Arts Movement through the Perspectives of Chicago Women Writers*. Her essays have appeared in *The Funk Era and Beyond: New Perspectives on Black Popular Culture* and *Journal of Lesbian Studies,* and she has forethcoming essays in the *African American Review,* and in a collection focusing on black writers and the Left.

Howard Rambsy II teaches African American literature and directs the Black Studies Program at Southern Illinois University, Edwardsville. His articles, blog entries, and mixed media exhibits focus on poetry, literary history, and afrofuturism. He is author of *The Black Arts Enterprise*.

Alice Randall is the author of *The Wind Done Gone, Pushkin and the Queen of Spades,* and *Rebel Yell*. She is Writer-in-Residence at Vanderbilt

University, where she teaches courses on country lyric in American culture, creative writing, and soul food as text and in text.

Richard Schur is Associate Professor of English Studies at Drury University. His articles on African American literature and critical race theory have appeared in journals such as *Contemporary Literature, American Studies, Biography,* and *Law & Inequality.* He is also the author of *Parodies of Ownership: Hip Hop Aesthetics and Intellectual Property Law,* which focuses on how intellectual property issues have affected African American literature, art, music, and cultural criticism.

Evie Shockley is Associate Professor of English at Rutgers University–New Brunswick. She is author of *Renegade Poetics: Black Aesthetics and Formal Innovation in African American Poetry.* She has also published two books of poetry: *the new black* (2011)—one of *Library Journal*'s Best Books of 2011—and *a half-red sea* (2006). Her poetry and essays have appeared in such journals and anthologies as *African American Review, Contemporary Literature, Callaloo, esque, The Nation, Harvard Review, TriQuarterly Online,* and *Black Nature: Four Centuries of African American Nature Poetry.* Shockley's honors include the 2012 Holmes National Poetry Prize (awarded by Princeton University's creative writing faculty), an American Council of Learned Societies (ACLS) Fellowship (2008), and a Schomburg Scholars-in-Residence Fellowship from the Schomburg Center for Research in Black Culture (2007).

Martha Southgate is the author of four novels. Her newest, *The Taste of Salt,* was published in September 2011 and was named one of the best novels of the year by the *San Francisco Chronicle* and the *Boston Globe.* Her previous novel, *Third Girl from the Left* won the Best Novel of the Year award from the Black Caucus of the American Library Association and was shortlisted for the PEN/Beyond Margins Award and the Hurston/Wright Legacy Award. Her novel *The Fall of Rome* received the 2003 Alex Award from the American Library Association and was named one of the best novels of 2002 by Jonathan Yardley of the *Washington Post.* She is also the author of *Another Way to Dance,* which won the Coretta Scott King Genesis Award for Best First Novel. She received a 2002 New York Foundation for the Arts grant and has received fellowships from the MacDowell Colony, the Virginia Center for the Creative Arts, and the Bread Loaf Writers Conference. Her July 2007 essay for the *New York Times Book Review*, "Writers Like Me," appears in the anthology *Best African-American Essays 2009*. Southgate has published nonfiction articles in the *New York Times Magazine*, *O*, *Premiere*, and *Essence*.

L. H. Stallings is Associate Professor of Gender Studies at Indiana University-Bloomington. She is author of *Mutha Is Half a Word!: Intersections of Folklore, Vernacular, Myth, and Queerness in Black Female Culture*, which critically engages folklore and vernacular theory, black cultural studies, and queer theory to examine the representation of sexual desire in fiction, poetry, stand-up comedy, neo-soul, and hip-hop created by black women. She is also co-editor and contributing author to *Word Hustle: Critical Essays and Reflections on the Works of Donald Goines*, which offers a critical analysis of street literature and its most prolific author Donald Goines. She is completing *Funk the Erotic: Black Erotica, Freaks, and Funk Studies*.

Alexander G. Weheliye is Associate Professor of African American studies at Northwestern University. He is the author of *Phonographies: Grooves in Sonic Afro-Modernity*, which was awarded the Modern Language Association's William Sanders Scarborough Prize for Outstanding Scholarly Study of Black American Literature. Currently, he is working on two projects. The first, *Habeas Viscus: Race, Bare Life, and the Human*, concerns the relationship between black studies, political violence, and alternate conceptions of humanity. The second, *Modernity Hesitant: The Civilizational Diagnostics of W. E .B. Du Bois and Walter Benjamin*, tracks the different ways in which these thinkers imagine the marginal as central to the workings of modern civilization. His work has been published in journals such as *American Literary History; boundary 2; CR: the New Centennial Review; Public Culture; Social Text; Diverse Magazine;* the *Journal of Visual Culture; re/visionen: Postkoloniale Perspektiven von People of Color auf Rassismus; Kulturpolitik und Widerstand in Deutschland;* and *Black Europe and the African Diaspora*.

Dana A. Williams is a specialist in contemporary African American literature and Chair of the Department of English at Howard University. She is author of *"In the Light of Likeness—Transformed": The Literary Art of Leon Forrest* and *Contemporary African American Female Playwrights: An Annotated Bibliography.* She is the editor of *Contemporary African American Fiction: New Critical Essays, African American Humor, Irony, and Satire: Ishmael Reed, Satirically Speaking, Conversations with Leon Forrest,* and co-editor of *August Wilson and Black Aesthetics.* Her work has been published in numerous journals and edited volumes. She is currently completing a book on Toni Morrison's Random House editorship tentatively titled "Toni at Random."

INDEX

AALBC. *See* African American Literature Book Club

"acting white," 221–222, 223, 230n19. *See also* passing narratives

action in graphic novels, 298

Adams, Grace, 77

Adell, Sandra, 312–313, 325n7

Adisa, Opal Palmer, 293

aesthetic integrity of Hip Hop culture, 94–95, 96–97

Affirmative Actions: How to Define Black Culture in the 21st Century (Monica Miller), 250–251

"Africa Signs and Spirit Writing" (Mullen), 139

African American experience: aural/oral importance to, 141–143; continuity within, 4–5, 78; in graphic novels, 287; narrative frame of, 303–305

African American literature: achievement of, 1–2; Africana Studies approach to, 302–326; challenges of applying conceptual categories to, 312–314; changing definitions of, 56–57; clichés in, 50–51; commercial potential of, 71–72; and "criteria of Negro art," 2; diversity in, 3–4; graphic novels as, 297–298; ideas of liberation in, 311–312; intellectual space of, 57–69; and normative conceptual categories, 314–317; obsolescence of, 52; professional legitimacy in, 61–65; relationship with urban fiction, 114; self-publishing of, 76; trends in, 49, 72; uncomfortable truths in, xi; validity of urban fiction as, 93–94; value of, 63; visual arts in, 139. *See also* popular fiction

African American Literature Book Club (AALBC), 73, 76–77, 113

African American Literature: The Reconstruction of Instruction (Stepto and Fisher, eds.), 62–65

African American Review, 65–66, 195–196

Africana Studies, 325n2; Conceptual Category approach, 305–314; and contemporary historical fiction, 317–324; and early African American literature, 314–317

"Afro-American Literature: From Critical Approach to Course Design" (1977 conference), 62

Afro-Blue: Improvisation in African American Poetry and Culture (Bolden), 142

Afro-Diasporic culture, "soul" and, 217–219

Against the Grain (Freeze), 118, 119, 127

Alfred A. Knopf publishing, 49

alienation, 159, 199–200, 206

Alkalimat, Abdul, 57–58

Allen-Agostini, Lisa, 26

Always Out Numbered, Always Outgunned (Mosely), 343–344

Ambike massacre, 21

American Civil Liberties Union (ACLU), 22

American Negro Slave Revolts (Aptheker), 289

Amistad publishing, 51

angry black woman cliché, 119

Another Good Loving Blues (Arthur), 336

Another Way to Dance (Southgate), 257–258

"Ant of the Self, The" (Packer), 262

Aptheker, Herbert, 289

Armah, Ayi Kwei, 302

art, high *vs.* low, 66, 93–94, 95

art as resistance, 143–144, 148–149

Art Sanctuary, 72

Arthur, Artist (A. C.), 80

artistry as agency, 146–147

àshe, 38n27

Ashe, Bertram, 196, 229n5

Atlanta Child Murders, 269, 272–282

Atlanta Child Murders, The (1985 film), 275

"Atlanta Child Murders, The: A Case

Study of Folklore in the Black Community" (P. Turner), 274
audiences, female, 47–48
aural/oral components in African American culture, 141–143. *See also* oral *vs.* written word
"authentic blackness," 143, 219, 229n10, 240–245, 251–252
Authentic Blackness (Favor), 236–237
authenticity, concept of, 225–236; and biracial Americans, 239–240; critique of, 245–246; and fighting, 249–250; and hip-hop music, 242–243, 247–248; and post-Civil Rights generation, 237–238, 248–249, 251; and racial identity, 236; and responsibility to community, 244. *See also* "authentic blackness"
Autobiography of An Ex-Colored Man, The (J. Johnson), 270, 296

"Baaad Nigger" figure, 171–172
"baby plot," 328–329
Bad-Brother-Man figure, 169, 172, 174–176, 177, 183
"badman" folk figures: and authenticity, 170–171; *vs.* "Baaad Nigger," 171–172; destructive nature of, 171, 172–173; in graphic narratives, 176; in Hip Hop culture, 168; historical emergence of, 170; rappers as, 169–171, 173. *See also* Bad-Brother-Man figure
Badu, Erykah, 91
Bailey, Ronald, 57–58
Baker, Calvin, 83
Baker, Houston A., Jr., 142, 312–313, 351–352; chapter by, 17–39
Baker, Kyle: images of resistance by, 290–291; and imagination, 300; self-publishing by, 286–287; use of action, 298; use of facial expressions, 297; use of focalization, 176–178. See also *Nat Turner* (Baker)
Baldwin, James, 259, 271, 276–277
Banks, Adam, 70
Baraka, Amiri (LeRoi Jones), 141–142, 194–195, 290
Barnes and Noble bookstores, 72, 97

Barthes, Roland, 127
Bean Eaters, The (Brooks), 270
Beatty, Paul: in annotated bibliography, 333; and blackness, 41–44; focus on sound, 193; and posterizing, 199; rejection of New Black Aesthetic, 197, 200; use of German identity, 202–203, 206. See also *Slumberland* (Beatty); *White Boy Shuffle, The* (Beatty)
Before Columbus Foundation, 72
Behind Those Books (2011 documentary), 88n47
Bell, Bernard, 140, 152n6, 160–161
Beloved (1998 film), 41
Beloved (T. Morrison), 41, 147, 289, 329–330
Berry, Bertice, 81
bibliography, annotated, 6, 333–349
Big Machine, The (Lavalle), 341–342
biracial Americans, 239–240, 241–242
Black, Daniel, 272, 333
Black Arts Enterprise and the Production of African American Poetry, The (Rambsy, II), 64
Black Arts Movement (BAM), 2, 12n4, 42, 59, 61, 63, 65, 71
Black Atlantic, The (Gilroy), 38n27
Black Authors and Publishers International Directory (Adams), 77
black bodies as spectacles, 108–109, 121
Black Boy (R. Wright), 296
"Black Crisis Shuffle: Fiction, Race, and Simulation" (R. Murray), 199
black cultural production, visual/visionary tradition in, 142–144
black culture, fragmentation in, 225
black entertainment industry, rise of, 60
black experience fiction, 87n37
black geeks, 214–215, 221–227, 223, 230n13, 230n18, 230n22, 252n1. *See also* geeks
Black German identity, 189, 202–206
"Black Graphix," 184n9
Black Issues in Higher Education journal, 83
black literary journals, history of, 65–66, 87n25
Black on Both Sides (1999, Def), 99–101
black poetry, 63–64, 293–294, 300n8

Black Power movement, educational reform and, 57

black print culture, 69–77; chasm within, 77, 82–83; diversity in, 75; double standards in, 79–80; growth of, 77; implications of, 70; limited data on, 76–77; myths about the poverty of, 78–79; organizing of, 71; and technology, 69–70; validity as literature, 80–81. *See also* publishing industry

"Black Radical Tradition, The" (Robinson), 302

black student enrollment, 58, 262

black studies, 57–58, 78, 85n7

Black Studies Program (Southern Illinois University Edwardsville), 285

Black Subjects: Identity Formation in the Contemporary Narratives of Slavery (Keizer), 140–141

black vernacular tradition: domestic violence in, 161–163; LGBTQI perspectives in, 156, 157, 159, 160–161, 165–166

black writers. *See* writers

BlackbooksDirect, 76–77

Blackman, Marci, 155–160, 164

blackness: and constructs of time, 190; and contemporary writers, 257; end of, 200; and interracial relationships, 165; and literature, 42–44, 189; and modernity, 210n2; music as metaphor, 191–193. *See also* "authentic blackness"; indeterminate blackness; racial identity

blaxploitation films, 82, 87n37

blog format of reading groups, 299

"Blood-Burning Moon" (Toomer), 270

Blues, Ideology, and Afro-American Literature: A Vernacular Tradition (H. Baker), 142, 312–313

blues music, 102, 213

Bluest Eye, The (T. Morrison), 25–26, 255, 256

Bolden, Tony, 142, 208

Bombingham (Grooms), 338

Boni & Liveright publishing, 49

book buying, 97

book clubs, 42, 75

Books of Soul website, 113

Boondocks, The (McGruder), 214, 285, 296, 298

Borders bookstores, 72

boundary crossing of black texts, 81–82

break beats, 209, 210n1

Brief and Wondrous Life of Oscar Wao, The (Diaz), 334

Broadside Press publishing, 71

Brooks, Gwendolyn, 18, 63, 270

Brown, Cecil, 178

Brown, Fahamisha Patricia, 142

Brown, James, 207

Brown, Kaven, 88n47

Brown, Sterling, 64

Brown Girl in the Ring, The (Hopkinson), 338

Broyard, Bliss, 97, 100

Bucholtz, Mary, 220, 230n16

Buck, Stuart, 230n19

Buffalo Dance: The Journey of York (F. Walker), 293

Burns, Ken, 44

Butler, Octavia E., 79, 156, 163–164, 271, 333–334

Byrnes, Peter, 210n7

Campt, Tina, 189, 205

Cane (Toomer), 270

Carby, Hazel, 102, 103

Carr, Greg E., 352; chapter by, 302–326

Cary, Lorene, 72

Caucasia (Senna), 235, 238–245, 250–251

Cavalcade: Negro American Writing from 1760 to the Present (A. Davis and Redding), 64

"Celebrating African American Literature: The Novel since 1988" conference, 5, 255, 331

Césaire, Aimé, 21

Check It While I Wreck It: Black Womanhood, Hip-Hop Culture and the Public Sphere (Pough), 73–74

children's books, 300n7

Chiles, Nick, 95–96, 98, 114–115

Chocolate Flavor (Zane), 75

Christian fiction, 49

"Civil Disobedience" (Thoreau), 44

Civil Rights movement: and educational reform, 57; and "soul," 217. *See also* post-Civil Rights generation

Clark, Wahida, 120

class: in black print culture, 79; and digital revolution, 82; intellectual class, 58–59; intraracial divisions of, 67–68, 262; in *Love,* 33; middle class, 204, 240

clichés in African American literature, 50–51, 119

Clifton, Lucille, 63, 293

Clinton, George, 198

clothing, social meaning of, 138–139

Cobb, Jelani, 171, 173

Cohen, Seth, 230n13

Cold Drank (Laymon), 96

Coldest Winter Ever, The (Souljah), 124–125, 329

Colfax Riot (1873), 317, 326n10

College Language Association, 62, 86n13

College Language Association Journal, 66

Collins, Patricia Hill, 92, 119, 158

colonialism, 21

Color Purple, The (A. Walker), 255, 256

Colored Museum, The (Wolfe), 50

colored people's time, 193, 194, 198–199, 210n6. *See also* CP time

comics, 168, 299–300. *See also* graphic novels

"Coming of John, The" (Du Bois), 223–224

commercial potential of black literary production, 71–72

"comparative criticism," 32–34

Confessions of a Ex-Doofus-Itchy-Footed Mutha (Van Peebles), 82

Confessions of Nat Turner, The (Gray), 176, 287

conscious people's time, 194–198. *See also* CP time

consumerism: and authenticity, 238; in gangsta rap, 184n8; and racial identity, 242

Contemporary African American Novel, The: Its Folk Roots and Modern Literary Branches (Bell), 160–161

contemporary African American literature. *See* African American literature; graphic novels; urban fiction

contemporary narratives of slavery, 137–153, 139–141. *See also* neo-slave narratives

continuity within black experience, 4–5, 78

contributor summaries, 5–6, 351–358

Cornell University, 85n7

"countercultures of modernity," 25, 38n27

CP time, 193–199; and break beats, 209; colored people's time, 193, 194, 198–199, 210n6; conscious people's time, 194–198; and indeterminate blackness, 205–206; in *Slumberland,* 202; and sound, 198–199

"Crisis in Black American Literary Criticism and Postmodern Cures of Houston A. Baker, Jr. and Henry Louis Gates, Jr." (Adell), 312–313

"criteria of Negro art," 2

"critical geography," 55

critical literacy, 56

critical pedagogy, 56

"critical problematics," 66

critical refusal, 37n10

criticism, literary: academic, xi–xii; "comparative criticism," 32–34; and graphic novel, 168–169; journalistic, 17–19, 23–24, 30–31, 35; and oral *vs.* written word, 98–99

crossover authors, 79

cultural meaning making: as category of human institutions, 310–312; in *Red River,* 323–324

"cultural mulatto," 60, 215, 216, 221, 223, 257

Culture of Sentiment, The (Samuels), 80

Dafina publishing, 51

Daniel, Yvonne, 311

Danticat, Edwidge, 334

Dark Rain (M. Johnson), 339–340

"darky" connotations, 191–192

David, John, 178

Davis, Arthur P., 64

Davis, Thadious, 77–78

Dayan, Colin (Joan), 17

"Dear Mama" (Tupac song), 173

Deas, Pia, 352; section by, 333–349

Debord, Guy, 130n33

deconstruction in African American scholarly discourse, 65

Def, Mos, 99–101

Delaney, Samuel, 156

Deleuze, Gilles, 225, 231n25

depression, 156–157

desire, 36

Dessa Rose: A Novel (S. Williams), 271, 349

deviancy, 160, 165–166

Dew Breakers, The (Danticat), 334

diaspora, 25–27

Diaspora critique, importance of, 36

Diaspora Studies, 25, 37n9

Diaz, Junot, 263, 334

Dickey, Eric Jerome, 49, 74

Dickson-Carr, Darryl, 252n1, 352–353; chapter by, 41–54

didactic function of spectacular writing, 122–125, 128, 131n39

digital technology. *See* internet; technology

directories of publishers and writers, 77

Discourse on Colonialism (Césaire), 21

diversity in African American literature, 3–4, 75

Dixon, Colleen, 82

DJs, 202

Does Your Mama Know?: An Anthology of Black Lesbian Coming Out Stories (Moore, ed.), 166

Domestic Allegories of Political Desire (C. Tate), 102–103

domestic novels, 102–103, 105–106

domestic violence, 161–163

Douglass, Frederick, 63, 65, 86n24, 270, 279–280, 289–290, 296

Douglass's Women (Rhodes), 346

Dr. Dre, 170

drama queen figure, 119

dramatic mode in urban fiction, 116–122, 128

Dreamer (C. Johnson), 339

Drinking Coffee Elsewhere (Packer), 259, 344

"Drinking Coffee Elsewhere" (Packer), 260–262

Drop (M. Johnson), 50

Drucker, Johanna, 184n9

Du Bois, W. E. B., 2, 49–50, 217, 223–224, 231n23, 325n3

duality, 222

Dubey, Madhu, 67, 78–79, 84

Due, Tananarive, 79, 335

Dunbar, Eve, 353

Dunbar, Paul Laurence, 270

Dunbar-Nelson, Alice, 157

Dunning, Stefanie K., 165

Durham, David Anthony, 81, 335

dynamics of production, 59

Dyson, Michael Eric, 106

eBlack Studies group, 78, 88n49

educational reform, 57–59

Eglash, Ron, 220, 230n18

Elkins, Stanley, 20

Ellis, Trey: in annotated bibliography, 335–336; "cultural mulatto," 60, 216, 221, 257; "New Black Aesthetic," 196–197, 216; "post-soul," 215, 217, 222, 229n5

Ellison, Ralph, 199, 230n20, 230n22, 252n6, 259, 271, 296

Eloquence of the Scribs, The (Armah), 302

Emerson, Ralph Waldo, 44

Encyclopedia of Slave Resistance and Rebellion (Rodriguez, ed.), 289

Entertainment Weekly magazine, 287

epilogues in urban fiction, 122–124, 126–127, 131n52

Erasure (P. Everett), 44–46, 47–48, 96, 336

erotica, black, 75

Eroticism, Spirituality, and Resistance in Black Women's Writings (Weir-Soley), 38n27

"Eruptions of Funk" (Willis), 199–200

"Erzulie: A Women's History of Haiti" (Dayan), 17, 36

Eshun, Kodwo, 207, 209

Essence Magazine, 113

"ethnopoetics," 63

Everett, Hugh, 210n7

Everett, Percival, 44–46, 48, 50, 96, 336
Evidence of Things Not Seen, The (Baldwin), 276–277
exilic relocation, 25
expatriate fiction, 190–191
exploitation, female, 65, 86n24, 92
extraordinary black boys, 296

Facebook, ix
facial expressions in *Nat Turner,* 291–293, 297
Fall of Rome, The (Southgate), 257–258
false consciousness in gangsta rap, 173–174
Family Matters (sitcom), 214
Fanon, Frantz, 217
Faulkner, William, 18, 32
Favor, J. Martin, 237
fear, capturing, 275–276
"featuring" practice, 103–104
"femiphobia," 106, 107–108
fictionalizing of history, 275
50 Cent, 104
fighting, racial authenticity and, 249–250
film rights, 41–42, 43
FIRE!! journal, 2
first-person perspective: in *Leaving Atlanta,* 279–280; in *Nat Turner,* 294–295
Fisher, Dexter, 62, 64, 66
Fledgling (Butler), 333–334
Flight to Canada (Reed), 294
Flowers, Arthur, 336
"Flying Underground *(for the children of Atlanta)*" (Giovanni), 276
Flyy Girl (Tyree), 347–348
focalization theory, 176, 177–181, 184n10
folk communities in *Leaving Atlanta,* 275
"folk," concept of, 237
forgetting, logic of, 24
Forgotten Readers: Recovering the Lost History of African American Literature Societies (McHenry), 80
Forman, Murray, 192
Freeze, 118, 119, 127
Fresh Prince of Bel-Air, The (sitcom), 221
From Trickster to Badman: The Black Folk Hero in Slavery and Freedom (Roberts), 172

"From 'Uncultivated Barbarian' to 'Poetical Genius': The Public Presence of Phillis Wheatley" (Nott), 326n9
Frye, Northrop, 63
"Fuck tha Police" (N.W.A. song), 173
funk, ethos of, 199–206; Beatty's use of, 200; in hip-hop culture, 208; and indeterminate blackness, 201, 202, 207–210
Funkadelic, 201

Gaines, Ernest, 328, 336–337
"gangsta" films, 46
gangsta rap, 170, 173–174, 184n8
Gates, Henry Louis, Jr., 1, 4, 63, 142, 312–313, 325n7
"geek genre," 295–296
geeks, 219–220, 228n2, 229nn11–12, 230n14; black geeks, 214–215, 221–227, 230n13, 230n18, 230n22, 252n1
gender dynamics of Hip Hop music, 98
gendered critiques of *Narrative of the Life of Frederick Douglass,* 65
gendering of artistic control, 48
Genette, Gérard, 119, 184n10
George, Nelson, 215–216, 217
Geto Boys, 170
Getting Mother's Body (Parks), 344
"ghetto realistic fiction," 113. *See also* urban fiction
Gilda Stories, The (Gomez), 337–338
Gilmore, Ruth Wilson, 22
Gilroy, Paul, 25, 38n27, 196, 210n2, 229n8
Gilyard, Keith, 70
Giovanni, Nikki, 63, 276
Girls From Da Hood book series, 93, 102–108
Glassie, Henry, 4
Glave, Thomas, 337
Glissant, Edouard, 17, 25
Go Tell It on the Mountain (Baldwin), 271
God Says No (Hannaham), 259, 264–265
Goertz, Karein K., 208
Goines, Donald, 98–99, 108–109, 113
Golden, Marita, 81
Golden, Thelma, 197–198
Golden Gulag: Prisons, Surplus, Crisis, and Opposition in Globalizing California (Gilmore), 22

Gomez, Jewelle, 337–338
governance: as category of human institu-
    tions, 307–308; in "On Being Brought
    from Africa to America," 315–316; in
    Red River, 319–320
Graaff, Kristina, 113–132, 353
Graham, Maryemma, 94, 353–354; chap-
    ter by, 55–88
Gramsci, Antonio, 235
graphic novels: African American history
    in, 287; "badman" folk figure in, 168–
    185, 176; as boundary crossing, 81–82;
    vs. canonical novels, 297–298; imagi-
    nation in, 291; incorporation into
    courses, 292; and reading practices of
    black men, 285–286; scholarly writ-
    ing on, 168–169; use of action in, 298;
    visual narrativity in, 178–181, 291. See
    also *Incognegro: A Graphic Mystery*
    (M. Johnson and Pleece); *Nat Turner*
    (Baker); *Stagger Lee* (McCulloch and
    Hendrix)
Gray, Thomas, 176, 286, 287, 294
"Great Pax Whitey" (Giovanni), 63
Green, David F., Jr., 333–349, 354
Griffin, Farah Jasmine, 58, 72, 73
Griggs, E. Sutton, 76
Grimke, Angelina Weld, 157
Grooms, Anthony, 338
Guardian, The, 18
Guattari, Felix, 225, 231n25
*Gumbo: An Anthology of African American
    Writing* (M. Golden and E. Harris), 81
G-Unit Books imprint, 104
guns, racial authenticity and, 249–250

Habiba, Ibrahim, 240
Hachette publishing, 49
hair, significance of, 28–29
Halberstam, Judith, 193
Hall, Stuart, 235
handshakes as racial identity, 246–247
Hankins, Leslie, 144
Hannaham, James, 259, 264–265
Harcourt Brace publishing, 49
Harlem Moon publishing, 51
Harlem Renaissance, 224

Harper, Frances Ellen Watkins, 76, 270
Harper, Michael, 63
Harper Trophy publishing, 51
Harris, E. Lynn, 76, 81
Harris, Norman, 210n6
Harris, Trudier, 354; chapter by, 269–283
Hartman, Geoffrey, 63, 86n24
Hartman, Saidiya, 140
Hayden, Robert, 21, 26
"Healer, The" (Badu song), 91
Henderson, Stephen, 63–64
Hendrix, Shepherd, 168, 175, 178–181
Henry's Freedom Box (Levine and K. Nel-
    son), 300n7
Herman, David, 176
"Hip Hop" (Def song), 99–101
Hip Hop culture, 183n2; aesthetic integ-
    rity of, 94–95; authenticity of, 237, 247–
    248; "badman" folk figure in, 168, 169–
    171, 173; and black authenticity, 251–252;
    black women's bodies in, 108–109, 120;
    high *vs.* low art, 93–94; importance
    of funk in, 208; scholarly writing on,
    168–169; sexist origins of, 92; Stagger
    Lee in, 180, 181; and urban fiction, 114;
    and women, 91–111; women writers in,
    98–102
Hip Hop fiction. *See* urban fiction
Hip Hop music: as far-reaching, 109n8;
    "featuring" in, 103–104; gender dynam-
    ics of, 98; lack of access to women, 101–
    102; and pornography, 97–98; as proxy
    for racial authenticity, 242–243; rela-
    tionship to urban fiction, 104; role of
    writing in, 99–102
Hip Hop Revolution (Ogbar), 170–171
historical events: and African American
    writers, 282; fictionalizing of, 275; in
    graphic novels, 287; in novels, 269–272,
    273–275
historical fiction, normative conceptual
    categories and, 317–324
Hit Me Fred: Recollections of the Sideman
    (Wesley), 207
Holloway House publishing, 71–72, 87n37
Holmes, Shannon, 117, 122–123, 126
hooks, bell, 68, 161, 236

Hopkins, Pauline, 76
Hopkinson, Nalo, 338
Horton-Stallings, LaMonda, 98–99, 108
"How Ya Livin?: Notes on Rap Music and Social Transformation" (Pinn), 170
Hughes, Langston, 2, 63, 270
humanism: end of, 226; and race, 218; secularization of, 217, 229n7
humor, African American, 263
Hunting in Harlem (M. Johnson), 46–48, 50, 52, 53, 340
Hurston, Zora Neale, 2, 38n27, 41, 93, 96, 118
Hurston/Wright Foundation, 81
Hustler's Wife, A (Nikki Turner), 105
"hyperwhite," 220–221

"I Ain't Tha 1" (N.W.A. song), 169–170
"I Hate Reading" fanpage, ix
Ice Cube, 169–170
Iceberg Slim, 113
identity. See racial identity
Illmatic (1994, Nas), 99
illustrated narratives, 286, 292. See also graphic novels
imagination: as agency, 145–146; and comics, 299–300; and graphic novels, 291; and novels, ix
imagined readership, 96, 104
In a Queer Time and In a Queer Place: Transgender Bodies, Subcultural Lives (Halberstam), 193
"inauthentic blackness," 219, 229n10. See also "authentic blackness"
Incidents in the Life of a Slave Girl. Written by Herself (Jacobs), 74, 137, 270
Incognegro: A Graphic Mystery (M. Johnson and Pleece), 168, 175, 181–183, 182
Independent Publishers Group, 72
independent publishing, 49, 59, 70–71, 72–73, 88n42
indeterminate blackness, 190–191, 198, 201, 202, 205–206, 207–210, 253n7
Indiana State University's School of Education, 66
institutions, black student enrollment in, 58, 262

insults as racial identity, 246
integration, 213, 226. See also post-integration literature
intellectual space of African American literature, 57–69
"intellectual terrorism," 37n10
intelligent slaves, 293–296, 300n8
International Monetary Fund (IMF), 23
internet, 72, 74–75, 299
interpersonal relationships in urban fiction, 118
interracial relationships, 165, 203, 205–206
Introduction to African American Studies, A Peoples College Primer (eBlack Studies), 88n49
Invisible Man (Ellison), 230n20, 252n6, 271, 296
isolation, sense of, 281

Jackman, Marvin X., 63, 86n16
Jackson, Candice Love, 77, 79
Jackson, Lawrence, 64
Jacobs, Harriet, 74, 137–139, 152nn3–4, 270
Jahn, Manfred, 176
James, Darius, 338–339
James, Marlon, 26
Japanese by Spring (Reed), 52
Jarrett, Gene, 12n3
jazz, 207
Jazz (2001 documentary), 44
Jazz at Lincoln Center, 43–44
Jenkins, Candace, 237, 252n2
Jim Crow era, literary production and, 1–2
John Crow's Devil (M. James), 26
John Henry Days (Whitehead), 348–349
Johnson, Charles, 271, 294, 339
Johnson, E. Patrick, 236
Johnson, Georgia Douglass, 157
Johnson, James Weldon, 270, 296
Johnson, Lemuel, 37n10
Johnson, Mat: in annotated bibliography, 339–340; contributor bio, 354–355; Hunting in Harlem, 46–48, 52; market forces of black literature, 50, 52; section by, ix–xii. See also Incognegro: A Graphic Mystery (M. Johnson and Pleece)

Jones, Edward P., 51, 139, 141, 143, 148–150, 271, 340–341
Jones, Suzanne, 240
Jones, Tayari, 256, 272, 273, 341. See also Leaving Atlanta (T. Jones)
journalistic criticism, 30–31; of Love, 17–19, 23–24, 35
Jubilee (M. Walker), 271
Jump at the Sun publishing, 51

Kakutani, Michiko, 17–18
Karen Hunter Publishing, 73
Keane, John, 83
Kecht, Maria Regina, 61
Keizer, Arlene, 139–141
Kellner, Doug, 70
Kemp, J. T., 82
Kimani Books, 74
Kimani TRU imprint, 80
Kindred (Butler), 79, 156, 163–164
King, Lovalerie, 351
KMT: In the House of Life (Armah), 302
Knight, Keith, 285
knowing, ways of: in "On Being Brought from Africa to America," 316; in Red River, 320–321
Known World, The (E. Jones), 51, 139, 140, 141, 148–151, 340–341
Kubrick, Stanley, x
künstlerroman, 144

Labov, William, 170
Lane, Alycee, 157
language: capacity of, 55; diversity of, 70
Larsen, Nella, 157, 190–191
Lavalle, Victor, 341–342
Laymon, Kiese, 96–97
Leary, Joy Degruy, 22
Leaving Atlanta (T. Jones), 269–283; in annotated bibliography, 341; folk communities in, 275; narration styles in, 273, 279–281
Lee, Jarena, 143, 153n16
Lee, Ulysses, 64
Legba's Crossing: Narratology in the African Atlantic (Russell), 38n27
lesbian themes, 157, 158–159, 162, 166

Lesson Before Dying, A (Gaines), 336–337
Lethem, Jonathan, 295
Levine, Ellen, 300n7
Lewis, David Levering, 325n3
LGBTQI perspectives in black vernacular tradition, 156, 157, 159, 160–161, 165–166
Lhamon, W. T., 236
Li, Stephanie, 152n4
liberation in African American literature, 311–312
Life and Religious Experience of Jarena Lee, The (J. Lee), 143, 153n16
linguistic competency, 70
literacy, 69–70, 71, 87n33
literary achievement, middle-class privilege and, 83
literary criticism: academic, xi–xii; "comparative criticism," 32–34; and graphic novel, 168–169; journalistic, 17–19, 23–24, 30–31, 35; and oral vs. written word, 98–99
literary fiction vs. "popular fiction," 59–60, 66, 95–96
literary journals, history of, 65–66, 87n25
"literary slumming," urban fiction as, 121
literary studies, institutionalization of, 60–67
Lolita (Nabokov), ix–x
"long-view" memory, 302–303
Lorde, Audre, 157
Lott, Eric, 79
Love (T. Morrison), 27–36; "comparative criticism" of, 32–34; journalistic criticism of, 17–19, 23–24, 35; mainstream criticism of, 29–30; modernism in, 26; narrative perspectives in, 31; and Transatlantic Slave Trade, 21
Love, Monie, 101
Loving Her (A. Shockley), 156, 161–163
lynching, 121, 183, 270
"Lynching, The" (McKay), 270
Lyne, Adrian, x
Lyte, MC, 101

Madhubuti, Haki (Don L. Lee), 71, 86n22
Mahmood, Saba, 108
Malcolm X, 293

Mama figure, 50
Man Who Cried I Am, The (J. Williams), 190–191
Manley, Michael, 23
Mansbach, Adam, 94–95
maps, 150–151
marketing strategies of paperback publishers, 103–104
Marquez, Garcia, 18
Marsalis, Wynton, 43–44, 196–197
masculinity, 175
Matson, R. Lynn, 326n9
Matthews, Frank, 73
Maultsby, Portia, 171
Mbembe, Achille, 25
McCulloch, Derek, 168, 175, 178–181
McDowell, Deborah, 65, 86n24
McFadden, Bernice, 342
McGruder, Aaron, 214, 228n2, 285, 296, 298
McHenry, Elizabeth, 80
McKay, Claude, 49–50, 270
McKinney-Whetstone, Diane, 342–343
McMillan, Terry, 45, 74, 76, 95–96
Medgar Evers College, 85n7
media culture, gaps in, 56–57
media outlets, Atlanta Child Murders and, 278–279
media saturation, meaning of literacy and, 69–70
memory: as category of human institutions, 310; in *Red River*, 322–323; time/space coordinates of, 302–303
Meridians journal, 92
"Message to the Grassroots" (Malcolm X), 293
Middle Passage (C. Johnson), 294
"Middle Passage" (Hayden), 21, 26
middle passage in *Nat Turner*, 176–177
middle-class privilege, literary achievement and, 83
middle-class women, sexual propriety of, 102–103
Midnight: A Gangster Love Story (Souljah), 346–347
migration, Northern, 270–271
Miller, Bob, 72

Miller, Laura, 18–19
Miller, Mills, 88n47
Miller, Monica, 250–251
Miller-Young, Mireille, 97–98
Minaj, Nicki, 91
miscegenation, 181, 205
"Misogynistic/Harmatia" flaw, 29, 30
misogyny in music industry, 92, 173–174
misrecognition, 208–209
Modern Language Association (MLA), 62, 86n13
modernism, 19, 24–25, 30–31
Monk, Thelonious, 45
Moody-Turner, Shirley, 351
Moore, Lisa C., 166
morality tales, urban fiction as, 107, 123–124, 131n52
More Brilliant than the Sun: Adventures in Sonic Fiction (Eshun), 209
Morgan, Joan, 92
Morrison, Mary B., 49
Morrison, Toni, xi, 55, 147, 255–256, 259, 328; in annotated bibliography, 343; *Beloved*, 41, 147, 289, 329–330; on black middle class, 204; *Bluest Eye*, 25–26, 255, 256; and "countercultures of modernity," 38n27; and diaspora, 27; employed at publishing house, 45; "eruption of funk," 199–200; modernism, 24–25; and neo-slave narratives, 271; on sexuality, 205; *Song of Solomon*, 28–29. See also *Love*
"Morrison Modernism," 26, 28, 31
Morriss, Bentley, 87n37
Mosely, Walter, 343–344
Moses: When Harriet Tubman Led Her People to Freedom (Weatherford and K. Nelson), 300n7
Moss, Thylias, 139, 141, 143, 293–294. See also *Slave Moth: A Narrative in Verse* (T. Moss)
Moss, Wil, 287
motherhood, significance of, 152n4
movement and memory: as category of human institutions, 310; in *Red River*, 322–323

"Mugshots"—Wayne Williams and the Atlanta Child Murders (2000 documentary), 277
"Mulatto Millennium, The" (Senna), 245
mulattos, 243. See also "cultural mulatto"
Mullen, Harryette, 139, 142–143, 151, 152n2, 153n18
multicultural paranormal young adult fiction, 80
Murray, Albert, 213
Murray, Rolland, 199
music: and "blackness," 42; as metaphors for understanding blackness, 191–193; primacy of in African American culture, 141–142; to re-imagine time, 198–199. See also funk, ethos of; Hip Hop music
M.W.I. (Multiple Worlds Interpretation) concept, 198, 210n7
My Soul to Keep (Due), 335
"Myth of a 'Negro Literature,' The" (Baraka), 141–142

Nabokov, Vladimir, ix–x
Narcisse, Evan, 287
narration styles, 31, 279–281
Narrative of the Life of Frederick Douglass, An American Slave (Douglass), 65, 270, 279–280, 296
Nas, 98–99
Nat Turner (Baker), 285–301; "badman" folk figure in, 168, 175, 183; depictions of slavery in, 290–291, 296–297; facial expressions in, 291–293, 297; first-person perspective in, 294–295; focalization in, 177–178; imagination in, 300; intelligent slave in, 294–296; middle passage in, 176–177; publishing of, 287; Turner's confessions in, 291; use of action in, 298
"Nation Time" (Baraka), 194–195
National Urban League, 299
Native Son (R. Wright), 46, 99, 270
Native Tongues, The, 230n21
Naylor, Gloria, 41
Neal, Mark Anthony, 196, 215, 216–217

Negro American Literature Forum journal, 66
Negro Caravan (A. Davis, U. Lee and S. Brown), 64
"Negrobilia," 241–242, 252n6
Negrophobia: An Urban Parable (D. James), 338–339
Nelson, Kadir, 300n7
Nelson, Marilyn, 272, 276
neo-slave narratives, 139–141, 152n6, 271–272. See also contemporary narratives of slavery
nerds vs. geeks, 219–220, 228n2, 229n11, 230n14. See also geeks
Nervous (Zane), 75
Never Go Home Again (Holmes), 117, 122–123, 126
New Amerykah, Part One: 4th World War (2008, Badu), 91
"New Black Aesthetic, The" (Ellis), 196–197, 216, 257
New Black Aesthetic (NBA) movement, 60, 196–197, 200, 229n5
New Black Cultural Practices, 217
New Negro Renaissance, 46, 49–50
"New New Black Aesthetic," 250–251
New York Times, 17–18, 18–19
Newsweek magazine, 72
Nielsen, Aldon, 2
Nigger Heaven (Van Vechten), 50
Noire, 49
normative conceptual categories: application to contemporary historical fiction, 317–324; application to early African American literature, 314–317, 326n9
Nothing But a "G" Thang (Quinn), 173–174
Nott, Walt, 326n9
novels: historical approaches to, 273–275; and imagination, ix, 269–272; intelligent slaves in, 294; in visual media era, ix–x. See also graphic novels; romance novels; urban fiction
Nugent, Benjamin, 220
Nugent, Richard Bruce, 2
numbness, 163–164
Nunez, Elizabeth, 73

N.W.A. (Niggaz Wit Attitudes), 169–170, 173, 184n3
"n-word," 175
"N.Y. State of Mind" (Nas song), 99

Obama, Barack, 219, 221, 229n10
oceanic critical consciousness, 19–27. See also Post-Traumatic Slavery Syndrome (PTSS)
Ogbar, Jeffery, 170–171, 173, 251
O'Hehir, Andrew, 23–24
Okra, Ben, 73
"On Being Brought from Africa to America" (Wheatley), 315–316
"On Lit Hop" (Mansbach), 94–95
Once Upon a Time When We Were Colored (Taulbert), 194
155-The Atlanta Child Murders (2000 documentary), 275
One World publishing, 51
oppression, 4, 256, 259
Oprah Winfrey Show, The, 42
"Oprah's Book Club," 42
"optic blackness," 236
oral vs. written word, 66, 98–99, 102–103
oral/aural components in African American culture, 141–143
Oreo (Ross), 222
Oshinsky, David, 23
Osiris Rising (Armah), 302
"overeducated" black subjects, 223–224
OWN (Oprah Winfrey Network), 42

Packer, ZZ, 259, 260–262, 344
paperback publishers, marketing strategies of, 103–104
Paradise (T. Morrison), 343
paranormal romances, 80
Parks, Suzan-Lori, 344
Parliament (musical group), 207
party DJs, 202
passing narratives, 221–222, 240–241, 245, 265, 270. See also "acting white"
Paz, Octavio, 63
"Peeling off the Skin" (Adisa), 293
Pennington, Dorthy L., 210n6

performance art, 149–150
Performing the Word: African American Poetry as Vernacular Culture (F. Brown), 142
periodization, 194
Perry, Imani, 92, 106, 171, 173, 175
Perry, Phyllis Alesia, 344–345
persona poems, 300n8
Peterson, James Braxton, 168–185, 355
Petry, Ann, 270
P-Funk, 198, 201, 207–208
Phelps, Carmen, 155–166, 355
Philadelphia Fire (Wideman), 348
"Phillis Wheatley—Soul Sister?" (Matson), 326n9
Pinn, Anthony, 170, 173
Platitudes (Ellis), 50, 222, 335–336
Playing in the Dark (T. Morrison), 55
Pleece, Warren, 168, 175, 181–183
Po Man's Child (Blackman), 155–160, 164, 165
Poems on Various Subjects, Religious and Moral (Wheatley), 314–317
poetry, black, 63–64, 293–294, 300n8
popular culture studies, 76
popular fiction: clichés in, 46; vs. literary fiction, 59–60; reading of, 132n55; rise in production of, 72; role of women in, 91; sexualization and degradation of, 128. See also graphic novels; romance novels; urban fiction
pornography: Hip Hop music and, 97–98
"Portrait of the Black Male" (National Urban League report, 2007), 299
Post Black: How a New Generation is Redefining African American Identity (Womack), 251
Post Traumatic Slave Syndrome (Leary), 22
Post Traumatic Stress Disorder (PTSD), 21
post-black, 197, 198, 200, 210n5
"Post-Black, Old Black" (Taylor), 195
post-Civil Rights generation, 237–238, 248–249, 251, 259
posterizing, 195, 197–198, 200
post-integration literature, 213–231; syllabus example, 227–228, 228n1

"Postmodern Blackness, Yearning: Race, Gender, and Cultural Politics" (hooks), 68
post-oppression fiction, 252n5, 255–266
"post-soul" aesthetic, 195–196, 215–219, 229n5, 229n8
Post-Traumatic Slavery Syndrome (PTSS), 21–23, 24, 26
Potter, Russell, 202
Pough, Gwendolyn, 73–74, 92
Pratt, Mary Louise, 79
Precious (2009 film), 42, 255
prison literature, 73
prisons, 22–23, 123, 125
professional legitimacy, discourse of, 61, 62
Professor's Daughter, The (Raboteau), 345
Project on the History of Black Writing electronic database, 77
prologues in urban fiction, 122–124, 126–127, 131n52
"prolyretry" genre, 82
"propagandistic positivism," 60
Psychoanalysis and Black Novels: Desire and the Protocols of Race (Tate), 12n3
PTSS (Post-Traumatic Slavery Syndrome), 21–23, 24, 26
public intellectual phenomenon, 67–68
Publishers Weekly magazine, 49, 51–52
publishing industry: and Black Arts Movement, 59, 71; and black authors, 49–50, 52–53, 72–73; independent publishing, 49, 59, 70–71, 72–73, 88n42; and LGBTQI literature, 166; as profit driven, 96; repositioning of, 70–71; risk taking by, 51–52; self-publishing, 76, 286–287; technology as tool, 74–75; and urban fiction, 95–96, 97. See also black print culture
Publishing Trends journal, 72–73
Push (Sapphire), 41, 46, 255, 256, 329
Pym (M. Johnson), 340

"quadrilogy," 82
Queer in Black and White (Dunning), 165
Quicksand (Larsen), 190–191
Quinn, Eithne, 169, 173–174, 184n8

Raboteau, Emily, 345
race: and geek identity, 220; and humanism, 218
"Race and Ethnicity in America" (ACLU report), 22
"race-time continuum," 194. See also CP time
racial climate in Atlanta, 278
racial community, 60
racial identity: absence of homogeneity of, 67–68; and authenticity, 236; consciousness of, 195; and consumerism, 242; as multi-step process, 246–247; and sampling, 193; and stereotypes, 251; and tragic mulatto novels, 237, 252n2. See also blackness
racial stereotypes in literature, 121–122, 130n27, 251
racial-betrayal, 32
Radway, Janice, 80
Railroad Bill (Morris Slater), 170, 172, 184n6
Rambsy, Howard, II, 285–301, 355
Randall, Alice, 345–346, 355–356; section by, 328–331
Randall, Dudley, 71
Random House publishing, 45, 49
rap DJs, 202
rap music, roots of, 169–170
rappers: as "badman," 169–171, 173; and black authenticity, 251; women as, 91–92, 101–102, 109n1; as writers, 99
reader-identified books, 79–80
readers, 49, 330
reading groups, online, 299
reading practices of black men, 285–286
Reading the Romance (Radway), 80
"reality effect" of urban fiction, 127–128
Rebel Yell (A. Randall), 331, 346
Reckless Eyeballing (Reed), 50, 52
Red River (Tademy), 317–324; cultural meaning making in, 323–324; governance in, 319–320; movement and memory in, 322–323; science and technology in, 321–322; social structures in, 318–319; ways of knowing in, 320–321

Redbone Press, 166
Redding, J. Saunders, 64, 87n29
Rediker, Marcus, 20
Reed, Ishmael, 50, 52, 72, 294
resistance to slavery: art as, 143–144; depictions of, 289–291, 296–297; feminine forms of, 137–139
Respect the Jux (Matthews), 73
Revenge of the Nerds (1984 film), 230n17
"Reversion and Diversion" (Glissant), 17
Rhodes, Jewel Parker, 346
Riggs, Marlon, 191
Roberts, John W., 170, 171, 172–173, 175
Robinson, Cedric, 302
Rodriguez, Junius P., 289
romance novels, 74, 80, 81
Romantic Writers of America, 81
Roots (1977 miniseries), 290
Rose, Tricia, 92, 101
Ross, Fran, 222
Roth, Philip, 18
Rummell, Kathryn, 240
rumors, 274, 277
Run-DMC, 175
Rushdy, Ashraf, 139–140, 152n6
Russell, Heather, 38n27

Sacred Place, The (Black), 272
sadomasochistic practices, 155, 157–160
Sag Harbor (Whitehead): and authenticity, 235, 238–239, 240; humor in, 262–263; "New New Black Aesthetic" in, 250–251; and racial identity, 245–250; success of, 51; white gaze in, 263–264
Salon.com, 23–24
"Sambo Personality," 20
sampling, 192–193, 201, 206, 208, 253n8
Samuels, Shirley, 80
Sanchez, Sonia, 152n2
Sapphire, 41, 45, 46, 255, 328
Scenes of Subjection (S. Hartman), 140
Schur, Richard, 235–253, 356
science and technology: as category of human institutions, 309–310; in *Red River*, 321–322
Selected Poems (Brooks), 18

self-expression, democratization of, 70
self-publishing, 76, 286–287
"Self-Reliance" (Emerson), 44
Senna, Danzy, 83, 238–240, 245, 251
sensational writing, 116–122, 128, 130n33
separatism, black geeks and, 226
sexual alienation, 199–200
sexual harassment, 137
sexual objectification, 92
sexual performance in black vernacular tradition, 156
sexual propriety of black middle-class women, 102–103
sexuality: indeterminate blackness and, 205–206
Shakur, Tupac, 171, 173
Sharpley-Whiting, Denean, 92
Shockley, Ann Allen, 156, 161–163, 164
Shockley, Evie, 3, 12n4, 137–153, 356
Showalter, Elaine, 18
"Showing Her Colors: An Afro-German Writes the Blues in Black and White" (Goertz), 208
Signifying Monkey, The: A Theory of Afro-American Literary Criticism (Gates), 142, 312–313
Simon & Schuster publishing, 49, 75, 76, 96
Simpson, Louis, 18
Slave Moth: A Narrative in Verse (T. Moss), 139, 140, 141, 144–148, 151–152, 293–294
slave narratives, 65, 86n24, 137, 152n2, 270. *See also* contemporary narratives of slavery; neo-slave narratives
Slave Ship, The: A Human History (Rediker), 20
slave ships, 20, 176–177. *See also* Trans-atlantic as space of dread
"slaveship" (Clifton), 293
slaves/slavery: and African American writers, 271; children's book about, 300n7; familial fragmentation of, 177–178; in graphic novels, 287; as intelligent, 293–296, 300n8; physical trauma of, 163–164; resistance to, 137–139, 143–144, 289–291, 296–297
Slumberland (Beatty), 41–44, 189–210; in

annotated bibliography, 333; "blackness" in, 42–44; CP time in, 202; female audiences in, 48; focus on sound in, 193; posterizing in, 199, 200; Wynton Marsalis in, 196–197

Smith, Barbara Herrnstein, 66

Smith, Danyel, 114, 125, 252n2

Smith, Zadie, 222–223

Smitherman, Geneva, 70

social document fiction, 51

social mobility, 67

social networking, 74, 76

social structures: as category of human institutions, 306–307; vs. governance, 307–308; in "On Being Brought from Africa to America," 315; in Red River, 318–319

social/spatial geographies, 77–84

Song of Solomon (T. Morrison), 28–29

"soul," Afro-Diasporic culture and, 217–219

Soul Kiss (Youngblood), 349

Souljah, Sister, 124–125, 328, 329, 346–347

"souls of black folk," 219

Souls of Black Folk, The (Du Bois), 217, 231n23

sound, 192, 198–199. See also music

Southern Illinois University Edwardsville, 285

Southgate, Martha, 252n5, 257–258, 347, 356–357; chapter by, 255–266

Space is the Place (1974 film), 198

space music, 198

"Speaking in Tongues" (Packer), 262

Spectacular Vernaculars: Hip-hop and the Politics of Postmodernism (Potter), 202

spectacular writing, 128, 130n33; concept of, 114; didactic function of, 122–125; as entertainment, 125–128; as political tool, 123, 124–125; sensationalism, 116–122; urban fiction as, 115–116

Spillers, Hortense, 156, 165

spirit writing, 139, 142–143, 148, 153n18

Stag Shot Billy (C. Brown), 178

Stagger Lee (McCulloch and Hendrix), 168, 175, 178–181, 179, 180, 183

Stagger Lee/Stagolee/Stack-o-Lee character, 46, 169, 170, 178–181

Stallings, L. H., 189–210, 357

Stepto, Robert, 62, 63, 64, 66

stereotypes, racial, 121–122, 130n27, 251

Stigmata (P. Perry), 344–345

Strebor Books publishing, 74, 75

Street, The (Petry), 270

Street Chronicles Volume I and II book series, 104

Street in Bronzeville, A (Brooks), 270

street lit. See urban fiction

Strivers Row publishing, 51

Studio Museum, 197

Sugar (McFadden), 342

suicide, 209, 288–289

Sula (T. Morrison), 33–34

Sun-Ra, 198, 207

"superstandard" English, 220–221, 230n16

Tademy, Lalita, 317–324, 326n10

Tarpley, Natasha, 83

tastes, literary, 79

Tate, Claudia, 12n3, 102–103, 229n5

Tate, Greg, 215, 243

Taulbert, Clifton, 194

Taylor, Paul, 195

technology: and black print culture, 69–70; and black studies, 78; as category of human institutions, 309–310; and class, 82; and critical literacy, 56–57; as publishing tool, 72, 74–75; and reading groups, 299; social and intellectual space, 79; as venue for production, 59

temporal spatialization, M.W.I. and, 198

Their Eyes Were Watching God (2005 film), 41–42

Their Eyes Were Watching God (Hurston), 38n27, 41

They Tell Me of Home (Black), 333

Third Girl from the Left (Southgate), 257–258, 347

Third World Press publishing, 71, 88n42

Thompson, Robert Farris, 311

Thoreau, Henry David, 44

thought, systems of: as category of human

institutions, 308–309; in "On Being Brought from Africa to America," 316

"thug life" ethos, 171

Thugs and the Women Who Love Them (Clark), 120

Thurman, Wallace, 2

time, concepts of: and blackness, 190, 198; as culturally coded, 193–194; and music, 198–199. *See also* CP time

time/space coordinates of memory, 302–303

To the Break of Dawn (Cobb), 171

toasting, 169–170

Toomer, Jean, 270

Total Chaos: The Art and Aesthetics of Hip-Hop (Chang, ed.), 95

Toure, 197

tradition, 4–5; desire for, 313–314

tragedy, profiting from, 279

tragic mulatto novels, 237, 252n2

Transatlantic as space of dread, 19–27. *See also* Post-Traumatic Slavery Syndrome (PTSS)

Triple Crown publishing, 102

True to the Game trilogy (Woods), 123, 131n47

Tubman, Harriet, 290

Tumbling (McKinney-Whetstone), 342–343

Tupac Shakur, 171, 173

Turner, Darwin, 62, 86n13

Turner, Nat, 177, 286, 287, 294–296

Turner, Nikki, 49, 104, 105, 106–107, 108, 110n30, 127

Turner, Patricia A., 274

Two Thousand Seasons (Armah), 302

Tyree, Omar, 46, 347–348

"Ugly Beauty" (Monk composition), 45

Understanding the New Black Poetry (Henderson), 63–64

upper-middle class African Americans, visibility of, 240

Urban Books publishing, 103

urban fiction, 109n5, 113–132; and academic establishment, 76; as controversial, 114–115; critical view of, 88n47;

dramatic components of, 116–122, 128; as entertainment, 125–128; epilogues and prologues in, 126–127, 131n52; integrity of, 96–97; as "literary slumming," 121; as literature, 93–98; morality in, 107, 131n52; as performative act, 118–119; popularity of, 51–52, 97, 113; as productive literary genre, 93; proliferation of, 60; publishing of, 95–96; racist stereotypes in, 121–122, 130n27; readership of, 96–97, 104, 129n1; "reality effect" of, 127–128; relationship to Hip Hop music, 97, 104, 114; and small publishers, 49; as spectacular writing, 115–116; white gaze in, 121; women characters in, 119, 120; women writers of, 98–102

urban sensationalism, 51

Urkel, Steven (character), 214

"Urkel syndrome," 214–215

Van Peebles, Melvin, 82

Van Vechten, Carl, 49–50

Vansina, Jan, 307

violence, racialized, 178

visibility: of blacks, 155; of race and sexuality, 158; of upper-middle class African Americans, 240

visual arts in contemporary narratives of slavery, 137–153

visual narrativity, 176, 178–181, 291

visual/visionary tradition in black cultural production, 142–143

Vodoun, 36, 308

Waiting to Exhale (McMillan), 74

Walcott, Rinaldo, 210n2

Walk Through Darkness, A (Durham), 335

Walk Worthy publishing, 51

Walker, Alice, 259

Walker, Frank X., 293

Walker, Margaret, 271

Warren, Kenneth W., 1, 68–69

Weatherford, Carole B., 300n7

Weheliye, Alexander G., 252n1, 357; chapter by, 213–231

Weinstock, Ralph, 87n37

Weir-Soley, Donna, 38n27
Wesley, Fred, 207
West, Abby, 300n2
West, Cornel, 78
What Was African American Literature? (Warren), 1, 68–69
Wheatley, Phillis, 314–317, 326n9
When Winter Come: the Ascension of York (F. Walker), 293
White, Jaleel, 214
White Boy Shuffle, The (Beatty), 44, 50, 224–225, 296
white gaze, 26, 39n35, 121, 261, 263–264
white supremacy, 317
White Teeth (Z. Smith), 222–223
Whitehead, Colson: in annotated bibliography, 348–349; as contemporary writer, 259; critique of authenticity, 238–239, 245–246; and middle-class privilege, 83; and post-black, 197, 251; on *Sag Harbor*, 262–264; success of, 51. See also *Sag Harbor* (Whitehead)
Whose Song? And Other Stories (Glave), 337
Wideman, John Edgar, 348
willed amnesia, 37n10
Williams, Dana A., 357–358; chapter by, 302–326
Williams, John A., 190–191
Williams, Sherley Anne, 63, 271, 349
Williams, Wayne Bertram, 276, 277, 282n3
Willis, Susan, 199–200, 201, 205

Wind Done Gone, The (A. Randall), 345
Winfrey, Oprah, 41–42, 43, 44
"Wise 1" (Baraka), 290
Wolfe, George, 50
Wolk, Douglas, 291, 299–300
Womack, Ytasha, 251, 253n12
women: as characters in urban fiction, 120; in Hip Hop culture, 98, 100–102, 108–109, 120; pathologizing of, 119; role of in black popular fiction, 91
Women of Brewster Place, The (1989 film), 41
Women of Brewster Place, The (Naylor), 41
Woods, Teri, 123, 124, 131n47
World Bank, 23
Wreath for Emmett Till, A (Nelson), 272, 276
Wright, Michelle M., 204
Wright, Richard, 46, 99, 217, 224, 259, 270, 296
writers: black male, 46–48; definitions of blackness, 257; female writers of urban fiction, 98–102; and historical events, 282; need for readers, 330; and publishing market, 52–53; and slavery, 271
written literacy *vs.* orality, 66, 98–99, 102–103
Wynter, Sylvia, 218, 226, 229n7

Youngblood, Shay, 349

Zane, 49, 74, 76, 80

CPSIA information can be obtained at www.ICGtesting.com
Printed in the USA
LVOW13s0530060813

346333LV00004B/4/P

9 780253 006264